Agriculture in
the Postbellum South

M.I.T. Monographs in Economics

Agriculture in the Postbellum South: The Economics of Production and Supply

Stephen J. DeCanio

The MIT Press
Cambridge, Massachusetts, and London, England

HD
1773
.A5
D4

Bancroft

This book was set in Monotype Times Roman,
printed on Fernwood Opaque,
and bound in Columbia Millbank Vellum MBU-4317
by Halliday Lithograph Corp.
in the United States of America.

Library of Congress Cataloging in Publication Data

DeCanio, Stephen J
  Agriculture in the postbellum South.

  (M.I.T. monographs in economics, 12)
  Includes bibliographical references.
  1. Agriculture—Economic aspects—Southern States—History. 2. Agriculture—
Economic aspects—Southern States—Mathematical models. I. Title. II. Series.
HD1773.A5D4   338.1'0975   74–9636
ISBN 0 262 04047 6

To the landless and the poor farmers of the South whose names never appear in accounts of the history they made

Contents

Figure

Tables

Acknowledgments

This monograph consists essentially of my doctoral dissertation, with substantial revisions and additions. The dissertation was completed at the Massachusetts Institute of Technology in August 1972. The two principal members of my thesis committee, Peter Temin and Franklin M. Fisher, provided constant encouragement, an inexhaustible supply of helpful ideas, and the constructive criticisms I needed while working on the dissertation and the revisions. Credit for any of the accomplishments of this investigation should be shared with them. Robert Hall, the third member of my committee, also made several suggestions which I have tried to incorporate. Other members of the economics faculty at M.I.T. provided worthwhile comments at various stages in the research, especially Richard S. Eckaus, Evsey Domar, Matthew Edel, and Harold Freeman. I would like to convey my special appreciation to the entire faculty of the Department of Economics at M.I.T., for maintaining their confidence in me through all difficulties, even when this work was slow to progress.

Many other economists, in conversations, seminars, conferences, and correspondence, have contributed to the development of my ideas regarding Southern agriculture. A partial list would include Charles Bischoff, Lucy Cardwell, Thomas F. Cooley, Clarence Danhof, Paul David, Stanley Engerman, Robert Fogel, Claudia Goldin, Robert Higgs, Edith Lang, Joel Mokyr, William Parker, Roger Ransom, Joseph D. Reid, Jr., Nathan Rosenberg, Joseph Stiglitz, and Richard Sutch. My thinking was sharpened by discussions which took place at the monthly meetings of the Greater Cambridge Economic Historians organized by Peter Temin during 1971 and 1972. Responsibility for all remaining errors is mine, however.

I owe much to my late father, Dr. John DeCanio, and to my mother, Mrs. Alice DeCanio, who provided both moral and material support.

The early evolution of the project benefited from the insights of Michael Schwartz, however much our interpretations may have diverged since then. I would also like to thank Joe Schwartz, Helen Davidoff-Hirsch, Peter Kaiser, John Gliedman, and all my other friends who assisted me at various times.

An arduous task of keypunching was accurately accomplished by Emily Albanese, and large portions of the manuscript were typed by Mrs. Aimée v. Károlyi and Mrs. Norma Larson.

The work was begun while I was a graduate student at M.I.T. under an NDEA Title IV Fellowship. Keypunching was financed largely by a Tufts University Faculty Research Grant, and the computation time was supported by the M.I.T. Department of Economics.

Parts of Chapter 7 have appeared as "Cotton 'Overproduction' in the Post–Civil War South," *Journal of Economic History,* 33, no. 3 (September 1973), and some of the results of Chapters 4 and 5 are presented in "Productivity and Income Distribution in the Post-Bellum South," *Journal of Economic History*, 34, no. 2 (June 1974).

I would like to express a final thanks to Carol B., whose contribution was greater than she imagines.

Stephen DeCanio
Yale University
New Haven, Connecticut
March 1974

Agriculture in
the Postbellum South

1
Introduction

The Main Questions of Postbellum Southern Economic History

The social and economic upheavals during and following the American Civil War were enormous in depth and magnitude. Not only did the nation stagger under the impact of the war itself, with its hundreds of thousands of battle deaths and millions of dollars of property damage, but the institutions, social conventions, and individual attitudes of both South and North were profoundly altered. More than four million slaves were freed. The federal government entered into massive welfare and reconstruction work. State governments rose, fell, and rose again during the political turbulence of reconstruction. The patterns of race relations which would characterize the next hundred years began to form. Waves of agrarian discontent periodically swept over the West and the South.

In particular, the course of Southern development after the Civil War was unique in the history of the nation. In the wake of defeat, that unhappy region was characterized by exceptional levels of political and racial violence. Lynchings, tortures, election frauds, night riding, and chain gangs were widespread. The newly freed blacks[1] were special targets of these outrages. Racial discrimination and castelike restrictions persisted

---

1. The proper designation for the Afro-American population is a sensitive matter. Most of the apellations used by nineteenth-century authors have racist overtones today, while those preferred by the Afro-Americans themselves have varied over time and across class and regional lines. What seems to be the simplest contemporary usage will be followed in the text, referring to members of the two races with the symmetrical "black" and "white," although occasionally blacks may be referred to as "Negroes," since this term is still acceptable in scholarly usage. Also, the ex-slaves will sometimes be referred to as "freedmen," a term which has disappeared from the vernacular, hence has no overtones at all. Of course, nineteenth-century sources will be quoted in their own language.

long after the abolition of the "peculiar institution" of slavery. These practices cannot be explained in economic terms alone, but an adequate description of the economic climate is a necessary precondition for understanding them.

It is natural to ask whether Southern social and legal institutions during this period were founded on some sort of economic imperative. Did the repressive atmosphere of rural life serve the economic interests of any group or groups? One promising approach to this question follows from Evsey Domar's suggestion that slavery and serfdom may originate in the availability of free land.[2] Domar's hypothesis rests on the obvious fact that if land is a free good (owing, for example, to the proximity of a fertile and unsettled frontier), then no landowner can collect any income by renting out his land. A prospective tenant would prefer to move to the untouched frontier and set up his own farm rather than to pay any positive rent at all. Because of this, Domar argues that if land and labor are the only factors of production, the coexistence of (1) free land, (2) a free peasantry (free in the sense of being able to move, bargain for wages, etc.), and (3) a nonworking class of agricultural owners who live by collecting rents is impossible. If the land is free, the nonworking class must draw its income from *exploitation* of the agricultural laborers, by paying them a wage less than the value of the marginal product of labor, and by controlling the state apparatus to enforce some form of slavery or serfdom on the peasants.

Domar recognizes that a more realistic model requires the inclusion of capital and management. Nevertheless, he argues that

so long as agricultural skills can be easily acquired, the amount of capital for starting a farm is small, and the per capita income is relatively high (because of the ample supply of land), a good worker should be able to save or borrow and start on his own in time. . . . But until land becomes rather scarce, and/or the amount of capital required to start a farm relatively large, it is unlikely that a large class of landowners . . . could be supported by economic forces alone.[3]

In this case as well as in the land-and-labor-only model, political intervention in the labor market to hold the wage below its market equilibrium level would be necessary for the maintenance of the landlords.

The Domar hypothesis seems attractive in explaining several concrete historical instances of slavery and serfdom, including the case of the

---

2. Evsey Domar, "The Causes of Slavery or Serfdom: A Hypothesis," *Journal of Economic History* 30, no. 1 (March 1970): 18–32.
3. Ibid., 20.

United States.[4] If the existence of the frontier accounts for why slavery took such deep root in the Southern states,[5] the postbellum period might well have been marked by the development of an alternative system of agricultural serfdom or peonage. The war did not abolish the frontier. If anything, it raised the land/labor ratio through the death of large numbers of actual and potential farmers. In addition, the Southern planter class did not disappear. Indeed, by the end of the 1870s, many of the same individuals who had played a prominent part in the Rebellion were again powerful in the Southern state governments.[6] The legal and social restrictions placed on the Southern farmer population, particularly the freedmen, may thus have constituted a reenslavement or enserfment of the type envisioned by Domar.

Interestingly enough, at least one Southern observer anticipated Domar's reasoning.[7] In 1869, S. W. Trotti of South Carolina wrote:

We think . . . nothing more certain to prevent this transformation [from laborer into proprietor] than the accumulation of population, and nothing so sure to bring it about as the present limited supply of laborers. If labor is scarce and high, and land abundant and cheap, there will soon be no laborers, but all proprietors. And when all are homesteaded, what will become of the present land-holder, the upper strata of society? They will suffer a degradation commensurate with the elevation of the lower orders. And who dare say, that because the hewers of wood and drawers of water are elevated, at the sacrifice of intelligence and refinement, that civilization has achieved a triumph?[8]

Mr. Trotti unmistakably captured the essence of the Domar hypothesis, that the South, sparsely populated but endowed with abundant and fertile land, would soon be transformed into a region of independent free-

4. Ibid., 23–30, for Domar's discussion of the United States case, as well as other historical instances suggestive of this hypothesis.
5. Of course, one of the problems with Domar's hypothesis applied to the United States is that it does not explain why slavery was not established in the North, and particularly in the West. Even if the West were thought to typify the independent freeholder case (and it hardly can, since tenancy was widespread), the Domar hypothesis does not explain why one or the other of his polar cases emerges as the "equilibrium" for a particular region.
6. Kenneth Stampp, *The Era of Reconstruction: 1865–1877,* pp. 10–11.
7. Domar cites several antecedents, among them V. Kliuchevsky, *Kurs russkoi istorii* (Moscow: Gosudarstvennoe sotsial'no-ekonomicheskoe izdatel'stvo, 1937; originally published in 1906), English translation by C. J. Hogarth, *A History of Russia* (New York: Russell and Russell, 1960); Herman J. Nieboer, *Slavery as an Industrial System: Ethnological Researches* (The Hague: Martinus Nijhoff). According to Domar, Nieboer refers to A. Loria, *Les Bases Economiques de la Constitution Sociale* (1893), and to E. G. Wakefield's, *A View of the Art of Colonization* (1834). Domar also finds "glimpses" of the hypothesis in Adam Smith's, *The Wealth of Nations.*
8. S. W. Trotti, "Immigration," *Southern Cultivator* 27 (December 1869): 372.

holders, given the abolition of slavery and the absence of any alternative mechanism for exploitation of labor.

Any straightforward application of the Domar hypothesis to postbellum conditions is beset with several difficulties, however. The main problem with the simple (land-and-labor-only) version is that its major premise, land's being an economically free good, was not satisfied. The price of land in the South was not zero either before or after the war. As for the more realistic version including capital costs, movement to the western frontier for purposes of homesteading was expensive. Danhof estimated that at least $1,000 was required to start a Western farm in the 1850s,[9] and even if the cost of starting a Southern cotton farm after the Civil War had been only half that figure, it was still probably beyond the reach of the penniless freedman or sharecropper.

The idea that there may be a link between repressive institutions and exploitation of labor does not require free land and negligible farm-making costs, however. Free land and existence of a nonworking landlord class may be sufficient conditions for the exploitation of labor, but they are not necessary conditions. Equality between the wage and the value of the marginal product of labor is not a logical consequence of the existence of a labor market. Political and economic freedoms may be abrogated to hold the wage below the value of the marginal product of labor whatever the factor ratios. A nonproductive landowning class could exert its influence to restrict labor mobility, restrain competition among employers for laborers, and deny labor bargaining rights, all to the economic disadvantage of the working population. Land could have a positive price and workers might exhibit some mobility, even given such exploitation of labor. Nevertheless, the labor market would be imperfect, and the society would reflect in its institutions and mores the formal and informal mechanisms of the landowners' market power.

The term "exploitation" is used here and throughout in its technical economic sense of labor's receiving a wage below the value of its marginal product. This "Robinsonian" definition of exploitation is different from the Marxian notion of "exploitation," in which the appropriation by private owners of the returns to nonhuman factors of production in itself constitutes "exploitation" of workers, whatever the relation between the free market wage rate and the actual wage rate. Exploitation in either sense is distinct from a situation in which farmers in general or blacks in

9. Clarence Danhof, "Farm-Making Costs and the 'Safety-Valve': 1855–1860," in *The Public Lands,* ed. Vernon Carstensen (Madison: University of Wisconsin Press, 1963).

particular were excluded from certain nonagricultural pursuits. If blacks
were restricted to farm labor, the competitive wage level for agricultural
workers might have been depressed as a result. The historical debates re-
volve primarily around conditions *within* the agricultural sector, however, and this investigation is directed toward describing the labor
market conditions in that sector only. Discrimination against blacks
outside of agriculture will not be considered explicitly.

Most past and present writers who are not economists use the term
"exploitation" much more loosely. It generally has some connotation of
"unfairness," but such a concept is vague. There is usually no way to
determine from purely textual analysis which meaning (or mixture of
meanings) is intended. A purely competitive economy in which all factors
receive payments corresponding to their marginal products may generate
institutions which maintain the status quo, but it is the Robinsonian
type of exploitation which necessitates extraordinary interventions and
distortions in the labor market.

Clearly, slavery before the war is consistent with this type of exploitation. It has also been implicit in the view of some historians that the
economic status of the freedmen was hardly an improvement over their
condition as slaves. According to John Hope Franklin,

> there can be no question that the majority of Negroes worked, despite
> Southern doubts of their efficiency as free workers. They had no other
> choice but to cast their lot with their former masters and assist them in
> restoring economic stability to the rural South. . . . As free workers,
> however, they gained but little. The wages paid to freedmen in 1867
> were lower than those that had been paid to hired slaves.[10]

If the wage paid to a hired slave was equal to the marginal product of labor (and there is no reason to think that it would not be, since the payment was made to the slaveowner), then one possible interpretation of
Franklin's argument is that the postemancipation wage was again set at
an exploitative level. W. E. B. DuBois reasoned along similar lines when
he wrote: "Property control especially of land and labor had always
dominated politics in the South, and after the war, it set itself to put
labor to work at a wage approximating as nearly as possible slavery
conditions."[11]

This conception of the course of Southern labor history is shared by
Paul S. Taylor, who believes that for the blacks the period following the
Civil War was an "intermediate phase" in their long transformation

10. John Hope Franklin, *From Slavery to Freedom,* p. 308.
11. W. E. B. DuBois, *Black Reconstruction in America,* p. 586.

from slaves to free men. During this transition, the blacks continued to be subjected to coercion and exploitation:

The failure of the Radical Republicans to carry through their program [of guaranteeing full freedom for the ex-slaves] left the freedmen with neither land nor the political equipment of free men for their own protection. And during the struggle to attain the northern program, southern whites forged an iron determination to reestablish and maintain what emancipation had loosened, namely, their strong controls over Negro laborers. . . .
. . . The plantation system was continuing to exert pressure to compel the freedmen to labor just as it had exerted pressure from its beginning in seventeenth century Virginia; and the planters were strong enough politically to enact laws to support this renewal of coercion of the laborer which seemed to them so unanswerably necessary and desirable.[12]

The persistence of the notion that emancipation brought few economic gains to the blacks is reflected in some of the conclusions of a recent article by the economic historians Roger Ransom and Richard Sutch:

Emancipation from slavery was obviously the necessary first step on what has proven to be an extremely long road toward economic equality for black Americans. Clearly, emancipation alone was not sufficient to assure the economic advancement of the freedmen, for emancipation did not change the white's deep-seated belief that the free Negro could never function in a market society. . . .
. . . After nearly fifty years of struggling within the South to achieve economic gains, the black saw migration to another region as the ultimate solution to his problems. The result, as we know all too well today, was not parity with whites. But the exodus [to the Northern industrial cities] probably did set in motion the first significant forces for Negro advancement in the history of America.[13]

In contrast with this view is the possibility that abolition destroyed the complex of labor market imperfections embodied in the slavery institution. Douglass North, while recognizing the impulse among white Southerners to continue to exploit the ex-slaves after emancipation, pointed to the operation of a powerful countervailing force:

Southerners were in competition for labor, and it was in the interests of an individual planter to offer a wage or a rental agreement that would attract labor. If a sufficient number of white farmers did compete, it

12. Paul S. Taylor, "Slave to Freedman," pp. 33, 35.
13. Roger L. Ransom and Richard Sutch, "The Ex-Slave in the Post-Bellum South: A Study of the Economic Impact of Racism in a Market Environment," *Journal of Economic History* 33: 145–146.

would push up the earnings of laborers and tenants to competitive levels and eliminate "exploitation."[14]

Recent work by Robert Higgs and Joseph D. Reid, Jr., certainly raises the possibility that postbellum Southern agriculture was characterized by competition and conventional maximizing behavior on the part of both landowners and laborers.[15]

Even so, competition in the labor market may not have been sufficient to guarantee prosperity or an adequate living standard for the laborers. Kenneth Stampp argues that the deficiencies and deprivations which followed the freedmen out of slavery were the origin of many of their subsequent difficulties:

To be sure, some of the radicals, especially those who had been abolitionists before the war, never lost faith in the Negro, and in the years after reconstruction they stood by him as he struggled to break the intellectual and psychological fetters he had brought with him out of slavery. . . .

Because the ante-bellum slave codes had prohibited teaching slaves to read or write, only a small minority of Negroes were literate. In this respect, as in most others, slavery had been a poor training school for the responsibilities of citizenship. It gave Negroes few opportunities to develop initiative or to think independently; it discouraged self-reliance; it put a premium on docility and subservience; it indoctrinated Negroes with a sense of their own inferiority; and it instilled in many of them a fear of white men that they would only slowly overcome. A writer in Harper's Weekly reminded friends of the Negroes that the freedmen were but "the slaves of yesterday . . . with all the shiftless habits of slavery [to be] unlearned. . . . They come broken in spirit, and with the long, long habit of servility."[16]

In the language of an economist, Stampp holds that the freedmen were deficient in human capital—education, work orientation, and entrepreneurship. Blacks possessed of nothing but their raw labor power would be bound to fare poorly in a competitive labor market after emancipation. Essentially the same pessimistic assessment of the freedmen's abilities is held by Ransom and Sutch:

The free Negro began his freedom with no familiarity with economic markets. The behavior of prices, the use of money, contractual commit-

14. Douglass C. North, *Growth & Welfare in the American Past,* second edition, p. 95.
15. Joseph D. Reid, Jr., "Sharecropping As An Understandable Market Response: The Post-Bellum South," *Journal of Economic History* 33: 106–130; Robert Higgs, "Race, Tenure and Resource Allocation in Southern Agriculture, 1910," ibid., pp. 149–169.
16. Stampp, *Era of Reconstruction* . . . , pp. 16, 120–121.

ments over time, and the other intricacies of commercial activity were completely new to him. Nor had his experience as a slave provided the freedman with the management skills necessary for independent farming. He was, of course, familiar with the tasks associated with the cultivation of cotton and corn. However, he was totally inexperienced with economic decision-making such as: how much of each crop to plant; when and how much fertilizer should be used; and how to market his crop to his best advantage. This lack of entrepreneurial experience was compounded by the absence of formal education: nine out of ten adult blacks in 1870 could not write.[17]

Related to the issue of black poverty is the problem of the condition of the white farmers. White incomes in the South were also lower than in the other regions,[18] and the agrarian unrest that swept through the South recurrently in the late nineteenth century was by no means confined to blacks alone. Whites also may have been plagued by exploitation in the labor market or inadequate human capital resulting from deficiencies in the Southern educational system. In addition, the agrarian unrest of the 1880s and 1890s has often been seen in terms of two related but separable issues: absence of crop diversification (cotton overproduction) and exploitation of farmers by merchants. In the standard account of the Populist movement, John Hicks has written of the South:

The evils of the one-crop system were compounded again and again. When prices went down, the farmer, with a mounting balance against him at the store, saw no way out except to rent more land and raise more cotton. By attempting to farm too much he of course cut down the effectiveness of his work and got a smaller return per acre. He found, moreover, that his expenditures for seed, fertilizers, and supplies had increased as much as the returns from his crop, and his debt at the store might be even more than it had been the year before. But with the lesson still unlearned he sought the next year to raise more bales of cotton rather than to devise means of cutting down his purchases. Could he have produced for himself even the corn and bacon and hay that he bought, he might have freed himself in a short time from the toils of the credit system. Little wonder that intelligent men campaigned earnestly for diversification. . . .
    . . . Those farmers who raised foodstuffs were generally in better condition financially than those who did not, but in spite of their example the hold of cotton upon the ordinary southern farmer remained unbroken.[19]

17.   Ransom and Sutch, "The Ex-Slave in the Post-Bellum South. . . ," p. 136. For the literacy figure, Ransom and Sutch cite United States Census Office, Ninth Census, *The Statistics of Population of the United States. . . Compiled from the Original Returns of the Ninth Census (June 1, 1870),* (Washington: G. P. O., 1872).
18.   Richard A. Easterlin, "Regional Income Trends, 1840–1950," in *The Reinterpretation of American Economic History,* eds. Robert William Fogel and Stanley L. Engerman, pp. 38–49.
19.   John D. Hicks, *The Populist Revolt,* pp. 48–49.

Hicks depicts the operation of the credit system and the exploitation of farmers by merchants in classical terms:

The effect of the crop liens [the main instrument of the credit system] was to establish a condition of peonage throughout the cotton South. The farmer who gave a lien on his crop delivered himself over to the tender mercies of the merchant who held the mortgage. He must submit to the closest scrutiny of all his purchases, and he might buy only what the merchant chose to sell him. He was permitted to trade with no other merchant except for cash, and in most cases his supply of cash was too meager to be worth mentioning. He must pay whatever prices the merchant chose to ask. He must market his crop through the merchant he owed until the entire debt was satisfied, and only then had he any right to determine the time and method of its disposal. If his crop failed to cancel his debt, as was the case with great regularity, he must remain for another year—perhaps indefinitely—in bondage to the same merchant, or else by removing to a new neighborhood and renting a new farm become a fugitive from the law. Estimates differ, but probably from three-fourths to nine-tenths of the farmers of the cotton South were ensnared to a greater or less degree by the crop-lien system.*

The high prices charged by the merchants on credit accounts contributed immeasurably to the distress of the Southern farmer. . . . [T]he fact that large margins of profit were realized from the credit trade is not open to question. . . .

The credit system contributed also to the one-crop evil, which did more than its full share to insure to the farmer a permanent condition of indebtedness. Cotton almost served the purpose of money, for it was always marketable, it was comparatively imperishable, it could not be consumed by the producer and thus destroyed, as could corn, for example, and it was comparatively easy to handle. The merchant, therefore, wished his customers to raise cotton, and he objected strenuously if they proposed to raise instead such articles as hay, corn, wheat, or potatoes. It was far more expedient, if not more profitable, for the farmer who found himself in need of credit to do what the merchant desired—plant nothing but cotton.[20]

In this traditional view, merchants' usury and the "one-crop evil" were the two major sources of economic hardship in the cotton South. Farmers clung to cotton both because of their own irrationality (planting more and more cotton as the price fell ever farther) and because they were forced to grow the staple by monopolistic merchants.

20. Ibid., 43–46. Hicks's references for the first paragraph (footnoted at the asterisk) are to Matthew B. Hammond, *The Cotton Industry: An Essay in American Economic History;* Matthew B. Hammond in the *Political Science Quarterly* 12:462; Alex M. Arnett, *The Populist Movement in Georgia* (New York: 1922, doctoral dissertation), pp. 57–58; and Charles H. Otken, *The Ills of the South; or Related Causes Hostile to the General Prosperity of the Southern People* (New York: 1894), pp. 76–78.

It would be possible to develop these themes further by examination of the historical literature, uncovering different points of emphasis and changes in nuance. More progress can be made, however, by posing a series of questions which embody the main points at issue:

1.   Was Southern agricultural labor exploited? Was labor paid (in the aggregate) a wage equal to the value of its marginal product?

2.   What were the relative productivities of white and black agricultural labor? If productivity differences did exist, were they attributable to human capital differences?

3.   Was cotton more productive and profitable than the alternative crops? Related to this question is a second one, that is, were Southern farmers inflexible or constrained in their concentration on cotton?

4.   To what extent did the rural furnishing merchants exercise a monopoly in the credit market?

To each of these questions of fact, there corresponds a pair of essentially distinct historical hypotheses which have broader implications in interpretation of the economic and political history of the South during this period. Because the competing hypotheses imply different answers to the factual questions 1–4, empirical determination of the answers to these questions would constitute a first critical test of the alternative descriptions of the historical reality. The hypotheses tested by answering them are the following:

1A.   The *exploitation hypothesis*. This is the economic interpretation of Southern social, legal, and political history which holds that political and economic freedoms were denied to the working population for the economic advantage of the landlord class. It identifies the various repressive laws and racial customs as the manifestations of legal and extralegal exercise of market power by employers.

1B.   The *competition hypothesis*. This alternative describes the postbellum labor market as relatively free of imperfections. Given the competition hypothesis, any explanation for the social tensions and racial discord of the postbellum period must fit within the context of a normally functioning labor market.

2A.   The *legacy of slavery hypothesis*. This consists of the notion that slavery deprived the blacks of the human capital required to achieve reasonable levels of productivity after emancipation. It predicts that blacks as a whole were less productive than whites as a whole. Given the establishment of the competition hypothesis, the legacy of slavery hypothesis would provide an explanation of a wage and income differential between whites and blacks.

2B.   The *land occupancy and ownership hypothesis*. The alternative in this case attributes productivity differences associated with the different groups of farmers to differences in the quality characteristics of the land they farmed, and income differences to unequal nonhuman factor ownership.

3A.   The *overproduction hypothesis*. This hypothesis summarizes the suggestions that Southern cotton farmers clung to cultivation of their staple because of either their own traditionalism or the merchants' insistence on cotton, in the face of adverse price movements and despite the benefits which would have followed diversification.

3B.   The *flexible specialization hypothesis*. This alternative holds that Southern farmers were rational in their concentration on cotton because of the suitability of Southern soil and climate for cotton as opposed to the other agricultural possibilities. Cotton enjoyed a "comparative advantage"[21] in the South in the sense that in areas where it could be grown it earned farmers higher returns than were obtained from comparable factor inputs in other areas of the South which grew alternative crops. In addition, however, farmers generally did respond flexibly to fluctuations in the relative price of cotton and the alternative crops, increasing their cotton plantings when they expected its price to rise and cutting back when they expected its price to fall.

4A,B.   The obvious alternatives are that furnishing merchants either were or were not monopolists in the rural credit market. However, factual question 4 cannot be answered here because of limitations in the investigator's resources and the paucity of data on Southern country stores. The issue of exploitation by merchants will be discussed in the context of question 3, but it cannot be settled with the same confidence as the other questions at this time.

Of course, these are not the only hypotheses which can be proposed concerning the structure of Southern agriculture. Nevertheless, they are in the spirit of both the contemporary accounts and the historical literature. In addition, the hypotheses seem to be reasonable a priori—none of them has the attributes of the implausible "straw man." Even when the hypotheses are mutually exclusive in the particular (for example, a farmer

---

21. "Comparative advantage" will be used here and throughout in a slightly different way than in standard international trade terminology. In trade discussions, the theory of comparative advantage explains why different countries or regions trading with each other tend to specialize in different lines of production. Here, "comparative advantage" refers to the particular advantages of cotton culture within a given region—the South. The term conveys the idea, common to both usages, of local conditions making specialization advantageous.

What about surplus value?

cannot be both exploited and paid a competitive market wage), examples of each might well be found to coexist side by side. Furthermore, black/ white productivity differences could have resulted from *both* human capital differences and land quality differences. For these reasons, the determination of the answers to questions 1–3 will focus on the *aggregate* situation. The settlement of questions 1–3 in the aggregate will be sufficient to reject some of the hypothesized descriptions of the nineteenth-century Southern economy and will provide a starting point for further investigation of the remaining hypotheses.

Results and Conclusions

The main findings of this study can be summarized as a series of established propositions.

a. The narrative, anecdotal, nonquantitative historical sources are insufficient to establish or disprove the hypotheses of postbellum Southern economic history proposed here. Convincing documentation can be found for both sides of factual questions 1 to 3—whether the labor market was imperfect or competitive, whether Southern farmers were rational or irrational in concentrating on cotton, and whether black labor suffered from a lower level of skill and productivity than whites. This negative conclusion is partly of a methodological nature. Non-quantitative tests simply do not have the power to resolve historical reality in enough detail to test the hypotheses at issue.

b. Nevertheless, more powerful statistical tests can be developed, based on estimation of agricultural production and supply functions for the postbellum period. It is possible to show that different ranges of parameter values in properly specified agricultural production and supply functions correspond to the different possibilities inherent in 1–3.

c. There is no evidence for overall aggregate exploitation of agricultural labor. Production function estimates indicate that marginal product factor pricing is entirely consistent with the known levels of wage and sharecrop payments. If anything, labor tended to receive a wage somewhat higher than the value of its marginal product.

d. Race-associated productivity differences did exist, even within counties of similar soil composition. Neither race was uniformly more productive than the other, however. In one specification of the production function, blacks in the border states on the periphery of the South seemed to possess a productivity advantage compared to whites in those states, while whites appeared to have a similar advantage over blacks in the cotton belt. In a more general specification allowing productivity differences within each racial group, whites who grew cotton were the farmers of greatest productivity, followed by black cotton farmers, black noncotton farmers, and white noncotton farmers in that order, with the black and white noncotton farmers roughly equal in productivity at the bottom of the scale. This ordering is essentially unchanged (though the strength of some of the relations is altered) if the states are grouped into subregions or if the counties in each state are not distinguished according to physical and chemical soil type.

e. Whatever the specification of the production function, cotton culture was more productive in value terms than the alternatives, other things being equal.

f. Regarding conclusions d and e, it is impossible to identify whether the productivity differences associated with crop and race were due to human capital differences or to differences in the quality of land farmed by the different groups of farmers. The productivity results do, however, contradict the simple legacy of slavery notion that blacks as a whole were less productive than whites as a whole. All the results are consistent either with the land occupancy and ownership hypothesis or with a more complicated human capital explanation which allows for differentiation of skill levels within each racial group.

g. Southern cotton farmers were about as price-responsive in the short run as American wheat farmers, and their speed of adjustment to changes in relative prices of the alternative crops was such that relatively full adjustment to once-and-for-all price changes would have been completed in only a few years' time. In addition, most of the Southern states showed a positive trend in share of planted acres devoted to cotton, as well as a low long-run price elasticity of cotton supply consistent with a comparative advantage for cotton.

h. The data and results presented here are insufficient to settle the question of exploitation of farmers by merchants.

These results have broader implications for the interpretation of postbellum Southern history. First, competition in the labor market cannot be rejected. Nothing in the results indicates any departure from marginal product factor pricing, at least after 1880. If the production function estimates are accepted, it follows that sharecroppers received a fair market wage. The various repressive laws and acts of violence perpetrated against blacks were indeed widespread but were not instruments of economic exploitation in the labor market.

A major source of economic inequality and relative poverty was the same as in any normally functioning private enterprise market economy —incomes were unequal largely because of unequal ownership of the nonhuman factors of production. Some productivity differences may have been due to human capital disparities, but these differences were small compared to the returns from ownership of land and capital. Income and standard of living depended more on an agriculturalist's nonhuman factor endowment than on anything else.

The sharecropping institution appears to have had little or no impact either upon the distributional shares of labor, land, and capital or upon patterns of resource allocation. While it is true that blacks and whites differed in total productivity, these differences can be explained by the land occupancy and ownership hypothesis, with the productivities of the different groups depending on their location on lands of different quality. Even if some of the productivity differences were the result of different amounts of human capital possessed by whites and blacks, there is still no evidence of any deviation from marginal product factor pricing. Both the production function and the supply function estimates indicate that Southern farmers' concentration on cotton was almost certainly not irrational or unreasonable. Cotton culture was associated with an unmistakable advantage in output as compared to the alternative uses of land. Cotton farmers were as elastic in their responses to relative price changes as wheat farmers of the West and North, and were neither slow nor inflexible in responding to market price signals.

It is reasonable to assume that the slave "wage" was lower than the value of the marginal product of labor. Given the exploitation of slave labor, the transition to competitive market determination of wage rates by 1880 constituted an important economic advance for the blacks. The elimination of exploitation was a major step in the direction of freedom regardless of the effects of emancipation and the Civil War on material standards of living in the South.[22] The social and political gains achieved with emancipation were also great, despite setbacks in the realization of full civil rights by all strata of the black population. Still, the defeat of the various land reform proposals made at the close of the Civil War was important in allowing a continued unequal distribution of wealth and

22.   Since emancipation placed the labor/leisure choice in the hands of the freedmen rather than the plantation owners, and since certain economies of scale appear to have been associated with slave agriculture, it is possible that black income levels measured in dollars may have declined after the Civil War. From the utility standpoint, however, elimination of slavery and its associated exploitation can only have benefited the freedmen. For a full discussion of these points and of the economics of American slavery in general, see Robert W. Fogel and Stanley L. Engerman, *Time on the Cross: The Economics of American Negro Slavery,* especially pp. 232–241 and 258–264, and the associated sections of *Time on the Cross: Evidence and Methods— A Supplement.*

income in the South, and this persistent inequality impeded the move- 11
ment of both blacks and poor whites toward full social and political
equality.

2
The Impressionistic Evidence

The first step in testing the hypotheses of the previous chapter is to determine what support for them can be found in the reports and accounts of Southern agricultural practices of the nineteenth century. It will be shown in this chapter that a strong case can be built on either side of the main questions. These questions will be taken up one at a time, with the mass of narrative and anecdotal sources summarized in as coherent a manner as possible. The objective is to show the breadth and variety of evidence that can be mustered for each of the opposing arguments rather than to present an exhaustive or rigorous survey of the nineteenth-century literature. The sources themselves are not always consistent—in many instances the same article or publication contains points in favor of both sides of the questions. These contradictions will be pointed out from time to time as they arise.

Exploitation in the Labor Market

Examination of the historical literature leaves no doubt that after the Civil War either the Southern labor market was characterized by widespread imperfection, or segments of the planter population exerted great effort to acquire market power. Before considering the equally convincing documentation of competition in the labor market, the entire case for exploitation will be presented, point by point.

Southern observers did not usually announce their exploitation of agricultural labor in modern terminology, and so it is necessary to decide exactly what kinds of evidence can be taken as indications of labor market imperfection. The following list may not include every trace of exploitative behavior or intentions, but it should serve as a useful guide:
1. Evidence of legal limitations placed on labor mobility or on the ability of laborers to seek out employment at the highest offered wage.

exploitation

2.   Other evidence of limitations on labor mobility or bargaining rights, in the form of intimidation, laws, and ad hoc punishments for labor organizing or bargaining activity.

3.   Direct and indirect evidence of planters' collusion to depress the wages of workers.

4.   Evidence of a consciousness on the part of either employers or workers of exploitative labor relations.

5.   Legal or informal attempts to eliminate or restrict institutions, such as labor agencies, which would increase the flow of job information and smooth the operation of the labor market.

6.   Use of forced labor in various forms such as convict labor, illegal slave labor camps, or similar types of involuntary servitude.

7.   Evidence of the closure or restriction of occupations outside agriculture to sections of the farm labor force, particularly blacks.

8.   Attempts by planters to bend the Freedmen's Bureau and other relief agencies into becoming organs for the enforcement of exploitative contracts.

Each of these manifestations of actual or potential employers' market power over laborers can be found in the latter half of the nineteenth century. Some appeared occasionally or infrequently, while others were almost constantly present.

The blacks were particular targets of real or intended exploitation. After the surrender of the Confederate armies, a series of interim state governments was set up according to the reconstruction plans of President Andrew Johnson.[1] Among the first acts of those governments was to pass a series of laws known collectively as the "Black Codes."[2] These laws were designed to regulate race relations, in particular black labor and contracts. In addition to the more notorious provisions of these codes limiting blacks' civil rights, prohibiting intermarriage, and regulating other social relations between the races,[3] many of the codes contained severe infringements of the freedom of black labor. It is worthwhile to cite these codes at some length, because many of the restrictive devices introduced in them were to reappear in various forms throughout the postbellum period.

Mississippi extended its statutory definition of vagrants to include "all freedmen, free negroes, and mulattoes in this State, over the age of eighteen years, found on the second Monday in January, 1866, or there-

---

1.   For a full account of Andrew Johnson's plans for reconstruction, see Eric L. McKitrick, *Andrew Johnson and Reconstruction.*

2.   Ibid., p. 169.

3.   Kenneth M. Stampp, *The Era of Reconstruction: 1865–1877,* p. 80.

after, with no lawful employment or business" and subjected such "vagrants" to a fine of fifty dollars and imprisonment for not more than ten days. If the "vagrant" was unable to pay the fine, he could be hired out to any person who would pay it, with the amount of the fine deductible from the freedman's wages. Thus, Mississippi blacks were denied the option of being unemployed at any time. Mississippi also levied a yearly $1 capitation tax on every freedman, nonpayment of which was prima facie evidence of vagrancy.[4]

Georgia also defined as vagrants those who "are able to work and do not work," and gave the courts the power to sentence such vagrants to be "bound out to some person for a time not longer than one year" upon posting of a bond not exceeding $300 (or less, at the court's discretion).[5] South Carolina required any "person of color" who was engaged in any type of work other than farm labor to obtain a license from the district judge and pay a fee ranging from $10 to $100 per year.[6] Florida also levied a head tax on all male inhabitants between 21 and 55 years old (except paupers and mentally defective persons) with the usual punishment of hiring out to follow on conviction of nonpayment.[7]

The hiring out of convicts was a recurring motif, and the definition of unemployed Negroes as criminals was not the only attempt by the defeated states to regulate the labor market through the criminal code. Violation of labor contracts was widely defined as a criminal offense. The Florida vagrancy law of 1866 provided that

when any person of color shall enter into a contract as aforesaid, to serve as a laborer for a year, or any other specified term, on any farm or plantation in this State, if he shall refuse or neglect to perform the stipulations of his contract by wilful disobedience of orders, wanton impudence or disrespect to his employer, or his authorized agent, failure or refusal to perform the work assigned to him, idleness, or abandonment of the premises or the employment of the party with whom the contract was made, he or she shall be liable, . . . to be arrested and tried before the criminal court of the county, and upon conviction shall be subject to all the pains and penalties prescribed for the punishment of vagrancy: *Provided,* That it shall be optional with the employer to require that such laborer be remanded to his service, instead of being subjected to the punishment aforesaid.[8]

4. Edward McPherson, *The Political History of the United States of America During the Period of Reconstruction, from April 15, 1865 to July 15, 1870,* p. 30. This source collection contains a compilation of the codes themselves; and the quotations are from the actual statutes.

5. Ibid., p. 33.

6. Ibid., p. 36.

7. Ibid., p. 40.

8. Ibid., p. 39.

Mississippi added that any person could earn a fee of $5 plus 10 cents a mile for arresting and returning a freedman, free Negro, or mulatto who quit his lawful employer before the expiration of his contract, the fee to be deducted, as usual, from the freedman's wages.[9] Louisiana restrained a laborer from leaving "his place of employment until the fulfillment of his contract, unless by consent of his employer, or on account of harsh treatment, or breach of contract on the part of the employer; and if they do so leave, without cause or permission, they shall forfeit all wages earned to the time of abandonment."[10]

The regulation of labor extended beyond the enforcement of contracts with criminal procedures. The South Carolina Black Code included the humiliating provision that "all persons of color who make contracts for service or labor shall be known as servants, and those with whom they contract as masters."[11] North Carolina in 1866 amended its apprentice law to apply to blacks in general, giving former masters the option of administering the "apprenticeship." Runaway apprentices could then be arrested for "desertion" and returned to their master or mistress.[12] South Carolina allowed the district judges to usurp the role of parents by providing that

Colored children between 18 and 21, who have neither father nor mother *living in the district in which they are found,* or whose parents are paupers, or unable to afford them a comfortable maintenance, *or whose parents are not teaching them habits of industry and honesty,* or are persons of notoriously bad character, or are vagrants, or have been convicted of infamous offenses, and colored children, *in all cases where they are in danger of moral contamination,* may be bound as apprentices by the district judge or one of the magistrates for the aforesaid term.[13]

Mississippi also gave the courts broad powers to apprentice out black children, with preference given to former owners.[14]

The regulation of labor extended in some cases to a detailed specification of exactly what behavior was required and prohibited on the job. Louisiana in 1865 legislated that "when in health, the laborer shall work ten hours during the day in summer, and nine hours during the day in winter, unless otherwise stipulated in the labor contract"; and that "bad

9.   Ibid., p. 31.
10. Ibid., p. 43.
11. Ibid., p. 36.
12. Ibid., p. 29–30.
13. Ibid., p. 36.
14. Ibid., p. 29.

work shall not be allowed." Injuries to farm animals were to be deducted from wages, the laborers were not allowed to leave home without permission of the employer, and "disobedience, impudence, swearing, or indecent language to or in the presence of the employer, his family or agent" were prohibited. Laborers were not to receive visitors during work hours, and they were to be allowed to keep no livestock without the permission of the employer.[15]

The Black Codes' regulation of the labor market was not confined to provisions applying only to freedmen. Also common in these codes were the antienticement provisions which made it a crime for landlords to compete for labor in the marketplace. Mississippi provided that

if any person entice away any apprentice from his or her master or mistress, or shall knowingly employ an apprentice, or furnish him or her food or clothing, without the written consent of his or her master or mistress, or shall sell or give said apprentice ardent spirits without such consent, said person . . . shall be deemed guilty of a high misdemeanor, and shall on conviction thereof before the county court, *be punished as provided for the punishment of persons enticing from their employer hired freedmen, free negroes, or mulattoes* [Emphasis added].[16]

Georgia similarly provided that it was a criminal offense "for any person to interfere with, hire, employ, or entice away, or induce to leave the service of another, any laborer or servant," as well as specifying that any laborer who left his employer without "justifiable excuse" should be guilty of a misdemeanor. The discovery of a person in another man's employ before expiration of a legal contract was taken as prima facie evidence of violation of the antienticement law by the new employer, and interestingly enough, the provisions of this act do not seem to have been restricted to employment of blacks by whites, but included all "laborers or servants."[17] Florida went even further in the severity of its antienticement law, providing that

if any person shall entice, induce, or otherwise persuade any laborer or employee to quit the service of another to which he was bound by contract, before the expiration of the term of service stipulated in said contract, he shall be guilty of a misdemeanor, and upon conviction shall be fined in a sum not exceeding one thousand dollars, or shall stand in the

15.   Ibid., p. 43.
16.   Ibid., p. 30.
17.   Ibid., p. 34.

pillory not more than three hours, or be whipped not more than thirty-nine stripes on the bare back, at the discretion of the jury.[18]

Considering this law in conjunction with the Florida vagrancy law, which defined unemployment as vagrancy and empowered the courts to bind out convicted vagrants for one year, the net effect was an attempt to legislate the labor market out of existence. This was one instance in which the freedmen and whites received equal treatment under the Black Codes—convicted vagrants could also be punished by whipping and the pillory.[19]

The Black Codes were short-lived, and were overturned either by the federal military authorities or by Congress when it swept away the Johnson reconstruction governments in 1867.[20] Still, the Codes indicate at the very least the determination of the leading Southern elements to retain control of the black labor force in the face of emancipation. It is also interesting that the messages of several of the federal military governors striking down the Black Codes contain explicitly antimonopoly language. Major General A. H. Terry's order commanding the nonenforcement of the Virginia Vagrant Act is worth quoting at length. General Terry first summarized the provisions of the Act, which were entirely similar to the Vagrancy Acts cited above. He then concluded:

Among those declared to be vagrants are all persons who, not having the wherewith to support their families, live idly and without employment, and refuse to work for the usual and common wages given to other laborers in the like work in the place where they are.

In many counties of this State meetings of employers have been held, and unjust and wrongful combinations have been entered into for the purpose of depressing the wages of the freedmen below the real value of their labor, far below the prices formerly paid to masters for labor performed by their slaves. By reason of these combinations wages utterly inadequate to the support of themselves and families have, in many places, become the usual and common wages of the freedmen. The effect of the statute in question will be, therefore, to compel the freedmen, under penalty of punishment as criminals, to accept and labor for the wages established by these combinations of employers. It places them wholly in the power of their employers, and it is easy to foresee that, even where no such combination now exists, the temptation to form them offered by the statute will be too strong to be resisted, and that such inadequate wages will become the common and usual wages throughout the State. The ultimate effect of the statute will be to reduce

18. Ibid., pp. 39–40.
19. Ibid., p. 39.
20. For a brief account of the repudiation of these governments, see Stampp, *Era of Reconstruction,* pp. 144–145.

the freedmen to a condition of servitude worse than that from which they have been emancipated—a condition which will be slavery in all but its name.

It is therefore ordered that no magistrate, civil officer or other person shall in any way or manner apply or attempt to apply the provisions of said statute to any colored person in this department.

By command of Major General A. H. Terry,

Ed. W. Smith, Assistant Adjutant General.[21]

Hardly a clearer perception of the efforts of the defeated Southern planters to maintain their monopoly control over labor could be found. Nor is General Terry's message the only example of the recognition by the Union authorities of the intent of the Black Codes. General Sickles, in disallowing the South Carolina Code, forbade the levy of any tax or fee for a license for the practice of lawful trades, and stated that

no person will be restrained from seeking employment when not bound by voluntary agreement, nor hindered from traveling from place to place, on lawful business. All combinations or agreements which are intended to hinder, or may so operate as to hinder, in any way, the employment of labor—or to limit compensation for labor—or to compel labor to be involuntarily performed in certain places or for certain persons; as well as all combinations or agreements to prevent the sale or hire of lands or tenements, are declared to be misdemeanors.[22]

Southern employers' efforts to exploit the emancipated blacks immediately after the war were not confined to passage of the Black Codes alone. There is some evidence of an attempt on the part of Southern opinion to influence the Freedmen's Bureau into becoming the agency for the enforcement of stringent and restrictive contracts on black labor. George Ruble Woolfolk uncovered a correspondence between William King, a Georgia planter, and Oliver O. Howard, Director of the Freedmen's Bureau, concerning ways in which the Freedmen's Bureau might make Negro labor more serviceable. According to Woolfolk, "King represented a group of planters who had met at Savannah for the purpose of effecting plans to solve the labor problem, and had written General Howard about it."[23] King recommended that "all freedmen who have not per-

21. McPherson, *Political History,* p. 42.
22. Ibid., pp. 36–37.
23. George Ruble Woolfolk, *The Cotton Regency: The Northern Merchants and Reconstruction, 1865–1880,* pp. 48–49. The letter referred to is cited by Woolfolk as *William King to Maj. General O. O. Howard,* Savannah, Georgia, 30 May, 1865. Woolfolk's reference (p. 210) states, "This letter, with the original planters' plan and the revisions after King's New England Conference . . ., were located in the Freedmen's Bureau MSS., War Department Archives, the National Archives, Washington, D.C." The letter will subsequently be referred to as the *King Letter.*

manent supporting employment, in cities, towns, and villages, . . . be required to remove to the country and make engagements for their labor," and that "all capable labor shall at once make engagements to labor in the country or agriculture, or otherwise for a term not less than 12 months from the date of contract at such wages as both parties may agree upon.[24] In King's plan, the Freedmen's Bureau was to avoid issuing rations to any freedman who was capable of working, and in the event that a freedman broke his contract, the response of the Bureau was to be severe:

Any Freedman who shall abandon in place of labor or fail to perform properly and faithfully the duties he has contracted to perform, or for other bad conduct, shall be reported to the nearest local superintendent, who shall immediately institute an examination of the case reported, and decide on its merits, and should such superintendent determine and decide, that the Freedman has been guilty of improper or unfaithful conduct, such Freedman shall be immediately placed in solitary confinement (and supplied only with bread and water) for such length of time as may be determined on, not however to exceed the term of his contract, and during the period of such absence from labor his wages shall cease and he shall yet be chargeable with the expense of supporting the non-supporting members of his family.[25]

Solitary confinement on bread and water was also the penalty recommended by King for freedmen who had neglected or refused to make a contract for a year's labor before the first of January of each year. In addition to enforcing the making and maintenance of labor contracts, the Freedmen's Bureau was admonished to punish any freedman who trespassed on the property of others, or made visits to farms or plantations other than the one where he was employed, without permission of his employer.[26] Needless to say, these recommendations were ignored, at least in the official policy of the Bureau. Nevertheless, such sentiments undoubtedly reflected a substantial segment of planter opinion, and there were instances when local Freedmen's Bureau officials carried out this sort of policy. For example, Brigadier General Fullerton, upon assuming control of the affairs of the Freedmen's Bureau in New Orleans immediately after the war, issued an order "that all persons of color in and about the city of New Orleans who did not produce evidence immediately of being employed should be arrested as vagrants. The consequence was that in the course of twenty-four or forty-eight hours a very large number of colored persons who were found upon the streets without evidence of

24. *King Letter,* Woolfolk, p. 71.
25. Ibid., p. 72.
26. Ibid., pp. 72–73.

employment with them were put in prison." General Fullerton's order was revoked within 48 hours by General Canby, commander of the district, but the incident was probably repeated in other cases.[27] One historian even found that

employers sometimes took advantage of the credulity of the Negroes to cheat them, or to offer better working conditions and induce them to break their contracts with another employer in order to take advantage of higher wages. Indeed, so common was this latter practice that the Freedmen's Bureau provided that planters should be fined from $100 to $500 for the offense.[28]

It is difficult to know whether the "offense" referred to was fraud or competition among employers for labor.

Reference to the exploitation hypothesis helps to explain the often-repeated complaint of Southern planters that they faced a "labor shortage." This cry was most often raised in the years just following the end of the war. A letter from a frustrated Mississippi planter to the *Southern Cultivator,* one of the most important agricultural magazines of the postwar period, is typical: "Labor is wanting; none of the plantations in this vicinity are fully stocked with hands."[29] *DeBow's Review* attributed the decline in the size of the plantation labor force to three causes:

We fear . . . that labor in cotton culture is fast diminishing. It is from three causes: Emigration from the cotton fields to the towns and cities; the deaths on the plantations; and, the retiring of women from cotton growing.[30]

This same article estimated the loss by death in the black population during the Civil War as between 500,000 and 1,000,000 persons.[31] But planters' compaints of a "scarcity of labor" implied in the simplest sense that they wished to employ more labor than was forthcoming at the offered wage. This is consistent with the offered wage's being below the market-clearing equilibrium wage, because of planters' obstinate refusal to

---

27. U.S. Congress, Joint Committee on Reconstruction, *Report of the Joint Committee on Reconstruction,* 39th Cong., 1st Sess. (1866), part 3, p. 25. This report will hereafter be referred to as the *RJCR.*
28. C. W. Tebeau, "Some Aspects of Planter-Freedman Relations, 1865–1880," *Journal of Negro History,* 21 no. 2 (April 1936): 143–144. Tebeau cites *Senate Executive Document,* no. 6, 39 Cong., 2d Sess., p. 141; and *House Executive Document,* no. 70, 39 Cong., 1st Sess., pp. 93–94 for this remarkable fact.
29. "H.," "Letter from Mississippi," *Southern Cultivator* 27 (June 1869): 181.
30. "Cotton Trade of the World," *DeBow's Review* (July 1869), p. 610. The numbering on the title pages and captions of *DeBow's Review* was somewhat irregular, so references to it will be cited by date only.
31. Ibid., p. 609. This estimate is almost certainly exaggerated.

if only they had cited marked

increase the offered wage. Instead, they attempted to force the blacks to work under compulsion, and found a "shortage" of labor.

It should be pointed out that an offered wage below the market wage in the years immediately following the war is also consistent with a slow adjustment by planters from paying slave wages to paying competitive wages, given a temporary labor market disequilibrium following emancipation. There is some evidence that the wage increased just after the war ended, and this will be discussed subsequently as part of the evidence that the labor market was operating competitively.

The belief that the blacks would not work without compulsion and the disposition of the planters to exploit them were linked. Carl Schurz's report on his fact-finding mission through the defeated Confederacy contained both direct and indirect evidence of this. Schurz himself drew the gloomy conclusion that

in at least nineteen cases of twenty the reply I received to my inquiry about their [southern whites'] view of the new system [of free labor] was uniformly this: "You cannot make the negro work without physical compulsion." I heard this hundreds of times, heard it wherever I went, heard it in nearly the same words from so many different persons, that at last I came to the conclusion that this is the prevailing sentiment among the southern people. . . .

A belief, conviction, or prejudice, or whatever you may call it, so widely spread and apparently so deeply rooted as this, that the negro will not work without physical compulsion, is certainly calculated to have a very serious influence upon the conduct of the people entertaining it. It naturally produced a desire to preserve slavery in its original form as much and as long as possible—and you may, perhaps, remember the admission made by one of the provisional governors, over two months after the close of the war, that the people of his State still indulged in a lingering hope slavery might yet be preserved—or to introduce into the new system that element of physical compulsion which would make the negro work. Efforts were, indeed, made to hold the negro in his old state of subjection, especially in such localities where our military forces had not yet penetrated, or where the country was not garrisoned in detail. Here and there planters succeeded for a limited period to keep their former slaves in ignorance, or at least doubt, about their new rights; but the main agency employed for that purpose was force and intimidation. In many instances negroes who walked away from the plantations, or were found upon the roads, were shot or otherwise severely punished, which was calculated to produce the impression among those remaining with their masters that an attempt to escape from slavery would result in certain destruction.[32]

32. Carl Schurz, *Report on the Condition of the South,* pp. 16–17. This *Report* was submitted by Schurz on December 19, 1865, and originally appeared as *U.S. Senate Ex. Doc. No. 2,* 39th Cong., 1st Sess. The Arno Press Reprint is an exact photographic reproduction of the original *Report,* and will be referred to hereafter as the Schurz *Report.*

Schurz then summarized the accounts which were sent to him of exploitative practices. Typical of these reports are those of Captain W.A. Poillon,
Assistant Superintendent of the Freedmen's Bureau in Mobile. In a letter
dated July 29, 1865, Poillon listed some of the murders, mutilations, and
other acts of violence perpetrated against Negroes who left the plantations of their former masters in his district, and concluded:

*Murder with his ghastly train stalks abroad at noonday and revels in un-
disputed carnage,* while the bewildered and terrified freedmen know not
what to do. To leave is death; to remain is to suffer the increased burden
imposed on them by the cruel taskmaster, whose only interest is their
labor *wrung* from them by every device an inhuman ingenuity can devise.
Hence the lash and murder are resorted to to intimidate those whom fear
of an awful death *alone* causes to remain, while patrols, negro dogs, and
spies (disguised as Yankees) keep *constant* guard over these unfortunate
people.[33]

In another letter, Captain Poillon reported that "laborers on the plantations are forced to remain and toil without hope of remuneration."[34]
Schurz's documents leave the distinct impression that white employers
recognized no limitation on the level of violence exercised to prevent free
travel and free labor contracting by blacks during the years immediately
following the conclusion of the war.

Schurz referred to a series of "attempted municipal regulations" in
Louisiana which had all the attributes of the statewide Black Codes, regulations "to prevent the freedmen from obtaining employment [away]
from their former masters" and "applying exclusively to the negro, and
depriving him of all liberty of locomotion":

The negro is not only not permitted to be idle, but he is positively prohibited from working or carrying on a business for himself; he is *compelled* to be in the "regular service" of a white man, and if he has no
employer he is *compelled* to find one. It requires only a simple understanding among the employers, and the negro is just as much bound to
his employer "for better and for worse" as he was when slavery existed
in the old form. If he should attempt to leave his employer on account of
non-payment of wages or bad treatment he is *compelled* to find another
one; and if no other will take him he will be *compelled* to return to him
from whom he wanted to escape. The employers, under such circumstances, are naturally at liberty to arrange the matter of compensation

33. Schurz, *Report,* p. 74.
34. Ibid.,p. 73. This letter was from Captain Poillon to General Carl Schurz, dated
September 9, 1865, from Mobile, Alabama.

according to their tastes, for the negro will be compelled to be in the regular service of an employer, whether he receives wages or not.[35]

Schurz was pessimistic about the willingness of the white South to accede to the full emancipation of Negro labor. His conclusion in this regard may be taken as an original statement of the exploitation hypothesis:

As long as a majority of the southern people believe that "the negro will not work without physical compulsion," and that "the blacks at large belong to the whites at large," that belief will tend to produce a system of coercion, the enforcement of which will be aided by the hostile feeling against the negro now prevailing among the whites, and by the general spirit of violence which in the south was fostered by the influence slavery exercised upon the popular character. It is, indeed, not probable that a general attempt will be made to restore slavery in its old form, on account of the barriers which such an attempt would find in its way; but there are systems intermediate between slavery as it formerly existed in the south, and free labor as it exists in the north, but more nearly related to the former than to the latter, *the introduction of which will be attempted.*[36]

Schurz included in his *Report* documentation of attempts by planters to restrain competition among themselves for black labor as well. A list of suggestions submitted to Schurz by a committee of planters on November 24, 1864, recommended "a law to punish most severely any one who endeavors, by offering higher wages, gifts, perquisites, &c., &c., to induce a negro to leave his employer before the expiration of the term for which he has engaged to labor without the consent of said employer."[37] A letter from T. Gibson of the N.O. and O. Railroad dated December 1, 1864, urged Schurz that

wages, rules, and regulations should be fixed and uniform; nothing left to discretion. A penalty should be inflicted on every employer who deviates from the established rates, *maximum* rates. . . . Wages should be extremely moderate on account of the unsteadiness of labor and exceeding uncertainty of crops of all sorts, but especially of cane and cotton.[38]

Needless to say, these overt and unsubtle efforts on the part of the defeated South to resubjugate the black population did not meet with favor among the abolitionist, radical, and even moderate Unionist population

35. Schurz, *Report,* pp. 23–24.
36. Ibid., p. 32.
37. Ibid., p. 84.
38. Ibid., p. 86.

of the North. The Black Codes were nullified, the provisional state governments dissolved, and the progress of reconstruction was taken over
by the Congress. In preparation for this, Congress established in 1865
the Joint Committee on Reconstruction, composed of members of both
Houses "who shall inquire into the condition of the States which formed
the so-called Confederate States of America, and report whether they, or
any of them, are entitled to be represented in either house of Congress."[39]
This Joint Committee included prominent Radical Republicans, among
them Thaddeus Stevens, but it was actually controlled by the moder-
ates.[40] Testimony before it supports in some places the exploitation
hypothesis, in others the competition hypothesis. The evidence for competition will be presented later, in keeping with the organization of the
material in this chapter.

The Joint Committee on Reconstruction, like Schurz, found abundant
grounds for believing that large segments of Southern opinion favored
reestablishment of some kind of slavery. Richard Hill, an ex-slave living
in Hampton, Virginia, testified that "it seems to be a prevalent idea, that
if their [the Southern states'] representatives were received in Congress
the condition of the freedmen would be very little better than that of the
slaves, and that their old laws would still exist by which they would reduce them to something like bondage. That has been expressed by a
great many of them."[41] This opinion was shared by Major General
George H. Thomas, commander of the military division of Tennessee,
who said that "if all restraint should be removed, the freedmen would be
thrown back into a condition of virtual slavery; that is, they would be
compelled by legislative enactments to labor for little or no wages, and
the legislation would assume such a form that they would not dare to
leave their employers for fear of punishment."[42] Such opinions were not
confined to proabolition spokesmen. Major General Clinton B. Fisk, a
Mississippi Freedmen's Bureau official, related that he had attempted to
obtain the release to her mother of a little girl being held by a Mississippi
planter. General Fisk entered into the record of his testimony the close
of the letter he received in reply from the planter:

As to recognizing the rights of freedmen to their children, I will say there
is not one man or woman in all the south who believes they are free, but

39. *RJCR*, p. i.
40. Stampp, *Era of Reconstruction*, p. 110.
41. *RJCR*, part 2, p. 56.
42. *RJCR*, part 3, p. 27.

we consider them as stolen property—stolen by the bayonets of the damnable United States government. Yours truly, T. Yancey.

General Fisk characterized the Yancey letter thus: "That is a sample of very much of the correspondence we have with that class of people."[43] The theme that the freedmen would not work without compulsion was also reiterated by several witnesses before the Joint Committee.[44]

The Committee uncovered many "outrages" committed against the free black population in attempts to regulate the labor market. Madison Newby, a black resident of Surrey County, Virginia, testified to a bizarre perversion of wage bargaining:

In Surrey county they [the employers] are taking the colored people and tying them up by the thumbs if they do not agree to work for six dollars a month; they tie them up until they agree to work for that price, and then they make them put their mark to a contract.
QUESTION. Did you ever see a case of that kind?
ANSWER. Yes, sir, I did.
QUESTION. How many cases of that kind have you ever seen?
ANSWER. Only one; I have heard of several such, but I have only seen one.
QUESTION. What is the mode of tying up by the thumbs?
ANSWER. They have a string tied around the thumbs just strong enough to hold a man's weight, so that his toes just touch the ground; and they keep the man in that position until he agrees to do what they say. A man cannot endure it long.
QUESTION. What other bad treatment do they practice on the blacks? Do they whip them?
ANSWER. Yes, sir; just as they did before the war; I see no difference.[45]

Captain J. H. Matthews, a provost marshal or subcommissioner of the Freedmen's Bureau in Mississippi, reported that in "ninety-nine cases out of a hundred" the freedmen were driven from the plantations at the end of the year without payment for their work, and that the old system of flogging was practiced extensively, "inhuman flogging, to the extent,

43. Ibid., p. 31.
44. See, for example, the testimony of Brigadier General Charles H. Howard, Inspector in the Freedmen's Bureau and brother of Major General O. O. Howard, Chief of the Freedmen's Bureau, *RJCR*, part 3, p. 36; also the testimony of Brigadier General James S. Brisbin, U.S. Army Captain stationed in Arkansas, *RJCR*, part 3, p. 70; and the testimony of Thomas Conway, Assistant Commissioner of the Freedmen's Bureau in New Orleans who testified that in effect the Louisiana Black Codes simply substituted the word "negro" for the word "slave" wherever it appeared, *RJCR*, part 4, p. 79.
45. *RJCR*, part 2, pp. 54–55.

in some cases, of 350 lashes."[46] Major General David S. Stanley remembered "four or five instances where negroes were killed for trying to leave their masters" in the state of Texas.[47]

The Joint Committee on Reconstruction also found direct evidence of planters' collusion to maintain low wage levels. Major General Clinton B. Fisk, the Alabama Freedmen's Bureau official quoted previously, contributed this account of wage-fixing, under questioning by Representative Boutwell of Massachusetts:

QUESTION. Do you know of any combinations among employers for the purpose of regulating the price of labor among the freedmen?
ANSWER. There were such combinations made early in the summer, among the planters in their conventions, fixing a very low rate of compensation for the labor of the freedmen. But the combinations were broken up by the officers of the Freedmen's Bureau. My orders prohibited any combinations of the people, or of communities, fixing any rate of wages. My directions to my subordinates were, to let labor, like any other commodity, compete in an open market.[48]

Major General Thomas of Tennessee also reported that he had received rumors of such combinations of employers, and had warned the officers of the Freedmen's Bureau to "take steps to prevent any undue advantage being taken by employers over the laborers they employ."[49] The tension between the opposing forces—the employers striving for market advantages and the federal occupation armies acting to prevent it—is highlighted in these testimonies, with the ultimate resolution in doubt. It seems likely that the Union generals would claim success in their campaign against the "combinations" even if the planters had been able to sidestep all efforts to break them up. In any case, Major General Edward Hatch had little doubt that many of the planters' "combinations" formed to begin reestablishing slavery had as their main objective the regulation of wages:

The men there [in Tennessee] who dislike the present state of things do not like to give up the negro. They think that by some kind of legislation they can establish a kind of peonage; not absolute slavery, but that they can enact such laws as will enable them to manage the negro as they please—to fix the prices to be paid for his labor. That is a very general idea among that class of men. But those men of broad views who know

46. *RJCR*, part 3, p. 142.
47. *RJCR*, part 4, p. 39.
48. *RJCR*, part 3, p. 30.
49. Ibid., p. 27.

that labor will find its level, are in favor of hiring the negro and paying him fairly. But they are in the minority.[50]

Reports of planter collusion during the 1860s were not confined to accounts and testimony of hostile Northerners. *DeBow's Review,* organ of the most respectable planter opinion, reported an 1868 meeting of citizens in Summerville, Alabama, which resolved, among other things:

Whereas, The present disorganized and inefficient System of Labor is causing great loss to the citizens of this community and county, and must ultimately result in the entire destruction of the agricultural interests of the country; and whereas the interests of the whites and blacks are identical; therefore,

1st. *Resolved,* That concert of action is indispensable among those hiring laborers for the ensuing year.

2nd. That every one hiring laborers should impress upon them the necessity of complying with the terms of their contract; and in the event of their failure to do so, they should be discharged.

3rd. That as good citizens, and acting in good faith towards each other, we pledge ourselves not to employ any laborers discharged for a violation of contracts, without a certificate of recommendation from the person last employing them. . . .

6th. That we should adopt a schedule of prices equalizing the wages paid laborers; and that we recommend the following classification: for 1st class field hands $10 per month; 2d class $8 per month; 3d class $6 per month.[51]

At about the same time, the planters in Amite County, Mississippi, recommended that if a freedman be discharged for poor work, or for attending "club meetings" without permission, the planters should "pledge ourselves not to hire or give such freedmen employment under any circumstances."[52]

All these quotations point unmistakably to a will on the part of the former Southern slaveholders to interfere with the free operation of the labor market. The existence of the will does not imply that a way was found, however. The provisional governments were dissolved, the Black Codes were overturned, Republican reconstruction governments were established throughout the defeated Confederacy with black participation, and the great fourteenth and fifteenth amendments to the Constitution were passed. The immediate postwar codes and combinations may

50. *RJCR,* part 1, pp. 107–108.
51. "Treatment and Pay of the Freedmen," *DeBow's Review* (February 1868), p. 213.
52. "How They are Settling the Labor Question in Mississippi," *DeBow's Review* (February 1868), p. 224.

have been futile efforts to maintain an advantage lost with abolition. But if so, the planters were persistent. The same sorts of oppressive laws and practices were tried over and over throughout the nineteenth century.

It would be impractical here to attempt to summarize the provisions of Southern legislation regarding agricultural labor relations for the period between the Civil War and World War I. Fortunately, other scholars have done this work, and their findings will be drawn on here. Oscar Zeichner, writing in the *Political Science Quarterly* in 1940, surveyed Southern laws regarding agricultural labor from the time of the Civil War through the thirties, and concluded that in addition to the crop lien laws, "the laws dealing with labor contracts, false pretenses, emigrant agents, and the enticing of laborers have assured the planter of legal support in his effort to secure a stable labor supply during the agricultural year."[53] It is interesting to see exactly how these laws guaranteed a "stable labor supply."

Several Southern states passed "false pretenses" laws "to keep agricultural laborers on the plantation for the duration of their contracts." The North Carolina law was typical:

In North Carolina it is a criminal offense, punishable by fine or imprisonment, for anyone to obtain advances "with intent to cheat or defraud. . . " from a person or corporation, and then "willfully fail, without a lawful excuse, to commence or complete such work according to contract. . . . "* It constitutes a like violation in twenty-one counties of the state for a tenant or sharecropper to receive supplies from his landlord and then refuse to cultivate the crop or abandon it "without good cause and before paying for such advances."**

As of the dates indicated, Alabama (1928), Georgia (1933), and South Carolina (1932) had similar "false pretenses" laws on the books.[54] All the "false pretenses" laws were designed to make violation of labor contracts a criminal offense. The Mississippi Supreme Court in 1912 had struck down a Mississippi law which made it a crime for a laborer, renter, or sharecropper to break a written contract without securing the landlord's permission, and to make another contract without notifying the second employer of the existence of the first agreement,[55] and the U.S. Supreme Court had overturned a similar Alabama law in 1911.[56] Since

53. Oscar Zeichner, "The Legal Status of the Agricultural Laborer in the South," *Political Science Quarterly* 55, no. 3 (September 1940): 428.
54. Ibid., p. 424. Zeichner's notes are
* North Carolina Code (1935), par. 4281.
** North Carolina Code (1935), par. 4481.
55. Zeichner, "The Legal Status . . . ," pp. 423–424, fn. 33.
56. Ibid., p. 425, fn. 38. Zeichner's reference is to Bailey *v.* Alabama, 219 U.S. 245 (1911).

the courts had declared it unconstitutional to make the mere breach of a labor contract a criminal offense, the "false pretenses" statutes were drawn up ostensibly to punish fraud.[57]

The "false pretenses" laws were not the only echo of the Black Codes. Zeichner's description of the "antienticement" laws could scarcely be more graphic:

Complementing the false pretense laws are those prohibiting the "enticing" of croppers, tenants and laborers from their employers. Farm hands might be kept on the plantation by threat of economic loss and legal punishment, but planters still had to eliminate the danger of outside interference with their tenants and croppers. The chief competitors for the cheap and tractable labor supply on the plantations were, first, the industrial enterprises of the North and to a lesser extent those of the South, and, secondly, farm operators, who because of labor shortages or other crises had to secure immediate extra help. In order to eliminate the danger from the first source, some states, notably Alabama, Georgia, Mississippi and South Carolina, have placed prohibitory restrictions upon employment agents who solicit and send labor out of the state. In Alabama all "emigrant agents," as they are usually called, and their assistants, partners and employees are required to pay an annual tax of $5,000 to the state. Each county of the state in which the agent operates can levy an additional tax up to a maximum of $2,500.* In Mississippi, labor agents must pay a fee of $500 for each county in which they work.** Georgia requires emigrant agents to post a bond acceptable to the Commissioner of Commerce and Labor "conditioned to pay any valid debt" owed by the solicited laborer to a citizen of the state. In addition they are taxed $1,000 for every county in which they carry on business.*** South Carolina also requires that emigrant agents be licensed by state and county. In both cases the licenses are renewable annually. The state fee is $500 for each county in which labor is solicited, while every county demands $2,000 for the similar privilege within its jurisdiction.**** Violations of these provisions in all of the above states are punishable by heavy fine or imprisonment.*****[58]

In addition, as of the dates indicated, Alabama (1928), Arkansas (1937), Georgia (1933), Louisiana (1932), Mississippi (1930), certain counties of North Carolina (1935) and South Carolina (1932) forbade "the 'enticing'

57. Zeichner, "The Legal Status . . . ," p. 425.
58. Ibid., pp. 426–427. Zeichner's references are
*   Ala. Code (1928), par. 696, 697, 3980.
**   Miss. Code (1930), Supplement, Appendix, p. 442.
***   Ga. Code (1933), sec. 92–506; see also sec. 54–9902.
****   S.C. Code (1932), par. 1377, 1378.
***** For further reference, see S. M. Harrison, *Public Employment Offices* (New York: 1924), p. 606; and R. S. Baker, *Following the Color Line* (New York: 1908), pp. 79–80.

or employment of tenants, sharecroppers and laborers . . . already under contract, and whose period of work has not ended."[59]

The United States Congress in 1898 set up an Industrial Commission
to "investigate questions pertaining to immigration, to labor, to agriculture, to manufacturing, and to business,"[60] and its investigation revealed
that Kentucky, Arkansas, South Carolina, Georgia, Tennessee, North
Carolina, Mississippi, Florida, and Alabama all had antienticement statutes on the books at that time.[61] One witness before the Industrial Commission argued that North Carolina's "Landlord and Tenant Act," a law
ostensibly designed to provide a "homestead exemption" of $1,000 worth
of real estate and $500 worth of personal property "not liable to execu-
tion for debt on any judgment acquired," had the result of virtually en-
slaving tenants to landlords. The Landlord and Tenant Act preserved the
"homestead exemption" by making nonpayment of debts a criminal offense, and this law was apparently used by some landlords to prevent labor mobility:

I believe that the homestead law in our section of the country is really a
hindrance and trouble rather than a benefit to the poor man, whom it
was intended to benefit. These technical violations of the criminal law,
however, are not, as I should like to emphasize, invoked by the better
element of our landlords. They are, as a rule, liberal; it is only by some
shyster fellow who wants to stop me when I am disposed to go elsewhere
with a view of bettering my condition. He finds that I have technically
violated some of these laws. It is difficult for a man to live on premises
for a time without violating any law—if not the spirit, some part of the
letter. He uses that as a lever to hold them over, under a promise of im-
munity from prosecution in the courts. . . .
     . . . The law is in favor of the landlord, and, if need be, he can use it
to the detriment of the tenant. That is the general trend of the law
through North Carolina.[62]

59. Zeichner, "The Legal Status, . . ." pp. 427–428, including fns. 48–54 for State
Code References.
60. U.S. Industrial Commission, *Reports of the Industrial Commission,* vol. 11:
Report of the Industrial Commission on Agriculture and Taxation in Various States
(1901), p. ii. Hereafter referred to as *ROIC,* 11.
61. U.S. Industrial Commission, *Reports of the Industrial Commission,* vol. 5: *Report of the Industrial Commission on Labor Legislation* (1900), pp. 74–77. Hereafter
referred to as *ROIC, 5.*
62. U.S. Industrial Commission, *Reports of the Industrial Commission,* vol. 10:
Report of the Industrial Commission on Agriculture and Agricultural Labor (1901),
pp. 416–421, passim. Hereafter this volume of the Industrial Commission's Reports
will be referred to as *ROIC,* 10. The quotations here are all from the testimony before the Industrial Commission of the Honorable George Henry White, the only
black man in Congress at that time, representing the Second District of North
Carolina.

Charles S. Mangum, Jr., in his 1940 monograph, *The Legal Status of the Negro,* chronicled the seesaw balance between the Southern states' attempts to restrict the freedom of agricultural labor through various types of peonage laws, and the federal courts' overturning of those laws.[63] In a Florida case decided in 1905, the federal court found that if an employer charged a runaway debtor with a crime for the sole purpose of having the debtor released to his custody to work off the debt, the federal antipeonage statutes were violated. Similarly,

In a South Carolina case a federal court held that one is guilty of peonage who by reason of his superior economic and social position induces a party to labor for the purpose of paying debts by threats of prosecution under criminal statutes, if by reason of such threats the will of the party is overcome.* Again, it has been said that one is guilty of peonage if he falsely pretends to another that the latter is accused of a criminal offense and offers to prevent his conviction if he will pay the prosecutor a sum of money in satisfaction, thus inducing him to sign a labor contract to reimburse the one who is supposed to have paid such sum for him and to submit to a deprivation of liberty in the meantime.**[64]

It should be noted that all these cases (as well as certain others not cited here) were decided in the first decade of the 1900s, just at the close of the period under study here. Clearly, the peonage issue was the subject of much adjudication in the South around the turn of the century, and where there is so much smoke, there is likely to be a substantial amount of fire. Mangum concluded that as late as 1940, "Situations exist . . . in the South as well as in other sections of the nation where Negroes are held in circumstances which approach involuntary servitude."[65] In his judgment, at least, the outcome of the legal struggle over labor peonage was not entirely in favor of the blacks.

These laws were not simply dead letters, remaining on the books because no one bothered to repeal them. A. B. Hart was one of the most perceptive observers of the South in the late nineteenth century. In 1910 he wrote *The Southern South,* based on his correspondence with South-

63.   It should be noted that this can be taken as evidence either for the legal embodiment of market power of landlords, or as the legal destruction of such power. Which proved ultimately the more effective: the operation of the laws while they were in force, or the striking down of the laws? There is no way to determine this from the legal history alone.
64.   Charles S. Mangum, Jr., *The Legal Status of the Negro,* p. 165. Florida reference is to *In re* Peonage Charge, 138 Fed. 686 (C.C.N.D. Fla. 1905). The other references are to *United States v.* Clement, 171 Fed. 974 (D.S.C. 1909), and **Peonage Cases, 123 Fed. 671 (M.D. Ala. 1903).
65.   Mangum, *The Legal Status of the Negro,* p. 172.

erners, conversations with his students at Harvard, and "in the last twen-
ty-five years . . . a dozen or more visits to various parts of the South
ranging in length from a few days to four months," as well as a journey
through rural parts of the South during the winter of 1907–1908.[66] Hart
found ample evidence of practices completely consistent with the laws
discussed previously. "Of recent years a new or rather a renewed cause
of race hostility has been found, because the great demand for labor,
chiefly in the cotton fields, gives rise to the startling abuse of a system of
forced labor, commonly called peonage, which at the mildest is the practice of thrashing a hand who misbehaves on the plantation, and in its
farthest extent is virtually slavery."[67] Also, "the conditions of the old
slavery times are more nearly reproduced in the cotton field than anywhere else in the South."[68] Part of this peonage system was the expected
collusion among employers:

It is unwritten law among some planters that nobody must give employment for the remainder of the year to a hand who is known to have left
his crop on another plantation; and still further, that no contract should
be made at the beginning of the year with a family which, after account-
ing for the previous crop, is still in debt to a neighbor.[69]

Possibly more remarkably, the peonage system also "began to be applied
to Whites."[70] Hart also noted the operation of the "false pretenses"
laws, and gave some typical examples of their operation, usually through
the subsequently outlawed device of having a runaway employee
arrested, fined, and remanded to the employer. In one instance, a woman
made a contract; before it expired, she married a man she had not yet
met when the contract was made. Her marriage was held to prove that
she did not intend to fulfill her contract when she made it, and she was
found guilty of "false pretenses" in signing the contract.[71]

   Even more appalling were some of the barbarities committed against
blacks for purposes of enforcing exploitative contracts. In "the most
frightful case of peonage as yet recorded,"

a woman was accused of a misdemeanor; it is doubtful whether she had
committed any; but at any rate she was fined fifteen dollars; Turner [a
Southern planter] paid the fine; she was assigned to him and he set her

66. Albert Bushnell Hart, *The Southern South,* p. 3.
67. Ibid., p. 278.
68. Ibid., p. 261.
69. Ibid., p. 280.
70. Ibid.
71. Ibid., p. 284.

to the severe labor of clearing land. And then what happened? What was a hustling master to do with a woman who would not pile brush as fast as the men brought it, but to whip her, and if she still did not reform, to whip her again, and when she still would not do the work, to string her up by the wrists for two hours, and when she still "shirked," God Almighty at last came to the rescue; she was dead![72]

The popular magazines of the period contain much support for the exploitation hypothesis. In the *Atlantic Monthly* just after the turn of the century, "Nicholas Worth" observed that "a large part of the Southern people have persuaded themselves that the Negro must be kept to a level reminiscent of slavery, forgetting that on this level he can only be a burden."[73] This opinion was also expressed in a series of articles appearing in *The Outlook* at about the same time. An anonymous Episcopalian clergyman of Virginia is quoted there as saying, "I suppose I'll shock you, when I tell you that I still believe in slavery. I believe slavery was of divine origin."[74] The author of the *Outlook* series went on to observe that disagreements over wage rates and labor supplied were the main source of friction between the races:

At any rate, it was clear that employers wanted better work than the negroes would do, and everywhere negroes wanted higher wages than they could get. This labor situation in a region where there are plenty of negroes to do the work needed, and at a time when there seemed to be plenty of work for negroes to do, was oftener mentioned than any other cause—than even criminal assault and mob reprisals—as occasion for mutual distrust between the races, especially for distrust of the negroes by the whites.[75]

Another article in the *Atlantic Monthly,* this one dealing with the famous "Negro Exodus" from the lower Mississippi Valley to Kansas during the late 1870s, indicated that the Southern opposition to this "exodus" went so far as to try "influencing the regular lines of steamboats not to carry the refugees."[76] This "influence" apparently involved more than words, because it was reported elsewhere that "four or five of the Mississippi steamboats which carried colored emigrants North while the

72. Ibid., pp. 284–285.
73. Nicholas Worth (pseud.), "Autobiography of a Southerner," *Atlantic Monthly* 98 (1906): 486.
74. Ernest Hamlin Abbott, "The South and the Negro," *The Outlook* 77 (May 28, 1904): 226. "The South and the Negro" was a seven-part serialized article beginning in the May 21, 1904, issue of *The Outlook*.
75. Ibid. (July 23, 1904): 692.
76. James B. Runnion, "The Negro Exodus," *Atlantic Monthly* 44 (August 1879): 230.

exodus was at its highest last spring [of 1879], have been seized and libeled for violation of the law in taking more deck passengers than their registers allowed them to carry."[77]

Support for the exploitation hypothesis can be found in popular farmers' magazines as well. The eminently practical agricultural trade journal, the *Southern Cultivator,* included in its helpful advice to farmers recommendations for collusion to regulate labor. In a letter to the editor titled "Concert of Action Among Farmers" in 1869, F. A. Dulany of Camden, Alabama, advised the readers of the *Southern Cultivator* thus:

Is it not important that cotton growers should also organize in some manner? Not only the farmers of the North, but professional men everywhere, can see the necessity of association, consultation, and concert of action, but mention the matter to some of our planters, (as I have done here) and just ask them to subscribe for the *Cultivator,* and they begin to decry at once "book-farming."[78]

This writer did not indicate whether he was referring to concert of action with respect to setting wages, marketing, or whatever, but a subsequent letter to the *Cultivator* a few months later left no doubt:

There should be, as there is in almost all other countries, a certain agreed price for all classes of labor, or some system in relation to the matter. As it is, we are all working against each other, and cannot prosper as a country, so long as it lasts. . . . Would it not be well to organize ourselves in the only field that we can operate? The only help is within ourselves, God, and our Mother Earth.[79]

Another letter to the editor extolling the benefits of agricultural associations contained the following prescription:

Laborers might be introduced [to the members of the Association] and those among us better controlled and made more reliable. . . . Our system must be improved. The time was, when planters relied on physical force to make up for all the deficiencies, but now every furrow plowed and every hill hoed must be paid for in money, and but few [are] willing to plow or hoe.[80]

In other words, planters' collusion could substitute for the physical force that served to "control" agricultural labor prior to the abolition of slavery.

77. "Exodus Notes," *Southern Workman* 7 (October 1879): 102.
78. *Southern Cultivator* 27 (May 1869): 149.
79. Alabama [pseud.], "What is Our Interest," ibid. (October 1869): 312.
80. C. M. Vaiden, "Agricultural Association," ibid. (September 1869): 275.

It is interesting to point out that the implication of the second letter quoted above is that the planters at that time were actively *competing* for labor. Indeed, that is consistent with the main point of this examination of the historical sources—a convincing argument can be made for either the exploitation hypothesis or the competition hypothesis. For the moment, however, only the existence of a desire by some planters to exploit the agricultural laborers and a consciousness of how that might be accomplished needs to be shown.

Advocacy of collusion by planters was repeated much later in the pages of the *Southern Cultivator*. W. J. Northen, President of the State Agricultural Society of Georgia,[81] a frequent contributor to the *Cultivator* and subsequently governor of Georgia,[82] wrote in an article entitled "The Situation":

All efforts to recover our losses, by tinkering on outside issues, will be worse than vain, until we strike the fundamental trouble and control the labor on our farms. Come together in communities, and counties and sections and determine what is fair and just and honest as to wages and service, and then demand it until it is given. There is no necessity for unkind or unreasonable exactions; these would be unworthy of an honorable man; but it is the high duty of every man to do his part in protecting the community against idleness, pilfering and vagrancy, and to encourage and demand, as far as his authority may go, such industry and application as will bring thrift and preserve the good order of society.[83]

The rhetoric is high-sounding, but the advice is to combine for the control of labor. Northen was an influential Georgia planter, and must have represented the sentiments of a wide section of that population. He repeated his advice in even stronger terms later in 1889:

Not only in the matter of trusts, but in the management of labor do farmers need uniform discipline and control. Hired help, on the farm, cannot be controlled when its worthless services will be accepted in a neighboring field, with great latitude in idleness and general indulgence. A laborer who leaves the farm and abandons his contract, without just cause, at a . . . hurtful time for the farmer, ought not to have opened to him a paying position on another farm in the same community, until his wrongs are adjusted. The labor in a community of farms should be managed under a fair and just policy, determined by farmers in council; and its requirements should be adhered to and strictly enforced.

81. "State Agricultural Society," *The Southern Cultivator and Dixie Farmer* (formerly *Southern Cultivator*) 47 (August 1889): 394.
82. Northen is referred to as the "ex-governor of Georgia" in *The Crisis* 4, no. 1 (May 1912): 17.
83. *Southern Cultivator and Dixie Farmer* 47 (January 1889): 20–21.

The management of the labor is the most important element in farm economy. It cannot be successful if farmers are not uniform and cooperative. . . . [Our] farms must be controlled by the superior intelligence of the landlord, and through a firm discipline, that should be enforced by the uniform management of the neighborhood.[84]

At the height of the Populist movement in Georgia, a Democratic Party county chairman went so far as to urge the "Democratic Farmers and Employers of Labor in Wilkes County" to use their market power to avert the impending danger of a Populist electoral victory:

This danger however can be overcome by the absolute control which you yet exercise over your property. It is absolutely necessary that you should bring to bear the power which your situation gives over tenants, laborers, and croppers. . . . The success [of the Populists] . . . means regulation of control of rents, wages of labor, regulation of hours of work, and at certain seasons of the year strikes. . . .

The peace, prosperity, and happiness of yourselves and your friends depend on your prompt, vigorous and determined efforts to control those who are to such a large extent dependent upon you.[85]

A distinctive part of the afterimage of the late nineteenth-century South is the chain gang. What is sometimes lost among the grisly descriptions of the abuses which characterized this forced-labor system is that the convict laborers were paid at best a subsistence wage (and sometimes, apparently, not even that). This fact was not lost on contemporary observers, however. "It [the convict lease system] proved profitable both to the state and to the lessee, as the latter could almost always underbid free labor."[86] A. B. Hart wrote that

the men on the chain gang are perhaps employed on city or county work, and if their terms expire too fast, the authorities will run out of labor; hence, the Negroes believe, perhaps rightly, that judges and juries are convinced of their guilt just in proportion to the falling off of the number of men in confinement; and that if necessary, innocent people will be arrested for that purpose. . . .

On the whole, one would rather not be a negro convict in a Southern state, or even a white convict, for many state and county prisons are simply left-over examples of the worst side of slavery. . . .

84. "Organization Among Farmers," ibid. (February 1889): 88.
85. The text of this circular, dated September 8, 1892, is from the Watson manuscripts cited by C. Vann Woodward, *Tom Watson: Agrarian Rebel*, p. 236.
86. William O. Scroggs, "Convict and Apprenticed Labor in the South," *The South in the Building of the Nation*, vol. 6, prepared by The Southern Historical Publication Society (Richmond: 1909): 48. This volume hereafter will be referred to *SBN*, 6.

The first trouble with the Southern convict system is that it still retains the notion, from which other communities began to diverge nearly a century ago, that the prisoner is the slave of the state, existing only for the convenience and profit of those whom he serves. . . . They [convicts] used to be rented to cotton growers, and a planter could get as few as two convicts or even one, over whom he had something approaching the power of life and death. This was a virtual chattel slavery. . . . Governor Vardeman in a public message in 1908 thought it necessary to say that "Some of the most atrocious and conscienceless crimes that have been perpetrated in this State are chargeable to the county contractor. I have known the poor convict driven to exhaustion or whipped to death to gratify the greed or anger of the conscienceless driver or contractor. The tears and blood of hundreds of these unfortunate people cry out for this reform."[87]

Blacks were not the only victims of this system,[88] but they were certainly the most frequent victims. Hart concluded that the convict lease system was tantamount to slavery:

Most of the cases of peonage arise out of the practice of selling the specific services of a convict to an individual; and it carries with it practically the right to compel such a person to work by physical force. What is to be done with a bondman who refuses to touch a hoe, except to whip him, and to keep on whipping him till he yields? The guards and wardens of prisons in the South use the lash freely, but they are subject at least to nominal inspection and control. To transfer the distasteful privilege to a contractor or farmer is to restore the worst incidents of slavery.[89]

It is difficult to know exactly how widespread this practice was, but in 1900, all the Southern states still had provisions in their penal codes providing for the use of convict labor in agriculture. The South was not unique in this regard, as many Northern and Western states also allowed use of convicts in farming. Some Northern states, however, such as California, Illinois, Iowa, Minnesota, and New York, did *not* allow the use of convict labor in agriculture.[90]

The extent to which convict labor constituted a significant source of agricultural labor is hard to assess, because the exploitation of chain-gang convicts by planters was only one facet of the entire labor market situation. Nevertheless, an anonymous black editorialist eloquently expressed the economic and legal oppression which must have been felt by many of the victims of chain-gang justice:

87. Hart, *Southern South*, pp. 200–202.
88. Ibid.
89. Ibid., pp. 286–287.
90. *ROIC*, 5, pp. 202–204.

Colored men are punished in this state [Georgia] without intelligent discrimination; old and young, thug and mischief maker, and often men and women, are herded together after unfair trials before juries who would rather convict ten innocent Negroes than let one guilty one escape. The sentences inflicted are cruel and excessive; 25 percent of the convicts are condemned for life and 60 percent for ten years and more. White men often escape conviction or are promptly pardoned. These slaves of the state are men sold body and soul to private capitalists for the sake of gain, without the shadow of an attempt at reformation, and are thrown into relentless competition with free Negro laborers. The fortune of many a prominent white Georgia family is red with the blood and sweat of black men justly and unjustly held to labor in Georgia prison camps; the state today is receiving $225,000 a year of this blood money and boasting of her ability to make crime pay.[91]

This passage raises the general question of whether the blacks themselves believed they were exploited in the labor market. The answer is by no means easy to give, especially since Southern black farmers left few records, and had scant access to any medium by which they might articulate their grievances. On the basis of scattered sources that do survive, however, there is strong evidence that many blacks did believe landlords unfairly exerted market power against them.

The *Southern Workman,* newspaper of the Hampton Institute and the organ of the "Hampton-Tuskegee" philosophy of Negro advancement through education and self improvement,[92] was hardly a radical journal. Nevertheless, the *Southern Workman* contains many expressions of perceived exploitation by blacks during the 1870s, 1880s, and 1890s. The editors of the *Workman* apparently believed that on the whole competition prevailed in the labor market (see the subsequent discussion in the next section of this chapter), yet they opened the pages of their newspaper to statements such as the following:

The colored people are being robbed, cheated, insulted, bulldozed and murdered. What will remedy this? . . . The colored people perform all the labor at the South, make all the corn, raise all the cotton and tobacco, the substance of immense revenue to the white tyrant. Notwithstanding this, the colored people are styled the "pauper class" and twitted by the whites as an improvident, shiftless and worthless class. They are reviled, spit upon, tyrannized over and persecuted. They are branded

91. *Alexander's Magazine* 1, no. 11 (March 1906): 18.
92. According to C. Vann Woodward, *"The Southern Workman* (Hampton, Va., 1872–1939) was the organ of the Hampton-Tuskegee school of race and labor philosophy." "Critical Essay on the Authorities," *Origins of the New South: 1877–1913,* vol. 9 of *A History of the South,* edited by Wendell Holmes Stephenson and E. Merton Coulter (Baton Rouge: Louisiana State University Press, 1951), p. 499.

as cowards and petty thieves. This they have borne with a "patient shrug" and humiliation which are disgusting and which outrage every instinct of true bravery and true manhood; which have been the cause of much unfavorable comment from our friends and more ridiculous criticisms from our enemies.

We have increased the cotton crops steadily until the yield has reached prodigious figures and we deserve commendation. But what do we get? The blood of our fathers is the price we receive for our labor. Profaned thresholds we receive for our fidelity and forbearance. Night is made hideous with the yells of denunciation and anathemas directed against us. Riot, racking in blood; mad rapine and organized bands of relentless murderers track us to our homes, our churches, our places of business and our public meetings, and there is no retreat, no succor, no commiseration for us. We must submit to this or take the only alternative—defend ourselves with our manhood, our valor and, if need be, with our blood. We are shot down like dogs, let us shoot back. We are cheated out of our earnings, let us demand remuneration and apply the torch when the demand is not acceded to as the means of removing the subject of contention. We can no longer afford to lie supinely upon our backs to be tread upon by ruthless robbers.[93]

One of the main features of the *Southern Workman* was the reprinting of articles and news dealing with Negroes from other periodicals. Several of these references allude to either the desire or actual attempts by Southern planters to reenslave the blacks. The following excerpt from an unnamed Southern newspaper was given as an example of a body of Southern opinion:

We know several of our largest planters who treat the negroes working for them exactly as they did their slaves, working them from daylight to sundown, allowing no idling; and if a darkey trespasses any of the rules he is tied up and a sound thrashing administered to him; then, if he leaves, the employer hunts him up, brings him back, and doubles the dose. This generally makes an effectual cure, and the offender resumes work, makes a good hand, and is anxious to hire to the same man another year. The employer has got value received out of his hands, and is, consequently, able to pay full wages. Govern your hands, and all sides will be better satisfied. Let them govern you, and the country will soon go to the dogs.[94]

In a similar vein, the *Workman* reprinted a long article from the *New York Times* dealing with the same subject:

93. Argus [pseud.], "Protect Yourselves," originally appearing in the black newspaper *The People's Advocate* (n.d., n.p.) and reprinted in *Southern Workman* 13 (January 1884): 5.
94. "Two Sorts of Southern Sentiments," *Southern Workman* 5 (May 1876): 38.

There are, indeed, in several of the cotton States, notably in South Carolina, Alabama, and Louisiana, a number of so-called leaders who freely express the belief that the negro, to be made useful, must be kept in a state little better than bondage, in short, as nearly in a condition of slavery as is possible under the law.

To bring about this result, the Rifle Clubs of South Carolina and a number of the most prominent Democrats in Alabama and Louisiana are engaged in a determined effort to reorganize the old Labor Leagues, and secure such legislative enactments as will place the unfortunate black laborer absolutely under their control. . . . They ask, in the first place, that [laborers' contracts] . . . be drawn by individual employers, or drawn by them and approved by the Labor Leagues . . . every violation by a colored man of such a contract would be considered a misdemeanor, to be punished by imprisonment, forfeiture of crops, or, as is proposed, in Edgefield and other White League strongholds, by the lash. Further than this, it is proposed that all colored men found out of employment or trespassing upon the lands of the whites shall be regarded as vagrants and punished accordingly. Should such laws go into effect, and their advocacy by the powerful Labor Leagues of South Carolina, and the secret organization known as the State Grange of Louisiana, leaves no doubt that there is grave danger of this being the case, the Southern black men would be almost as completely at the mercy of their white masters as they were twenty years ago. . . .

The Labor Leagues threaten, as a last resort, to openly take the law into their own hands, as they have already substantially done in secret, and agree among themselves not to rent land or give work to any laborer without the consent of his former master, or to buy corn, cotton, or produce of any kind from any employee without the consent of the proprietor of the land upon which it has been raised. In the same way, that is by an agreement among themselves, it will be a very easy matter for the Labor Leagues to determine what rates of wages they will pay their laborers.[95]

Interestingly enough, the editors of the *Southern Workman* commented on this article by criticizing its major premise. In keeping with the Hampton-Tuskegee philosophy, they argued that the main problem of the Southern black was an "internal" one, a lack of education rather than exploitation by Southern whites. "They [the *Times,* and certain Northern politicians, presumably] can make votes for themselves by showing that the black man is in danger of reenslavement, but would lose votes rapidly by passing around the hat for funds to relieve the negro from his bondage to ignorance."[96] The interchange is a striking example of the clash of the exploitation hypothesis and the legacy of slavery hypothesis. This theme recurred in subsequent issues of the *Workman:*

95. *Southern Workman* 7 (February 1878): 11.
96. Ibid.

In discussing the schemes of colored emigration, the real issue is quite neglected. The complaint of the colored men in Louisiana, in North Carolina and Mississippi, is, that they are not protected in their political rights, are charged high and excessive rentals for land, or are compelled to pay exorbitant prices for it, when purchased, and that, in short, their condition is very intolerable. There is truth in this statement of grievances, but there are other facts which should modify an opinion based solely on these *ex parte* statements. Land in the South is cheap enough, and the colored man's money will buy it as quickly as the white man's. We have yet to hear of a case where, under ordinary circumstances, his money has been refused. And in view of the utterly exhausting way all rented land is tilled by the tenant, the rental money is not high. Many white men at the South are at the same disadvantage as the Negro in the matter of paying high rents, and in the inability to purchase land. It is the misfortune of poverty, and there is no exception on race account.[97]

Despite its editorial position, the *Southern Workman* continued to report the statements and activities of more militant black spokesmen. In 1886, an article from Timothy Thomas Fortune's *Freeman's Journal* was reprinted, in which Mr. Fortune argued the exploitation hypothesis in the strongest terms:

We assert, without fear of successful contradiction, that nowhere else in the world can there be found a more odious, unjust and tyrannical landlord system than that which obtains in the South. It is a virtual continuation of the slave system, with the landlord relieved of the obligations and responsibilities to the laborer imposed upon him by the laws of the slave system and his right in the person as well as the labor of the slave.

All the land laws in the South are made in favor of the planters, and it is notorious that the wages paid by them to their employees are simply pauper wages; and this is aggravated by the store account and order system by which the laborer seldom ever sees a dime of cash and is frequently allowed to overdraw his account, or is overcharged, for the purpose of being held at the pleasure of the planter.[98]

This same Timothy Thomas Fortune was an active and radical black spokesman in the 1880s and 1890s. He has been described as "the foremost Negro journalist of his time."[99] *Black and White,* written by Fortune in 1885 "during the most radical phase of his career,"[100] contains

97.   W. N. A. [W. N. Armstrong?], "About Emigration," ibid. 9 (Feburary 1880): 15–16.
98.   Ibid. 15 (August 1886): 87.
99.   The descripton was applied by James M. McPherson in his Introduction to the Arno Press reprint edition of Timothy Thomas Fortune, *Black and White: Land, Labor and Politics in the South*, p. i.
100.   James McPherson, Introduction to *Black and White . . .*, p. ii.

some of the most passionate denunciations of capitalism and exploitation to appear in the United States before or since:

What are millionaires, any way, but the most dangerous enemies of society, always eating away its entrails, like the vultures that preyed upon the chained Prometheus? Take our own breed of these parasites; note how they grind down the stipend they are compelled to bestow upon the human tools they must use to still further swell their ungodly gains! Note how they take advantage of the public; how they extort, with Shylock avarice, every penny they possibly can from those who are compelled to use the appliances which wealth enables them to contrive for the public convenience and comfort; how they corrupt legislatures and dictate to the unscrupulous minions of the law. The Athenians were wise who enacted into law the principle that when a citizen became too powerful or rich to be controlled within proper bounds, the safety of society demanded that he should be exiled—sent where his power or riches could not be used to the detriment of his fellow-citizens.[101]

Fortune also argued that the wage is driven down to subsistence, "to the lowest possible point at which he [the worker] can live and still produce."[102] He brought similar charges against landowners:

Every hamlet, town, city, and state in the Union is in the grasp of the individual land holder. Starting with his fellows as a pioneer two hundred and fifty years ago, with his pickaxe on his shoulder, he has steadily grown in size and importance, so that to-day he holds in his hands the destinies of the Republic and the life of his fellow citizens. His bulk has become mastodonian in proportions and his influence has shrivelled up the energies of the people. More absolute than the Iron Prince of Germany, he pays no taxes; he limits production, not to the requirements of the population but to the demand of the market, at such figures as he can extort from the crying necessities of the people through the operations of "corners"; he regulates the wheels of government, State and Federal, and dictates to the people by making them hungry and naked.[103]

It should not be thought that Fortune was an isolated fanatic. He was editor of the New York *Age*, which, after two changes of name, became "the leading Negro paper in the country during the 1880's and 1890's," and "in 1887 Fortune founded the Afro-American League, an equal rights organization that antedated the Niagara Movement and the NAACP."[104] The *Southern Workman* reported the 1890 convention of the Afro-American League, of which Fortune was elected temporary chair-

101. Fortune, *Black and White.* . . , p. 151.
102. Ibid., p. 150.
103. Ibid., p. 232.
104. James McPherson, Introduction to *Black and White.* . . , p. i.

man. One of his speeches at this convention was "frequently interrupted by loud and long continued applause" from the 200 black participants:

We are met here to-day, the representatives of eight million freedmen, who know our rights and have the courage to defend them. We are here to emphasize the fact that the past condition of helplessness and dependence upon men who have used us for selfish and unholy purposes, who have murdered, and robbed, and outraged us, must be reversed.

We have been robbed of the honest wages of our toil; we have been robbed of the substance of our citizenship by murder and intimidation; we have been outraged by our enemies and deserted by our friends. It is time to call a halt. It is time to begin to fight fire with fire. I speak as an Afro-American, first, last, and all the time, ready to stab to death any political party which robs me of my confidence and my vote and straightway asks me what I am going to do about it."[105]

Another fiery champion of black rights during this period was William Sinclair; ex-slave, missionary, physician, and financial secretary of Howard University.[106] His book *The Aftermath of Slavery* is, if anything, more damning an indictment of white "outrages" against the black South than Fortune's book, because of its more explicit catalogue of crimes of all kinds perpetrated against the freedmen. In his chapter devoted to "Negroes and the Law," Sinclair quoted a series of Southern spokesmen advocating a return to slavery of some form, mild or otherwise, and observed:

As might be expected, illustrations in the concrete of the operation of this bitter persecution abound on every hand. Laws are enacted and enforced in the spirit of persecution, and the colored people are the victims of such laws; often they are condemned without even the form or semblance of law.

Regarding the latter, planters have combined or conspired—in defiance of the law—to arrest under false charges the number of colored men needed for service, hold mock trials, one of the conspirators acting as judge, condemn and sentence the helpless creatures to penal servitude; and then divide the laborers among themselves, put them in chains, and work them for long periods of time on their plantations. And this crime is committed against liberty and humanity rather than pay the small wages which agricultural laborers command in the South![107]

Sinclair next traced out the practices that have already been referred to: penal enforcement of labor contracts, forced labor to repay debts, and collusion between police and planters to secure slave-wage convict labor.

105. "The Negro Press," *Southern Workman* 19 (February 1890): 15. The speech was quoted from the Washington *Bee*, n.d.
106. William A. Sinclair, *Aftermath of Slavery*, pp. ix-x.
107. Sinclair, *Aftermath of Slavery*, pp. 223–224.

He recounted examples of Negroes beaten for attempting to leave the plantations they were working, and noted that "The Department of Justice is preparing to take up again the subject of peonage in the South."[108] But perhaps the most harrowing passage in Sinclair's book is the first-person narrative of a black man who had been for thirteen years a prisoner in a "peon camp" owned by a Southern state senator. This first-hand account originally appeared in the *Independent* of New York City, but the quotations are in the words of the victim. After working as free laborers for a period of years for the senator, and being forced to buy all supplies from his commissary, the narrator and several of his friends decided to leave and seek work elsewhere. The senator said they were free to go, so long as they signed "acknowledgments" of their accumulated debts to the commissary. Anxious to leave, the black men made their marks, only to find

in the papers we had signed the day before, we had not only made acknowledgment of our indebtedness, but that we had also agreed to work for the senator until the debts were paid by hard labor. And from that day forward we were treated just like convicts. Really we had made ourselves lifetime slaves, or peons, as the laws called us. But, call it slavery, peonage, or what not, the truth is we lived in a hell on earth what time we spent in the senator's peon camp.

The wife of the man telling his story was made a concubine of the white men who operated the camp, as were the wives of some of the other Negroes. His wife bore two children by some of the "white bosses," but at least she was able to live in a house. The other women were forced to live and work with the male peons, in dwellings he described as "cesspools of nastiness." Whippings and other tortures were performed on recalcitrant or exhausted peons, with the result that "many came away maimed and bruised, and, in some cases, disabled for life."

Recruits to the peon camp were obtained by sending agents to the local courts, who advised blacks charged with petty offenses to plead guilty and work off their fines at the peon camp; but the charges made against their accounts at the commissary always exceeded their wages, so that "by the time he has worked out his first debt another is hanging over his head, and so on and so on, by a sort of endless chain, for an indefinite period; as in every case the indebtedness is arbitrarily arranged by the employer." One of the commonest "crimes" leading to the peon camp was adultery. After his release from the peon camp, while his wife was still held in concubinage, the black narrator summed up his experience:

108. Ibid., pp. 224–227, passim.

I have been here in the district since they released me, and I reckon I'll die either in a coal mine or an iron furnace: it don't make much difference which. Either is better than a Georgia peon camp. And a Georgia peon camp is hell itself![109]

Blacks' concern over exploitation, intimidation, and forced labor was reflected by the new civil rights organization, the National Association for the Advancement of Colored People. *The Crisis,* official magazine of the NAACP, carried in each issue a "crime report" giving as much information as was available on the lynchings and "outrages" which had taken place during that publishing period. In the majority of instances reported, blacks were lynched for rape, assault, or for no apparent reason at all. The causes of "race wars" or fights between individual blacks and whites resulting in a lynching were often not specified. But at least one case confirmed the observation made earlier that labor disputes were a significant cause of deadly violence:

On June 13, near Rochelle, in Wilcox County, Ga., McHenry, a Negro who wounded a planter, C. S. Ritchie, was lynched.

McHenry was a tenant of Ritchie's and the two quarreled, the Negro shooting Ritchie, but not inflicting a serious wound.

McHenry was taken to the Ritchie home and identified by the wounded man. Then the mob of "leading citizens" hanged the Negro to a tree near the Ritchie home and cut the body to pieces with bullets.

When Ritchie was shot he was attacking the Negro because the latter was tardy in going to work.[110]

Forced labor did not always end in the extreme of murder. *The Crisis* also reprinted the following letter from the *Savannah Tribune,* regarding the "large number of Negroes . . . being arrested as vagrants":

Is it because there are no loafers among the other races? Or is it on account of the explicit order from the chief of police to arrest Negroes only? A week or ten days ago 108 able-bodied men were arrested and detained in the barracks on suspicion—men who are working every day, or at least whenever an opportunity for work is offered. The "milk in the cocoanut" is that the farmers want cotton pickers at starvation price and and worst treatment, and at the same time there will be races with automobiles very soon—convict labor as opposed to free labor is required to further the money-making scheme of a body of enterprising citizens.[111]

109. Ibid., pp. 229–232.
110. "Crime," *The Crisis* 4, no. 4 (August 1912): 167.
111. "The Burden," ibid. 3, no. 5 (March 1912): 209.

Also published periodically was a list of the number of "Colored Men Lynched Without Trial," which gave the following figures from 1885 through 1911:[112]

1885	78
1886	71
1887	80
1888	95
1889	95
1890	90
1891	121
1892	155
1893	154
1894	134
1895	112
1896	80
1897	122
1898	102
1899	84
1900	107
1901	107
1902	86
1903	86
1904	83
1905	61
1906	64
1907	60
1908	93
1909	73
1910	65
1911	63
Total	2,521

If economic history were written according to the advocacy system, the case for the exploitation hypothesis could be rested at this point. Surely the evidence presented is overwhelming that Southern labor relations after the Civil War included elements of exploitation. That is an important fact, but it does not settle the question of whether exploitation was prevalent *in the aggregate.* There is no way of knowing whether the previously detailed instances were typical or exceptional, and no way of assessing whether some planters' intentions to control labor forcibly were shared by the entire employing class. Even if planters were all of a single mind, it does not necessarily follow that they were able to translate their desires into social reality.

112. Ibid. 4, no. 1 (May 1912): 39.

Even these objections would remain rather abstract, were it not for the fact that a similar and, it seems, equally persuasive, brief can be written for the competition hypothesis. Using many of the same sources, and the same procedure of seeking out direct and indirect evidence of competition in the labor market, it can be "proved" in the same way that the Southern labor market was largely free of imperfections after the surrender of the Confederate armies.

Competition in the Labor Market

As with the exploitation hypothesis, it is useful to indicate the kinds of evidence which could be considered support for competition in the labor market. The following list also is not exhaustive, but should be roughly comparable with the list supporting exploitation. Traces of competition for labor will be found in:

1. Evidence of labor mobility, particularly in response to the prospect of higher wages and/or better working conditions.

2. Direct evidence of planters' competition for labor.

3. Expressions of a consciousness or awareness of competition in the labor market, either on the part of the employers or on the part of the agricultural workers. Included in this category would be arguments introduced in debates on policy proposals such as whether to encourage actively immigration into the South.

4. Evidence of a rise in wage levels just following the war, as the market presumably changed from one of slave labor to one with free labor.

5. Evidence of the existence of alternative employment for agricultural workers, including blacks.

Examples of each of these manifestations or preconditions of competition can be found without much difficulty.

The planters' complaint of a scarcity of labor just after the war was paralleled by objections to freedmen's moving throughout the countryside, refusing to remain and work in one place.

The first effect of emancipation upon many individuals of the [black] race was to inspire them with a desire to abandon the scenes that had been familiar to them as slaves, and they promptly acted upon this impulse; separated from their former homes by their own determination, they obtained employment elsewhere—in many instances in distant parts, of which they had no previous knowledge. Some even doubted whether they had been really liberated until they had tested their ability to leave the old localities without opposition from their former owners.

Even if they were confident that they could do so just then, they anticipated that their present liberty would be curtailed so much in the future
that they would practically be reduced to their original condition again.
An emotion of fear, therefore, urged them to depart. Fidelity, timidity, or
sound judgment induced a few to remain permanently where they had
always lived, but the vast majority of negroes changed their habitations
either immediately or in the course of the first years after they were set
free. Many of the largest plantations were almost depopulated of their
former laborers, the places they vacated being filled by those who had
immigrated from other sections or had come in from the same countryside.

At present, the laborers are not inclined to emigrate to a great distance
by the mere force of a migratory instinct; a few do so under the terms of
temporary contracts into which they have been tempted to enter by the so-
licitations of agents, but a large number are rarely influenced to remove
in a body to far off States in the mere hope of improving their condition.
Within the circle of an extensive division of country, however, they are
constantly shifting; they will rent land for one year and set up on their
own account as mechanics the next, or they will work for one planter
a month and labor in the employment of another for twelve months, or
attach themselves to the same plantation for many years, and then sud-
denly announce their intention to leave . . . they start anew as if they
were untrammeled, and their ability to do so, is a strong inducement to
them to rid themselves of their burdens in one locality by settling in another at a distance.[113]

The author of this passage shared the low opinion of the freedmen
held by many other Southerners of his time. In actuality, many blacks
were motivated to travel by the "impulse" to find family members from
whom they had been forcibly separated in the slave market. Even so,
observers more sympathetic to the freedmen noted the same phenomenon of widespread black mobility. For example, although Carl Schurz
disagreed on the proportions of freedmen involved, he found that

as soon as the struggle was finally decided, and our forces were scattered
about in detachments to occupy the country, the so far unmoved masses
began to stir. . . . Large numbers of colored people left the plantations;
many flocked to our military posts and camps to obtain the certainty of
their freedom, and others walked away merely for the purpose of leaving
the places on which they had been held in slavery, and because they
could now go with impunity. Still others, and their number was by no
means inconsiderable, remained with their former masters and continued their work on the field, but under new and as yet unsettled conditions, and under the agitating influence of a feeling of restlessness.[114]

113. Philip A. Bruce, *The Plantation Negro as Freeman,* pp. 176–178.
114. Schurz, *Report,* p. 15.

This evidence of considerable mobility should be evaluated in light of the fact that not *all* workers have to move in order for competitive conditions to prevail in the labor market. Only enough need to move to equalize wages between regions and to allow the market-clearing wage to be reached.

Just as the planters' lament that Negroes would not work without compulsion was evidence of a continued desire to exploit them, the many statements that freedmen were perfectly willing to work for "fair" wages show planters' willingness to pay the market rate. Schurz wrote that "in the reports of officers of the Freedmen's Bureau, among the documents annexed to this [report], you will find frequent repetitions of the statement that the negro generally works well where he is decently treated and well compensated. Nor do the officers of the Freedmen's Bureau alone think and say so. Southern men, who were experimenting in the right direction, expressed to me their opinion to the same effect." Schurz observed that the number of these satisfied planters was small, but that it corresponded to those who "gave free negro labor a perfectly fair trial," and also that Northern men engaged in cotton planting "almost uniformly speak of their negro laborers with satisfaction."[115]

These findings were echoed in the testimony before the Joint Committee on Reconstruction. Major General George H. Thomas, commander of the military division of Tennessee, testified:

QUESTION. Do the freedmen generally find employment in Tennessee?
ANSWER. I do not know of any difficulty in their finding employment.
QUESTION. And at fair wages?
ANSWER. Yes, sir; and there is a general understanding among the negroes and among the whites that each is to comply with his part of the contract, so that there is no difficulty and no dissatisfaction.[116]

The very next witness before the Joint Committee was a Colonel William Spence, a Tennessee farmer and former slaveowner. His testimony corroborated General Thomas's:

In the county where I live the condition of the freedman is very good. There is an agency of the Freedmen's Bureau there, but there have been very few cases that have to be taken before it for adjustment. The freedmen have behaved exceedingly well, and have obtained fair wages.[117]

Brigadier General James S. Brisbin, a U.S. Army officer stationed in Arkansas, recognized that even though an inclination to reestablish slavery

115. Ibid., p. 28.
116. *RJCR*, part 1, p. 109.
117. Ibid., p. 117.

still existed, the general practice was to pay fair wages, and freedmen were perfectly willing to work for those wages.[118] Dr. James P. Hambleton, an Atlanta physician, who had lived in Georgia for fifteen years and who admitted that "all my interests are in Georgia," went even further, actually regretting the new-found bargaining power of the freedmen:

QUESTION. What has been the conduct of the negroes during and since the war?
ANSWER. I have seen very little difference. They were very humble and obedient during the war; no people ever behaved better. After the war they were under the impression that freedom meant freedom from labor, and everything of that sort; most of them quit work, and refused to do anything until cold weather came last winter. They fully expected the United States government to clothe and feed them. Since then, a great many of them have made contracts, and are working very well; but the great difficulty is that they will not stick to a contract; they are fickle; they are constantly expecting to do better; they will make a contract with me to-day for twelve or fifteen dollars a month, and in a few days somebody will come along and offer a dollar or two more, and they will quit me—never saying anything to me, but leave in the night and be gone. They are constantly striking for higher wages.[119]

Just as the Joint Committee on Reconstruction received testimony that planters' organizations had been formed with the intent of regulating wages, it also heard witnesses say that no such organizations existed. Dr. M. M. Lewis of Alexandria, Virginia, testified:

QUESTION. Is there not, generally, among their [freedmen's] employers a disposition to constrain the freedmen to work at low wages?
ANSWER. I rather think not. Like everybody else, they like to get labor as cheap as they can. That is the disposition pretty much everywhere.
QUESTION. Do you know of any combinations among employers to keep down the wages of freedmen?
ANSWER. No, sir; I do not.
QUESTION. There is no general understanding to that effect?
ANSWER. No, sir.[120]

The same negative response was elicited from David C. Humphreys of Huntsville, Alabama.[121] Major J. W. Smith, an army paymaster from Little Rock, Arkansas, did "not see much disposition on the part of the landholders to oppress them [the freedmen], nor do I think there is much

118. Ibid., part 3, p. 70.
119. Ibid., part 3, p. 167.
120. Ibid., part 2, p. 77.
121. Ibid., part 3, p. 65.

danger of it at this time, from the fact that they want their labor."[122] According to another Congressional report, it was not unknown for planters' competition for labor to result in the exchange of blows over the hiring of another man's former employees.[123]

The complaints of Southern planters went much further than dissatisfaction with the new mobility of the freedmen. Many of the points listed above as potential evidence for a competitive labor market were raised explicitly by the perceptive "Southerner" writing in the *Galaxy* in 1871. "Southerner's" article deserves to be quoted at length, not only because it contained evidence for competition, but also because it showed the depth of planters' dismay at the turn of events. "Southerner" also addressed various admonitions to other planters to reverse the labor situation.

Migratory and fond of change, sure of a home whenever willing to work on account of the great demand for farm labor, the freedman manifests a singular indifference to contracting, and many of them rarely live two years in succession on the same place. It seldom or never occurs that a man works exactly the same force in different years both as to numbers and individuals. . . .

The employer or his overseer, though giving good wages, by persuasion, begging, or complimentary encouragement, has to induce the freedmen to work. Often he possesses no power of coercion and cannot even attempt its exercise. All he can do is to control his freedmen by moral influence, persuasion, or example; get an overseer or agent to look after the hands, or dock each freedman for every half hour of lost time. A threat to discharge, or even a discharge itself, would prove of little avail, because in the first place the laborer is wanted, and in the second place he could readily procure another situation. . . .

With all these drawbacks, it is still absolutely necessary for the planter to have laborers. . . . So he speaks to one freedman after another, mounts his horse and rides hither and thither, sends an agent back and forth day after day, announces his willingness to make liberal contracts, does make large offers, bribes his own hands to hire others for him, goes to the towns and villages and addresses the many colored loiterers on the streets, stops at railway stations and sounds the freedmen he always finds strolling near, and thus by one means and another gradually obtains as many hands as he wants, or failing in that, as many as he can. . . .

. . . Occasionally an advertisement appears in a newspaper, declaring that such and such a freedman has broken his labor contract, and that whoever hires him shall be prosecuted according to law; but it

122. Ibid., p. 99.
123. John Cornelius Englesman, "The Freedmen's Bureau in Louisiana," *The Louisiana Historical Quarterly* 32, no. 1 (January 1949): 185. Englesman cited the Truman report in *Senate Executive Documents*, 39 Cong., 1st sess., no. 43, p. 89. The incident referred to took place during 1866.

rarely or never occurs that such a prosecution takes place, though the freedman is hired by some other planter. Indeed, it is a difficult matter to discover an absconded freedman, for he can readily find a home go where he will, so great is the demand for laborers. . . .

Without delay all Southern planters should agree upon some general plan of hiring, some well-understood rate of wages, and some mode of discovering and punishing deliquent laborers. There should be an entire stop put to the custom, now common and considered not altogether unfair, of enticing another man's laborers from him by offering higher wages. A trespass law of general application is needed, which will prevent strange freedmen from intruding upon the premises of others, engaging in mischief, stealing, or tempting the laborers to leave their employers and contract with some one else.[124]

"Southerner" also pointed out among the reasons for the disastrous (for the planters) situation that freedmen were being used to build the new railroads, and that "the rich lands of Mississippi, Louisiana, and Texas have drawn many freedmen from other portions of the South, because the larger the yield the higher the wages."[125]

The planters' and agricultural magazines also contained evidence of labor market competititon. *DeBow's Review,* in addition to favoring arguments encouraging immigration to freshen competition among the farm workers (the immigration debate will be separately discussed), contained explicit references to competition for labor in the years following the war. For instance, the "Report on Cotton" in the September 1869 issue argued that planters should make the best of the new situation:

Inducements to large planting [of cotton] will open employment to every person able and willing to work, and may renew a hurtful competition for labor, leading to excessive wages. All this, however, must be left to adjust itself under the operation of demand and supply, and further results will complete the imperfect demonstration of the past year, that cotton-growing by labor left free to assert its own price, and not burdened by unwise imposts, is cheaper and more profitable to the individual planter than planting by slave labor could be under its most favorable circumstances, while the community will gain in wealth, and the best uses of wealth, beyond anything conceived by men of the past generations.[126]

Another writer, arguing against Chinese immigration largely on social and political grounds, reasoned that a Chinese would not necessarily

124. Southerner [pseud.], "Agricultural Labor at the South," *The Galaxy* 12, no. 3 (September 1871): 329, 332, 334, 337, and 339.
125. Ibid., p. 335.
126. *DeBow's Review* (September 1869), pp. 787–788.

continue to work at the wage he was "imported" to work for, in the face
of competition among planters:

We may remark here, that many persons with whom we have con-
versed are of the impression that the coolie will always labor at the same
rate at which he is imported. Why the coolie should labor alongside of
the negro, at less wages than the negro receives for doing the same a-
mount of work, we cannot understand. It would be still more incompre-
hensible that no planter would bid more for the coolie than the low rate
at which the importer held him. Have we peonage here? Can a man hold
a laborer against his will? If he break his indentures and go away, can
the employer follow him with a fugitive slave law? It is rather our impression that if planters, cultivating the earth, should hear that there was
half price labor on the plantation of anybody else that they would explain to those laborers their rights, and inveigle them to leave their half
price situation. There would be Joss houses and an opium stupefactory,
and birds' nests would be sold in the shops. Every inducement would be
offered, and it is not reasonable to suppose that a faithless heathen, who
quits his own country to make money, would resist the temptation to
double his wages. We do not say that a day's work of a coolie would be
equal in value or price to a day's work by a white man or an African, but
that the coolie would receive, before he had made the second crop, as
much for planting, plowing, and picking an acre as any one else would.[127]

This writer apparently missed the main point of the immigration proponents, that increased population would drive down the market wage
(see discussion below), but he exhibited no sentimentality about the
lengths Southern gentlemen would be willing to go to in order to secure the
labor they desired. Writing of conditions in Louisiana, another contributor to *DeBow's* stated:

If we consider that all the labor in the sugar districts is and has been fully
employed, the question arises, where is the labor to come from for the
increased planting? There is room for double the amount if the projected
increase is carried out. Can it be obtained for bidding higher for it? We
should think it might to a certain extent. Since the war there has been
a rush of all classes to the towns, especially of negroes, and that is one of
the reasons why some of the plantations have been depopulated. It is
now the time for such to return to their proper avocation instead of
eking out a miserable existence in the towns. Under the circumstances,
we may anticipate what will occur in the country. Those planters who are
already under way and able to pay, will outbid their poorer neighbors,
and there will necessarily occur a rise in wages. The high prices offered
may secure a sufficiency of laborers to those who bid for them. But those
from whom they are taken from may well inquire where they are to get

127. William M. Burwell, "Science and the Mechanic Arts Against Coolies,"
ibid. (July 1869), pp. 564–565.

others, and they should look the thing squarely in the face at once. It will not do to imagine that by cunning management and paying a little more, one may obtain the number of hands that he wants. He may be disappointed by the better management of another. In the squabble, for squabble there will be, it will be each one for himself and the devil take the hindmost.[128]

Disapproval of this sort of competition for labor was not confined to the aristocratic *DeBow's*. The more "down-home" *Southern Cultivator* referred both explicitly and offhandedly to competition among planters for agricultural workers. A "Subscriber" wrote the *Cultivator* in 1869:

> Go to the city of Memphis—and I expect it is so at other places—and you will find farmers from all the country around, hunting up freedmen, and offering them wages that they cannot afford to pay, to go to the country, for the purpose of cultivating cotton. Last year, when farmers determined to raise meat and bread enough to supply them, and some to spare, it was not so. Labor was then dependent upon the farmer—now the farmer is dependent upon the laborer, and the laborer knows it, and it makes him careless and indifferent; for he knows that if discharged at one place for indolence, his labor is in such demand, he can readily find employment at another.[129]

Another writer in the same issue argued for yearly contracts but weekly wage payments, on the grounds that such a payment system was superior because it discouraged agricultural workers from moving at the end of the year and "exorcised the evil spirit of discontent that possesses them."[130]

The *Southern Cultivator* also decried the increased bargaining power of the blacks. A Georgia planter complained, "Once we had reliable labor, controlled at will. Now, we depend upon chance for labor at all. It is both uncertain and unreliable; and our contracts must often be made at great disadvantage."[131]

Calls for "concert of action" on the part of planters to control the wage rate were usually accompanied by admissions of the difficulty of accomplishing such combinations. "Acorn" wrote in 1869:

---

128. J. C. Delavigne, "The Labor Question," ibid. (February 1870), pp. 168–169.
129. "Grain and Stock vs. Cotton Culture," *Southern Cultivator* 27 (July 1869): 214.
130. Agricola [pseud.], "The Labor Question," ibid., p. 207.
131. J. Dickson Smith, "Revolution in Southern Agriculture," ibid. (February 1869), p. 53.

It is very ridiculous to charge our people with a want of sagacity or public spirit, because they don't see the necessity of organization. Of all classes, the agricultural is the least disposed to act in concert, because it does not feel the necessity. And at the South, where our population is sparse, and every man lord of his own manor, it is not easy to get up social gatherings, at which farmers can exchange opinions and compare notes.[132]

Also, the operation of a competitive labor market is hinted by S.W. Trotti, the same contributor who anticipated the Domar hypothesis (see above, chapter 1):

It is true, under the present order of things, the Southern planter is seldom presented with the alternative of giving higher wages or a cessation of labor; but as a substitute for strikes, he is blessed with what we may call quits, under the operation of which he wakes up some fine morning and finds that half his hands or perhaps all of them, without warning on their part, or sufficient provocation on his, have gone into the employment of his neighbor.[133]

Planters' awareness of the improved competitive position of the black agricultural workers was even expressed in verse appearing in the *Cultivator*. A poem titled "Coronation Ode" attempted to ridicule the improved situation of the blacks. One stanza dealt with planter-freedman relations:

> Before his throne proud planters bow,
> For help to wield the hoe and plough,
> See him in social confab now
> > Beside the Digger—
> His antecedents disavowed,
> > To please the nigger.[134]

The author of this doggerel was trying to satirize the extent to which the "proud planters" had been laid low—they were forced actually to speak personally to the blacks in order to elicit needed labor from them! To modern eyes, of course, it is the would-be satirist who appears ridiculous.

There is some scattered evidence that the compensation of black agricultural workers rose immediately after emancipation. An article, "Condition and Wants of the Cotton Raising States," in the February 1869 *DeBow's Review* included the following highly suggestive passage:

132. Acorn [pseud.], "Diversity of crops, &c," ibid. (June 1869), p. 174.
133. "Immigration," ibid. (December 1869), pp. 372–373.
134. "Coronation Ode," ibid. 32 (July 1874): 291.

We have been compelled for some time past, to recognize the fact that the whole question of labor rests in the hands of the negro. This has been fully illustrated by their conduct since the year 1865, when first they fully comprehended that they were a free people. That year, the hands, with few exceptions, remained in their old situations, and were contented with a share in the cotton and corn crops, ranging from an eighth to a twelfth. In 1866, many, influenced by a desire for change, or a prospect of doing better elsewhere, left their homes, and hired themselves to others. The experience of the preceding year had made them afraid of contracting for a share in the crop; consequently, they demanded money wages, and, of course, money wages had to be paid. The scale of wages, graduated according to the capability of the hand, ranged from six to eight dollars for women, from eight to twelve dollars for men. However, in 1867,they again demanded a share in the crops. But their estimate of the value of their labor had risen, instead of an eighth of the cotton and corn, they demanded a *fourth* of every thing raised on the plantation. They demanded it, and, of course they got it. If a planter demurred to accede to it, he immediately found himself without hands. Notice, that there was no concert of action on the part of the planters to oppose these ever increasing exactions; had this been done in the first instance, the negro would not have imbibed the idea that his services were indispensable to the planter, and that he had only to name his terms to have them accepted. On the contrary, every man tried to out bid his neighbor, and to fill up his requisite quota of hands at the expense of every one else.[135]

It would certainly be difficult to find a clearer example of what could be expected to happen during the transition from an imperfect labor market (slavery) to a competitive one (after emancipation).

Other contemporary observers apparently saw the same phenomenon:

Harry Hammond attached significance to the fact that as early as 1866 a freedman in the upper pine belt had come to believe that the share of the laborer should be one-fourth of the produce plus food and shelter. By 1869, however, a Negro labor organization was asking half the crop for tenants, and wages of fifteen to twenty dollars for laborers, presumably with state supervision of contracts. Gradually contracts were on their faces liberalized until many of them provided that three-fourths of the crop should go to the tenant and one-fourth to the landlord—an arrangement that was characteristic, it will be recalled, of white tenancy in Chester District as early as 1842.[136]

135. A. R. Lightfoot, "Condition and Wants of the Cotton Raising States," *DeBow's Review* (February 1869), p. 153.
136. Marjorie S. Mendenhall, "The Rise of Southern Tenancy," *Yale Review* 27, no. 1 (Autumn 1937): 126. Unfortunately, Mendenhall cites no source for Harry Hammond's observation. It should also be pointed out that she does not specify whether the final sharecrop arrangement in this instance (with 3/4 of the crop going to the tenant) was based on the tenant's provision of animals, fertilizer, and other

Southern attitudes towards immigration also revealed the belief of large segments of the population that competition prevailed in the labor market. Both *DeBow's Review* and the *Southern Cultivator* contained a large amount of material devoted to a debate on the pros and cons of encouraging immigration into the South after the war. *DeBow's Review* was generally favorable to immigration. Each issue contained a "Department of Immigration and Labor."[137] In some cases, immigration was advocated on social or political grounds, usually as a way of strengthening white hegemony by increasing the proportion of white population.[138]

DeBow's also advocated immigration specifically to introduce workers to compete with the black labor. A. R. Lightfoot, the same man who observed in *DeBow's* the increase in wage rates between 1865 and 1867, concluded his article with a defense of immigration on these grounds:

It is evident that until some competition is produced by the importation of labor, the negro element will have the question of wages pretty much in their own hands. Their demands are already so exorbitant, that cotton raising has nearly ceased to be a money making business. As the price of labor goes up, the price of land declines. Cotton lands that were formerly estimated at $30, can now be bought for $10. Rents have fallen proportionally.

Did the tide of emigration set towards the Southern States, instead of from them, these evils would be remedied. Labor would be cheapened, lands would increase in value, and cotton raising would once more be-

---

capital. On the same page of her article, Mendenhall observes that "The model of contracting preferred in South Carolina. . . required the payment of one-third of the crop to the laborer who furnished his own rations." So there is a certain amount of confusion on her part as to the terms for division of output between landlord and tenant. Most reports of share contracts show 1/4 to 1/2 of the crop as the return to labor alone (see appendix D below). Hammond's observation of a *rising* share to labor is what is of interest here.

137. See, for example, *DeBow's Review* (February 1868), pp. 207–213 in which the "Department of Immigration and Labor" included (1) the Report of General Wagener of South Carolina, who was that state's Commissioner of Immigration. General Wagener's Report covered his attempts to induce Germans, Scandinavians, and Irish to emigrate to the South, and gave the budget of the South Carolina Bureau of Immigration as well; (2) an article titled "Traduction of the South in Europe," in which John L. Zundstron, agent in Stockholm for the Louisiana Bureau of Immigration, described the "slanders" spread about the South by unscrupulous rival Northern and Western agents, to dissuade emigration to the South; and (3) a sample lette written to the Louisiana Bureau of Immigration showing opportunities available for immigrants.

138. See, for example, William M. Burwell, "Science and the Mechanic Arts against Coolies," *DeBow's Review* (July 1969), pp. 560–564, which opposed Chinese immigration while arguing for white immigration; or the article titled "Immigrants Wanted," *DeBow's Review* (March 1869), pp. 243–244, which stated: "we need the moral and intellectual influence of white foreigners in addition to our own people."

come remunerative. We want men of capital to come among us, and introduce white labor. . . . We see afar off, a brighter future, separated
from us, it is true, by years of privation and endurance, but it is a future
of peace and prosperity.[139]

The *Southern Cultivator* also served as a forum in the immigration debate. The "immigration for competition" argument was typified by this
excerpt from a letter by "Policy" in 1869:

Chinese immigration would operate beneficially in preventing the industrious negro from relaxing from industrious habits, owing to the bad
example of the idle and intemperate; while the latter would see the necessity of reforming, as they no longer commanded the labor market, and
must therefore work or starve; while the improved general industry
would operate beneficially on the rising generation. An amount of Chinese immigration adequate to effect these objects, would doubtless prove
very salutary. War and emancipation reduced the available amount of
agricultural labor considerably, and there is a constant tendency to its
lessening still more. . . .
    . . . It is desirable, in his own interest, that the negro should con-
tinue industrious, but what security is there that he will, and how is this
to be best insured. The introduction of another race, equally capable of
laboring under a Southern sun, though comparatively few in numbers,
would, by the operation of the spirit of competition, effect the desired
object, to the mutual advantage of all parties.[140]

David Dickson (a frequent contributor to the *Southern Cultivator*), even
in arguing *against* immigration on the grounds that cotton production
should be curtailed and not expanded, made the unusual point that competition between Negro and immigrant labor would drive down wages
and thereby lead to *strikes* which would be to the overall detriment of
the planter class.[141] Another contributor anticipated the salutary effects
of Chinese competition on Negro labor:

Bring them [Chinese] here in competition with the negroes, and the latter may find it to their interest to quit stealing and going to the Legislature,
and go to work in the cotton fields where they belong. If the negroes
could be induced to quit loafing about the towns and country, and could
all be brought to the plantations, the South would have laborers enough.[142]

139. A. R. Lightfoot, "Condition and Wants of the Cotton Raising States," *De-
Bow's Review* (February 1869), pp. 153–154.
140. "Cotton and Labor," *Southern Cultivator* 27 (November 1869): 338.
141. David Dickson, "Mr. Dickson on Immigration," ibid. (August 1869): 238–
239.
142. G. D. H. "Immigration," ibid. (September 1869): 281.

It is not the purpose of this discussion to chronicle the entire course of the immigration debate in the postwar South. The point of these examples is to illustrate how some spokesmen who advocated bringing immigrants into the South during these years argued as though they believed that a shift of the labor supply curve to the right would lower the wage. Such a position is compatible with thinking a more numerous labor force would be easier to control and exploit, but given the language of the proposals, which often mention benefits such as the "spirit of competition" which immigration would foster among workers, it seems safe to conclude that at least some immigration proponents held a competitive labor market model in their minds.

The Southern immigration movement has been discussed by other historians,[143] and it is interesting to note that many of their conclusions are consistent with what would be expected given the competitive model. Fleming's theory that prior to 1880 the South "desired no immigration either from the North or from foreign countries"[144] was rejected by Loewenberg, who concluded instead that "there was a definite desire for immigration throughout the whole period which expressed itself in many ways."[145] Immigration was generally favored by the Southern periodicals, state laws were passed between 1865 and 1876 favoring immigration, travelers' recorded impressions showed a "dominant trend of opinion in favor of immigration, certain Southern real estate firms became agents for labor (immigration) and even after 1880, strong official support continued to be given to immigration bureaus and projects."[146]

Perhaps more to the point is Berthoff's finding that immigration was supported by certain economic interests, and opposed by others. "Plantation owners led the movement to bring in foreigners."[147] The reason was that "cheap foreign labor seemed likely not only to replace emigrating Negroes but also to break down Negro monopoly of unskilled labor and so keep wages low."[148] On the other hand, the majority of Southern

143. For example, Walter Fleming, "Immigration to the Southern States," *Political Science Quarterly* 20, no. 2 (June 1905): 276–297; Bert James Loewenberg, "Efforts of the South to Encourage Immigration, 1865–1900," *South Atlantic Quarterly* 33, no. 4 (October 1934): 363–385; Rowland T. Berthoff, "Southern Attitudes Toward Immigration, 1865–1914," *Journal of Southern History* 17 (1951): 328–360.
144. Fleming, "Immigration to the Southern States," p. 276.
145. Loewenberg, "Efforts of the South to Encourage Immigration. . . ," pp. 363–364.
146. Ibid., pp. 368–380, *passim*.
147. Berthoff, "Southern Attitudes. . . ," p. 328.
148. Ibid., p. 331. Berthoff cites *Public Opinion* (Washington, 1886–1906), 38 (1904): 47; *Railway World* (Philadelphia, 1856–1915), 48 (1904), pp. 1491–1492; Caroline E. MacGill, "Immigration into the Southern States," in *The South in the Building of the Nation* (13 vols., Richmond, 1909–1913), 6: 593–594, in support of his assertion.

people opposed immigration for the same economic reason that prompt-
ed the landlords to support it:

The campaign to develop southern economy on a base of white immigrant labor failed in two ways. First, of the millions of Europeans who
came to the United States between 1865 and 1914, only an incidental
number entered the South. Second, the economic interests which hoped
to profit from immigrant laborers or land buyers never reconciled most
of the southern people to an influx of foreigners. In fact, Southerners,
though they had little experience with immigrants, in this period became
as outspoken xenophobes as those old-stock Northerners who objected
to the masses of foreigners actually in their midst. . . .
    . . . When confronted with actual groups of foreigners or with visions
of a mass immigrant invasion, Southerners, unless they hoped for immediate profit from the immigrants, rallied to defend their race and culture or to repel the supposed threat of economic competition.[149]

The Farmers' Alliances, forerunners of the Populist Party, displayed
growing opposition to immigration in the late 1880s and early 1890s.[150]
Hostility to immigrants even reached violent proportions—Italians were
lynched in Louisiana and Mississippi in the 1890s.[151]

    Other evidence that different economic groups held opposing views
on immigration exists. Theodore Saloutos found that

determined and tireless as the larger and more influential planters were
in their quest for foreign labor, the small white farmers, and to some
extent the Negroes, opposed it. The small whites, in particular, were ap-
palled by a fear that the country would be overrun by inferior peoples,
and that they, as small producers, would be placed at a competitive
disadvantage. Apprehensions were also voiced by them over dangers that
would arise from the "jealousies and prejudices of races widely differing
in character, taste, and traditional customs."[152]

149. Berthoff, "Southern Attitudes. . . ," p. 343.
150. Ibid., p. 345.
151. Ibid., p. 344, citing Henry Cabot Lodge, "Lynch Law and Unrestricted Immigration," *North American Review* (Boston, 1815–1938), 152 (1891): 602–605; and
James Basset Moore, *A Digest of International Law* (8 vols., Washington, 1906), 6:
843–849.
152. Theodore Saloutos, "Southern Agriculture and the Problems of Readjustment:
1865–1877," *Agricultural History* 30, no. 2 (April 1956): 70. Saloutos cites "Coolie
Labor at the South," *The Nation* 1 (August 31, 1865): 264–265; "The Chinese Problem," *The Rural Carolinian* 1 (April 1870): 434; *New Orleans Price Current* 41 (October 16, 1869): 2; *DeBow's Review* 2 (August 1866): 215–217; 4 (October 1867):
362–364; 5 (January 1868): 82.

The *Southern Cultivator* as late as 1889 reported that the Farmers' Alliance of Tuskaloosa County, Alabama, "memorialized" the legislature of Alabama against proimmigration influence exerted on it by the Alabama Agricultural Society and the Southern Interstate Immigration Convention. The Alliancemen asked, "Will the Legislature spend time and money in an effort to secure cheap labor and salubrious homes for men of other countries, or will it labor to promote the welfare and happiness of the people who are here, and are also those whom the Legislature is supposed to represent?"[153]

Nor was Alliance opposition to immigration schemes confined to the local level:

An important meeting was held in Meridian, Mississippi, on December 5th [1888]. The National Alliance, the National Wheel, and the Cooperative Union of Farmers and Laborers, merged into one body to be known as the Farmers and Laborers Union, of America, with a consolidated membership of 1,500,000. . . .
A great many matters of vital importance were passed upon. On the subject of emigration a resolution was adopted, to the effect that while we will welcome emigrants from the Northwest particularly, and from other parts of the world, we deprecate any attempt to colonize this country with ignorant and pauper population.[154]

Berthoff also found evidence of blacks' opposition to immigration. "More directly threatened than white farmers were Negroes, who might have been driven out of southern agriculture and industry if some immigration promoters had realized their plans. Though almost inarticulate, Negroes were said in 1907 to oppose immigration."[155] It is true that the black population was "almost inarticulate," but a few instances of their opposition to immigration do survive.

And so in the matter of immigration. The material interests of the State [S.C., 1871] clearly demand it. But the blacks are against it, as they fear its political consequences. A late debate in the [state?] Senate illustrated this. A bill was up to exempt new railroad enterprises and various enumerated kinds of manufactures from taxation. A black leader debated it, and in the course of his remarks took occasion to say he had heard, or overheard, a good deal from the class of people whom this legislation was designed to benefit; that it was intended to overslaugh and crowd out the blacks by foreign immigrants, to be introduced into the State by

153. "A Vigorous Protest," *Southern Cultivator and Dixie Farmer* 47 (March 1889): 144.
154. "Concentrating Their Efforts," ibid. (February 1889): 87.
155. Berthoff, "Southern Attitudes. . . ," pp. 347–348, citing Fleming, "Immigration and the Negro Problem," *World Today* 12 (1907): 96; *Southern Lumberman* 49, no. 578 (1906): 22–23.

wholesale. Now, he wanted everybody to understand that the blacks did
not intend to be crowded out, but that they proposed to stand their
ground and, "fight this thing out to the bitter end." He said they might
bring on their immigrants, and they would find the blacks ready for
them.[156]

The *Southern Workman* printed an editorial (December 1880) and a
letter (May 1883) identifying the cheapness of Chinese labor as a potential factor in depressing all wages, even though the editorial policy of
the *Workman* was one of not opposing immigration, since it would ex-
pose the Chinese to Christianity.[157] And the *Southern Workman* was not
the only black periodical to register opinion against immigration. *Alexander's Magazine* in 1906 realized that "it has been one of the pleas of
southern senators in congress to increase the influx of immigrant Poles,
Italians, Swedes, etc., in the United States in order that the South might
get a sufficient stock of cheap labor to supplant the Negro." The article
went on to deplore the displacement of Negro day labor by immigrants—
barbers, bootblacks, railroad hands, street gangs, and brickyard forces:

The South will have its choice of cheap European labor or that of the
despised Negro. In a choice between a white man and a Negro, for the
same position, in the South the Negro must suffer, whatever his qualifications. . . .
    Many times the South has threatened to import foreigners to force
out Negro labor. This move on the part of the government will accomplish what the South has longed for—it will make Negro labor no longer
a necessity. The common laborer being forced out of employment, the
existence of the professional class will inevitably be undermined. Sooner
or later the Negro must turn to some other corner of the earth to work
out an existence.[158]

Alexander's apparently held a strange view of how competition works—
rather than the tide of immigrants depressing wages, the magazine
thought it would only result in blacks being displaced by immigrants.
Whatever its economic theory, *Alexander's* feared the competition of
immigrants and correctly perceived the motivations of many white
Southern immigration boosters.

156. Walter L. Fleming, *Documentary History of Reconstruction: Political, Military, Social, Religious, Educational and Industrial, 1865 to the Present Time* (2 vols.,
Cleveland: Arthur H. Clark Company, 1907), 2: 310. The passage is from J. S. Pike,
Prostrate State, p. 55, dealing with South Carolina in 1871.
157. *Southern Workman* 9 (December 1880): 121–123; 12 (May 1883): 55.
158. "Immigration and the Negro," *Alexander's Magazine* 2, no. 2 (June 15, 1906):
16–17.

Leaving the immigration debate, references to competition in the labor market continued through the last decades of the nineteenth century. Charles Nordhoff, a correspondent for the *New York Herald,* concluded on the basis of a tour through the cotton belt in 1875 that

the system of planting on shares, which prevails in most of the cotton regions I have seen, appears to me admirable in every respect.* [*Most economists consider it a bad system.] It tends to make the laborer independent and self-helpful, by throwing him on his own resources. He gets the reward of his own skill and industry, and has the greatest motive to impel him to steadfast labor and self-denial.

I have satisfied myself, too, that the black man gets, wherever I have been, a fair share of the crop he makes.[159]

Similarly, the *Report* of the Industrial Commission contains testimony that would indicate that neither the law nor the market situation was entirely unfavorable to the agricultural worker. The Honorable O.B. Stevens, Commissioner of Agriculture in the State of Georgia, indicated that it was very easy for tenants to move from farm to farm, despite previously contracted indebtedness.

Q. Is the indebtedness any design on the part of the government or the renters holding to a condition of poverty, or is it the result of some other influence?

A. There is nothing whatever to force a man to stay on the farm. They usually rent these lands from year to year. . . . If the tenant is dissatisfied for any cause, he has a perfect right to go whenever he wants to. The landlord has no lien and no claim upon the property of the tenant whatever except for rent and advances, and those only apply to the present crop. . . .

Q. . . . What would be the position of a man, however, who had defaulted on one farm? What would be his probability of being able to get another farm in that locality, provided he did not liquidate his indebtedness in the first instance?

A. Oh, he would not be regarded as a first-class tenant. But there is always plenty of room there for everybody, and he always gets a place and gets along in some way. Some people always take him up. . . .

. . . Sometimes you have a tenant on a place, and he finds he can do a little better somewhere else, and he moves off and goes to the next place. Sometimes the landlord finds that he can get a better tenant than the one he has. He lets this fellow go and gets the other fellow. They are continually moving around from place to place.

---

159. Fleming, *Documentary History of Reconstruction.* . . , 2: 320, citing Charles Nordhoff, *The Cotton States in 1875,* pp. 21, 107.

Stevens went on to inform the Industrial Commission that "the law in our state protects the laborer in every instance," and he attributed the poverty of the blacks to "the fact of bad management upon the part of ignorant tenants," rather than to exploitation by whites:

A. The garnishee law does not apply to wages. The law provides that wages for labor of any kind can not be garnisheed. Labor is protected all around. . . .

Q. . . . I would like to learn what is the cause of the fact as you stated, that at the end of each year a great many of the tenants make no money—they are in debt. Is it because of the oppressive disposition of the white people to drive hard bargains, or is it because of the bad management of the tenant when freed from the general management and direction of the white people? Or is it because of the bad system? Are the system and the law bad?

A. The law has nothing whatever to do with the systems that are adopted for farm labor; nothing whatever. The only law that we have is the law that protects a laborer in collecting his wages, either one way or the other.

Q. Now, may I take the liberty of suggesting that that is a sufficient answer to that phase of the question. It is not the law. But is it the oppressive disposition of the white people?

A. No.[160]

Another witness confirmed the existence of the Alabama law making it a misdemeanor to break a contract, but also noted that this law was seldom enforced.[161] Such potentially biased testimony must be taken at something less than face value, but it is none the less indicative of the existence of a body of opinion favorable to the competition hypothesis.

Wages of Farm Labor in the United States, an 1892 Department of Agriculture compilation of investigations and inquiries concerning agricultural wages and labor conditions, contains extensive evidence of a competitive labor market in the South. While the Department of Agriculture surveys did not generally distinguish between black and white agricultural workers, the compilers nevertheless asserted that "a very large proportion of those working for wages in agricultural operations in the Southern states may be assumed to be of the colored race."[162] The

160. *ROIC,* 10: 908–911. The questions and answers have been arranged in separate paragraphs instead of being run together as in the *ROIC.*
161. Ibid., p. 925, testimony of the Honorable Robert Ransom Poole, Commissioner of Agriculture of the State of Alabama.
162. United States Department of Agriculture, Division of Statistics, *Wages of Farm Labor in the United States,* Miscellaneous Series, Report no. 4 (Washington: Government Printing Office, 1892), p. 12.

section of the report titled "Abundance or Scarcity of Labor" includes a long list of descriptions of the local agricultural labor markets given by the county boards of observation in the various states. In numerous counties throughout the South, agricultural labor was reported to be "scarce" because of the monetary inducements offered by nonagricultural competitors. The alternative employment opportunities responsible for drawing labor off the farms included public works, railroads, sawmills, turpentine farms, phosphate mines, iron furnaces, coal mines, shops, oyster fisheries, and salt works. The higher wages offered in these and other alternative occupations were the most frequently mentioned cause of the scarcity of labor in agriculture.

The movement of agricultural workers, both black and white, to other regions or to cities was also cited frequently in this report as contributing to labor scarcity. These migrations were often ascribed to economic responses. For example, the correspondent from from Lee County, Mississippi, reported that labor was "very scarce. Better lands, better wages, and a desire among colored people to huddle together has caused thousands to leave here for the Mississippi bottoms and for Arkansas." Competition operated in other forms as well. Several Texas counties claimed an abundance of agricultural labor "owing to close proximity to Mexico, where labor is cheap." In at least one case, labor was scarce because people had fled certain "local disturbances."

Many of the county reports implicitly referred to alternation by agricultural workers between the different forms of land tenure, depending on the relative returns to each. In some localities wage laborers were "scarce, owing to the loose way of renting land," while in other places they were scarce because they "prefer to work for part of the crop" or because "land has been so cheap and abundant that almost every one owns his own land and farms for himself." Elsewhere, it was apparently "more profitable for laborers to work for others than to farm for themselves," and they sometimes reverted to wage labor because there was "difficulty in getting credit so as to farm for themselves."[163]

It has already been noted that the history of Southern labor legislation fluctuated between the passage and nullification of repressive laws. One legal scholar writing in 1910 gave a fairly optimistic assessment of the legal situation of black labor. His case was based on the difference between laws pertaining to race *distinctions* (the "Jim Crow" separate facilities laws) and the laws directly restricting the economic freedom of labor:

163. Ibid., pp. 30–38. The quotations are scattered through the section of the report on the "Abundance or Scarcity of Labor" dealing with the Southern states.

Race distinctions do not appear to be decreasing. On the contrary, distinctions heretofore existing only in custom tend to crystallize into law. As a matter of fact, most of the distinctions which are described above as the "Black Laws of 1865–68" [the infamous Black Codes] are no longer in force. No state now carries statutes prescribing the hour when a Negro laborer must arise, requiring his contracts to be in writing, prohibiting him from leaving the plantation or receiving visitors without his employer's consent, or exacting a license fee of him before he can engage in certain trades. These laws were vestiges of the slave system and survived but a short time after that system had been abolished.[164]

The authors of several modern monographs dealing with the South during this period have also come to the conclusion that strong elements of competition were prevalent in the labor market. According to Roger Shugg, in Louisiana after the war "the free Negro did not work as hard as a slave,* [and] had less supervision and discipline. . . .** Trouble often arose because planters would compete with one another in bidding for hands. This practice almost demoralized Negroes on the sugar plantations, according to Bouchereau,*** and led to unorganized strikes and much dalliance before signing contracts for a new year."****[165]

LaWanda Cox uncovered one such strike of agricultural workers for higher wages in 1880:

Attempts on the part of Negro field labor to strike and organize were infrequent after Reconstruction. There exists, however, an interesting account of a strike for higher wages by Negro workers on Louisiana sugar plantations in 1880. The Negroes went from plantation to plantation getting others to join them. The State militia was sent out and the ringleaders were arrested, tried, and imprisoned for trespass. Petitioning the governor for pardon, they stated that they had thought it within their rights to go where other laborers were working, even though on the property of an individual, and induce those laborers to join them. They now understood this to be a violation of the law. "When laborers differ with their employers hereafter about the price of their labor," the petition read, "it will be in a peaceable manner and with law always on their side." They were released and "quiet was restored."* . . . Conflict between southern laborer and landowner took forms other than overt

164. Gilbert Thomas Stephenson, *Race Distinctions in American Law* (New York: AMS Press, 1969; reprinted with permission of Appleton-Century-Crofts, New York, 1910), p. 351.
165. Roger W. Shugg, *Origins of Class Struggle in Louisiana: A Social History of White Farmers and Laborers during Slavery and After, 1840–1875,* ([Baton Rouge]: Louisiana State University Press, 1939 and 1968), 252. Shugg's references are
* *DeBow's Review* 3: 356.
** E. g., [New Orleans] *Crescent,* January 22, 29, 1869.
*** *Statement of the Sugar and Rice Crops Made in Louisiana,* 1869–70, ix–x.
**** [New Orleans] *Crescent,* February 11, 1869.

clashes. Most notable was the continued bargaining throughout the period over wages, shares, or cash rentals, with each party trying to obtain whichever arrangement would assure him the largest income.[166]

Enoch Banks's *Economics of Land Tenure in Georgia* is an old though still useful economic account of the Southern postbellum agricultural economy. Banks, writing in 1905, observed the frequent movement of blacks following emancipation, although he attributed much of this mobility to a "political motive" distinct from response to wage differentials or other economic incentives.[167] However, he did comment on the economic motive (wage incentive) involved in migration of laborers off the farm, whites to cotton-manufacturing industry, and blacks into the cities, both responding at least in part to the lure of higher wages.[168] Interestingly, Banks apparently anticipated the major result of this investigation, namely, that agricultural labor received a wage equal to the value of its marginal product:

The same fundamental economic law works . . . the laborer tends to get that part of the product for which he is economically responsible.[169]

He also believed, however, that this result would only be obtained when the plantation-wages system of labor payments replaced the sharecropping system, and that the laborer

is economically responsible for a larger absolute amount under the plantation system than under the cropping system and fundamental economic law will tend to give this larger amount to him.[170]

Thus, Banks believed in marginal product factor pricing under a straight wage payment system, which he felt was more efficient than a sharecropping system. It will be shown later that under plausible assumptions the form of agricultural tenure has no impact on distribution or efficiency. (See below, chapter 3). For the moment it is sufficient to point out Banks's conviction that some measure of competition prevailed in Southern agriculture at the time he wrote.

166. LaWanda Cox, "The American Agricultural Wage Earner, 1865–1900," *Agricultural History* 22, no. 2 (April 1948): 97.
* Cox's source for this episode is apparently *Appleton's Annual Cyclopaedia. . . 1880*, p. 482.
167. Enoch M. Banks, *The Economics of Land Tenure in Georgia*, Studies in History, Economics and Public Law, vol. 23, no. 1 (New York: Columbia University Press, 1905): 78–79
168. Ibid., p. 115.
169. Ibid., p. 113.
170. Ibid.

Vernon Wharton, in his meticulous study *The Negro in Mississippi,* found that after 1867 there

was a change in the attitude of the planters, and especially of the editors and public leaders. They had become reconciled to the fact that slavery was dead, and that codes to enforce peonage could not be applied. It had become apparent that the Negroes must be paid, and that their right to move about in search of better contracts could not be blocked.[171]

However, some of Wharton's other evidence shows that this acquiescence may have been superficial. During the great Negro "Exodus" of the late 1870s, the "small white farmers and their representatives, a majority of the white population, probably wish to see the Negroes removed from the state as rapidly and as thoroughly as possible" because "they could not compete with the Negroes in the production of cotton and could have no hope until the freedmen were gone."[172]

The attitude of the employer group was an entirely different matter. They prophesied general ruin for the state if the Exodus continued, and quickly turned to newspaper progapanda [*sic*] to try to dissuade the emigrants.* When propaganda failed, some did not hesitate to use violence. This included the use of irregular courts,** the breaking up of crowds of Negroes waiting for boats,*** the arrest of emigrants on charges of vagrancy and of obtaining goods under false pretenses,**** and the beating and kidnapping of Negro leaders.*****[173]

The same tension between imperfection and competition in the labor market is evident here as elsewhere. The care and conscientiousness of Wharton's research in effect uncovered both conflicting tendencies. Nevertheless, he felt confident to summarize the consequences of emancipation thus:

171.   Vernon Lane Wharton, *The Negro in Mississippi, 1865–1890,* volume 28 of The James Sprunt Studies in History and Political Science (Chapel Hill: University of North Carolina Press, 1947): 120.

172.   Ibid., p. 114. Wharton refers to the Hinds County *Gazette* (January 22, 1879).

173.   Wharton, *The Negro in Mississippi,* pp. 114–115. The references are:

* Hinds County *Gazette,* November 27, December 11, 25, 1878, January 5, February 5, 19, March 5, 26, April 2, 1879.

** Jackson *Weekly Clarion* April 23, 1870.

*** Ibid., May 14, 1879, quoting the Greenville (Miss.) *Times.*

**** Ibid., April 23, 1879; *Senate Reports,* no. 693, 46th Cong., 2nd Sess., part ii, p. 501.

***** *Senate Reports,* no. 693, 46th Cong., 2nd Sess, part ii, p. 500.

The chief advantage that freedom brought to the Negro was the ability to move about, and thus to establish among the employer class a certain amount of competition for his labor.[174]

Finally, it is again possible to examine statements by blacks themselves regarding their view of the operation of the labor market. Again, it is difficult to find Southern black spokesmen. In keeping with the Hampton-Tuskegee philosophy, the *Southern Workman's* editors generally believed that the labor market was competitive, and that blacks could increase their income only by increasing their level of education and following that up with hard work. In an 1875 review of the Southern press, the *Workman* prefaced its compilation by remarking that Southern blacks were "deeply stirred by recent political events," and that in addition, "like any other people, they will in the end collect in those regions where they are best treated and best paid."[175] Later that same year, the *Workman* carried an article entitled "A Few Words on the Labor Question," written by a planter who saw unmistakable evidence of employers' competition for black labor:

If, as owners of the soil, possessors of what little capital there is in the South, and with a superior intelligence, we do not control the labor of our land, the fault lies at our own doors. We have no system, no concert of action. To the contrary, we are constantly pulling against each other. We are the employers, but every farmer has his own notion of things, and cares nothing for his neighbor's plans. If I hire hands for wages, one of them may at any time conclude to leave. If so, he only goes across my line fence and my neighbor hires him.[176]

Beginning in 1878, the *Workman* carried a series of articles on economics by T. T. Bryce, and in these articles, Bryce put forward what essentially amounted to a competitive model of the determination of wages, interest, and other prices. For example, Bryce argued that the wage rate is determined by supply and demand:

The next great law of exchange that I would apply to labor, is the law of demand and supply. . . . If there be two men wanting to buy labor (that is, to hire it), and only one man to sell his labor, it is certain the man who offers most in exchange will secure the labor. If, on the other hand, there be two men to sell their labor, and only one to buy it, it is equally certain that the one will be hired who will sell his labor the cheaper. This law of demand and supply is a law of nature, and no amount of legislation can change it, any more than it could prevent the earth turning on its axis. . . .

174. Wharton, *The Negro in Mississippi*, p. 106.
175. *Southern Workman* 4 (January 1875): 2.
176. Ibid. (September 1875): 67.

Labor has its market price, just as corn or cotton; if there be a large
supply and small demand, prices will be low; if there be a small supply
and a large demand, prices will be high— and no amount of law making,
nor mass-meetings, will prevent it. Everyone tries to buy as cheaply and
sell as dearly as possible; the man with labor to sell will take the highest
price he can get; the man with labor to buy, will give as little as possible;
the price they may agree upon is the market price, and neither close the
bargain if they really think they can do any better for themselves. Buyer
and seller *together* make the price, *neither* can do it *alone;* and a Government has no more to do with the price of labor (that is, the rate of wages)
than it has with the price of potatoes. No Government can fix the price
of labor, that is, it cannot say wages shall be so much or so little. No
man can be compelled to employ labor he doesn't want; and no man
can be compelled labor for wages that do not suit him.[177]

Would-be exploiters of labor may have had an easier task than trying
to "prevent the earth turning on its axis," but Bryce clearly had legal
controls and labor associations in mind when denouncing the futility of
"law making" and "mass-meetings." Bryce also condemned both forced
labor and violent strikes:

Everyone who attempts to steal another's purse, or deprive him of his
life, is seized and punished by the law. So, too, with a man's labor; he
has a right to the peaceable enjoyment or employment of it, and anyone
who attempts to interfere with such peaceable enjoyment or employment
by the use of threats, violates the law, and should be punished by it, as
much as if he had tried to wrest from him his purse or his life. . . .
That all men with particular interests in common should unite for
mutual protection and encouragement is most proper; that they should
endeavor to get the best pay, or, in other words, the most in exchange
for their services, is right and just; but their efforts must be through reasoning, and the means of the market-place—and not through violence
or threatenings.[178]

Bryce also believed that "no 'strike' is ever successful, unless the wages
being received by the help are under the market rate."[179] The soundness
of Bryce's economic reasoning is not at issue here; what is important is
the prominence given to his articles in the *Southern Workman.* In addition to the article titled "Labor" from which the excerpts quoted
above were taken, subsequent issues of the *Workman* contained articles
on "Capital" and "Wages," all emphasizing the same theme, that competitive conditions were the rule in all markets.[180]

177. "Labor," ibid. 7 (October 1878): 77.
178. Ibid.
179. Ibid.
180. Ibid. 7 (November 1878): 85; 8 (February 1879): 16.

Most of the *Workman's* references to the causes of the various "Exodus" black mass migrations of the 1870s and 1880s emphasized response to wage incentives. An article reprinted from the *Newberry* (North Carolina) *Herald* stated:

The Texas fever has laid a strong hold upon the Newberry Negroes. The week before last one hundred and fifty left this place for Texas; we learn that a large party will go to-morrow, and another party on the following Friday. Some of these emigrants are well-to-do Negroes, but they say that labor is too cheap here and their wages too hard to collect after they have been earned.[181]

A similar analysis was offered by the *Workman* itself, later in the same decade:

The exodus again in progress among the colored people—from North Carolina into Arkansas, Mississippi and Louisiana, at the invitation of land companies who pay their way and sell them land at nominal prices —may result, like former movements of the kind, in considerable individual suffering and disappointment, but also, like those, in more of general benefit. It has at least several encouraging suggestions—as showing, for instance, that the Negroes are wanted and welcomed in some parts of the country at any rate, and furthermore, that they are capable of taking hold of their own problem, and settling their questions for themselves. The motive for emigration seems to be chiefly in depression of labor and wages, from failure of crops on the worn out tobacco fields.[182]

As with the other issues, however, the *Southern Workman* was not single-minded. In May 1879, it carried with a favorable preface a letter to the *New York Herald* of April 14 from "a clergyman and native of the South," who argued that the exodus (which must have been the great Mississippi Valley to Kansas exodus) was due not so much to "political intimidations and even outrages against the negro in the South," as to exploitation:

They [blacks] realize the fact that their emancipation in the South has only lifted them from slavery to serfdom.
Behind all this stands the fact that the negro in the South is systematically cheated out of his wages. . . . He rents a tract of land and the landlord has a lien against the whole crop for the rental. It is a penitentiary offence to move any part of the crop from the place before the landlord is satisfied for his rents. The landlord has the first claim on what the negro makes. . . .

181. "Another Negro Exodus," ibid. 13 (February 1884): 17.
182. Ibid. 18 (April 1889): 1.

. . . Of course under these circumstances emancipation is a huge disappointment to the negro. He is in a worse condition than he was in
slavery. The white money lender gets all the fruit of his labor, and is
under no obligation to feed and care for him and his wife and children.
   The ultimate effect of all this will be disastrous to the South. . . . It is
already having the effect to drive the negro out of the South. . . . The
remedy is very simple—even-handed justice to the negro as a laborer.
This will hold him in the South. Nothing else will.[183]

This contradictory note is an appropriate one for ending this discussion of the competition hypothesis versus the exploitation hypothesis. It has been shown that on the basis of only the narrative accounts
surviving from the postbellum period, a strong case could be made for
either hypothesis. There is no doubt that the incidents related here did
actually take place—there were peon camps and there were blacks who
responded to wage incentives in moving from place to place. At times
the repressive laws were part of the state penal codes, and at other times
these laws were overruled by the courts.
   The fundamental question which cannot be answered by this sort of
investigation is whether Southern agricultural labor was exploited *in the
aggregate*. At any point in history, a society is likely to generate unusual,
even extraordinary injustices. The problem of historical interpretation is
not primarily concerned with these exceptional cases, but with the general tendency or trend. Enough reported instances of both exploitative and
competitive behavior exist to support either hypothesis about the Southern agricultural labor market. It remains to be shown, using quantitative
and statistical methods, which hypothesis prevailed for the South as a
whole.

The Relative Merits of Black and White Agricultural Labor

The degree of competition or imperfection in the labor market is not the
only interesting economic issue of the late nineteenth-century South.
Perhaps of equal interest, because of its connection with the legacy of
slavery hypothesis (that the black population emerged from slavery deficient in education, initiative, and enterprise and hence was low in productivity relative to the whites), is the question of whether there was any
significant quality difference between black and white labor during the
period. At least one careful historian, B. J. Loewenberg, has concluded
that Southern opinion after the Civil War was in agreement that free
black labor was inferior to white labor.[184] This assessment is derived

183. Ibid. 8 (May 1879): 51.
184. Loewenberg, "Efforts of the South to Encourage Immigration," p. 365.

from the often-repeated stereotype of the lazy, shiftless, irresponsible freedman, which was so common in the nineteenth-century literature. Because of the ubiquity of this stereotype, only a few typical examples of it in its "original" form will be presented here. It is no surprise that many planters and other whites thought badly of the capabilities of the Southern blacks; what may be unexpected is the large number of planters' statements that black labor was equal or superior to that of whites.

It should be pointed out that for the "inferiority" of a certain type of labor to have an economic meaning, "inferiority" must refer to lower productivity, other things being equal. One type of labor will not be considered "inferior" in the context of this discussion if the employers simply have a taste for the other. Similarly, a difference in productivity attributable to differences in capital per man or the fertility of the land farmed cannot be counted as labor "inferiority." The legacy of slavery hypothesis refers only to deficiencies in human capital or acculturation which might have followed the freedmen out of slavery. Nineteenth-century observers rarely, if ever, conformed to the ceteris paribus requirement in their comparisons, so their evaluations of labor productivities are only of limited value. Nonetheless, their views on black as against white agricultural labor are still suggestive.

The land occupancy and ownership hypothesis (that productivity differences were associated mainly with soil quality differences) will not be discussed in this section at all. That discussion will be deferred until after the presentation of the econometric results, in order to be able to state with real precision what race-associated productivity differences must be explained by any proposed hypothesis. This section will be confined to a simple survey of the nineteenth-century comparisons of the effectiveness of the members of the two races in Southern agriculture.

Philip Bruce articulated one very common theme of the planters, that the blacks were simply incapable of farming successfully without white supervision:

The greatest injury which a planter can inflict upon the interest of the community in which he lives, is to rent the whole of his estate in small lots to colored tenants, especially if he abandons his home permanently to dwell elsewhere, leaving his property entirely in their hands. The quality of the soil begins at once to depreciate from improper usage and careless cultivation; the buildings and fences soon fall out of order from natural decay or the depredations of pilferers; the teams decline to the poorest condition; the crops produced are of an inferior quality. But this is not all: such an estate soon becomes the safe harbor of all the depraved negroes in the vicinity; the vicious habits of the women and men alike increase owing to their removal from the control of the proprietor;

thievish and superstitious practices are more common and open, and brawls and quarrels arise more often than elsewhere.[185]

Such a pessimistic view did not prevent Bruce from remarking elsewhere:

It is plain that in the general conflict between whites and blacks as laborers, the negro enjoys the chief advantages. He is physically as vigorous and stanch as the white man; and is more cheerful and more easily managed; he lives in happiness under material conditions that would be intolerable to the humblest white laborer: and has no sentiment or pride that will prevent him from seeking any kind of employment, however disagreeable that employment may be to ordinary sensibilities, or in what degraded situations, it may place him.

Not only can the negro successfully compete with the native white man, and drive him from the field, but he is also able to expel the immigrant competitor who does not shrink at all from working in his company and at he same tasks.[186]

Perhaps these alleged qualities explained why "the large planters prefer to make up their complement of hands by employing negroes alone."[187] Buried under the racial stereotypes, Bruce was grappling with two contradictory ideas. His notion of the racial inferiority of blacks required that they be incompetent farmers or tenants; yet he was also faced with an observed predilection of at least some planters for black workers. This contradiction reappeared, and undermined the attempt of many a postbellum planter spokesman to achieve consistency in his writings about the merits of various types of plantation labor.

Contributors to the *Southern Cultivator* also expressed doubts about blacks' capabilities:

Planters persist in giving a poor ignorant, lazy, superstitious being, who has no property and never intends to have anything if he can help it, an interest in their crops. . . .

The labor question is a vexed question in the cotton belt; yet I believe there is a sufficient amount of labor in the South, if it could be judiciously controlled, the opinion of a great many intelligent planters, to the contrary notwithstanding. If the negro with his ignorance, superstition and natural inferiority, can't be controlled by the planters of the South, we as a class are the poorest business men that we have ever read about.[188]

185. Bruce, *Plantation Negro as Freeman,* pp. 214–215.
186. Ibid., p. 188.
187. Ibid., p. 186.
188. Red Bone [pseud.], "Fertilizers and Labor," *Southern Cultivator* 30 (May 1872): 168.

A very extensive outline of this "black inferiority" argument is given in a much later issue of the *Cultivator,* in 1889:

Following up the communication in the last issue of *The Cultivator* . . . I am led to say, that the most marked difference between farm methods at the West, and those practiced at the South, will be found in the labor employed. Farm labor in Ohio is far superior to farm labor in Georgia. Ohio farmers positively decline to employ negroes in their fields, when it is possible to secure white labor. They say they have uniformly found negroes "indolent, careless, wasteful and destructive. Their idleness requires constant attendance to keep them at work; their carelessness, close supervision to see that their work is properly done; their wastefulness and destructiveness would bankrupt any man of moderate means, who is not constantly gathering up behind them." . . .

It has been frequently said that the South will never have any better farm labor than negroes. If so, I am sorry for the South, unless they are to be greatly improved. Negroes are thriftless, not caring to accumulate for themselves and, of course, indifferent to the accumulation of their employers. They are extremely idle, and, therefore, cannot be made profitable without expensive supervision. They are very destructive to property and abusive to stock. In these evils they have been indulged, until their character and conduct have become uniform for evil.[189]

It should be noted that even in the middle of his condemnation of black labor, the writer felt obliged to acknowledge that "it has been frequently said that the South will never have any better farm labor than negroes." Other magazine references to the alleged inferiority of black labor can be found. For example, "Nicholas Worth" in his *Autobiography* alleged that black labor actually *deteriorated* after emancipation:

The negro was the principal laborer in producing cotton, and, without training as farmer and as man, he was becoming a less efficient laborer. They practically forbade his training. The pitiful short-staple yield of impoverished acres was sold for the starving price of low grades because it was not skillfully nor promptly gathered from the fields; it was wastefully handled; it was sold to pay mortgages on itself. Life could rise no higher till efficiency and thrift came in.[190]

A similar opinion was voiced in *DeBow's Review:*

To work large plantations with our present labor is clearly impossible; and the greed for land will hardly endure while weeds choke up the broad acres once so productive. We have the soil and the market to

189. W. J. Northen, "Methods Compared," *Southern Cultivator and Dixie Farmer* 47 (December 1889): 605.
190. Nicholas Worth, "Autobiography of a Southerner," p. 166.

ensure successful farming; but we have very little of the skill and knowledge necessary to attain the highest results. . . .

It is evident enough that at present even a small plantation, or *farm*, as I presume they will in the future be called, cannot be successfully worked by Freedmen.[191]

The hearings before the Industrial Commission in the 1890s also included the same sort of testimony.

I think one of the causes of the depression in agriculture in the South is the presence of the negro. The negro does not know how to use improved implements, and does not want to know how, and it is almost impossible to teach him. If a man farming cotton on an extensive scale puts an improved implement in use, every darky says it is impossible to use it, and they do not. They enter very largely into the agricultural conditions of the South; the people rent to them, and work on shares with them. They are averse to making anything in the world except cotton. They do not want to make corn. They love watermelons better than any people or any nation on earth, and they do not know how to make watermelons. They do not care anything about knowing how, but they do love them. . . . I believe the presence of the negro in the South will retard its progress, its industrial and moral development, and its advantageous development, and its social development, agricultural development, and all other kinds of development; and the question is now, What are you going to do about it? Bishop Turner advocates a separation of the races. I am with him on it. . . . There is no question but that if the negroes were removed from our country their places would be filled in the future by more intelligent labor.[192]

One of the methods used to "demonstrate" this inferiority of black labor was to compare the output per man of blacks and some other group of farmers, and to conclude from lower black output per man that black labor was deficient. This dubious methodology was employed by an article in the *World's Work*, the June 1907 issue of which was devoted entirely to the South. The article, entitled "Immigration to the South," reported a "test" which was performed on "the 'Sunny Side' property, on the Mississippi River, in Chicot Country [*sic*], Arkansas." Negro work squads were compared with Italians, and it was found that "the Italian seems to have produced more lint per hand, by 1,410 pounds, or 120.1%, and to have exceeded the Negro's yield per acre by 170 pounds, or 72.9%. The difference in money value in favor of the Italian was $148.89 per hand, or 115.8%, and $18.41 per acre, or 69.8%." It was also found that the Italians had been more successful in accumulating

---

191. "Farming in the South," *DeBow's Review* (April 1868), pp. 367–368.
192. *ROIC*, 10:62, testimony of J. Pope Brown, President of Georgia State Agricultural Society.

work stock and in liquidating their debts at the end of the year.[193] There were several flaws in this "experiment." First, there was no control for the fertility of the land farmed by the two groups of workers. Second, there is no guarantee that the black farmers did not face some sort of discrimination that the Italians did not face, such as discrimination in purchases of capital equipment. Third, the Italian immigrants may not have been randomly selected representatives of white agricultural workers. They may have been particularly energetic and innovative simply because they were immigrants. These objections notwithstanding, the type of calculation presented in this Arkansas experiment was undoubtedly widely accepted as evidence of the inferiority of black farm laborers.

Fleming reported a similar calculation, made in the 1880 census. The main points of the census report were:

1. That where the blacks are in excess of the whites there are the originally most fertile lands of the state. The natural advantages of the soils are, however, more than counterbalanced by the bad system prevailing in such sections, viz., large farms rented out in patches to laborers who are too poor and too much in debt to merchants to have any interest in keeping up the fertility of the soil, or rather the ability to keep it up, with the natural consequences of its rapid exhaustion and a product per acre on these, the best lands of the state, lower than that which is realized from the very poorest.

2. Where the two races are in nearly equal proportions, or where the whites are in only slight excess over the blacks, as is the case in all the sections where the soils are of average fertility, there is found the system of small farms worked generally by the owners, a consequently better cultivation, a more general use of commercial fertilizers, a correspondingly high product per acre, and a partial maintenance of the fertility of the soils.

3. Where the whites are greatly in excess of the blacks (three to one and above), the soils are almost certain to be below the average in fertility, and the product per acre is low from this cause, notwithstanding the redeeming influences of a comparatively rational system of cultivation.[194]

Apparent white productivity advantages were attributed to superior white skills despite inferior soil, while black disadvantages were said to persist despite blacks' location on the most fertile soils. The census analysts partially anticipated some of the findings of chapters 4 and 5 below involving productivity differences associated with both race and

193. *World's Work* (June 1907), p. 8960.
194. Fleming, *Documentary History of Reconstruction. . . ,* 2: 324, citing E. A. Smith, "Cotton Production by Whites and Blacks," *Report on Cotton Production of the State of Alabama,* Census of 1880.

crop. The detailed identification of the productivity differences between the groups will prove to be somewhat different, as will the interpretation of those differences, however. Fleming also reported a productivity calculation based on the 1900 census. In this latter calculation, J. C. Hardy, president of the Agricultural College of Mississippi, found that predominantly black counties with high per-acre land values produced less output per acre than predominantly white counties with low per-acre land values.[195] Hardy also reported that the counties in which black farmers were more closely managed by whites were more productive than the black counties in which not many white managers were employed. While Hardy conceded that "this difference is partly caused by a difference in the fertility," he asserted, "the principal reason is due to the superior intelligence used in the management of the first group [where white management prevails]. This is proved by the fact that in every comparison made between a white county and a black one the black was the most fertile, yet the white was nearly twice as productive."[196] Apparently, Hardy believed that land prices are a better measure of fertility than output per acre. But just as output per acre is inadequate as a fertility measure because of possible differences in land/labor ratios and capital stocks across counties (as well as potential race-associated differences in labor productivity), so also land values might reflect factors such as transportation costs and other locational factors distinct from the intrinsic physical and chemical fertility of the soil. Land values could even reflect the market power of landlords. Clearly these calculations are inadequate, but Southern opinion supporting and conditioned by them was both substantial and influential.

Despite the prevalence of this stereotypic conception of black inferiority, the opposite view, that black agriculturalists were in no way deficient compared to whites, was surprisingly widespread. There is no dearth of statements testifying to the quality and skill of black farmers and agricultural workmen.

As early as 1863, a representative of the New England Educational Commission for Freedmen enthusiastically reported the progress of South Carolina blacks. This remarkable letter is worth reproducing in full:

195. Ibid. 2: 441, citing J. C. Hardy, *South's Supremacy in Cotton Growing*, p. 8.
196. Ibid., p. 442.

Ashdale, near Beaufort,
S.C., August 8th, 1863

The colored people are doing well generally. They are quite industrious, and well informed in all that appertains to raising the cotton and all the other productions of the soil. They are very much interested in all those products that form the means of their subsistence. They are laboring assiduously to procure in the coming harvest sufficient to supply all the wants of the body, with some amount to sell. The Governor of this department in the spring cut off the clothes and rations from all the people that were able to labor in the fields, and it has proved one of the most efficient means of promoting industrious habits among them. So long as they saw before them a source from which they could draw food and clothes, they were contented, and these contributions had a deleterious effect upon them. Now they are aware that if they do not produce sufficient to support themselves, and purchase their clothes, they must suffer, and they are quite ambitious to get as much as possible. It is quite surprising to see the ingenuity and tact which many of them exhibit to accomplish that end. They certainly have imbibed largely the spirit of trade and commerce, by which they increase their revenue. Their little fields are guarded with the strictest care, and the growth of all the products watched with much eagerness, and the profits calculated by them, as much as the cargo and the profits to accrue therefrom are, by the great shippers of our commercial marts. They are fast learning the value of money, and are acquiring an idea of property, whether it be in a horse or land. There is a growing desire among them to become owners of land. Hundreds of them are guarding their little stores with jealous care, and adding to their stock all they can, in order to have sufficient to make purchases at the next sales of land. To be able to receive all the proceeds of their labors, is one of the heights of their ambition. The adjoining plantation to the one where I live, was purchased last year by the negroes. They have worked it themselves without any direction from white people. They have exhibited all the skill, thus far, of those that have been worked by the Government. They have a large field of cotton, and a larger one of corn. I see them frequently, and converse with them about it. They are as proud of their labors as are any of the farmers of the North when success follows a period of industry. They have planted and brought to good growth by the necessary working three acres of cotton, each of which is, I am told, the maximum of one person's allotment, when other crops are worked by the same hand to the maximum. This condition of that plantation excites the emulation of all the surrounding people, and they frequently say that if they could work this land in the same way we could see some great crops. I have no doubt that if the negroes owned the land and could work it with the expectation of receiving all the proceeds, the cotton crop would have been increased one-third, if not one-half.

So far as the question of subsistence is involved with these people, there is not the least doubt about it. They are abundantly competent, and able and willing, to support themselves, and in a short time many of them will acquire a competence that will enable them to demand and supply themselves with many of the comforts of civilized life.

[signed] A.B. Plimpton[197]

The Joint Committee on Reconstruction heard many witnesses who thought the blacks were doing well after emancipation. The same Colonel Spence of Tennessee who told the committee that the freedmen worked well for fair wages (see above, note 117) described the poor *whites* in terms that were elsewhere applied only to the blacks:

The poorer classes of whites are not getting along so well. They have no schools, and where they have no land they cannot get employment as readily as the colored men can. The richer men will not employ them, for the truth is, they are not as valuable for laboring as the negroes are. According to my judgment the poorer classes of white people, not only in Tennessee, but all over the south, are scarcely able to take care of themselves. They are inclined to be idle and lazy, and think it degrading to work.[198]

Speaking directly to the issue of the "unwillingness of the negro to work," Colonel E. Whittlesey, Assistant Commissioner of the Freedmen's Bureau for North Carolina, was quite caustic:

QUESTION. What can you say in relation to the negro's love of labor? Is he inclined to work for fair wages, or is he, generally, an idler and a shirk?
ANSWER. I think that there is no more industrious class of people anywhere than the negroes of North Carolina when they have proper inducements held out to them. The idleness that has been witnessed during the last season was due in a great measure to the disturbed state of the community and to the uncertainty in their minds (an uncertainty very well founded, too) whether they would receive any pay at all for their work. I have heard no complaints of idleness or shirking in places where I have known that they were receiving fair and prompt payment for their work.[199]

Samuel Thomas, Colonel and Assistant Commissioner of the Freedmen's Bureau in Mississippi and northeast Louisiana, agreed in a letter to Carl Schurz:

It is nonsense to talk so much about plans for getting the negroes to work. They do now, and always have done, all the physical labor of the

197. *Extracts from Letters of Teachers and Superintendents of the New England Educational Commission for Freedmen*, vol. 39 of Pamphlets on Slavery, Harvard Widener Library Collection, p. 6.
198. *RJCR*, part 1: 117.
199. *RJCR*, part 2: 182.

south, and if treated as they should be by their government, (which is so anxious to be magnanimous to the white people of this country, who never did work and never will,) they will continue to do so. Who are the workmen in these fields? Who are hauling the cotton to market, driving hacks and drays in the cities, repairing streets and railroads, cutting timber, and in every place raising the hum of industry? The freedmen, not the rebel soldiery. The southern white men, true to their instincts and training, are going to Mexico or Brazil, or talk of importing labor in the shape of Coolies, Irishmen—anything—anything to avoid work, any way to keep from putting their own shoulders to the wheel.[200]

Such favorable assessments of black productivity were not made only by sympathetic observers. A Southern writer described the changed race and labor relations prevailing in Georgia after the war this way:

The confident prophecies of the croakers that Southern plantations would go to waste, and that nothing but ruin lay before us, have proved the merest bosh. The enormous increase in the cotton crop of the South alone shows that the colored people, as free laborers, have done well, for it is not to be disputed that they form very nearly the same proportion of the laborers in the cotton fields that they did when they were slaves. . . . under no circumstances could worthless labor have produced the enormous increase in this crop.[201]

This same Southerner went on to point out that the blacks did not live "in dread of the terrible Ku-klux," and that "very many negro farmers are capable of directing the working of their own crops," without any white supervision.[202] James Runnion, in his *Atlantic* article on the "Exodus" movement of 1879, repeated the observation that Southern whites loathed work and that "it is certain that negro labor is the best the South can have, and equally certain that the climate and natural conditions of the South are better suited to the negro than any others on this continent."[203]

According to Vernon Wharton, "It also soon became apparent to those who gave the matter an actual trial that the freedmen in agriculture furnished a more satisfactory type of labor than could be obtained from white workers, either natives or immigrants." Wharton's conclusion was based on statements such as this "Sensible Communication" to the *Raymond Gazette* from a landowner near Terry, Mississippi, written in 1886:

200. Schurz, *Report,* p. 82.
201. "A Georgia Plantation," *Scribner's Monthly* 21, no. 6 (April 1881): 830.
202. Ibid., pp. 830–831 and 833–834.
203. Runnion, "The Negro Exodus," p. 229.

I do not . . . decry white labor, for I like it, when of the right kind, but if either must go, give me the nigger every time. The nigger will never "strike" as long as you give him plenty to eat and half clothe him: He will live on less and do more hard work, when properly managed, than any other class, or race of people. As Arp truthfully says "we can boss him" and that is what we southern folks like. . . . I have worked both kinds of labor, side by side, with varying results. The nigger will do the most work and do it according to personal instructions. . . . I record Experience against Theory.[204]

In the 1890s, the Industrial Commission found planters satisfied with the quality and competence of black labor. J. H. Hale, who owned farms in both Georgia and Connecticut and who had direct experience with both Northern and Negro labor, was unstinting in his praise:

I count that the negro labor of the South is the best agricultural labor in America to-day. I will recommend them way ahead of our New England Yankee. The Yankee boys we think are perhaps a little smarter for some expert work, but for agriculture throughout the year I think the negro labor of the South, at least the section where I am located, the Black Belt, is the best agricultural labor in America to-day, and I can accomplish more work for $1 in Georgia than I can for $3 in Connecticut, and get the same crop result. . . .
. . . The extra advantage is in the efficiency and the honesty of purpose and the faithfulness of the negro labor as compared with what we can get in Connecticut. I went South with the idea that the negro was a rather stupid creature and could be used only in the grosser lines of work, and I have learned different by using them for a number of years. . . .
. . . I do not know how the South could live without negro labor. It is the life of the South; it is the foundation of its prosperity; and the great future prosperity I see in the South, and believe in the South, is because they have such splendid labor and such good labor. God pity the day when the negro leaves the South, or if they have to have labor from foreign countries to take the places of the negro.[205]

Mr. Hale went on to explain that Negroes required no more supervision than Northern workers, and that they were improving in efficiency. He closed his testimony on this subject by giving an example of the faithfulness of the blacks employed by him—they took care of his plantation and house while he was gone on trips, and voluntarily cut their wages when some of his orchard trees were killed by an unseasonable frost.[206]

204. Wharton, *The Negro in Mississippi*, p. 121, citing the *Raymond Gazette* (May 8, 1886).
205. *ROIC*, 10: 382–383. The quotation consists of relevant parts of Mr. Hale's answers to a series of questions put by the Commission.
206. Ibid., p. 383.

Not quite so enthusiastic as Mr. Hale was the Honorable Robert Ransom Poole, Commissioner of Agriculture of the State of Alabama, who nevertheless testified that, "If they [Negroes] were as economical as the white people they would absolutely own that country in a few years. It is getting so that in our section in the black belt the most of the lands are rented to negro tenants for the simple reason that they can afford to give more for them than the white man can. I own several plantations and I rent to the negroes because I can get more rent from the negro."[207] According to Mr. Poole, part of the reason for this was that Negroes did their own labor while whites hired it done,[208] but if that were the case, either blacks were better workers, or the vaunted advantages of white supervision were illusory. It should be recalled from the earlier part of this section that another witness before the Commission saw "one of the causes of the depression in agriculture in the South is the presence of the negro," so that it would only be fair to say that the Commission was receiving mixed information. This ambivalence of the sources was quite common.

Perhaps the most persuasive arguments for the high quality of black labor after the war were those given by practical farmers in the *Southern Cultivator*. In an 1869 article, "What is the Proper Labor for the South," a "Subscriber" discussed the quality of black labor compared to the alternatives:

Much has been said and written about the uncertainty and unreliability of free negro labor, and the necessity of superceding it by foreign white labor. To this end, Immigration Societies have been organized, to bring foreigners to take the place of the negro, in the cotton and rice fields of the South.

At the risk of joining issue with many wise and good men, who really have the welfare of the country at heart, I venture to controvert the wisdom and propriety of this movement. . . .

. . . He [the Negro] is already trained to the labor necessary for . . . production. He has his important part to perform in advancing the wealth and prosperity of the South. There is no adequate substitute for his labor. We have no faith in the availability of European emigrants, as a substitute for the negro, in the production of cotton. . . . Is it not true that he [the Negro] has proved himself the most patient and enduring laborer that can be brought into the cotton and rice fields of the South? Shall we give him up merely because his bonds have been broken? Shall we cast away an inestimable boon, which God in his unerring wisdom had bestowed upon us, in the labor of the negro, because the relation of master and slave has been destroyed by Puritanical fanaticism?[209]

207. Ibid., p. 926.
208. Ibid.
209. *Southern Cultivator* 27 (February 1869): 50–51.

As is apparent even from the text quoted, "Subscriber" was no believer in black social or political equality. Nevertheless, he admitted "there is no adequate substitute for his labor." This opinion was shared by another writer in the same issue of the *Cultivator*. Even though Negro labor was "both uncertain and unreliable" and contracts with it were made at great disadvantage to the planter, "Negro labor is all we have at present, and is decidedly preferable to any we are ever likely to have—all emigration societies to the contrary, notwithstanding."[210] Still another contributor held:

I agree with Mr. Dickson as to the labor question. Let the Germans stay where they are. They will do very well in the grain regions of the West, where they are hired by the day or week, and where such a thing as holding plow handles is out of date. There they jump into the seats of a Cultivator or mower and reaper, and drive "around" with a huge umbrella aboard if they wish, as if on a frolic. Just let him come down here, Mr. Editor, and try his hoe day after day in our "brilin sun," and he will heartily wish himself back in 'de farder land.' Give me cuffee, and I can give you cotton. There are no set of laborers on earth, save the sambo's, [*sic*] who can make a cotton and corn crop, on three pounds of bacon and a peck of meal per week. A German, on this diet would shrink up so promptly that a cut gourd vine would not even be a parallel.[211]

As might be expected, some of the strongest assertions of the capability of black farmers and agricultural laborers are to be found in the pages of the *Southern Workman*. The *Workman* advanced two main arguments—first, that black labor was in no way inferior to white, and second, that *free* black labor was superior to slave labor both in productivity and profitability. A self-described "enemy of the Negro" writing "A Few Words on the Labor Question" in the *Workman* of 1875 observed:

"Farming don't pay," has been a cant throughout the South since Lincoln's emancipation proclamation, and almost as universal has been the accusation, "our labor is too unreliable," meaning of course negro labor. Both observation and experience teach me that "white labor" is as unreliable as "negro labor" on the farm. . . . the high priced lands of the North are no evidence of agricultural thrift. Those farmers live very well it is true, but they work much harder, and are more troubled with unreliable labor than we of the South. I have heard northern farmers

210. J. Dickson Smith, "Revolution in Southern Agriculture," ibid., p. 53.
211. Dixie [pseud.], "Nut Grass—the Labor Question," ibid. (September 1869), p. 277.

say, time and again, that during their busiest season, they have today had all the "help" they wanted, and to-morrow it was gone.[212]

The *Workman* did seem to be sensitive to the possibility that its statements might be interpreted as special pleading on behalf of the Southern blacks. At any rate, it frequently printed statements by anti-Negro Southern spokesmen as to the progress and productivity of the blacks. An 1877 issue reprinted an article from the *Charleston News* which argued that white immigrants did not make a profit, whereas black workmen did:

> We are a "burnt child" on the question of immigration. We have tried white employees, beginning with the natives, and going all through the catalogue, even to those from the very back-doors of the Continent of Europe, and we are free to confess we have never found one that netted us a dime, while we know we made money out of Sambo, even though he persists in voting the Radical ticket.
> The principle we lay down is this: Any white man in this country who has attained to the age of maturity, and has never accumulated enough to buy him a home, will be more of a charge than a profit to me on my plantation. And this principle is adhered to because it is founded upon the experience of the past.
> Secondly. Field hands coming from another country to the "Sunny South" bring with them no experience as to the cultivation of our crops, are not climatized, have less muscle and endurance under our climate than the negro, have far more wants, which require a cash capital that the Southern farmer has not; and for these reasons are less profitable, even with their superior energy, than the thriftless negro to whom we have all our life long been accustomed.[213]

The height of irony was reached in reprinting a segment of an interview with none other than Jefferson Davis. Mr. Davis "spoke of the negro race in a rather patronizing way—as children, and not as men. . . . It was his opinion that, wherever the negro race was found, it must be as an inferior and servile race, and, in the long run, they would give way to the superior race under any and all circumstances." However, Davis acknowledged that he had

changed his mind entirely upon one question, viz., that the great staples of the South, cotton and sugar, could be produced with greater economy and in greater abundance by paid labor rather than by the labor of slaves. He said to your correspondent: 'This has already been demon-

212. *Southern Workman* 4 (September 1875): 64.
213. "Immigrants—Do They Pay?" ibid. 6 (May 1877): 35.

strated, and that fact alone goes far to prove the advantage which the abolition of slavery has been to the whites.'[214]

Three years previously a northern correspondent, "D.G.F." of Oswego, New York, related to the *Workman* a conversation he had had with a Texas gentleman during an extended train journey through the South. The Texas planter, who had lost 100 slaves by the Act of Emancipation, found that, after a period of transition,

among these liberated people there were many, perhaps a majority, or more, who were industrious, economical, and naturally thrifty. Adapting themselves to circumstances they have bent their energies to improve their own condition and that of their race. As a result, many have already made large progress in education, many are now landowners, and on every hand unmistakable evidences are beginning to appear of prosperity and comfort. To the race, as a whole, freedom has already proved a blessing.[215]

This planter also argued that emancipation had increased productivity in the South, because under the slave system, weight quotas for picking and workers' lack of any interest in the crop decreased both the quality and the quantity of the yield. He concluded that both whites and blacks had benefited from emancipation, even in those cases when whites were thrown back to reliance upon their own labor.[216] Finally, the 1878 *New York Times* article reprinted in the *Workman,* which was cited previously, concurred in the opinion that free labor was superior to slave. Noting that cotton output had increased and that planters were not as burdened by mortgage as they had been before Emancipation, the *Times* stated:

That the emancipation of the slaves has been the first great cause of this result, there can be no doubt. The free colored man, having more self-respect, a greater feeling of responsibility, more knowledge, and from the necessities of the case being more industrious and faithful, is much more valuable as a laborer than was the negro slave. Unfortunately, there is a very large class of persons in the South who are not willing to acknowledge these facts, or who are so blinded by prejudice that they cannot regard them as do practical business men in other parts of the country.[217]

214. Ibid. 8 (May 1879): 52.
215. "Northern and Southern Views of What Emancipation has Accomplished," ibid. 5 (October 1876): 78.
216. Ibid.
217. Ibid. 7 (February 1878): 10. For the previous reference to this article, see note 95.

Despite such reported improvements in the condition of freedmen, the *Southern Workman* did not fail to take every opportunity to put forward its particular prescription for Southern black progress:

When the war closed there were two sets of Radicals, divided in opinion on Negro labor. One of them claimed, in their own peculiar phraseology, that "Free niggers would not work"; the other claimed that the colored man would labor as well as the white man, and compete successfully with him in all branches of human effort. As usual, when extreme views are stated, there is some truth and some fallacy in both statements. . . .
. . . If the negro be not so good a laborer as the white man, it is his misfortune, not his fault. . . . During his enslavement the negro had no chance to learn to labor, although work was the only branch of education open to him. A man labors only when he puts forth an exertion in order to get something in return for it,—if a man put forth an exertion through fear of punishment or through the compulsion of some other man, he is not a laborer, he is only a worker. . . . if we would increase the usefulness of the negro to himself and to others, *he must be educated.*[218]

This comparison of the respective qualities of black and white agricultural labor would not be complete without an inquiry into whether the levels of wages differed between the races. There is no doubt that in some instances the preference expressed by planters for black labor rested on the cheapness of that labor as compared with white.[219] What is surprising is the infrequent mention of such a discrepancy, and even some explicit statements that the pay of white and black workers was the *same.* It may be that planter spokesmen felt that the obvious did not need to be repeated, but there may actually have been no difference in remuneration for identical work in many situations. For example, not a single case of black and white sharecroppers in the same county receiving a different share of the crop was found.

One of the few systematic collections of wage data was in the *Report* of the Industrial Commission. As usual, the evidence is contradictory. The digest of testimony of volume 7 of the *Report* summarized a preponderance of instances in which black mechanics were paid less than their white counterparts, although there were a few cases of equal pay for equal work. Black tradesmen were generally thought to depress the wages of whites because "they can live on much less." But one witness

218. T. T. B. [T. T. Bryce?], "Negro Labor," ibid. 9 (March 1880): 45.
219. See, for example, *ROIC*, 10: 378, testimony of J. H. Dale; Dixie [pseud.], 'Nut Grass—the Labor Question," *Southern Cultivator* 27 (September 1869): 277; H. H. G., "Immigration and the Labor Question," ibid. (December 1869): 374.

believed that in places where the blacks were organized, their wages were the same as whites. This witness concluded, "For that reason the white mechanics of the South are assisting the colored men to organize."[220]

The picture is even more confused when attention is focused on agricultural labor. For *farm* workers, most Industrial Commission testimony indicated that blacks and whites received equal pay for equal work. Some witnesses were explicit:

Q. . . . What is the difference between the competition of the white labor and black labor in South Carolina?
A.   The cotton is raised by colored people. The white people raise cotton in competition with the colored man and for the same work we do not pay any more. My whole place is arranged in so much for a day's work, and no matter who I have to plow I pay the same for the work. I have overseers and a colored foreman that I pay more.[221]

Another Southern farmer testified that "the greater portion of our field labor comes from our colored population. About 20 per cent are white. All share alike. The contracts are made on the same basis to each race."[222] On the other hand, another farmer told the Commission that the reason immigrants would not come to the South was that black labor was cheaper than any other type, with the possible exception of the Chinese.[223]

In its overall statistical summary of Southern wage levels, however, the Industrial Commission concluded that competition equalized wages for similar kinds of work, and that the only wage advantage enjoyed by whites over blacks was due to their concentration in the more skilled trades:

It would be desirable to show precisely the relative compensation of white and colored laborers. In these investigations it was not practicable to give averages by races. The returns were by counties, and averages of the whole body of laborers were calculated. As a very large proportion of them are of the colored race, especially in cotton-growing sections, and as any white labor of the same grade of service is leveled in the competition, a true average for exclusively colored labor would approximate these records of Southern labor, which by reason of higher pay of whites

220.   U.S. Industrial Commission, *Reports of the Industrial Commission,* vol. 7: *Report of the Industrial Commission on the Relations and Conditions of Capital and Labor Employed in Manufactures and General Business,* pp. 64–65. Hereafter referred to as *ROIC,* 7.
221.   *ROIC,* 10: 120, testimony of L. W. Youmans, a farmer and merchant from Fairfax, South Carolina.
222.   Ibid., p. 455, testimony of J. E. Nunnally, a farmer of Nunnally, Georgia.
223.   Ibid., pp. 46, 52, testimony of James Barrett, a farmer of Augusta, Georgia.

in a few more responsible positions would be somewhat higher than the average for the exclusively colored.[224]

Other comparisons between black and white wages for similar work are few and far between, though there are other scattered indications that equal work received equal pay. In one unusual instance, the man who was Superintendent of the Texas Military Institute just after the war alleged that freedmen were actually contracting for *higher* wages than free whites, but this case was exceptional.[225]

A. B. Hart wrote that whites and blacks were treated the same as laborers.

Nowadays some Whites are tenants or laborers on large plantations. Near Monroe, [Louisiana], for instance, is a plantation carried on by Acadians brought up from lower Louisiana, with the hope that they will like it and save money enough to buy up the land in small parcels. There are plantations on which white tenants come into houses just vacated by negro tenants, on the same terms as the previous occupants; the women working in the fields, precisely as the Negroes do; there are plantations almost wholly manned by white tenants. . . .

Outside of the administrative force and their families there are commonly no white people on a cotton plantation. The occasional white hands make the same kind of contracts, live in the same houses, and accept the same conditions as the Negroes; but their number is small and they are likely to drift out either into cotton mills or into sawmill and timber work.[226]

Even after the Jim Crow movement was well under way, whites and blacks worked side by side on the same jobs, though there is no way of gauging how frequently or how amicably this took place.[227] One modern investigator found just after the Civil War a rude equality extending down to overseers' treatment of black and white tenants alike.[228]

Even from this brief survey it should be apparent that there was no clear pattern of agreement on the relative merits of black and white agricultural labor after the Civil War. If blacks were less productive, it was due to a "legacy of slavery" rather than to any intrinsic deficiencies. However, even given the undoubted oppressions and deprivations of slavery, there is still copious evidence that the black agricultural worker

224. *ROIC*, 11: 123.
225. *RJCR*, part 4, p. 131, testimony of Caleb G. Forshey.
226. Hart, *Southern South*, pp. 45 and 264. Notice the contradiction between the two (widely separated) passages concerning the presence of whites on plantations.
227. For an example of this, see Abbott, "The South and the Negro," p. 229.
228. Shugg, *Origins of Class Struggle in Louisiana*, p. 266, citing the New Orleans *Picayune* (September 8, 1867).

was the equal or superior of the white in the postbellum years. As in the case of exploitation versus competition in the labor market, the anecdotal evidence is not sufficient to decide the question.

The Advantages and Disadvantages of Cotton Culture

The next major issue of the postwar Southern economy has to do with the complaint of "overspecialization" in cotton expressed by many agrarian reformers before 1900. These reformers advocated crop diversification to alleviate agricultural poverty and distress among both whites and blacks. By this point, it should be no surprise that the findings presented here will show that it is possible to support either the argument that cotton overproduction was the curse of the South, or that cotton was the most profitable crop available to the agricultural sector. While it is undeniably true that a host of critics and relatively impartial observers saw cotton culture as a source of low incomes and stagnation, it is also true that many similarly qualified commentators hailed cotton as the source of Southern wealth, not of its poverty.

"Overproduction" is a vague term, and in order to clarify its economic meaning, it is useful to summarize the main arguments that the South grew too much cotton:

1. First, there were simple and unqualified statements that cotton was not profitable to grow. It is easy to find statements of this type in the agricultural magazines, but the actual reasons for the alleged unprofitability were usually either not specified or are among the subsequent items of this list.

2. Farmers' speed of adjustment was too slow. That is, farmers displayed sluggish reactions to changes in prices or in other market signals. Sometimes this was combined with a notion that the farmers knew how to grow only cotton, or would only grow cotton, no matter what its price. In any case, the causes of "overproduction" were farmers' irrationality and ignorance rather than any "external" agency.

3. Cotton was overproduced because merchants and landlords insisted that their tenants grow cotton. Usually, the blame was laid at the door of the rural furnishing merchants. These merchants allegedly demanded that their tenants grow cotton because the cotton could not be eaten. Thus tenants had to buy all supplies at the country stores, at inflated prices and usurious rates of interest. Sometimes it was also argued that the merchants preferred cotton because of its salability. These arguments were variations on the theme that merchants forced farmers to

grow cotton, in order to exploit them in the rural credit market. As a result, farmers were "locked in" to cotton culture.

4. Related to these arguments, but on a larger scale, was the proposition that the South as a whole needed to diversify in order to escape its dependence on the rest of the country for food and other necessary supplies. Sometimes this was combined with a metaphysical argument that cash farming was somehow enervating, while agricultural self-sufficiency was ennobling.[229]

On the other side, the arguments that cotton deserved to remain "king" even after the war generally follow these lines:

1. Simple statements that cotton was the best crop of the South, and that its production should be increased, not decreased. Often such assertions were accompanied by crude projections of the world demand for cotton, which was undeniably increasing throughout the period.

2. More sophisticated arguments purporting to show that cotton had a comparative advantage in the South as against the alternative crops. These arguments were couched sometimes in terms of profitability, sometimes in terms of climate and physical conditions.

3. Finally, there is evidence that the farmers *were* price-responsive, economically rational decision-makers. Although not usually used to justify the cotton/noncotton crop mix, these indications are contrary to

---

229. The overproduction arguments were summarized in a similar way in volume 6 of *The South in the Building of the Nation:*

Though there was always in the South an insufficient production of home supplies by the average farmer and planter, the decrease in the production of food materials or home supplies marks a change in plantation methods of profound economic importance. Many causes have contributed to this condition. Among them we may note the following:
1. The almost exclusive use of cotton as the basis of credit to farmers, and the absence of adequate working capital in farming.
2. The want of foresight, a tempermental characteristic of a large body of the more ignorant and thoughtless class of negro renters.
3. The general prevalence of the renting system with its exemption from direction and control. This reduces the number of "hands" working for wages under the direction of those who have most foresight and intelligence and most interest in building up a more diversified and restorative system of agriculture, by which food crops would be grown.
4. The insufficiency of home supplies is partly due also to the indifference or approval of the advancing merchant, who, to sell supplies at a profit from his store, usually urges that the maximum acreage be put in cotton.
5. The greater familiarity of the body of agricultural laborers in the cotton belt with cotton culture than with diversified agriculture.
6. The almost universal system of annual or short term rentals and the absence of any general system of valuing the young grain crops that might be growing at the end of the renter's period of tenancy. This in many states keeps the more enterprising class of tenants from growing fall-sown crops, such as wheat or oats. (J. F. Duggar, "Areas of Cultivation in the South," *SBN* 6: 21–22.)

the view that Southern farmers were ignorant, irrational, "traditional" agriculturists.

It may be observed here that a failure by Southern producers to increase their incomes through collusion to restrict output should not be construed as "overproduction." If the South as a whole had acted as a monopolist or oligopolist in the world cotton market and had faced a less-than-infinitely-elastic world demand curve for cotton, then the profit-maximizing level of total cotton acreage would have been less than the acreage actually devoted to cotton. However, this cannot reasonably serve as a modern economist's definition of "overproduction." Any competitive industry could restrict output and gain higher total returns if its firms colluded, yet producers in competitive industries are not said to suffer from overproduction; rather, they are credited with being efficient. In weighing the evidence concerning the performance of nineteenth-century agriculturalists, overproduction can only mean that for some reason *individual* farmers were producing too much cotton, given their market frame of reference—that *given* the prices they faced (and could not affect), they chose an inefficient crop mix which included an excess of cotton.

The same kinds of contradictory evidence on both sides of the over-production question can be found, as in the previous cases of the two labor market hypotheses and the comparison of black and white agricultural labor. The form of the presentation on the cotton issue will be slightly different than in the two previous cases, however. Many of the pertinent statements on cotton culture contain the contradictory evidences side by side. Commentators were apt to conclude that diversification was necessitated by the growth of cotton revenues or that the suitability of Southern soils and climate created too great a temptation to specialize in cotton. For this reason, instead of presenting the arguments for overproduction first, and following them by the arguments for comparative advantage, both sides of the argument will be presented together. This format underscores the deep confusion of the nineteenth-century analysts on this subject.

A good starting point for this discussion is the *Southern Cultivator,* the practical farmers' magazine which was accessible to most literate Southern farmers.[230] The question of overproduction was probably the

230. The *Southern Cultivator's* subscription varied from $1 to $2 per year, compared to $6 per year for *DeBow's Review;* it claimed 200,000 readers (not all of whom were necessarily *subscribers*) every month in 1889 (May 1889: 230); and an examination of the advertisements for farm equipment, patent medicines, fertilizers, and clothing leaves no doubt that the *Cultivator* was aimed at the ordinary, if somewhat more prosperous than average, farmer.

greatest source of controversy in its pages. Most of the magazine every month was devoted to tips on various new techniques or agricultural experiments, but a huge number of letters and articles touched on the cotton issue.

The *Cultivator's* preoccupation with the overproduction debate even antedated the Civil War. In 1849, letters appeared advocating greater self-sufficiency, more working up of raw materials to be performed in the South itself, and investment in manufactures rather than in slaves.[231] An article later that year titled "Cotton—Too Much Planted" argued that "a less quantity would bring them more money," even though conceding that "this doctrine has and will be assailed by the great bulk of cotton planters, both by precept and example."[232]

After the war, the controversy resumed. In 1869 David Dickson argued both sides:

Now we can purchase fifty million dollars worth of guano in its raw state, and clear one hundred millions of dollars on it in nine months, and expend nothing additional in manufacturing cotton and grain out of it.—what say you to that? Are you not willing to have the money? I say let any foreigner have your dollars, when you can with certainty make two dollars in nine months, clear of cost, for every dollar spent.

It is in every man's mouth, keep your money at home. That is impossible—money is not productive, unless kept moving. *This* is the point: keep your *labor* at home—manufacture everything at home that you can make to any advantage—spin your cotton and wool in Georgia, and convert it into cloth—work up raw hides into shoes—lumber into ships—wheat into flour—corn into bacon and lard—grass into beef, mutton and wool—iron ore into all manner of useful implements, &c., &c.[233]

Part of Dickson's inability to make up his mind may have been due to the fact that he was a fertilizer and cottonseed magnate in Sparta, Georgia,[234] but the confusion extended far beyond him. The two opposing arguments ran parallel throughout the years of the 1870s and 1880s in the *Cultivator*.[235]

231. Sylvius [pseud.], "The True Policy of the South," *Southern Cultivator* 2 (January 1849): 10.
232. Whitman H. Owens, ibid. (October 1849): 103.
233. *Southern Cultivator* 27 (January 1869): 44.
234. See, for example his advertisement in this same January 1869 issue of the *Cultivator,* p. 45. Dickson ads appeared in many other issues of the *Southern Cultivator* as well.
235. The issues of the *Southern Cultivator* which were available to this writer covered the years 1849, 1869, 1872, 1874, 1878, and 1889. These volumes provide a sufficient sample to demonstrate the confusion that existed among the contributors.

In an 1869 article "What is the Proper Labor for the South," a "Subscriber" flatly stated "King Cotton re-asserts his power, and we who are to maintain him on the throne will see to it that we get our fair proportion of the benefits of his reign. Our redemption, under the favor of God, is in the cotton crop—out of it is to be realized the money power, the wealth of the South. By and through it we can and will control the commerce of this country."[236] Not quite so vainglorious, but of the same mind, was "Panola," who argued that at current prices, cotton was simply more profitable than other crops, particularly corn:

I say why plant an unremunerative corn crop, to be cultivated all the summer, and consumed in the cultivation of the succeeding cotton crop, when the same planter, with the same [labor] force, by leaving off the corn crop, can plant more cotton, and sow more largely of small grain, and finally put more money into his pocket, which is the gist of the thing, at last?[237]

"Acorn" wrote that his high hopes for diversification had been dashed by the prevailing high cotton prices, so that "the hoary despot still sways his sceptre supremely," that is, cotton remained king.[238] A Tennessee "Subscriber" made it clear that he did "not advocate the abandonment of the cultivation of cotton . . . it is eminently the crop of the South, but until we devote less of our land, time and attention to the cultivation of cotton, and more to the cultivation of grain, grass and clover, and to the raising of stock, we can never be an independent and prosperous people."[239] One "Random" of Egypt Station, Mississippi, told the readers of the *Cultivator* that of all the possible food crops for the South, corn was too expensive because it "has second choice only of good land and good work," wheat was uncertain, and rye, oats, barley, and buckwheat had not been adopted in the South as staple breadstuffs.[240] Another contributor reiterated the profitability of cotton, while cautioning that other crops should be substituted for the "presumptuous little Cotton King" should the relative profitabilities of the crops change.[241]

In 1872, the *Cultivator* reported extracts from an address by Governor DuPont delivered at Tallahassee in December 1871, in which the Governor advised that ". . . cotton be subordinated to the food crops"

236.   *Southern Cultivator* 27 (February 1869): 50–51.
237.   P[anola] [pseud.], "Letter from Panola—Corn *vs*. Cotton &c," ibid., p. 60.
238.   Acorn [pseud.], "Diversity of Crops, &c," ibid. (June 1869): 174.
239.   Subscriber [pseud.], "Grain and Stock *vs*. Cotton Culture," ibid. (July 1869): 214.
240.   Random [pseud.], "Bread for the South," ibid. (September 1869): 280.
241.   J. Quitman Moore, " 'Mr. Dickson on Immigration' Reviewed," ibid. (October 1869): 302.

because the extent of cotton planting precluded recovery of labor and other costs in cotton, and in order to avoid costs of transporting corn and meat from the Midwest.[242] Another writer in the same year urged diversification beyond both cotton and corn, to rejuvenate soil fertility and to decrease dependence on the North and West for other provisions.[243]

In 1874, "Acorn" wrote again to the *Cultivator* bemoaning the over-specialization in cotton because of its great profitability:

> There is a fascination about cotton planting that seems irresistible—people all around us are drawn into the vortex; and we are very much to blame for it—for our papers and politicians are always blowing about the millions the cotton crop brings into Southern pockets. It is a mistake, and the sooner we realize it the better. The profits belong to others—the loss is ours.[244]

"Acorn" probably believed that the farmers were not receiving the profits, which would be reason to switch crops if the returns to alternate crops could be retained, but he did not say why the farmers were unable to keep the cotton profits. The editors also reprinted an article from the *New York Financial Chronicle* (date not given) which noted the profitability of cotton in no uncertain terms:

> We have extremely little faith in any falling off in acreage, except what actually is enforced, either by want of capital, or through bad weather in spring, preventing the putting in of seed, or some cause beyond the will of the planter.
> And the reason for this is evident—it lies in the fact that cotton always has paid better, and even since the war does pay better, than any other crop.[245]

The *Chronicle* article went on to argue for diversification in any case, not because cotton was less profitable, but "to guard against unfavorable contingencies."[246]

The editors of the *Cultivator* began their 1874 volume with a denunciation of "money crops—cotton, as the representative of these, well-nigh absorbing the whole energy of our farmers."[247] Perhaps more significant

---

242. "Farm Policy—Reasons for a Change of, At the South," ibid. 30 (February 1872): 44–45.
243. P. C. Wilkes, "Cotton *vs.* Grain Crops and Stock-Raising," ibid. (April 1872): 126.
244. Acorn [pseud.], "The Philosopher's Stone—Pay as You Go," ibid. 32 (April 1874): 129.
245. "Extent of Cotton Planting for Next Crop," ibid. (May 1874): 173.
246. Ibid.
247. "Thoughts for the Month," ibid. (January 1874): 1.

are repeated references to Grange advocacy of diversification, the first contained in the "Declaration of Principles" by the National Grange, adopted at St. Louis, February 11, 1874, and reprinted in full in the April 1874 issue of the *Cultivator*.

> We shall endeavor to advance our cause by laboring to accomplish the following objects [among others]: . . .
> To reduce our expenses, both individual and corporate; to buy less and produce more, in order to make our farms self-sustaining.
> To diversify our crops, and crop no more than we can cultivate.[248]

In a similar tone, T. J. Smith, Master of the Georgia State Grange, addressed his Patrons in these words:

> Let me earnestly and affectionately entreat you not to abandon the policy of making an abundance of supplies for home, and heed earnestly the resolution as passed by the Cotton States Convention of November last year, and impressively reiterated in its session of July last, of planting one-third of our arable land in small grain, one-third in corn and one-third in cotton.
> Hearken to the warning voice of the past whose syren [sic] song of planting all cotton, hurled us into bankruptcy of property and well nigh of credit and character.[249]

A "Cotton-Planting Granger" from Alexandria, Louisiana, wrote the *Cultivator* that despite fair crops and good prices after the war, "three-fourths of the cotton planters were broke" because they had borrowed money and planted cotton exclusively. According to this Granger,

> cotton planters should make cotton with their own money, and not with borrowed capital; otherwise they are the slaves of manufacturers, middle men and capitalists generally, when really they should hold the commanding position, and be independent of all such classes, which most assuredly would be the case, did they make cotton with their own means.[250]

Another "Subscriber" depicted farmers' irrational predilection to plant cotton, in characteristically florid phrases:

> In spite of the rains and cold, people here put forth every effort to plant a full crop of cotton—as fast as it died or was washed away, they replanted, until there are no seed left. They have fought hard for the

248. Ibid. (April 1874): 137.
249. "Georgia Patrons of Husbandry," ibid. (October 1874): 391–392.
250. "Make Cotton on Your Own Capital—Borrowing Ruinous," *Southern Cultivator* 32 (November 1874): 420.

"Old King," and whilst badly disappointed in the old gentleman, don't seem disposed to give up their allegiance yet. For—although judging the future by the past,—he promises nothing but bankruptcy and ruin, they still rally under his time-honored banner, and persistently refuse to give up the fight.

Cotton is emphatically, their King—and though he kicks and spurns them, they hail him their Chief, and will die like dogs, licking the hand that smites them. We glory in their spunk—but must confess, we fail to see good judgment in it.[251]

In 1878 the same contradictory themes persist. One article claimed that a well-managed cotton farm on productive lands was capable of returning 30–50 percent on capital invested, *provided* that consumption expenditures (such as the purchases which made up most of the store account) were not counted as part of the cost of production.[252] Another, reprinted from *Savannah News,* provided the results of an experiment in which "broomsedge land" yielded a profit when planted in cotton, but not in corn.[253] On the other side, one contributor in that year repeated the argument, familiar by now, that diversification was necessary to achieve self-sufficiency,[254] while another claimed that cotton production was no longer profitable in North Carolina, South Carolina, and Georgia.[255]

The 1889 volume opened with the *Cultivator's* editorializing that money was not the proper objective of farming:

What is the fundamental error of our system, the underlying cause of the depression which prevails so generally among the agricultural classes? It is the fashion to say that we plant too much cotton and produce too many bales. Another form of the same reply is, that we plant too little in grain and other provisions crops and buy too much from abroad. These are both correct in fact, but they do not go back to the root of the matter. These errors of detail are based upon a deeper lying, fundamental error—a misconception of the true business of a farmer. . . .

The average Southern farmer has been prone to consider the production of cotton, or sugar, or tobacco, or rice (according to locality) as the *ultimate* of his aims and efforts, and to look upon the production of food supplies, the care of live stock, and the minor industries of the farm, as so many drawbacks or hindrances—more or less necessary evils—to his

251. "Crop Notes, &c.," ibid. (June 1874): 241.
252. R. I. McDowell, "The Cost of Cotton Culture," ibid. 36 (May 1878): 175, reprinted from *Southern Home* (n.p., n.d.).
253. "Corn and Cotton on Old Broomsedge Land," ibid. (October 1878): 378.
254. G. M. Stokes, "Encouraging Signs Among the Farmers," ibid. (April 1878): 153.
255. A Friend of the Cultivator [pseud.], "Cost of Cotton Production," ibid. (November 1878): 444.

full and abounding success. . . . The farmer has been striving to *recoup* his losses, or build up a competence or a fortune by making *money,* and he is little inclined to produce anything that will not always command the cash.

But the number is increasing of those farmers who believe that the essential of farming is to make a living on the farm.[256]

Other contributors continued the attack on overspecialization in cotton and the failure of farmers to achieve self-sufficiency.[257] Concentration on cotton was even satirized in an article contrasting Southern farming "Then and Now," in which specializing in cotton while purchasing "cheap" food and supplies from other regions was presumably ludicrous enough to discredit the "all-cotton plan" on its face.[258]

Of greater interest, however, is an article devoted to "American Cotton" which argued simultaneously that the South enjoyed a worldwide comparative advantage in cotton culture, but that nevertheless diversification should be practiced.

The true policy of the South is not to make less cotton, but to make it on less land, and therefore at less cost. It is the great money crop of the world. The American cotton is the one crop that can be shipped to all parts of the world. Wherever a bale of American cotton is turned out it will bring its value in gold. Our peculiar soil, and desirable climate together, give us an advantage over all other countries in producing it. . . .

The one thing now to be done in order to make the cotton producers the richest people in the world, is to bring their lands to the highest state of cultivation possible. To cultivate less land in cotton and to cultivate it better, and to put the balance of our lands in diversified crops.[259]

The unnamed writer of this article must have implicitly held an unusual notion of the agricultural production function, because he did not advocate expansion of the labor devoted to cotton at the same time the land planted in cotton was to be decreased. Such optimism about the unlimited productivity of the soil was not unknown in the *Cultivator.* This muddled reasoning went unchallenged, although a later article made the point that even though diversification might be desirable, "it requires both time and money to convert a cotton plantation into a grain and

256. "Thoughts for the Month—For the Month of January," *Southern Cultivator and Dixie Farmer* 47 (January 1889): 2.
257. Jno. H. Dent, "An Address to the Farmers," ibid., (February 1889): 75; Mr. Dent repeated his point in "The Farmers of the South must Reform," ibid. (April 1889): 163; see also Tar Heel [pseud.], "A 'Tar Heel's' Observations," ibid., p. 203.
258. Alpha [pseud.], "Then and Now," ibid. (September 1889): 446.
259. "American Cotton," ibid. (February 1889): 100.

stock farm."[260] W. J. Northen even admonished the farmers of Georgia to use the profits from the exceptionally good cotton crop of 1889 to get themselves out of debt and finance a changeover to more diversified farming![261] It is apparent that whatever view the *Southern Cultivator's* correspondents held on the relative profitability of cotton farming, they usually recommended diversification.

DeBow's also carried planter opinion in favor of diversification and self-sufficiency.[262] But consider the following passage:

Our soil and climate are pre-eminently adapted to the growth and cultivation of the cotton plant. Though this fact may be universally admitted, we would state in proof of it, that according to the census of 1860, the State of Mississippi produced that year one and a quarter million bales of cotton, it being more than one-fifth of the product of all the cotton States. This fact of itself is sufficient to prove that the soil and climate of Mississippi are both eminently adapted to the production of cotton. But while this is true, it is equally true that in past years, for nearly one-third of a century, we may say from the year 1830, the cotton planters of the Southern States have given to the cultivation of cotton an undue and disproportionate, excessive degree of care, attention, labor, capital and breadth of land, to the exclusion of other crops, such as cereals, vegetables, fruits, hay and stock of every description, to the great detriment of themselves and the ruin of our country.[263]

DeBow's did not recoil from an even more blatant *non sequitur* on this subject:

The following is what the Commissioner of Agriculture says in his annual report, just out, on Southern agriculture: The continued high price of cotton has made its culture more profitable than at any former period, and the crop of 1868 has yielded a larger amount of money than that of 1859. . . .

I regret to observe, from official correspondence and during a brief tour through the cotton states, the tendency to neglect other crops and concentrate all available labor and capital upon a single product, how-

260. R. J. R., "From Cotton to Grass and Stock Farming—Bermuda Grass—Burr Clover—Red Clover and Bermuda—Texas Blue Grass—Best Cattle," ibid. (August 1889): 385.

261. W. J. Northen, "Our Opportunity," ibid. (October 1889): 519.

262. For example, "What We Need," *DeBow's Review* (January 1868), reprinted from the Columbus, Georgia *Enquirer* (n.d.); also "Farming in the South," *DeBow's Review* (April 1868), p. 367.

263. "Industrial Association of Mississippi," ibid. (January 1868), p. 83. The quotation is from a report on a meeting of "a number of influential gentlemen recently met and organized at Jackson 'to encourage, develop, and improve the Agriculture, Horticulture, and the Manufacturing and Mechanic Arts of the State, as those upon which the comfort, prosperity, and happiness of all classes primarily depend.' "

ever profitable. The inevitable result will be more cotton and smaller net returns after the purchase of needed supplies and, as a further result, a slower improvement of neglected lands. This bane of Southern agriculture is still operative, and may cease to exist only when low prices, disaster, and despondency shall again arrest the impolitic and irrational course of production. I would not advise an attempt to keep up prices by limiting the yield; a somewhat larger supply of the staple is needed in the markets of the world; the present rates cannot be sustained indefinitely; but I would not foster the suicidal mania for cheapening the money-producing crop while rendering dearer every other that must be purchased as an auxiliary of its production.[264]

Other observers were not free of the inability to make up their minds about cotton's profitability. Henry W. Grady wrote in *Harper's* in 1881:

After sixteen years of trial, everything is yet indeterminate. And whether this staple is cultivated in the South as a profit or a passion, and whether it shall bring the South to independence or to beggary, are matters yet to be settled. Whether its culture shall result in a host of croppers without money or credit, appealing to the granaries of the West against famine, paying toll to usurers at home, and mortgaging their crops to speculators abroad even before it is planted—a planting oligarchy of moneylenders, who have usurped the land through foreclosure, and hold by the ever-growing margin between a grasping lender and an enforced borrower—or a prosperous self-respecting race of small farmers, cultivating their own lands, living upon their own resources, controlling their crops until they are sold, and independent alike of usurers and provision brokers—which of these shall be the outcome of cotton culture the future must determine.[265]

Grady went on to argue half-heartedly for diversification:

Those who have the nerve to give up part of their land and labor to the raising of their own supplies and stock have but little need of credit, and consequently seldom get into the hands of the usurers. But cotton is the money crop, and offers such flattering inducements that everything yields to that.[266]

Successive articles in the anthology *The South in the Building of the Nation* held, first, that "over-production of cotton and failure to raise the necessary food supplies on the plantation were the main causes for the depression, so far as it affected the Southern cotton growers,"[267] and next, that efforts by the United States Department of Agriculture to en-

264. "Agricultural Department," ibid. (February 1870), pp. 187–188.
265. Henry W. Grady, "Cotton and Its Kingdom," *Harper's New Monthly Magazine* 63 (October 1881): 719–720.
266. Ibid., p. 723.
267. Matthew Brown Hammond, "Cotton Production in the South," *SBN,* 6: 96.

courage diversification had failed because "the fact remains that the value per acre of the staples above mentioned [cotton, tobacco, rice and sugar] has been high compared with that of the cereals. The motive for keeping a large area in a single crop has been a strong one."[268]

Of course, not all sources are so conflicting. A. B. Hart evidently thought the South had a strong comparative advantage in cotton. "Since the South seems better fitted than any other part of the earth for the cultivation of cotton, since at any price above six cents a pound there is some profit in the business, and at the prices prevailing during the last five years a large profit, it seems certain that the Negro will be steadily desired as a cotton hand."[269] "Nicholas Worth" in his autobiography expressed a similar opinion:

It is a marvelous fact, unmatched anywhere under the sun, that these Southern states have a practical monopoly of one of the most valuable staple products of the earth. No other land has such an advantage. Wheat grows on our great prairies; it grows in many other countries also. So corn; so cattle; so wool; so even the minerals, gold and silver and copper. No one land has a monopoly even of tropical products. But the South is, and always will be, the great source of cotton.[270]

In 1907 an issue of the *World's Work* devoted entirely to the economy and investment prospects of the Southern states argued that the South exercised a practical monopoly in cotton production because that region's winters were cold enough to kill the pests that destroyed cotton, while its warm weather lasted long enough for a full growing season. The tropical countries warm enough for cotton did not enjoy the cold months.[271] This same issue of the *World's Work* included advertisements extolling the virtues of various cities and states of the South. Overproduction of cotton was not even hinted in one of these:

It costs $25 a year to cultivate an acre of cotton. Poor farmers can raise 250 pounds to an acre which with the seed is worth at least $32 or a profit [of] $7 an acre. A good farmer will make a bale (500 1bs.) to an acre or a profit or [*sic*] nearly $40 an acre and many make $1\frac{1}{2}$ bales to an acre, or about $65 (allowing for increased cost of good cultivation), an acre profit. Compare this with the profits from wheat growing and remember that because there is more land than population you can buy the land for

268. Thomas F. Hunt, "Cereal Farming in the South," *SBN*, 6: 113.
269. Hart, *Southern South*, p. 267.
270. Nicholas Worth, "Autobiography of a Southerner," p. 481.
271. D. A. Tompkins, "The South's Vast Resources," *World's Work* (June 1907), p. 8952.

from \$7 to \$40 an acre. As one farmer said: "The most shiftless Negro can make a living growing cotton. There is no reason why an intelligent white man should not get rich at it." And they do.[272]

The *Southern Workman* advocated diversification, both to stay out of debt[273] and as behavior towards risk:

All experience points to a diversified system as the really successful way of farming. Our Southern brethren have seen the folly of the one crop system, and are now raising their own grain, and it will not be long before they will be entirely independent. They will not rely on "King Cotton" any more. We have but little hope of the farmer who adheres, with such a tenacity to the one crop plan, never realizing that good time coming. Furthermore, we think the risk too great for a farmer to have all his capital in a crop of corn, wheat, oats, flax or grass, but should, as far as practicable, have a portion of his farm devoted to each. Then, should one crop fail, or the price thereof be low, he would not be among the sufferers from "hard times."[274]

The *Workman* also listed diversification as part of a 30-year program by which a man could start from scratch and become a prosperous farm owner.[275]

Government reports and testimony taken by investigating committees were more confused. A Senate-sponsored inquiry into the causes of the agrarian distress of the early 1890s concluded that overproduction, the failure to grow home supplies, speculation in cotton futures, and the demonetization of silver were the chief causes of the depression among the cotton farmers.[276] Regarding overproduction, the reasoning of the Committee was hardly razor sharp: "Overproduction in the sense that more cotton has been produced than can find an effective demand at fair prices, in the present condition of the finance and trade of the world, is undeniably true. Overproduction in the sense that the needs of the world

272. "Nature's Garden Spot," advertising section of *World's Work* (June 1907), pages not numbered. "Nature's Garden Spot" consisted of the eastern section of Virginia, the Carolinas and Georgia, Florida, and central Alabama.
273. "The Negro Question," *Southern Workman* 19 (June 1890): 65.
274. "Diversified Farming," ibid. 5 (March 1876): 22, reprinted from *Prairie Farmer* (n.p., n.d.).
275. F. Richardson, "Hints on Agriculture," ibid. 6 (September 1877): 69.
276. U.S. Congress, Senate, *Report of the Committee on Agriculture and Forestry on Condition of Cotton Growers in the United States, the Present Prices of Cotton, and the Remedy; and on Cotton Consumption and Production,* 53rd Cong., 3d Sess., Report 986. The discussion here is abstracted from the section summarizing the testimony and the Committee's findings, vol. 1: iii–xliv. This report will hereafter be referred to as *RCCG,* 1, and *RCCG,* 2.

for cotton and cotton manufactures have been more than met is denied."[277] The Committee did acknowledge "that considering our soil and climate, and the energy and industry and skill of our people, the American cotton raiser has the advantage over all others, and in the sharp competition in the future he will be the more successful." Nevertheless, the majority report recommended diversification to raise prices and escape the cotton credit system.[278]

The *Report* of the Industrial Commission, if anything, leaned in the direction of finding cotton the most profitable Southern crop. In the "Topical Digest of the Evidence" of volume 10, the Commission admitted, "Diversification of agriculture [is] difficult in the Southern States," primarily because of Southern land's unsuitability for the alternative food crops, the high salability of cotton and the ease with which credit could be obtained against it. The Commission reported that witnesses advocated diversification nevertheless.[279]

Examining the testimony itself, P. H. Lovejoy, a merchant and planter of Hawkinsville, Georgia, testified:

You can not jump right out of all cotton system and go into the other. They have not the means to do it with, and they must have help. The cotton crop is the only thing they can get ready money for in our section. . . . We have no market there for [corn and wheat and products of that kind]. . . .
. . . They can not make enough corn and wheat there to the acre to make it interesting to go in it. Ten or 15 bushels of corn is a good crop in our country. That is the reason why we stick to cotton.[280]

L. W. Youmans, a farmer and merchant of Fairfax, South Carolina, told the Commission that on the basis of experiment and "after mature reflection and an experience of 30 years, I thought the best promise would be in cotton." Youmans calculated that it was cheaper to buy some meat and horses from the West than to raise them at home, even though he did raise his own corn, forage, and bacon. He also found that "it is cheaper [that is, more profitable] in my section to raise cotton than wheat," and his experimentation can be summed up by his response to a question on diversification: "If I thought I could diversify to my advantage, I would do so, but there is no crop there that I can plant with more certainty of coming out even [than cotton]."[281]

277. Ibid., p. vi.
278. Ibid., p. xliii.
279. *ROIC,* 10: ccxlii-ccxliii.
280. Ibid., p. 78, testimony of P. H. Lovejoy.
281. Ibid., pp. 117–121, *passim.*

These examples could be multiplied.[282] How is it possible for such confusion to have existed? One explanation might be that the profitability of cotton versus alternative crops depended on the relative prices of the various crop outputs, and since these relative prices changed from year to year, assessments of profitability were bound to change. The references given above are not arranged chronologically, and many of them refer to different years. This objection does not apply to the internally inconsistent statements, however. Even so, it requires a jump in reasoning to go from temporary fluctuations in price and profitability to the overall conclusion that chronic "overproduction" was a major source of distress. That leap consists of some sort of assertion that farmers were slow to react or incapable of reacting to changes in relative prices by changing their crop mix.[283] Two sources of farmers' rigidity are usually cited: either farmers' ignorance, sluggishness, or irrational predilection for cotton; or insistence on cotton culture by merchants and landlords as a way of locking tenants and other poor farmers into an exploitative credit system. As before, both support and contradiction of these can be found.

A classic description of the existence and consequences of a very low speed of adjustment was given by W. J. Northen in the *Southern Cultivator:*

At these highly remunerative [1867, 1868, and 1869 cotton] prices, farming in Georgia offered unusual inducements and magnificent possibilities. Everybody began farming and everybody planted cotton exclusively. The price dropped from these high points, yet never low enough to lose hope that it would rally again. Year after year the delusion has lasted, until multitudes of men, confronting the horrors of debt, have seemed utterly unable to tear themselves away from its constantly fastening power. This is the history, concisely told, of the depression in Georgia since the war so far as we are personally connected with it. Under the long-continued system of one crop and clean culture, our lands have been made barren, and many who came from the cities, under the delusion of fifty cents for cotton have abandoned us to our poverty and the fearful solution of our problem. To the towns and the cities, and

282. To take an example almost at random, William E. Highsmith, "Louisiana Landholding During War and Reconstruction," *Louisiana Historical Quarterly* 38, no. 1, contains references to both the distress resulting from concentration on cotton and the profitability of cotton above that of alternative crops.
283. Overproduction due to farmers' price-response rigidity also requires that the properly deflated relative cotton price declined secularly. Examination of the price data used in chapter 7 reveals that there were periods of relative cotton price decline that lasted for several years. The deflated cotton price does not appear to have declined steadily after 1880, however.

away from the country and the farms, men and means, frightened as by a spectre, have been drifting, while debt, cruel and exacting, has wrung from us all but hope and honor. The country now languishes for the help that could easily make the wealth of the State.[284]

The economist Enoch M. Banks commented similarly in 1905:

Mortgages were made to secure debts; they were executed therefore only in those cases in which the debts lapsed. These cases were numerous, however, on account of the decline in the price of cotton from 1874 to 1898, and also on account of the slowness with which the farmers have been adjusting themselves in accordance with the best combination of the productive factors. . . .
 . . . The croppers do not as a rule make plans with reference to the future, and bend their energies toward the realization of those plans. They are content if they can make some arrangement whereby they may be enabled to get the bare necessaries of life throughout the year that immediately concerns them.[285]

Banks neglected to indicate whether the "decline in the price of cotton" was an absolute decline or decline relative to the other relevant prices.[286]

A more poetic expression of the same sort of farmers' ignorance and rigidity was given by "Nicholas Worth":

The people,—the people of these fertile states,—a vast multitude, far apart as they dwell from one another; pioneers yet (for the land is unsettled and their life is primitive and hard), but holding fast to the notion that they are a part of a long-settled life; fixed in their ways; unthinking and standing still; a grim multitude, though made up of jovial individuals; credulous of all old formulas and sayings, whether true or false, and incredulous of any new thing however obvious; sprawling in the sun of this happy climate; hungry without knowing it, and unaware of their own discomfort; ignorant of the world about them and of what invention, ingenuity, industry, and prosperity have brought to their fellows, . . . a stolid mystery these country people are in the mass.[287]

At times these pessimistic evaluations of the adaptability of the Southern farmers had racial overtones:

A remedy more and more looked to in all parts of the country is diversified or intensive farming. For this sort of farming the general opinion

284. "Mr. Northen's Address," *Southern Cultivator and Dixie Farmer* 47 (September 1889): 450. The address was delivered before the Georgia State Agricultural Society at Cedartown, Georgia, August 13, 1889.
285. Banks, *Economics of Land Tenure in Georgia*, pp. 51, 101.
286. See note 283 above.
287. "Nicholas Worth," *Autobiography of a Southerner*, p. 171.

seems to be that the negro laborer is not suitable. Testimony as to his capability is not all one way, it is true. . . .

Others say, however, that the negro can raise cotton and nothing else; that he can not be trusted to care for stock; that he is unable to use farm machinery (as has been noted); that he will not give the care and attention necessary for diversified and intensive farming. It is said that any negro renter will not even cultivate his own garden patch to any great result in providing supplies for his family.[288]

On the other hand, direct evidence of price responsiveness of the Southern farmers is somewhat harder to find. It does exist, nonetheless. Robert Somers, an English traveler, observed in 1870–1871:

The farmers of Tennessee have gone more extensively into the culture of cotton under the stimulus of high prices than was probably prudent, and Nashville of late years has been a brisk cotton market. The reduction of price this season will send many of the growers back to grain and stock, for which the soil and climate are well qualified. Yet the cultivators of the soil in Tennessee, as in other parts of America not supremely adapted by nature to the growth of any peculiar product for which there is a great demand in foreign markets, have difficulty in apportioning their crops, and are always ready to introduce or extend whatever promises a better return.[289]

Somers was not sure these adjustments were a good thing, however:

The old system of corn and cotton for ever on the same fields in uncertain proportions can no longer suffice to give a stable interest to the land; and if a large area and low price of cotton one year are followed by a small area and high price the next, and gambling in the cotton market is to be complicated by gambling in the growth of the staple, a most unfavorable blow will be given to cotton manufactures throughout the world.[290]

An Alabama Commissioner of Agriculture in the 1890s also had confidence in the long-term adaptability of the farmers in his state:

After the increase in price of cotton directly after the war, every farmer went into raising cotton, thinking there was more money in the production of cotton than in other products, and neglected the raising of pork and corn; but the decrease in the price of cotton forced them back to raise

---

288. U.S. Industrial Commission, *Reports of the Industrial Commission,* vol. 15: *Reports of the Industrial Commission on Immigration and on Education,* p. 553. Hereafter referred to as *ROIC, 15.*
289. Robert Somers, *Southern States Since the War, 1870–71* (London and New York: Macmillan and Co., 1871), p. 271.
290. Ibid., p. 268.

more corn, and now we are raising nearly all we consume in my State.[291]

Possibly farmers' reactions to price changes were among those things too obvious to mention. Attention to the market is implicit in the arguments that cotton was the favorite crop because of its profitability, just as a low speed of adjustment was one of the reasons advanced for "overproduction." Certainly *DeBow's Review* and the *Southern Cultivator* discussed farming techniques and economics endlessly, which indicates at least that readers of those magazines kept track of the economic situation. The incessant debates over diversification, crop rotation schemes, and the results of agricultural experiments throw doubt on the idea that Southern agriculture was cast into a "traditional" mold and was carried on in a spirit of not-so-blissful oblivion. And the demand for the publications of the agricultural experiment stations, as well as subscriptions to the agricultural papers of the South, was rising, increasing several hundred percent in the first decade of the twentieth century.[292]

The other agency blamed for overproduction of cotton was the Southern credit system, particularly furnishing merchants' insistence that farmers borrowing from them concentrate on cotton. The *merchants'* predilection for cotton was usually explained in terms of the low risk and salability of the cotton crop, the merchants' need for a cash crop to enable them to satisfy *their* creditors, or their desire to have the farmers indebted to them cultivating a crop which couldn't be eaten, so that the farmers would be forced to purchase all food and supplies from the merchants. Usually a connection was made between farmers' being exploited and their being locked in to cotton production.

Modern economic historians have developed and expanded this argument.[293] For example, Roger Ransom and Richard Sutch argue that monopolistic country store owners influenced farmers' crop choice decisions in a manner adverse to the farmers' interests:

[T]he local merchant by exercising this monopoly power was able to

291. *ROIC*, 10: 920, testimony of the Honorable Robert Ransom Poole.
292. J. F. Duggar, "Areas of Cultivation in the South," *SBN* 6: 22.
293. Roger L. Ransom and Richard Sutch, "Debt Peonage in the Cotton South after the Civil War," *Journal of Economic History* 32, no. 3 (September 1972): 641–669; William E. Laird and James R. Rinehart, "Deflation, Agriculture, and Southern Development," *Agricultural History* 42 (April 1968): 122; C. Vann Woodward, *Origins of the New South, 1877–1913*, volume 9 of *A History of the South*, ed. Wendell Holmes Stephenson and E. Merton Coulter (Baton Rouge: Louisiana State University Press, 1951), pp. 180–184. For an extensive nineteenth-century statement of the argument that the credit system was ultimately responsible for cotton overproduction, see Matthew Brown Hammond, *The Cotton Industry: An Essay in American Economic History* (Ithaca, N.Y., 1897), pp. 141–226.

prevent the production of agricultural commodities for home consumption and force the production of staple crops. . . .

. . . Apparently, the merchant was able to increase his volume of business and simultaneously strengthen his monopoly position by requiring his customers to concentrate on the production of cotton or some other cash crop and purchase their food from him. By virtue of his local monopoly he could refuse to supply credit on any crop other than cotton. . . .

The merchant's insistence on cotton and his monopoly of credit may have prevented the smaller farmers from diversifying even if it was in their own interest to do so. . . .

Apparently, then, the merchants were able to coerce their customers into excessive production of cotton in order to reap the profits of selling foodstuffs to the farmer.[294]

Two issues need to be separated. The first is whether the furnishing merchant was "a monopolist in a limited local market."[295] Whether or not the merchants actually exploited farmer consumers remains an open question and will not be settled here. The second question is whether the merchants in fact preferred cotton, and if they did; whether they insisted on cotton culture *to the detriment* of the farmers and tenants who did business at their stores. In other words, was it true, as Sutch and Ransom argue, that "the merchant's insistence on cotton and his monopoly of credit may have prevented the smaller farmers from diversifying even if it was in their own interest to do so"?

The difference between these two questions needs to be made clear, especially since it seems to have eluded almost every writer on the subject. Suppose, for purposes of argument, that the merchant actually did possess a credit monopoly in relation to the farmers in his area. This monopoly could have been due to spatial factors, barriers to entry, or the absence of alternative credit institutions.[296] Suppose further that because of relative prices or physical (soil and climatic) conditions, *corn* was the most profitable crop that could be grown by the farmers in that area. Would the merchant insist on cotton? Clearly not, if he truly possessed a credit monopoly. Corn was not the only commodity required by a farming family as working capital—they also needed clothing, seed, fertilizers, implements, notions; in short, all those necessities which could not be produced on the farm. *If* the merchant possessed a true credit monopoly, why would he not be able to realize his full monopoly profits

294. Ransom and Sutch, "Debt Peonage. . . ," pp. 643, 655, 656, 665.
295. Ibid., p. 655.
296. A careful and thorough discussion of possible sources of monopoly power in the hands of the rural furnishing merchants can be found in Ransom and Sutch, ibid., pp. 651–655.

from sales of those commodities which the farmer *still* was forced to buy from the merchant, excluding corn? Could the merchant not charge an exorbitant (monopoly) price for salt, or clothing, or harnesses? If the merchant possessed a monopoly claim to a portion of the farmer's income, due to the farmer's dependence on the merchant for credit and necessities not produced on the farm, the limit to the merchant's return would have been how much the tenant or farmer could bear to pay without moving away or revolting, *not* the amount of food purchased at the store. If corn were more profitable than cotton, monopolistic merchants would have insisted that their debtors grow corn, in order to maximize profits. Obviously, the same argument applies to whatever the most profitable crop mix actually was.

The idea that merchants insisted on cotton in order to force farmers to purchase food at the local stores has been questioned before, by Thomas D. Clark, a modern historian of the Southern country store:

The argument, which has been advanced on numerous occasions, that one main reason for cotton's becoming a staple crop in the post-war South was its inedibility, would seem to be wholly fallacious. Certainly no merchant ever hinted at such a thing in an interview with the author, and no such implication appears in the mercantile records examined. Instead, *many merchants have been known to advise customers to plant more food and feed crops in order to leave more of their cotton money clear.* . . . To argue that the inedibility of cotton was an important factor in production is ridiculous in the light of the fact that clothing was practically as much a matter of primary concern as food. In most communities of the post-war South spinning wheels and looms were not wholly unknown, and it was just as possible to lose money on cotton used for home consumption in the manufacture of clothing as it was on edible products. The whole point in the furnishing trade was profit, and an intensive examination of invoice and account books indicates that perhaps a greater profit was to be made in the sale of clothing and notions than in provisions. [Emphasis added].[297]

Clark continued that low risk and high liquidity *were* incentives favoring cotton culture,[298] but these would not necessarily imply a conflict of interest between merchant and farmer. A merchant who perceived that the greatest potential agricultural profits lay in raising cotton would be inclined to recommend or insist that his debtors cultivate the staple, *regardless* of any monopoly advantage he might have. Concentration on the most profitable crop would benefit both merchant and tenant.

Analogously, the preference of *landlords* for cotton or for alternative

297. Thomas D. Clark, "The Furnishing and Supply System in Southern Agriculture since 1865," *Journal of Southern History* 12, no. 1 (February 1946): 37.
298. Ibid., p. 37.

crops would seem to depend primarily on the relative profitability or productivity of the various crops, whatever the landlord's market position vis-à-vis the farmers or tenants.

Only the questions of the relative profitability of cotton as against alternative crops, and of the farmers' price-responsiveness, can be settled using the techniques of the subsequent chapters. The quantitative investigation required to determine the market position of the furnishing merchants awaits future investigators. Farmers' adaptability has already been discussed. As in all the previous cases, it is possible to uncover conflicting evidence on (1) whether or not country merchants and Southern landlords actually did insist on cotton and prohibit diversification, and (2) whether the merchants were monopolists or whether they charged competitive market prices. Because the monopoly position of the merchants will not be determined in this study, only evidence pertaining to (1) will be presented.

One of the most persistent proponents of the view that merchants insisted on cotton culture was the economist Matthew B. Hammond. He consistently argued that merchants distorted the crop-choice decision to the detriment of the farmers.

A still greater hindrance to the improvement of the farming system of the cotton belt was the credit system which had arisen, and which gave to merchants the power of deciding what crop should be planted, regardless of their effects upon the land, or their value to the producer.[299]

Elsewhere, Hammond said that

unfortunately, there were few of the cotton growers who were in a position to change from cotton to other crops. . . .
. . . The only security which the tenant farmer could give to the country merchant who advanced him his food, clothing, and other necessities, was a mortgage on his crops and as cotton, because of its ready sale was much to be preferred to other crops, the merchant was obliged to demand it as security for his advances. This preference shown to cotton by the advancing merchant led to its over-production and consequent fall in price. . . . Escape from this vicious circle proved impossible for most of the negro croppers and some of the white ones, and "the cropping system" and the system of "crop-liens" thus worked conjointly in causing over-production of cotton and agricultural depression in the South.[300]

299.   Matthew Brown Hammond, *The Cotton Industry: An Essay in American Economic History,* pp. 139–140.
300.   Hammond, "Cotton Production in the South," *SBN,* 6: 92–93.

In the Industrial Commission's summary of testimony concerning crop liens, the same theory was advanced:

It is a general custom of cotton planters and their tenants to use their credit with the neighboring merchants to obtain their plantation and family supplies in advance of the maturing of the crop, often even before the seed is planted. The farmer estimates about how much credit he wants, and the merchant tells him to produce so many acres of cotton, allowing a good margin against a possible crop failure. . . . It is a direct cause of the enormous production of cotton, with a constant tendency toward overproduction, and of the low price of cotton. . . . The store system of the South amounts to a sort of peonage with the cotton planter. The rate of interest on the liens of cotton crops averages at least 40 per cent a year, and the planters are at least a year behind.[301]

The Industrial Commission's summary also blamed an overextension of credit encouraged by the crop lien as a source of distress, but observed at the same time that the merchants did not prosper under the system, because of the high risks involved: "Merchants are not prosperous when the farmers are not, because they lose so much on their advances."[302]

The Congressional *Report on Condition of Cotton Growers* reported the most extreme statement of the inedibility argument. Major W. H. Morgan, a planter of LeFlore County, Mississippi, informed the investigators:

In short, I would say that it only pays to raise cotton in order to have a market at home for what you raise other than cotton. Your tenants or farm laborers are your patrons, and just so far as you can make them so, you are successful.[303]

Morgan attributed his success as a planter to the fact that he raised his corn and feed "at home."[304]

None of these statements is surprising, in light of the general acceptance of the merchants' preference for cotton by almost all modern historians. What may be surprising is that tenant diversifiers found *support* among the economically powerful classes. Some landlords not only permitted, but even encouraged, self-sufficiency on their plantations. There is strong evidence that the "garden patch" was an integral part of the small postwar farm.

301. *ROIC*, 10: cvi.
302. Ibid., pp. cvi-cvii.
303. *RCCG*, 1: 347.
304. Ibid.

In all cases the planter furnished a dwelling-house free, wood and water (paid for digging wells), and pasture for the pigs and cows of the tenant. In all cases the renter had a plot of ground from one to three acres, rent free, for a vegetable garden or "truck patch." Here could be raised watermelons, sugar-cane, potatoes, sorghum, cabbage, and other vegetables. Besides his pigs and cows, every tenant could keep chickens, turkeys, and guineas, and especially dogs, and could hunt in all the woods around and fish in all the waters.[305]

Naturally, landlords' encouragement of the garden patch would tend to weaken any "lock-in" desired by merchants. Tenant farmers may have been economically helpless, but landholding planters were surely not. The *Southern Cultivator* also reported some instances of planters permitting tenants to garden. In an article praising the agricultural practices on the South Carolina plantation of Captain W. Miles Hazzard, the *Cultivator* presented a long list of recommendations for dealing with free labor. Among the suggestions were:

10. To every household a garden spot is allotted; and to each laborer a portion of rice land—to full hands one acre, and to others in proportion. . . .

12. They [the laborers] are allowed to keep a reasonable number of hogs, and to raise poultry *ad libitum*.[306]

Captain Hazzard's plantation also included a store "where abundant and diversified supplies are kept," and the *Cultivator* reported that supplies were "sold to the laborers at the lowest cash prices, taking their due bills in payment."[307] Of course, this situation may have prevailed only until the planter/merchant learned the profits to be made in exploiting his laborers. But an article reprinted in the *Cultivator* from *Southern Plantation* in 1878 reported similarly a planter who "allows them [his employees] a certain amount of land to cultivate for themselves and in their own way."[308] Perhaps the most remarkable instance of the active promotion of self-sufficiency among tenants by a large Southern landowner is to be found in the Appendix of Timothy T. Fortune's polemical *Black and White*. Fortune appended the testimony of John Caldwell Calhoun before the Blair Senate Committee on Education and Labor

305. Walter Fleming, "The Economic Conditions During the Reconstruction," *SBN* 6: 7. As the title of the essay indicates, Fleming's description is applicable to the Reconstruction period.
306. Agricola [pseud.], "The Labor Question," *Southern Cultivator* 27 (July 1869): 207.
307. Ibid.
308. "The Labor System of the South," ibid. 36 (November 1878): 427.

taken in New York in September of 1883, "because of the uniform fairness with which he treated the race and labor problem in the section of [the] country where he is an extensive landowner and employer of labor."[309] John Caldwell Calhoun may have been a progressive planter, but he was surely no upstart, being the grandson of John C. Calhoun of South Carolina[310] and a man who, in his own words, had "been identified with the agricultural interest of the South from my earliest recollections, and . . . a practical cotton planter myself since the war, giving my own personal attention to my interests since 1869."[311]

Mr. Calhoun furnished his field hands

free of cost, a house, fuel, and a garden spot varying from half to one acre; also the use of wagon and team with which to haul their fuel and supplies, and pasturage, where they have cattle and hogs, which they are encouraged to raise.[312]

Calhoun continued:

We encourage him in every way in our power to be economical, industrious, and prudent, to surround his home with comforts, to plant an orchard and garden, and to raise his own meat, and to keep his own cows, for which he has free pasturage. Our object is to attach him as much as possible to his home. Under whatever system we work, we require the laborer to plant a part of his land in food crops and the balance in cotton with which to pay his rent and give him ready money. We consider this system as best calculated to advance him. . . .

. . . We have our own gardens, and generally raise our own supplies, but every planter interests himself to find a market for all the products of his laborers. For instance, we encourage them to raise poultry to a great extent. If they have a surplus of potatoes, or eggs, or chickens, we will buy it and create a market for it, and ship the articles off in order that if they have any surplus they may realize on it. On the Mississippi River we have nearly all the markets. . . . We make the best market we can for the products of our small farmers.[313]

Calhoun also stated that in the interior of his own state of Arkansas, the small farmers were more diversified, and that his own plantation practiced diversification "in case of a disaster to our cotton crops."[314]

309. Fortune, *Black and White*. . . , p. 243. Fortune's reference for this testimony is to the Blair Senate Committee on Education and Labor, *The Relations Between Capital and Labor* (vol. 2), pp. 157 ff.
310. Fortune, *Black and White*. . . , pp. 243–244.
311. Ibid., p. 244.
312. Ibid., p. 246.
313. Ibid., pp. 248, 253.
314. Ibid., pp. 250, 252.

These examples show that at least some landlords encouraged their tenants' self-sufficiency early in the postwar period. It does seem that it would have been rational for landlords operating farms on shares to maximize output. All this indicates (if such an indication were still needed) the danger of generalizing from anecdotal evidence. It is not the contention here that *some* merchants did not prefer cotton; only (a) that elements of one center of economic power, the planters, were not entirely opposed to diversification, and (b) that even if the merchants were monopolists exploiting the farmers who borrowed from them, it does not necessarily follow that farmers had to be "locked in" to cotton culture.

Again, it should be emphasized that the monopoly power of the merchants cannot be determined on the basis of either the literary evidence or the econometric estimates of the later chapters. The abundance of conflicting testimony precludes any definitive assessment of the "merchant monopoly hypothesis" on the basis of anecdotes or single instances alone. Furthermore, it will be shown in the next chapters that the future presumption must be in favor of the competition hypothesis with respect to the labor market, despite the array of individual incidents of exploitation which can be compiled. This finding suggests caution in accepting any generalization regarding market imperfections in the postbellum South. In any case, the question of merchants' monopoly power must be kept distinct from the preference of merchants or farmers for cotton or other crops.

Summary

The result of this none-too-systematic survey of the nineteenth-century sources is in the form of an "impossibility theorem." Traditional historical methods simply cannot resolve the postbellum Southern agricultural system sufficiently to distinguish which of the major alternative hypotheses were true in the aggregate. The extraordinary political and social tensions of that region may have had their origins in exploitation of agricultural labor and of the blacks in particular, but a search of the sources will never be able to determine if the documented instances of exploitation were general or exceptional. Similarly, the poverty of the black population may have been due to educational and entrepreneurial deficiencies rooted in the slavery experience, but conventional methods are incapable of even determining whether the blacks as a group were less productive than whites as a group. Cotton overproduction and farmers' traditionalism may have caused stagnation in the economy and contributed to the agrarian unrest of the 1880s and 1890s, but equally possible (on the basis of the statements of contemporary observers) is that the South's suitability for cotton culture was the main pillar of whatever prosperity its people were able to enjoy. Clearly, if further progress is to be made toward understanding these historical problems, more powerful techniques must be developed and applied. That endeavor constitutes the remainder of this book.

3
Some Theoretical Issues

The preceding chapter has established the impossibility of settling some of the outstanding questions of postbellum Southern economic history by reference solely to the writings of contemporary observers. Subsequent chapters will develop more powerful quantitative tests of the alternative hypotheses on the labor market, the overall productivity of whites and blacks, and the relative profitability of the alternative crops. The rationale of the tests will be outlined below. In addition, it is necessary to dispose of some theoretical difficulties involved in designing these tests. That is the purpose of this chapter.

Chapters 4 and 5 consist of estimates of agricultural production functions for each Southern state in each census year from 1880 to 1910. The specification of these production functions includes parameters which, depending on their values, express one or the other of the competing hypotheses. Estimation of the values of these parameters, combined with appropriate statistical tests of significance, will then determine which hypothesis is consistent with the quantitative historical data.

For example, given the production function estimates, it is possible to calculate the share of output which would have been received by labor had it been paid according to its marginal productivity. This "competitive" labor share, if compared with the share of output actually received in payment for labor services alone (which can be determined independently of the production function estimates), will support either the competition hypothesis or the exploitation hypothesis. If the marginal productivity labor share implied by the production function estimates is greater than what sharecroppers actually did receive in payment for their labor, the exploitation hypothesis is supported over the competition hypothesis. Conversely, if the competitive labor share implied by the estimated parameters of the production function is roughly equal to what agricultural workers actually did receive, it may be concluded that the data are at least consistent with labor market competition in the aggregate. It will be seen that the nature of the tests limits their power to absolutely reject or accept either hypothesis, and this limitation will be examined subsequently.

Similarly, the production function specification will explicitly parameterize potential productivity differences between the races, and the estimates of the productivity parameters will be used to test the hypotheses of systematic black/white productivity differentials. Finally, the overall productivity in value terms of cotton as compared to the alternative crops will be parameterized, to determine whether cotton "overproduction" was manifested in an output loss associated with concentration in cotton.

Chapter 7 uses time series price and acreage data to estimate farmers' price-responsiveness and speed of adjustment in their behavior as cotton suppliers, to further test the hypothesis that farmers were inflexibly committed to an unprofitable cotton crop.

The data which form the basis of the production function estimates are the published census county cross sections on agricultural inputs and output from 1880 to 1910. Because of the nature of the data and the special institutional arrangements in Southern agriculture (in particular, the existence of sharecropping), several theoretical difficulties arise in estimating agricultural production functions and interpreting the results:

1. Did the form of tenure make a difference? In other words, did the existence of sharecropping in agriculture distort the pattern of factor allocation or distribution of the output between the factors?

2. Is it possible to circumvent the identification problem associated with estimating production functions from input and output data? Alternatively, what error structure, model of producer behavior, and estimation technique can lead to well-behaved parameter estimates given only input and output data?

3. Is aggregation of the production functions possible? If so, do the aggregate county input and output data correspond to the appropriate aggregate variables in the aggregate production functions?

4. Is it possible to take account of the intrinsic differences in soil fertility? "Land" was not a uniformly homogeneous factor of production, so that serious errors of measurement would result from using acreage alone as the land input in the production function.

Before presenting the results of the estimations, each of these difficulties needs to be dealt with in turn. The models and approaches which will be employed in this chapter were all first introduced by other economists—no claim is being made that the general treatment of the theoretical questions contained here is new. The purpose of this chapter is to bring together results scattered through the literature and to show how they bear on the particular issues of Southern history which are being examined. Of course, the originators of the models should not be held responsible for their application or for any errors in what follows.

The general thrust of the recent theoretical work is that the existence of a sufficient degree of competition obviates difficulties 1 and 3 listed above. That is, competition rules out the possibility that sharecropping distorted allocation of resources and distribution of returns, and it permits aggregation of the production functions across crops and farms to the county level for which cross-sectional data exist. In a fundamental sense, therefore, the competition hypothesis must be taken as the null hypothesis in the subsequent tests, since competition is required to disregard the effects of sharecropping per se and to allow statistical estimation of aggregate production functions.

If the final estimated competitive share (computed from the production function estimates on the basis of marginal product factor pricing) diverges markedly from the actual observed labor share (computed independently from a sample of sharecrop contracts), it follows that the assumption of perfect competition must have been false. In other words, rough equality between the estimated competitive labor share and the actual labor share is a *necessary condition* for the competition hypothesis. On the other hand, if the estimated competitive labor share agrees with the actual observed share, there is no reason to doubt the operation of competition in the labor market, even though such a result cannot ultimately prove the competition hypothesis. A fortuitous combination of imperfections and immobilities could conceivably produce an apparent equality between the estimated marginal product of labor and the wage. But such an outcome can hardly be expected. Also, if the aggregation theorems, neutrality of tenure, and accuracy of the parameter estimates are robust to deviations from perfect competition (so that the production function estimates are close to the true production functions), a necessary condition for the *exploitation* hypothesis is that the calculated marginal productivity labor share be *greater* than the actual observed labor share. In the subsequent discussion, results will be loosely characterized as supporting either the exploitation hypothesis or the competition hypothesis, depending on the outcome of the comparison between the estimated marginal product of labor and the actual wage. The strict interpretation that only a necessary condition for the competition hypothesis is being tested should always be kept in mind, however.

Sharecropping and Tenure Institutions

Any model that purports to represent the behavior of agricultural workers and landlords in the late nineteenth-century South must allow for the coexistence of sharecropping, renting of land for cash, wage labor by agricultural workers, and owner-operated farms which sometimes employed hired laborers. Intuitively, if the production functions were constant returns to scale and if competition prevailed in the factor markets, the equilibrium *in the absence of risk considerations* should have been one in which both workers and landlords were indifferent between the various tenure arrangements. If workers were free to move about and to enter work arrangements voluntarily, and if landlords were free to operate their farms under any form of tenure they chose, no tenure arrangement would have been preferred by either workers or landlords in equilibrium, provided all the different forms of tenure were coexistent. In this case, the mere existence of sharecropping arrangements should not lead to allocational inefficiency, for if it did, it would be possible to increase the incomes of some members of the economy without decreasing the incomes of the others simply by abandoning the sharecropping or one of the other tenure forms. The conclusion that sharecropping coexisting with other tenure arrangements in a competitive setting leads to an efficient equilibrium has been reached by other investigators, using models which are formally very different from one another.[1] Of course, a landless laborer would prefer to *own* his land, in order to be able to draw the actual or imputed rent, but that is different from the issue of whether a landless laborer would rather rent a farm, work on shares, or work for wages.

The contrary "classical" supposition that sharecropping leads to allocational inefficiency has been incorporated into a general equilibrium model by Bardhan and Srinivasan.[2] Their model requires as an equilibrium condition that the marginal product of land in sharecropping be equal to zero,[3] which is implausible for the nineteenth-century South. The tenant farms of that period were small, and it seems unlikely that they were so extensively cultivated that additional acreage would have

1. Steven N. S. Cheung, *The Theory of Share Tenancy* (Chicago: University of Chicago Press, 1969); Joseph D. Reid., Jr., "Sharecropping and Agricultural Uncertainty," Department of Economics Discussion Paper No. 257 (Philadelphia: University of Pennsylvania, April 1973).
2. P. K. Bardhan and T. N. Srinivasan, "Cropsharing Tenancy in Agriculture: A Theoretical and Empirical Analysis," *American Economic Review* 61, no. 1 (March 1971): 48–64.
3. Ibid., p. 49.

contributed *nothing* to output. It is also easy to show that if the production functions are constant returns, a Bardhan and Srinivasan-type model has no interior solution and is therefore not consistent with the coexistence of wage labor, cash renting, and sharecropping.[4] Even with decreasing returns, the Bardhan and Srinivasan model cannot accommodate simultaneous cash rentals and sharecropping.[5] These properties make the Bardhan and Srinivasan model inappropriate for agriculture in the nineteenth-century South.

The model used here is similar to the one first proposed by Cheung,[6] but the development will be carried out along lines suggested by Temin.[7] The production functions will include three factors—land, labor, and capital—instead of only land and labor, but it will be seen that this modification is a minor one. The problem of nonhomogeneous soil inputs will be deferred, since the purpose of the present demonstration is to show that different tenure arrangements by themselves have no effect on resource allocation or distribution.

Assume a constant returns agricultural production function which is the same for each of the forms of tenure. Because of constant returns, the first-order conditions which will be derived from profit-maximizing behavior on the part of the producers are only sufficient to determine optimum factor ratios, not the scale of operations. It would be possible to express the first-order conditions in terms of factor ratios, but as long as it is remembered that the scale of operations is not determinate, either set of conditions is suitable for describing the results of the maximization. Assume further that the production functions are well behaved in the sense that the first-order conditions for an extremum lead to a profit maximum rather than to a minimum.[8] Also, suppose at first that

4. This result is due to Peter Temin. It follows from the fact that in a Bardhan and Srinivasan model with the three forms of tenure, both partial derivatives of the production function evaluated at the equilibrium quantities of land and labor used in sharecropping are greater than the corresponding partial derivatives of the production function evaluated at the quantities of land and labor employed in cash renting. Either the production functions are different under the different forms of tenure (and there is no reason to expect this to be so) or workers will not divide their time between sharecropping and working land rented for cash. Again, this result requires constant returns production functions.

5. Bardhan and Srinivasan, "Cropsharing Tenancy. . . ," footnote 8, pp. 51–52.

6. Cheung, *The Theory of Share Tenancy,* pp. 16–29.

7. Temin's suggestions were made in conversations and unpublished work during 1971–1972.

8. A full discussion of sufficient conditions for constrained maximization in models of the type used here (with more than one constraint) may be found in Kevin Lancaster, *Mathematical Economics* pp. 52–54. The production functions specified and estimated in subsequent chapters are "well-behaved" in the sense in which this term is used in the text, bearing in mind the proviso that given constant returns, only the optimum factor ratios are determined.

the landlord provides all the capital equipment in sharecropping, with the sharecroppers providing only their labor.

Write the production function for a given farm (without any subscript denoting the farm) as

$$q_i = F^i(l_i, h_i, k_i) \qquad i = s, p, w \qquad (3.1)$$

where

q = output

l = labor input

h = land input

k = capital input

and the indexes s, p, and w designate the outputs and inputs in share-cropping, cash renting, and owner operation with the use of hired labor, respectively. Let l_o = the labor contribution of the owner-operator himself.

For a landlord operating all three types of farm simultaneously, profit can be written

$$\begin{aligned} \pi = & \, rF^s(l_s, h_s, k_s) + ph_p + F^w(l_w, h_w, k_w) \\ & - w(l_w - l_o) - v(k_s + k_w) \end{aligned} \qquad (3.2)$$

where

r = share received by landlord under sharecropping

p = the rental rate for land

w = the wage rate for hired labor

v = the price of capital

The landlord's leisure will be ignored, which amounts to fixing l_o and excluding it from the landlord's set of decision variables. Inclusion of leisure would not alter the model, except that the landlord would maximize utility instead of profits and l_o would be a decision variable. The results of the analysis would be substantially unchanged. Also, the landlord whose profit function is given in (3.2) above is one who operates farms under all three forms of tenure. It will be seen momentarily that the argument is unchanged even if he is operating under only one or two of the alternative tenure forms.

This landlord maximizes profits. But if competition prevails in the labor market, he will face the constraint that no laborer will work under any form of tenure which earns less income for the laborer than an alternative form. These constraints can be expressed as

$$(1 - r) \, F^s(l_s, h_s, k_s) = wl_s \qquad (3.3)$$

$$(1 - r) F^s(l_s, h_s, k_s) = F(l_s, h_x, k_x) - ph_x - vk_x \qquad (3.4)$$

where h_x and k_x represent the optimal amounts of land and capital which a laborer would rent at the market rates should he choose to rent a farm for cash rather than work as a sharecropper. Constraints (3.3) and (3.4) represent the condition that the sharecropper could earn an equivalent income working either as a wage hand or as a cash tenant. The requirement that h_x and k_x be optimal amounts of land and capital for the renter imply

$$F_2(l_s, h_x, k_x) = p \qquad (3.5)$$

and

$$F_3(l_s, h_x, k_x) = v \qquad (3.6)$$

Constraints (3.3) and (3.4), and conditions (3.5) and (3.6), embody the assumption of competition in the factor markets. The competition takes the form of workers enjoying the mobility to seek out employment at the market wage rate w or to rent land as an alternative to sharecropping, and of renters being able to hire as much land and capital as they desire at going rental rates.

The constraint on the amount of land owned by the landlord can be expressed as

$$h_s + h_p + h_w = h \qquad (3.7)$$

Of course, the landlord could rent additional land and hire labor to work it, but with perfect competition and constant returns, any additional output generated by this procedure would be divided by the owners of these factors; so no increase in profits could be obtained. Hence, this possibility will be ignored.

Thus, the landlord maximizes profits (3.2) subject to (3.3), (3.4), and (3.7). This leads to the Lagrangean expression

$$\mathcal{L} = rF^s + ph_p + F^w - w(l_w - l_o) - v(k_s + k_w)$$
$$- \lambda[h_s + h_p + h_w - h]$$
$$- \mu_1[(1 - r)F^s - wl_s] \qquad (3.8)$$
$$- \mu_2[(1 - r)F^s - F(l_s, h_x, k_x) + ph_x + vk_x]$$

The first-order conditions for an interior maximum (with all three tenure forms present) and with all land utilized will be

$$\frac{\partial \mathcal{L}}{\partial l_s} = rF_1^s - \mu_1(1 - r)F_1^s + \mu_1 w - \mu_2(1 - r)F_1^s$$
$$+ \mu_2 F_1(l_s, h_x, k_x) = 0 \qquad (3.9)$$

$$\frac{\partial \mathscr{L}}{\partial l_w} = F_1^w - w = 0 \tag{3.10}$$

$$\frac{\partial \mathscr{L}}{\partial h_s} = rF_2^s - \lambda - \mu_1(1 - r)F_2^s - \mu_2(1 - r)F_2^s = 0 \tag{3.11}$$

$$\frac{\partial \mathscr{L}}{\partial h_p} = p - \lambda = 0 \tag{3.12}$$

$$\frac{\partial \mathscr{L}}{\partial h_w} = F_2^w - \lambda = 0 \tag{3.13}$$

$$\frac{\partial \mathscr{L}}{\partial k_s} = rF_3^s - v - \mu_1(1 - r)F_3^s - \mu_2(1 - r)F_3^s = 0 \tag{3.14}$$

$$\frac{\partial \mathscr{L}}{\partial k_w} = F_3^w - v = 0 \tag{3.15}$$

The landlord's decision variables are the amounts of land allotted to each of the tenure forms, the labor desired for sharecropping and as wage help, and the capital employed on the sharecropped and owner-operated farms. In addition to these first-order conditions, landlord equilibrium also requires that no money be lost to the landlord as a result of his use of the sharecropping form. In Cheung, the assumption is made that the sharecrop share r is itself another decision variable.[9] Here it will simply be assumed that the equilibrium r be such as to maximize profits, since otherwise sharecropping would be abandoned. (Landlords are free to choose the tenure forms they operate with.) In either case, the additional equation

$$\frac{\partial \mathscr{L}}{\partial r} = F^s + \mu_1 F^s + \mu_2 F^s = 0 \tag{3.16}$$

must be added to the list of first-order conditions. These first-order conditions together imply ordinary marginal product factor pricing:

$\mu_1 + \mu_2 = -1$	from (3.16)	(3.17)
$F_1^w = w$	from (3.10)	(3.18)
$F_2^s = p$	from (3.11), (3.12), and (3.17)	(3.19)
$F_2^w = p$	from (3.12) and (3.13)	(3.20)
$F_3^s = v$	from (3.14) and (3.17)	(3.21)
$F_3^w = v$	from (3.15)	(3.22)

In addition,

9. Cheung, *The Theory of Share Tenancy*, pp. 19–21.

$F_1^s = -\mu_1 F_1^w - \mu_2 F_1(l_s, h_x, k_x)$ from (3.9), (3.17), and (3.18)   (3.23)

In order to complete the demonstration of ordinary marginal product factor pricing under all tenures, it remains to be shown that

$$F_1^w = F_1(l_s, h_x, k_x) \tag{3.24}$$

From (3.5) and (3.20) and from (3.6) and (3.22), respectively,

$$F_2^x = p = F_2^w \tag{3.25}$$
$$F_3^x = v = F_3^w \tag{3.26}$$

if $F(l_s, h_x, k_x)$ is written as F^x.

But since F is constant returns, (3.25) and (3.26) together imply the equality of the factor ratios

$$\frac{h_x}{l_s} = \frac{h_w}{l_w} \tag{3.27}$$

$$\frac{k_x}{l_s} = \frac{k_w}{l_w} \tag{3.28}$$

Therefore (3.24) also follows from the properties of constant returns production functions.[10] Combining (3.17), (3.18), (3.23), and (3.24)

10. For any constant returns production function F with three factors, $q = F(l, h, k)$ can be written

$$\frac{q}{l} = F\left(1, \frac{h}{l}, \frac{k}{l}\right), \text{ or}$$

$$q = lF\left(1, \frac{h}{l}, \frac{k}{l}\right)$$

Therefore

$$\frac{\partial q}{\partial h} = lF_2\left(1, \frac{h}{l}, \frac{k}{l}\right) \cdot \frac{1}{l} = F_2\left(1, \frac{h}{l}, \frac{k}{l}\right), \text{ and}$$

$$\frac{\partial q}{\partial k} = F_3\left(1, \frac{h}{l}, \frac{k}{l}\right)$$

Thus, since $\partial q/\partial h$ and $\partial q/\partial k$ are functions of h/l and k/l only,

$F_2^x = p = F_2^w$ and

$F_3^x = v = F_3^w$

together imply

$\dfrac{h_x}{l_s} = \dfrac{h_w}{l_w}$ and $\dfrac{k_x}{l_s} = \dfrac{k_w}{l_w}$

But

$$\frac{\partial q}{\partial l} = F\left(1, \frac{h}{l}, \frac{k}{l}\right) + lF_2\left(1, \frac{h}{l}, \frac{k}{l}\right)\left(-\frac{h}{l^2}\right) + lF_3\left(1, \frac{h}{l}, \frac{k}{l}\right)\left(-\frac{k}{l^2}\right)$$

$$= F\left(1, \frac{h}{l}, \frac{k}{l}\right) - \left(\frac{h}{l}\right)F_2\left(1, \frac{h}{l}, \frac{k}{l}\right) - \left(\frac{k}{l}\right)F_3\left(1, \frac{h}{l}, \frac{k}{l}\right)$$

which is also a function of only the two factor ratios h/l and k/l. Hence $F_1^w = F_1^x$.

shows that $F_1^s = w$ and thus completes the demonstration that the marginal product of labor is equal to the wage under each tenure arrangement.

Modification of the model to allow the capital costs in sharecropping to be divided between landlord and tenant does not change the conclusion of marginal product factor pricing in all tenures. The profit function and the competitive labor market constraints become in this case

$$\pi = rF^s + ph_p + F^w - w(l_w - l_o) - vk_w - rvk_s \tag{3.29}$$

$$(1 - r)F^s - (1 - r)vk_s = wl_s \tag{3.30}$$

$$(1 - r)F^s - (1 - r)vk_s = F^x - ph_x - vk_x \tag{3.31}$$

The only first-order conditions which are altered are the partial derivatives with respect to k_s and with respect to r. These become

$$\frac{\partial \mathcal{L}}{\partial k_s} = rF_3^s - rv - \mu_1(1 - r)F_3^s + \mu_1(1 - r)v - \mu_2(1 - r)F_3^s$$

$$+ \mu_2(1 - r)v = 0 \tag{3.32}$$

$$\frac{\partial \mathcal{L}}{\partial r} = F^s - vk_s + \mu_1 F^s - \mu_1 vk_s + \mu_2 F^s - \mu_2 vk_s = 0 \tag{3.33}$$

or

$$(F_s - vk_s)(1 + \mu_1 + \mu_2) = 0 \qquad \text{from (3.33)} \tag{3.34}$$

Now vk_s is the total capital cost in sharecropping, so as long as this cost does not constitute the entire output, (3.17) follows from (3.34). From (3.32),

$$F_3^s[r + (1 - r)(-\mu_1 - \mu_2)] + v[-r + (1 - r)(\mu_1 + \mu_2)] = 0 \tag{3.35}$$

So combining (3.17) and (3.35) yields (3.21) again, provided (3.30) and (3.31) hold so that μ_1 and μ_2 are not zero. Hence, none of the marginal product factor pricing conditions is changed when the capital costs are shared in sharecropping in the same proportion as the output.

It is easy to see that the essential steps in the reasoning are unchanged if only one or two of the forms of tenure employed by the landlord. If only cash renting and wage labor are involved, there is no doubt that competition will result in marginal product factor pricing. If only sharecropping and one of the other tenure forms coexist, then profit maximization under the appropriate constraint (either (3.3) or (3.4)) will again yield marginal product factor pricing in all tenure forms. Also, if the landlord only operates sharecrop farms but his sharecroppers can quit and earn wage w or rent land and capital at market rates, the same results apply. The essential point is the same—if workers are free to move from farm to farm, and if landlords are free to choose the form of tenure under which they operate their farms, then constant returns to scale is sufficient to guarantee that sharecropping has no impact on distribution or allocation.

Of course, this somewhat bland result does nothing to explain the locational pattern of sharecropping throughout the South. Considerations of risk and incentives are probably crucial in determining the incidence of cropsharing.[11] The model developed here and the estimates based on it do not deal with these risk and incentive elements at all. The arrangements made for risk sharing are not directly relevant to the issue of static imperfection in the labor market. A risk premium in addition to ground rent accruing to landlords, for example, cannot be considered to be exploitation. Sharecropping may have amounted to a crude form of insurance, and insurance premiums are not monopoly profits. In actuality, one might expect the sharecrop share received by workers to be somewhat *higher* than their purely competitive share exclusive of risk, for in a sharecropping arrangement the tenant and landlord share the risk, while if the landlord simply hires for wages, the workers bear none of the risk. Similarly, if the function of sharecropping is to *reduce* risk (rather than to disperse it) by facilitating revision of expectations, it would have the effect of increasing the incomes of both landowners and laborers, rather than to change the distribution of income in agriculture.

For the same reason, it is not necessary to consider the incentive effects of the different tenure institutions. If sharecropping was practiced in order to motivate the labor force or to encourage cooperation between landowners and laborers, its effects on the distribution of income presumably would have been neutral. The incentive question should be pursued in further research, but it need not be definitively answered in the present limited context of deciding whether exploitation or competition prevailed in the labor market.

11. This seems to be the consensus among all the recent investigators. See Cheung, *The Theory of Share Tenancy;* Bardhan and Srinivasan, "Cropsharing Tenancy in Agriculture. . . "; Reid, "Sharecropping and Agricultural Uncertainty"; and Stiglitz, "Incentives and Risk-Sharing in Sharecropping." The abbreviated discussion that follows cannot begin to do justice to the ideas developed by these economists; its only purpose is to suggest that the difficult issues involved in explaining the incidence of sharecropping do not have to be settled for purposes of the present investigation.

It should be added that not all the writers on this subject agree on precisely the role played by risk in determining the incidence of sharecropping. For example, Reid contrasts his own view with that of Cheung when he argues that "sharecropping's potential for risk *reduction*—derived from the encouragement a share contract gives cooperating factor owners to similarly respond to revisions in expectations over the crop season—rather than its unnecessary capability for risk dispersion emerges as a major impetus to sharecropping." (Reid, p. 39.)

Least Squares and Identification

The production functions ultimately estimated are all of a generalized Cobb-Douglas form. The difficulties in estimating Cobb-Douglas production functions from cross-section input and output data are well known.[12] If the Cobb-Douglas production function to be estimated is written (with the subscript i denoting the unit of observation) as

$$Q_i = CL_i^\alpha \, T_i^\beta \, K_i^\gamma \, e^{u_i} \tag{3.36}$$

then ordinary least squares applied to cross-section data on inputs and output will yield consistent and unbiased estimates of the parameters only if the disturbance u_i is not correlated with either the inputs or with the "human errors" leading to random deviations from optimum input choices. This is consistent with profit maximization if the producers do not know the value of the disturbance before making their input decisions and consequently behave as if the value of the error term were equal to one. Such a model "is applicable in situations where there is a lag between the application of inputs and the realization of output."[13] Certainly most of the inputs to the Southern crops of this period (particularly land and capital inputs) had to be chosen early in the growing season, before the consequences of weather, pest infestations, and many other "acts of nature" could be known.

Alternatively, suppose the production process were entirely nonstochastic (so that $u_i = 0$). Proper maximizing behavior by the producers with competition in the factor and output markets would result in every producer's choosing identical factor ratios, and no surface could be fitted by least squares to the input and output data. But if management failures and other random disturbances led to deviations of actual input choices from the optimum input combinations, it would be entirely appropriate to estimate the parameters of (3.36) by ordinary least squares. If these "human errors" are large (leading to large variation in the actual input combinations of the different producers) or at least if the variation in the inputs from this source is large compared to the variation arising from producers' response to the stochastic component of the production process itself, then least squares applied to the input and output data will yield acceptable estimates of the production function parameters. This

12. See, for example, Marc Nerlove, *Estimation and Identification of Cobb-Douglas Production Functions*.
13. Yair Mundlak and Irving Hoch, "Consequences of Alternative Specifications in Estimation of Cobb-Douglas Production Functions," *Econometrica* 33, no. 4 (October 1965): 817. In the same article, these authors point out that if the production function disturbance is "partially transmitted" to the inputs (as is most likely in agriculture), both least squares and an alternative estimator proposed by them will be biased.

situation is likely to be descriptive of postbellum Southern agriculture, which was characterized by a large number of small farms operated with uneven levels of managerial skill.

Estimation techniques other than ordinary least squares are beset with practical or theoretical difficulties. The detailed factor price data required to estimate the parameters of the production function by the factor shares method[14] do not exist. (Systematic records of input prices at the county level would be needed.) A production model similar to (3.26) described by A. Zellner, J. Kmenta, and J. Drèze[15] has the property that if decision-makers maximize *expected* profits, then ordinary least squares applied to the input and output data produces consistent and unbiased estimates of the parameters, provided the production function exhibits decreasing returns to scale. The presumption that agricultural producers maximize expected profits would be plausible, but unfortunately the proscription of constant returns is contrary to what is required to be able to ignore tenure arrangements and to carry out aggregation to the county level. On balance, it would seem that any bias in the least-squares estimates resulting from correlation between u_i and the inputs is likely to be small, and that ordinary least squares is the most practicable statistical technique for utilizing the available cross-sectional data in the published censuses to obtain meaningful estimates of the parameters of the production functions.

Aggregation

The producing units of the Southern agricultural sector were individual farms, yet the published censuses over the postbellum period contain only data on inputs and outputs aggregated to the county level. Also, during this period agricultural output consisted of several different crops, each potentially exhibiting a different technology of production. The first aggregation question is whether it is possible to represent the "output" of an individual farm as a single function of the total inputs on that farm, regardless of the mix of different crops produced. The second aggregation question is whether, given the existence of such functions at the farm level, it is possible to aggregate them to a county-level production function which has the same parameters as the single farm function.[16] These two questions will be considered in reverse order.

14. For a description and discussion of this method, see Nerlove, *Estimation and Identification.* . . , pp. 61–85.
15. A. Zellner, J. Kmenta, and J. Drèze, "Specification and Estimation of Cobb-Douglas Production Function Models," *Econometrica* 34, no. 4 (October 1966): 784–795.

First, suppose the farmwide production functions do exist. It is then possible to show that the functions of the type specified in the later chapters all belong to the class of functions for which aggregation to the county level is possible under competitive conditions. In addition, the aggregate inputs are the natural sums of the single farm inputs added over the entire county. The proof below follows the proof first given by Solow.[17] Within any given county, let F be the constant returns production function characteristic of the farms within that county, so that for farm i,

$$Q_i = F(L_i, T_i, K_i) \tag{3.37}$$

with L_i, T_i, and K_i the labor, land, and capital inputs, respectively, and Q_i the output of the farm. Anticipating the specification of the later chapters, let the labor and land inputs be "composite" inputs, with

$$L_i = aW_i + bB_i \tag{3.38}$$

$$T_i = cH_i + dJ_i, \tag{3.39}$$

where

W_i = input of white labor on farm i

B_i = input of black labor on farm i

H_i = cotton land input

J_i = other improved land input

and the constants a, b, c, and d are parameters of the production function representing the productivity levels of the respective inputs. Detailed discussion of this specification of the inputs will be deferred to chapter 4; the only purpose here is to show that the Solow aggregation result holds for a general constant returns production function whose inputs are specified as in (3.38) and (3.39).

Since the production function is assumed to be well behaved, competition and maximizing behavior will lead to marginal productivity factor pricing and an equalization of the factor prices within the county:

$$\frac{\partial Q_i}{\partial W_i} = aF_1(L_i, T_i, K_i) = \frac{\partial Q_j}{\partial W_j} = aF_1(L_j, T_j, K_j) \qquad \text{all } i, j \tag{3.40}$$

16. For a survey of the aggregation problem, see Franklin M. Fisher, "The Existence of Aggregate Production Functions," *Econometrica* 37, no. 4 (October 1969): 553–577.

17. Robert M. Solow, "Capital, Labor, and Income in Manufacturing," in National Bureau of Economic Research Conference on Research in Income and Wealth, *The Behavior of Income Shares*, Studies in Income and Wealth 27, pp. 104–105.

$$\frac{\partial Q_i}{\partial H_i} = cF_2(L_i, T_i, K_i) = \frac{\partial Q_j}{\partial H_j} = cF_2(L_j, T_j, K_j) \qquad \text{all } i, j \qquad (3.41)$$

$$\frac{\partial Q_i}{\partial K_i} = F_3(L_i, T_i, K_i) = \frac{\partial Q_j}{\partial K_j} = F_3(L_j, T_j, K_j) \qquad \text{all } i, j \qquad (3.42)$$

Since F is constant returns, these equations imply the equality of the generalized factor ratios across farms:[18]

$$\frac{aW_i + bB_i}{cH_i + dJ_i} = \frac{aW_j + bB_j}{cH_j + dJ_j}; \qquad \frac{K_i}{cH_i + dJ_i} = \frac{K_j}{cH_j + dJ_j}$$

and

$$\frac{aW_i + bB_i}{K_i} = \frac{aW_j + bB_j}{K_j}; \qquad \text{all } i, j \text{ within a given county.} \qquad (3.43)$$

Let

$$a\sum W_i + b\sum B_i = L$$

$$c\sum H_i + d\sum J_i = T \qquad (3.44)$$

$$\sum K_i = K$$

where the summation runs over all the farms in the county. Further define

$$\lambda_i = \frac{aW_i + bB_i}{L}; \ \mu_i = \frac{cH_i + dJ_i}{T}; \ \eta_i = \frac{K_i}{K} \qquad (3.45)$$

If the "adding up" rule for proportions is applied, then

$$\frac{\sum(aW_i + bB_i)}{\sum(cH_i + dJ_i)} = \frac{aW_i + bB_i}{cH_i + dJ_i} \quad \text{or} \quad \lambda_i = \mu_i \qquad (3.46)$$

Similarly, $\lambda_i = \eta_i$. Now

$$aW_i + bB_i = \lambda_i L, \quad cH_i + dJ_j = \mu_i T \text{ and } K_i = \eta_i K \qquad (3.47)$$

Thus

$$\begin{aligned}
Q = \sum Q_i &= \sum F(\lambda_i L, \mu_i T, \eta_i K) \\
&= \sum F(\lambda_i L, \lambda_i T, \lambda_i K) \\
&= \sum \lambda_i F(L, T, K) \quad \text{(because of constant returns)} \\
&= F(L, T, K) \sum \lambda_i \\
&= F(L, T, K) \quad \text{since} \quad \sum \lambda_i = 1 \qquad (3.48)
\end{aligned}$$

Hence the aggregate production function exists, and the input aggregates are the "natural" sums of the farm inputs.

18. See note 10 of this chapter.

The first question of aggregation, whether it is possible to represent the potential multiple outputs of a single farm's production as a single function of its total inputs, cannot be answered so easily. The root of the difficulty is a deficiency in the data. While most counties of the South grew several crops (and presumably many farms grew multiple crops as well), the census enumerators collected only data on the amount of acreage devoted to each crop and did not record separately the amounts of labor or capital devoted to the cultivation of the various crops. Thus, while the technology of production of each of the different crops may have been different, there is no way to estimate separately different production functions for each crop. The data deficiency is not one which could be rectified by recourse to the census manuscripts, because even at the farm level no reporting was made of the amounts of labor and capital on each farm devoted to the cultivation of the various products. To be able to estimate agricultural production functions then, it is almost a necessity that the functions have the property that some stable function of the separate outputs must be expressible as a function of the *total* of the inputs on each farm. That is, if $q_1, q_2, \ldots, q_n$ are the amounts of the different crops produced, and $x_1, x_2, \ldots, x_m$ are the total of the inputs of labor, land, capital, etc. used on the farm, then in order to be able to estimate production functions from the input and output data provided in the published or manuscript censuses it is necessary to be able to express the relation between the outputs and inputs as

$$g(q_1, q_2, \ldots, q_n) = h(x_1, x_2, \ldots, x_m) \tag{3.49}$$

whatever the mix of outputs might be. This restriction on the form of the production function is known as *separability,* and a production function exhibiting it is said to be a separable production function.[19]

Another piece of terminology must be introduced before proceeding further. A multiple-output production process is defined as being *nonjoint* if the process can be represented by a set of distinct production functions, with no economies or diseconomies of jointness. In the example of outputs q and inputs x above, these distinct production functions might be denoted by $f^{(1)}(x_1^{(1)}, x_2^{(1)}, \ldots, x_m^{(1)}), f^{(2)}(x_1^{(2)}, x_2^{(2)}, \ldots, x_m^{(2)}), \ldots, f^{(n)}(x_1^{(n)}, x_2^{(n)}, \ldots, x_m^{(n)})$. Nonjointness does not require that the outputs be produced by physically distinct processes; it

---

19. This definition of separability is given in Robert E. Hall, "The Specification of Technology with Several Kinds of Output," *Journal of Political Economy* 81, no. 4 (July/August 1973): 880. The concept of separability was originally introduced by Yair Mundlak, "Specification and Estimation of Multiproduct Production Functions," *Journal of Farm Economics* 45, no. 2 (May 1963): 433–443.

is only necessary that the $f^{(i)}$ exist as functions.[20] Nevertheless, if the production processes *are* physically distinct, then the nonjointness property is characteristic of production.

The following useful theorem on multiple-product technologies is due to Hall:

Impossibility Theorem for Separable Nonjoint Technologies:
No multiple-output technology with constant returns to scale can be both separable and non-joint. That is, the individual production functions in such a technology are identical except for a scalar multiple, implying that there is effectively only a single kind of output.[21]

This theorem is related to the aggregation problem under consideration for the following reasons: (1) The absence of a breakdown on the inputs of labor and capital to the various crops necessitates specification of a separable production function if estimation is to be carried out. (2) On technical grounds, however, there is good reason to believe that the production of the different agricultural outputs in the postbellum South was essentially nonjoint. The two most important crops were corn and cotton, and these crops were produced by two essentially distinct biological processes. When both were grown on the same farm, they were most often grown in different fields, so that it is possible at least conceptually to separate the production processes for the two crops into two distinct production functions, each with distinct inputs. But given these two propositions, the Hall impossibility theorem establishes that the distinct production functions characteristic of cotton and corn production must be specified to differ by at most a scalar constant. This restriction, plus the assumption of competition in the product markets, allows aggregation of the different outputs at the farm level.

Suppose for simplicity that the only two agricultural outputs are cotton and corn. Consider only the case of constant returns Cobb-Douglas production functions for the two crops. This will be the type of specification proposed in the later chapters. Also, consider only the case of two factors of production, labor and land. (The proof would be essentially unchanged in the case of more than two inputs and outputs.) Then, according to the Hall theorem, the most general form of the production functions for cotton and corn will be

---

20. For nonjointness, the individual production functions $f^{(i)}$ must have the following two properties: (1) There are no economies of jointness: if the vector of inputs x can produce the vector of outputs q, there exists a factor allocation $x^{(1)} + x^{(2)} + \ldots + x^{(n)} = x$ such that $f^{(i)}(x^{(i)}) \geq q_i$, $i = 1, 2, \ldots, n$. (2) There are no diseconomies of jointness: if $q_i = f^{(i)}(x^{(i)})$, all i, then $x = x^{(1)} + \ldots + x^{(n)}$ can produce q. Hall, "Specification of Technology. . . ," p. 884.
21. Ibid., p. 885.

$$Q_1 = A_1 L_1{}^\alpha T_1{}^{1-\alpha} \tag{3.50}$$

$$Q_2 = A_2 L_2{}^\alpha T_2{}^{1-\alpha} \tag{3.51}$$

with the subscript 1 denoting cotton and 2 denoting corn. The Hall theorem guarantees that if the production process is separable and non-joint, the exponent α will not differ between the two functions.[22]

Now, let p_1 and p_2 be the prices of cotton and corn in the (competitive) output markets, and define $V_i = p_i Q_i$, $i = 1, 2$.
Then

$$V_i = p_i Q_i = L_i{}^\alpha (\mu_i T_i)^{1-\alpha} \tag{3.52}$$

with

$$\mu_i = (p_i A_i)^{\frac{1}{1-\alpha}} \tag{3.53}$$

Competition in the labor market and profit maximization guarantees that

$$w = \alpha L_1{}^{\alpha-1}(\mu_1 T_1)^{1-\alpha} = \alpha L_2{}^{\alpha-1}(\mu_2 T_2)^{1-\alpha} \tag{3.54}$$

Hence $L_1/(\mu_1 T_1) = L_2/(\mu_2 T_2)$, so that the aggregation of V_1 and V_2 follows just as in the previous discussion of aggregation over all the farms in a county, namely,

$$V_1 + V_2 = (L_1 + L_2)^\alpha (\mu_1 T_1 + \mu_2 T_2)^{1-\alpha} \tag{3.55}$$

Thus in the case of production functions for cotton and corn differing only by a scalar constant, with competition in the output markets, it has been shown that the total value of output is the appropriate output variable, and that an aggregate production function with the same input elasticities α and $1 - \alpha$ as the individual crop production functions does exist. This production function has the property that its labor input is simply the total labor input of the farm, while its land input is a linear combination of the land inputs to cotton and corn, with the coefficients of the linear combination equal to the products of the production functions' constant terms and the market prices of the two crops.

This is precisely the type of production function which will be introduced in the subsequent chapters. As mentioned before, the census enumerators did collect data on T_1 and T_2; so equations of the form of (3.55) can be estimated. It has therefore been shown that in the case of separable and nonjoint production functions, aggregation at the farm

22. It might be noted that the technology described by (3.50) and (3.51) actually can be written in the form of a separable production function. For given total labor and land inputs $L = L_1 + L_2$ and $T = T_1 + T_2$, the production possibility frontier for the two outputs can be easily shown to be
$(Q_1/A_1) + (Q_2/A_2) = L^\alpha T^{1-\alpha}$
which is of the form of equation (3.49), the definition of separability.

level can be carried out, and that an aggregate production of the form of (3.55) is the *most general* Cobb-Douglas specification that is possible.

Hall has developed statistical tests for the properties of separability and nonjointness.[23] Unfortunately, his tests require knowledge of the factor prices at the level of observation of the test sample, and this detailed information on factor prices does not exist for the postbellum South. Unless other tests which do not require such information can be developed, the question of whether the proposed specification is entirely adequate in representing the joint production possibilities of the individual farm production functions will remain open. In the special case of separable and nonjoint production functions, it is the most general Cobb-Douglas specification, however.

This means that at one level, the solution to the aggregation problem for a multi-product farm is imperfect. But at another level, the difficulty may not be so serious. Up to this point, it has been assumed that the true "underlying" production functions describe processes in which the ultimate output is the quantity of the crop produced (cotton, corn, or some other agricultural product). But in a situation in which the null hypothesis is one of competition and efficiency, it is possible also simply to specify that the total dollar value of farm productions not fed to livestock is the "output" of agricultural production. This amounts to assuming that farmers combined their inputs in the most efficient way to maximize their production of this "output" given the technical constraints, and that the resulting relationship between various input combinations and output is the "production function." This concept of the production function may not be immediately suggestive of a Cobb-Douglas form, but the main justification for using a Cobb-Douglas form in the first place is that it is an approximation for a wider class of production functions including the CES which have various desirable properties.[24] It may be that there simply is no underlying model of production relating quantity of outputs to the inputs, and that the postulated relation between the value of output and the inputs is the most accurate specification. In conclusion then, under the null hypothesis of competition in the local factor and output markets, aggregation to the county level is theoretically permissible.

23. Hall, "The Specification of Technology," pp. 886–889.
24. J. Kmenta, "On Estimation of the CES Production Function," *International Economic Review* 8, no. 2 (June 1967): 180–189; see also Michael D. McCarthy, "Approximation of the CES Production Function: A Comment," ibid., pp. 190–192; J. Kmenta, "The Approximation of CES Type Functions: A Reply," ibid., p. 193.

Heterogeneity of Soils

This problem was treated by allowing the constant term in the production function to vary from county to county according to the physical and chemical properties of the soil. Southern soils were assayed and classified in the 1880 census.[25] The existence of this 1880 geographic survey is in some sense a fortunate accident, since it provides a ready-made means of identifying intrinsic fertility differences of the various types of Southern soil. Variation of the production function constant term across counties belonging to different soil type categories allows for overall fertility differences associated with physically heterogeneous soils.

With these difficulties out of the way, it is possible to proceed to the estimation of the production functions.

25. U.S. Census Office, *Tenth Census, 1880,* vols. 5–6: *Report on Cotton Production in the United States; also Embracing Agricultural and Physico-geographical Descriptions of the Several Cotton States and of California,* ed. Eugene W. Hilgard.

4
Specification and Estimation of the Agricultural Production Functions

Specification

It is useful to begin by reviewing the information sought by estimation of Southern agricultural production functions:

1. The estimates should allow calculation of the share of output received by workers if they were paid according to their marginal productivity, so that the hypothesis of competition in the labor market can be tested. It has been shown in the previous chapter that for constant returns production functions, competition in the factor markets allows the distributional and allocative impact of sharecropping to be ignored, and the farm production functions to be aggregated to the county level. It is desirable but not necessary that the production function have reasonably simple distributional properties, so that the competitive labor share will not be too difficult to calculate.

2. Potential differences in black and white labor productivity should be allowed. However, the specification should not require that both types of labor be present in order for production to take place. This latter requirement rules out the black and white labor force variables from entering multiplicatively.

3. Similarly, the function should allow for productivity differences associated with the cultivation of different crops. This will allow testing the hypothesis that cotton had lower overall profitability (to the entire agricultural sector) than the alternative crops. Again, there should be no requirement that all crops be produced in order to achieve a positive level of output, since many counties reported no cotton grown at all.

4. Intrinsic soil fertility differences due to physical, chemical, and possibly climatic differences should be allowed for.

5. Finally, the specification of the production function should permit

constant returns to scale. Constant returns is necessary for the theorems on tenure and aggregation to hold true. Estimation of the production functions without imposing the constraint of constant returns will allow a test of the constant returns assumption. As in the test of competition, if the unconstrained estimates do not deviate from constant returns, it may be concluded that constant returns is consistent with the data. The constant returns requirement cannot be proved by this test, however.

6. The error structure should be such as to allow consistent estimation of the parameters by ordinary least squares applied to the county cross-section input and output data.

A production function possessing properties 1–6 is the following:

$$Q = A_1^{S_1} A_2^{S_2} \ldots A_N^{S_N} (aW + bB)^\alpha (cH + dJ)^\beta K^\gamma e^{u_o} \tag{4.1}$$

where

Q = value of all agricultural output net of intermediate products fed to livestock

S_i = a set of dummy variables, one for each of the N soil types in each state, with the property that $S_i = 1$ when the county described by the production function is of soil type i, and $S_i = 0$ otherwise

W = white agricultural labor input

B = black agricultural labor input

H = cotton land input

J = agricultural land input for all usages other than cotton culture

K = agricultural capital input and

u_o = a random disturbance term, normally distributed with mean 0 and variance σ^2.

For a full discussion and detailed definitions of these variables, see appendix A. Also, this aggregate production function is defined for each county, but the county subscripts on the variables are omitted for simplicity in notation. The constant terms will vary between counties belonging to the different soil-type categories, but will be the same for all counties with a given soil type.

In accordance with the discussion of estimation in the previous chapter, either u_o is uncorrelated with the inputs or the "human errors" leading to deviations from optimum factor ratios have large effects compared to producers' responses to u_o. The producing units are the individual farms, but the tentative assumption of perfect competition within counties allows aggregation to the county level. The sample of counties for each estimate consists of the counties making up each of the ten major cotton-producing Southern states in each of the four census years 1880–1910. If Texas is omitted in 1890 and 1900, and Virginia altogether,[1] there are 38 production functions estimated in all. The choice of single states in single census years as the sample boundaries was essentially arbitrary although the correspondence between the political units (states) and county samples is convenient for discussing the results.[2]

In most of the subsequent discussion, the production function (4.1) will be represented in its logarithmic form. Hence

$$\log Q = \sum_{i=1}^{N} B_i\, S_i + \alpha \log(aW + bB) + \beta \log(cH + dJ)$$
$$+ \gamma \log K + u_o \qquad (4.2)$$

with

$$B_i = \log A_i;\ i = 1, 2, \ldots, N$$

will also be referred to as "the production function." The results of estimating the parameters of (4.1) or (4.2) will be designated the Group I results. In addition, for purposes of discussion of the static and distributional properties of the model, the disturbance term will be ignored.[3]

It is easy to verify that production function (4.1) satisfies requirements 1–6. Suppose both whites and blacks are paid the value of the marginal products of their respective labors. Then labor's share of output is given by

$$S = \frac{1}{Q}\left[\frac{\partial Q}{\partial W} \cdot W + \frac{\partial Q}{\partial B} \cdot B\right] = \frac{\partial Q}{\partial W} \cdot \frac{W}{Q} + \frac{\partial Q}{\partial B} \cdot \frac{B}{Q} \qquad (4.3)$$

But

$$\frac{\partial Q}{\partial W} = \alpha a\, \frac{Q}{aW + bB} \qquad (4.4)$$

$$\frac{\partial Q}{\partial B} = \alpha b\, \frac{Q}{aW + bB} \qquad (4.5)$$

1.   Production functions for Texas in 1890 and 1900 were not estimated because the census tabulations of the Texas county cross sections in those two years were extremely difficult to code in a form suitable for machine processing. Virginia was not included in the sample of states because by 1880 hardly any cotton was grown there.
2.   But see appendix E on the essential arbitrariness of this breakdown of the data into manageable samples.
3.   The assumptions made about the disturbance term allow consistent estimation of the production function parameters from the input and output data. If *uncertainty were eliminated* (set $u_o = E(u_o)$), the production function remaining would have the same parameters as (4.1) but it would contain no random disturbance. (Even the constant terms would be the same, since $E(u_o) = 0$.) Thus discussion of the distributional properties of the production function omitting the disturbance term corresponds to exploring the properties of the model in the absence of uncertainty, which is exactly the objective of the present investigation.

Therefore,

$$S = \alpha a \frac{Q}{aW + bB} \cdot \frac{W}{Q} + \alpha b \frac{Q}{aW + bB} \cdot \frac{B}{Q} = \alpha \qquad (4.6)$$

which is the same as the ordinary Cobb-Douglas result. By an analogous argument, $\beta = $ land's share in output if both types of land are rented at the value of their marginal products. The share of capital is given by γ, and as in the ordinary Cobb-Douglas function, returns to scale is given by the sum $\alpha + \beta + \gamma = \nu$.

Differences in white and black labor productivity are embodied in the values of the parameters a and b. Similarly, crop-associated productivity differences are captured by the values of c and d. Two notes of caution in interpreting these parameters are needed, however. First, a fundamental identification problem arises here and throughout the discussion. A difference in the estimated values of a and b may represent different levels of skill or human capital differences associated with the two races. It could also represent a systematic difference in the fertility of the land farmed by blacks and whites. In the same way, a difference between c and d could represent a skill differential between cotton farmers and farmers of other crops, as well as a difference in land quality associated with crop. Because of this, productivity differentials captured by different estimated values of a and b or c and d will be designated only as "race-associated productivity differences" and "crop-associated productivity differences."

The second warning concerns the interpretation of c and d. The finding that $c > d$ might indicate that cotton tended to be located on land of greater fertility than other crops, that cotton was a high-value cash crop which could not be grown everywhere (that is, that certain lands could not sustain a cotton crop, whatever its price), or that cotton farmers enjoyed some other sort of productivity advantage that could not easily be dispersed throughout the South. Conversely, if $c < d$, Southern farmers should have been able to produce a greater value of output by shifting out of cotton, *had they been able to*. If they could not diversify, it was presumably due to a soil specificity or to some other rigidity, such as being required to grow cotton to obtain credit from the local furnishing merchant. In either case, a difference between c and d cannot represent an advantage resulting simply from an unconstrained *decision* to plant cotton or the alternatives, since if it did, the South would either have grown cotton exclusively or would not have grown it at all.

The coefficients of the dummy variables represent levels of productivity of the different physical and chemical soil types. Since race- and crop-associated productivity differences may also be attributable to soil quality differences which are systematically associated with race or crop, the coefficients of the dummy variables will be said to represent the "net residual fertility" or simply the "net fertility" of the different soils. The overall significance of these coefficients compared to a single constant in the production function constitutes a test of whether such residual productivity differences were actually important.

Thus, requirements 1–6 are satisfied. However, the production function (4.2) is not linear in all the unknown parameters. In particular, a, b, c, and d enter the function in a nonlinear way. A nonlinear technique could be used to estimate a, b, c, and d, but in view of the large amount of data to be processed and the difficulty in deciding on an initial point from which to start any search process, it was decided to approximate the production function by linearizing it in a Taylor series expansion. Let

$$f(a,b) = \log(aW + bB) \tag{4.7}$$

Expand $f(a, b)$ in Taylor series around (a_o, b_o). Let this point be chosen such that $a_o = b_o$. This could be considered to be "the point of insufficient reason" if no a priori judgments are to be made about the productivity differences between the races. The first few terms of the Taylor series expansion of this function of two variables are

$$f(a,b) = f(a_o, b_o) + (a - a_o)\frac{W}{a_oW + b_oB} + (b - b_o)\frac{B}{a_oW + b_oB}$$

$$+ \frac{1}{2!}\left[(a - a_o)^2(-1)\frac{W^2}{(a_oW + b_oB)^2} + 2(a - a_o)(b - b_o)(-1)\right.$$

$$\left. \times \frac{WB}{(a_oW + b_oB)^2} + (b - b_o)^2(-1)\frac{B^2}{(a_oW + b_oB)^2}\right] \tag{4.8}$$

+ higher-order terms

If a_o is set equal to b_o, this expansion becomes

$$f(a,b) = \log(a_oW + a_oB) + \left(\frac{a}{a_o} - 1\right)\left(\frac{W}{W + B}\right) + \left(\frac{b}{a_o} - 1\right)\left(\frac{B}{W + B}\right)$$

$$- \frac{1}{2!}\left(\frac{a}{a_o} - 1\right)^2\left(\frac{W}{W + B}\right)^2 - \frac{2}{2!}\left(\frac{a}{a_o} - 1\right)\left(\frac{b}{a_o} - 1\right)\left(\frac{W}{W + B}\right)$$

$$\times \left(\frac{B}{W + B}\right) - \frac{1}{2!}\left(\frac{b}{a_o} - 1\right)^2\left(\frac{B}{W + B}\right)^2 \tag{4.9}$$

+ higher-order terms.

Inspection of the first few terms of this Taylor series reveals a sufficient condition for convergence, as follows:

$$\frac{W}{W + B} + \frac{B}{W + B} = 1 \tag{4.10}$$

Also, the higher-order terms will be of the form

$$\frac{(-1)^{k-1}}{k} \left[\left(\frac{a}{a_0} - 1 \right) \left(\frac{W}{W + B} \right) + \left(\frac{b}{a_0} - 1 \right) \left(\frac{B}{W + B} \right) \right]^k \tag{4.11}$$

Therefore, the series will converge absolutely if

$$\left| \frac{a}{a_0} - 1 \right| < 1 \text{ and } \left| \frac{b}{a_0} - 1 \right| < 1 \tag{4.12}$$

by comparison to a convergent geometric series.[4]
If these inequalities are rewritten as

$$-1 < \frac{a}{a_0} - 1 < 1 \text{ and } -1 < \frac{b}{a_0} - 1 < 1 \tag{4.13}$$

this sufficient condition for convergence becomes

$$0 < a < 2a_0 \text{ and } 0 < b < 2a_0 \tag{4.14}$$

Since a_0 can be picked arbitrarily, these conditions can always be met. However, the series will converge more rapidly the closer a_0 is to a and b. Since a_0 can be picked at will, it can always be close to a or to b, but can be close to both only if a is close to b. Hence, the linear approximation of $f(a, b)$ obtained by dropping the quadratic and all higher-order terms will be a better approximation the closer a is to b. But the linear approximation can still be used even if a and b are greatly different, since the Taylor series *always* converges for *some* value of a_0.

Thus, if all nonlinear terms are omitted,

$$f(a, b) = \log a_0 + \log (W + B) + \frac{a}{a_0} \cdot \frac{W}{W + B}$$

$$+ \frac{b}{a_0} \cdot \frac{B}{W + B} - 1 \tag{4.15}$$

But

$$\frac{W}{W + B} = 1 - \frac{B}{W + B}$$

4. George B. Thomas, *Calculus and Analytic Geometry*, p. 603.

So

$$f(a,b) = \left(\log a_0 + \frac{a}{a_0} - 1\right) + \log (W + B) + \frac{1}{a_0} (b - a) \frac{B}{W + B} \quad (4.16)$$

So that

$$\alpha \log (aW + bB) = C' + \alpha \log (W + B) + \frac{\alpha}{a_0} (b - a) \frac{B}{W + B} \quad (4.17)$$

A similar argument can be made to show

$$\beta \log (cH + dJ) = C'' + \beta \log (H + J) + \frac{\beta}{c_0} (c - d) \frac{H}{H + J} \quad (4.18)$$

Combine all these results, write $W + B = R$ and $H + J = T$, rename the constants, and note that for any constant D,

$$\sum_{i=1}^{N} B_i S_i + D = \sum_{i=1}^{N} (B_i + D)S_i \quad \text{since} \quad \sum_{i=1}^{N} S_i = 1 \quad (4.19)$$

Therefore, the final linear approximation of (4.2) is

$$\log Q = \sum_{i=1}^{N} C_i S_i + \alpha \log R + \beta \log T + \gamma \log K + \frac{\alpha}{a_0} (b - a) \frac{B}{R}$$

$$+ \frac{\beta}{c_0} (c - d) \frac{H}{T} + u_0 \quad (4.20)$$

Several comments can be made about this approximation technique. First, because the values of a_0 and c_0 are absorbed by the constant term, there is no need to guess a priori values of a_0 and c_0 close to the actual values of a and c. On the other hand, this advantage is partially offset by the fact that since a_0 and c_0 are not distinguishable from the constants (or each other), there is no way to recover any information on the absolute magnitudes of a and b or c and d. It might be thought that a and c could be scaled arbitrarily at, say, $a = 1$ and $c = 1$ since scaling can be absorbed in the C_i constants. This would be possible except that it would necessitate constrained estimation of the coefficients of B/R and H/T. Unconstrained estimation would admit the possibility of *negative* estimated values of b and d, which would make no economic sense.

For suppose the scale were set so that $a = 1$. Then expand

$$f(b) = \log(W + bB) \quad (4.21)$$

in Taylor series around $b = 1$. Ignoring the higher-order terms as before, the result is

$$f(b) = \log (W + B) + (b - 1) \frac{B}{W + B} \quad (4.22)$$

Thus the coefficient of B/R in the estimated equation would be

$$\theta = \alpha(b - 1) \tag{4.23}$$

So that

$$b = \frac{\theta}{\alpha} + 1 \tag{4.24}$$

If θ is not constrained it is possible for the estimated values of b to be less than zero, which is economically meaningless. In fact, $b < 0$ if $\theta < 0$, $\alpha > 0$, and $|\theta| > \alpha$. Unconstrained estimation could well generate estimates of θ and α in this range, and indeed examination of the results below shows a large number of cases of θ and α combinations which imply $b < 0$ if $a = 1$. Since the purpose of the Taylor series approximation is to simplify the estimations and to avoid costly search procedures or intractable constrained estimation, the arbitrary scaling of $a = 1$ cannot be used.

Therefore, the only information that can be extracted from the estimates of the coefficients of B/R and H/T are the signs of the differences $(b - a)$ and $(c - d)$, and whether these differences are significantly different from zero. Not being forced to guess values of a_o and c_o a priori guarantees that the Taylor series approximation will converge (and hence that linearization is feasible) but because a_o and c_o are unknown, the actual magnitudes a, b, c, and d cannot be recovered.

The Group I results of estimating (4.20) are presented in table 4.1.

TABLE 4.1   The Group I Regressions

Each column consists of the production function estimates for the indicated state in the census year at the head of the column. The numbers in parentheses just to the right of the parameter estimates are the standard errors of the estimates; the numbers in square brackets just below the standard errors are the associated t-statistics for testing the null hypothesis that the coefficient is zero. The only exception to this is that the t-statistic reported along with the estimate of ν, the returns to scale, is actually $\hat{\nu} - 1$ divided by its standard error, and hence is appropriate for testing the hypothesis that $\nu = 1$.

R^2 is the miltiple correlation coefficient. The F statistics with m and n degrees of freedom directly below the R^2 values test the overall significance of the regressions.

obs. $=$ the total number of observations (that is, the number of counties in each state for the particular census year).

$u^{*\prime}u^* =$ the sum of squared residuals when the soil-type dummy variables are included in the regression, and

$u'u =$ the sum of squared residuals when the soil-type dummy variables are all replaced by a single constant term in the regression. $u^{*\prime}u^*$ and $u'u$ will be used subsequently in testing the overall significance of the coefficients of the soil type variables.

The estimates of the coefficients of the soil-type dummy variables are reported for each state separately from the estimates of the input variables' coefficients, for ease in reading the tables. The numbers directly beneath the soil-type coefficient estimates are the *ranks* by size of the respective coefficients for each state and each census year.

TABLE 4.1   (Continued) North Carolina—Group I

Estimated Parameter	1880	1890	1900	1910
α	.260(.0819) [3.175]	.448(.0936) [4.790]	.325(.0640) [5.087]	.345(.0685) [5.037]
β	.407(.0674) [6.036]	.335(.114) [2.937]	.500(.0773) [6.473]	.518(.0725) [7.149]
γ	.326(.0682) [4.780]	.275(.116) [2.372]	.156(.0879) [1.773]	.143(.0840) [1.706]
$\dfrac{\alpha}{a_0}(b-a)$	.687(.173) [3.965]	.372(.189) [1.963]	.424(.134) [3.156]	.452(.146) [3.103]
$\dfrac{\beta}{c_0}(c-d)$	1.219(.226) [5.389]	.438(.262) [1.674]	.488(.191) [2.559]	1.307(.190) [6.868]
ν	.993(.0470) [−.149]	1.058(.0585) [.991]	.981(.0377) [−.504]	1.006(.0406) [.148]
R^2	.961	.919	.958	.966
$F(m,n)$	255.4(8,84)	122.4(8,86)	244.0(8,86)	288.5(8,82)
obs	93	95	95	91
$u^{*\prime}u^{*}$	2.38447	3.75025	1.68962	1.86561
$u'u$	2.53224	3.93311	1.98743	2.18748

TABLE 4.1   (Continued) South Carolina—Group I

Estimated Parameter	1880	1890	1900	1910
α	.203(.157)	.415(.185)	.200(.135)	−.186(.137)
	[1.292]	[2.237]	[1.480]	[−1.357]
β	.277(.135)	.517(.186)	.537(.142)	.645(.109)
	[2.047]	[2.777]	[3.780]	[5.926]
γ	.407(.0995)	.148(.159)	.227(.150)	.447(.0908)
	[4.087]	[.931]	[1.518]	[4.916]
$\dfrac{\alpha}{a_o}(b - a)$	.292(.232)	−.212(.268)	−.441(.145)	−.455(.145)
	[1.258]	[−.790]	[−3.050]	[−3.137]
$\dfrac{\beta}{c_o}(c - d)$	1.044(.371)	.930(.469)	1.265(.262)	1.800(.236)
	[2.812]	[1.985]	[4.823]	[7.623]
ν	.887(.0794)	1.080(.102)	.964(.0544)	—
	[−1.423]	[.784]	[−.662]	
R^2	.967	.936	.965	.978
$F(m, n)$	71.76(9,22)	39.08(9,24)	86.24(9,28)	143.4(9,29)
obs	32	34	38	39
$u^{*\prime}u^*$	.286584	.592397	.240073	.186624
$u'u$	.396139	.951389	.605753	.823080

TABLE 4.1   (Continued) Georgia—Group I

Estimated Parameter	1880	1890	1900	1910
α	.590(.0671) [8.795]	.444(.0589) [7.534]	.450(.0677) [6.641]	.164(.0467) [3.520]
β	.283(.0645) [4.385]	.407(.0590) [6.893]	.377(.0676) [5.573]	.524(.0378) [13.857]
γ	.243(.0536) [4.544]	.170(.0495) [3.427]	.221(.0715) [3.090]	.333(.0437) [7.633]
$\dfrac{\alpha}{a_o}(b-a)$	−.116(.0991) [−1.168]	.221(.0824) [2.685]	−.258(.0730) [−3.531]	−.0604(.0595) [−1.015]
$\dfrac{\beta}{c_o}(c-d)$	1.124(.208) [5.407]	1.521(.178) [8.526]	.905(.177) [5.120]	1.294(.124) [10.409]
ν	1.116(.0362) [3.204]	1.021(.0316) [.665]	1.048(.0283) [1.696]	1.021(.0211) [.995]
R^2	.960	.970	.968	.986
$F(m, n)$	244.6(12,121)	317.1(12,119)	301.3(12,118)	759.4(12,128)
obs	134	132	131	141
$u^{*\prime}u^*$	3.07850	2.27590	1.67515	1.18222
$u'u$	3.75645	2.53452	2.12863	2.44083

TABLE 4.1   (Continued) Florida—Group I

Estimated Parameter	1880	1890	1900	1910
α	.364(.126) [2.889]	.521(.158) [3.300]	.227(.156) [1.452]	−.335(.230) [−1.460]
β	.365(.110) [3.301]	.107(.181) [.592]	.0400(.102) [.392]	.159(.147) [1.085]
γ	.201(.0783) [2.573]	.484(.141) [3.429]	.745(.120) [6.227]	1.133(.165) [6.871]
$\dfrac{\alpha}{a_0}(b-a)$	−.413(.378) [−1.092]	−.132(.437) [−.302]	−.497(.317) [−1.565]	.163(.546) [.298]
$\dfrac{\beta}{c_0}(c-d)$	2.004(.799) [2.507]	.454(.815) [.557]	2.469(.735) [3.358]	1.229(1.036) [1.186]
ν	.930(.0921) [−.760]	1.112(.0924) [1.212]	1.012(.0884) [.136]	—
R^2	.955	.919	.935	.915
$F(m, n)$	77.21(8,29)	49.35(8,35)	57.69(8,32)	45.85(8,34)
obs	38	44	41	43
$u^{*\prime}u^*$	1.62567	4.30723	1.83362	3.84342
$u'u$	2.38727	5.00741	2.46329	4.81499

TABLE 4.1   (Continued) Tennessee—Group I

Estimated Parameter	1880	1890	1900	1910
α	.404(.112) [3.613]	−.0319(.0640) [−.499]	.247(.0628) [3.935]	.240(.0619) [3.885]
β	.137(.118) [1.156]	.659(.0821) [8.024]	.503(.0712) [7.065]	.453(.0805) [5.630]
γ	.421(.0892) [4.716]	.339(.0656) [5.175]	.238(.0676) [3.520]	.333(.0729) [4.574]
$\dfrac{\alpha}{a_o}(b-a)$	.266(.195) [1.367]	.270(.157) [1.722]	−.148(.168) [−.880]	.105(.182) [.577]
$\dfrac{\beta}{c_o}(c-d)$	1.369(.330) [4.145]	.493(.257) [1.916]	.481(.299) [1.612]	.206(.314) [.655]
ν	.962(.0344) [−1.105]	—	.988(.0276) [−.435]	1.026(.0298) [.872]
R^2	.978	.984	.980	.980
$F(m, n)$	211.3(16,75)	285.1(16,75)	223.7(16,75)	222.5(16,74)
obs	92	92	92	91
$u^{*\prime}u^*$	1.34740	.792777	.838624	1.04603
$u'u$	2.56976	1.51585	1.25621	2.56563

TABLE 4.1   (Continued) Alabama—Group I

Estimated Parameter	1880	1890	1900	1910
α	.808(.126) [6.400]	.434(.0993) [4.372]	.443(.0820) [5.400]	.187(.0598) [3.127]
β	.340(.103) [3.294]	.539(.0644) [8.376]	.541(.0585) [9.251]	.635(.0573) [11.082]
γ	−.0183(.0827) [−.222]	.158(.0700) [2.256]	.108(.0829) [1.305]	.264(.0607) [4.353]
$\dfrac{\alpha}{a_0}(b-a)$	−.194(.187) [−1.041]	−.114(.114) [−1.003]	−.284(.0859) [−3.308]	−.453(.0766) [−5.914]
$\dfrac{\beta}{c_0}(c-d)$	1.669(.381) [4.383]	1.087(.272) [3.990]	1.024(.227) [4.503]	1.125(.198) [5.694]
ν	—	1.131(.0607) [2.158]	1.092(.0429) [2.145]	1.086(.0398) [2.161]
R^2	.974	.982	.984	.979
$F(m, n)$	144.5(13,51)	200.3(13,49)	231.7(13,49)	171.6(13,49)
obs	65	63	63	63
$u^{*\prime}u^*$	1.01875	.524055	.250262	.209915
$u'u$	1.37078	1.53858	.344849	.381332

TABLE 4.1　(Continued) Mississippi—Group I

Estimated Parameter	1880	1890	1900	1910
α	.212(.104) [2.042]	.118(.103) [1.140]	.357(.0522) [6.839]	.228(.0597) [3.811]
β	.295(.0986) [2.993]	.672(.108) [6.193]	.334(.0426) [7.844]	.396(.0557) [7.101]
γ	.529(.0815) [6.489]	.150(.106) [1.415]	.303(.0654) [4.636]	.364(.0752) [4.838]
$\dfrac{\alpha}{a_o}(b-a)$	−.225(.284) [−.792]	.585(.207) [2.833]	−.122(.0823) [−1.483]	−.309(.0895) [−3.451]
$\dfrac{\beta}{c_o}(c-d)$	1.707(.450) [3.792]	.842(.309) [2.726]	.976(.126) [7.728]	1.475(.178) [8.293]
ν	1.036(.0709) [.508]	.940(.0648) [−.926]	.994(.0278) [−.216]	.988(.0320) [−.375]
R^2	.959	.960	.989	.990
$F(m, n)$	107.2(13,60)	112.1(13,61)	403.3(13,61)	457.2(13,63)
obs	74	75	75	77
$u^{*\prime}u^*$	2.90427	2.07485	.355923	.490952
$u'u$	3.11330	3.81807	.639033	1.15984

TABLE 4.1 (Continued) Arkansas—Group I

Estimated Parameter	1880	1890	1900	1910
α	.410(.101)	.301(.105)	.277(.103)	.239(.102)
	[4.065]	[2.871]	[2.691]	[2.341]
β	.377(.0967)	.315(.0911)	.138(.110)	.376(.0884)
	[3.898]	[3.459]	[1.257]	[4.258]
γ	.199(.0702)	.307(.0661)	.633(.0965)	.365(.0751)
	[2.837]	[4.649]	[6.553]	[4.864]
$\dfrac{\alpha}{a_o}(b-a)$	−.408(.134)	.168(.117)	−.0822(.114)	−.527(.106)
	[−3.054]	[1.446]	[−.718]	[−4.949]
$\dfrac{\beta}{c_o}(c-d)$	2.281(.214)	1.358(.157)	1.244(.185)	1.972(.168)
	[10.666]	[8.627]	[6.739]	[11.744]
ν	.986(.0362)	.923(.0321)	1.048(.0361)	.980(.0458)
	[−.387]	[−2.399]	[1.330]	[−.437]
R^2	.957	.970	.964	.968
$F(m, n)$	139.0(10,62)	204.7(10,63)	169.7(10,63)	183.3(10,61)
obs	73	74	74	72
$u^{*\prime}u^*$	.839847	.595576	.569946	.628253
$u'u$	1.00982	.675252	.644752	.982887

TABLE 4.1   (Continued) Louisiana—Group I

Estimated Parameter	1880	1890	1900	1910
α	.202(.159) [1.268]	.393(.112) [3.516]	.335(.113) [2.972]	.229(.106) [2.157]
β	.374(.144) [2.607]	.220(.0779) [2.819]	.476(.110) [4.333]	.290(.0904) [3.209]
γ	.448(.0935) [4.788]	.378(.0608) [6.213]	.167(.0553) [3.028]	.424(.0782) [5.414]
$\frac{\alpha}{a_o}(b-a)$	.673(.378) [1.779]	.664(.248) [2.674]	.294(.212) [1.386]	−.0123(.224) [−.0552]
$\frac{\beta}{c_o}(c-d)$	.501(.409) [1.224]	.600(.255) [2.353]	.495(.324) [1.525]	1.127(.425) [2.649]
v	1.024(.0959) [.250]	.991(.0724) [−.124]	.978(.0651) [−.338]	.943(.0716) [−.796]
R^2	.916	.927	.924	.924
$F(m, n)$	44.71(11,45)	53.25(11,46)	50.88(11,46)	49.68(11,45)
obs	57	58	58	57
$u^{*\prime}u^*$	3.83072	2.16770	1.75323	1.77907
$u'u$	4.58390	2.61086	2.65074	2.32386

TABLE 4.1 (Continued) Texas—Group I

Estimated Parameter	1880	1910
α	.157(.0760) [2.070]	.263(.0907) [2.903]
β	.313(.0683) [4.584]	.703(.0778) [9.033]
γ	.681(.0943) [7.225]	.172(.105) [1.631]
$\dfrac{\alpha}{a_o}(b-a)$	.500(.815) [.614]	.487(.450) [1.080]
$\dfrac{\beta}{c_o}(c-d)$	2.474(1.442) [1.715]	2.049(.339) [6.051]
v	1.151(.0819) [1.844]	1.138(.0597) [2.312]
R^2	.954	.911
$F(m, n)$	286.4(15,206)	148.5(15,218)
obs	222	234
$u^{*\prime}u^*$	275.199	72.5995
$u'u$	289.358	77.8685

TABLE 4.1   (Continued) North Carolina—Group I

Estimated Parameter	1880	1890	1900	1910
C_1	2.021(.409) 4 [4.944]	1.630(.535) 4 [3.050]	2.656(.351) 4 [7.578]	2.777(.381) 2 [7.282]
C_2	2.125(.439) 2 [4.841]	1.687(.579) 3 [2.914]	2.850(.378) 1 [7.547]	2.879(.411) 1 [7.013]
C_3	2.171(.447) 1 [4.853]	1.788(.581) 2 [3.076]	2.725(.378) 3 [7.205]	2.702(.407) 3 [6.642]
C_4	2.103(.429) 3 [4.900]	1.789(.561) 1 [3.189]	2.774(.362) 2 [7.656]	2.563(.385) 4 [6.653]

TABLE 4.1   (Continued) South Carolina—Group I

Estimated Parameter	1880	1890	1900	1910
C_1	3.443(.766) 4 [4.495]	1.730(1.044) 4 [1.658]	3.009(.543) 3 [5.543]	3.297(.509) 2 [6.477]
C_2	3.660(.748) 1 [4.895]	2.207(.951) 1 [2.322]	3.265(.542) 1 [6.028]	3.458(.523) 1 [6.615]
C_3	3.595(.811) 2 [4.434]	1.936(1.101) 2 [1.759]	3.100(.560) 2 [5.532]	3.257(.508) 3 [6.414]
C_4	3.439(.775) 5 [4.436]	1.684(1.057) 5 [1.593]	2.861(.549) 4 [5.208]	3.137(.505) 4 [6.209]
C_5	3.542(.808) 3 [4.384]	1.742(1.108) 3 [1.572]	2.767(.551) 5 [5.024]	2.906(.505) 5 [5.754]

TABLE 4.1 (Continued) Georgia—Group I

Estimated Parameter	1880	1890	1900	1910
C_1	1.588(.353) 6 [4.500]	2.143(.312) 7 [6.868]	2.179(.285) 7 [7.642]	2.128(.224) 8 [9.498]
C_2	1.423(.336) 7 [4.240]	2.043(.304) 8 [6.725]	2.149(.277) 8 [7.759]	2.150(.213) 7 [10.113]
C_3	1.653(.349) 5 [4.734]	2.191(.312) 4 [7.028]	2.203(.280) 6 [7.874]	2.221(.219) 6 [10.128]
C_4	1.664(.347) 4 [4.801]	2.173(.309) 5 [7.024]	2.322(.287) 3 [8.098]	2.3177(.223) 5 [10.402]
C_5	1.343(.368) 8 [3.653]	2.210(.328) 3 [6.745]	2.257(.306) 5 [7.366]	2.3180(.237) 4 [9.766]
C_6	1.681(.338) 3 [4.971]	2.164(.304) 6 [7.124]	2.295(.286) 4 [8.026]	2.380(.223) 2 [10.657]
C_7	1.695(.324) 2 [5.236]	2.302(.293) 1 [7.866]	2.351(.276) 2 [8.506]	2.468(.218) 1 [11.306]
C_8	1.732(.311) 1 [5.572]	2.228(.276) 2 [8.074]	2.375(.255) 1 [9.331]	2.344(.208) 3 [11.285]

TABLE 4.1 (Continued) Florida—Group I

Estimated Parameter	1880	1890	1900	1910
C_1	3.028(.821) 3 [3.686]	1.816(.900) 3 [2.018]	2.114(.808) 4 [2.617]	1.621(1.236) 4 [1.312]
C_2	2.961(.714) 4 [4.150]	1.609(.757) 4 [2.127]	2.276(.753) 3 [3.023]	2.057(1.153) 2 [1.783]
C_3	3.192(.752) 2 [4.244]	1.824(.799) 2 [2.282]	2.335(.745) 2 [3.135]	1.795(1.130) 3 [1.588]
C_4	3.550(.682) 1 [5.207]	2.102(.704) 1 [2.985]	2.766(.697) 1 [3.970]	2.345(1.079) 1 [2.174]

TABLE 4.1   (Continued) Tennessee—Group I

Estimated Parameter	1880	1890	1900	1910
C_1	3.575(.387) 1 [9.229]	2.334(.284) 1 [8.203]	3.010(.334) 1 [9.022]	3.138(.372) 1 [8.428]
C_2	3.076(.379) 2 [8.107]	2.149(.276) 3 [7.772]	2.827(.325) 2 [8.708]	2.654(.341) 2 [7.782]
C_3	3.014(.388) 4 [7.759]	2.021(.277) 5 [7.304]	2.733(.318) 3 [8.591]	2.387(.333) 4 [7.161]
C_4	2.961(.393) 5 [7.542]	2.070(.273) 4 [7.572]	2.638(.312) 6 [8.460]	2.343(.325) 5 [7.200]
C_5	3.053(.358) 3 [8.535]	2.162(.257) 2 [8.409]	2.711(.287) 4 [9.438]	2.403(.304) 3 [7.894]
C_6	2.948(.363) 6 [8.111]	2.019(.257) 6 [7.873]	2.612(.289) 7 [9.025]	2.325(.306) 6 [7.600]
C_7	2.736(.377) 9 [7.267]	1.875(.265) 11 [7.066]	2.580(.295) 8 [8.732]	2.233(.312) 8 [7.148]
C_8	2.912(.385) 7 [7.573]	1.886(.271) 10 [6.954]	2.684(.301) 5 [8.925]	2.262(.316) 7 [7.163]
C_9	2.644(.341) 12 [7.754]	1.889(.241) 9 [7.832]	2.510(.270) 10 [9.286]	2.164(.284) 9 [7.605]
C_{10}	2.745(.364) 8 [7.534]	1.943(.254) 8 [7.637]	2.508(.282) 11 [8.879]	2.062(.301) 11 [6.852]
C_{11}	2.728(.379) 10 [7.202]	1.815(.264) 12 [6.869]	2.501(.294) 12 [8.512]	1.988(.310) 12 [6.405]
C_{12}	2.699(.372) 11 [7.254]	1.946(.262) 7 [7.412]	2.511(.294) 9 [8.550]	2.084(.312) 10 [6.676]

TABLE 4.1 (Continued) Alabama—Group I

Estimated Parameter	1880	1890	1900	1910
C_1	1.594(.653) 4 [2.441]	1.146(.565) 4 [2.026]	1.727(.416) 3 [4.148]	1.654(.422) 4 [3.923]
C_2	1.602(.655) 2 [2.448]	1.079(.580) 6 [1.860]	1.644(.427) 6 [3.848]	1.573(.426) 7 [3.693]
C_3	1.406(.638) 9 [2.205]	.950(.562) 8 [1.690]	1.614(.422) 9 [3.824]	1.545(.429) 9 [3.605]
C_4	1.598(.660) 3 [2.421]	.786(.568) 9 [1.385]	1.624(.425) 8 [3.826]	1.595(.431) 6 [3.703]
C_5	1.635(.639) 1 [2.561]	1.068(.553) 7 [1.931]	1.730(.411) 1 [4.207]	1.564(.415) 8 [3.766]
C_6	1.499(.627) 7 [2.392]	1.179(.557) 3 [2.119]	1.686(.417) 5 [4.044]	1.664(.418) 3 [3.978]
C_7	1.529(.634) 6 [2.410]	1.277(.562) 2 [2.274]	1.710(.418) 4 [4.088]	1.700(.421) 2 [4.041]
C_8	1.419(.649) 8 [2.186]	1.139(.569) 5 [2.001]	1.640(.420) 7 [3.902]	1.608(.419) 5 [3.833]
C_9	1.586(.565) 5 [2.806]	1.371(.529) 1 [2.592]	1.727(.403) 2 [4.291]	1.734(.412) 1 [4.208]

TABLE 4.1   (Continued) Mississippi—Group I

Estimated Parameter	1880	1890	1900	1910
C_1	1.815(.678)	2.239(.595)	2.674(.274)	2.542(.337)
	8 [2.676]	9 [3.765]	9 [9.763]	8 [7.535]
C_2	1.821(.692)	2.310(.607)	2.733(.278)	2.620(.339)
	7 [2.632]	8 [3.808]	5 [9.842]	6 [7.727]
C_3	1.963(.675)	2.360(.594)	2.734(.272)	2.756(.331)
	2 [2.908]	7 [3.975]	4 [10.061]	2 [8.319]
C_4	1.887(.665)	2.623(.590)	2.717(.272)	2.591(.334)
	5 [2.837]	4 [4.447]	7 [10.006]	7 [7.752]
C_5	1.781(.645)	2.615(.573)	2.786(.269)	2.388(.325)
	9 [2.763]	5 [4.563]	2 [10.358]	9 [7.352]
C_6	1.884(.634)	2.778(.560)	2.970(.269)	2.948(.341)
	6 [2.972]	2 [4.964]	1 [11.050]	1 [8.657]
C_7	1.933(.659)	2.501(.588)	2.703(.271)	2.709(.332)
	3 [2.934]	6 [4.252]	8 [9.992]	5 [8.167]
C_8	1.892(.655)	2.723(.587)	2.742(.273)	2.719(.336)
	4 [2.888]	3 [4.636]	3 [10.057]	4 [8.101]
C_9	1.986(.583)	2.911(.549)	2.727(.265)	2.745(.320)
	1 [3.408]	1 [5.306]	6 [10.283]	3 [8.574]

TABLE 4.1 (Continued) Arkansas—Group I

Estimated Parameter	1880	1890	1900	1910
C_1	2.671(.341) 2 [7.832]	3.221(.283) 1 [11.400]	1.882(.332) 1 [5.673]	2.868(.429) 1 [6.692]
C_2	2.720(.333) 1 [8.167]	3.099(.284) 4 [10.905]	1.796(.332) 2 [5.413]	2.756(.423) 2 [6.521]
C_3	2.612(.348) 3 [7.514]	3.150(.297) 2 [10.622]	1.730(.341) 6 [5.074]	2.490(.429) 6 [5.809]
C_4	2.576(.337) 6 [7.643]	3.065(.285) 6 [10.754]	1.737(.330) 4 [5.267]	2.632(.413) 3 [6.373]
C_5	2.591(.346) 5 [7.480]	3.105(.294) 3 [10.575]	1.731(.339) 5 [5.114]	2.556(.419) 5 [6.095]
C_6	2.608(.340) 4 [7.665]	3.087(.290) 5 [10.644]	1.769(.334) 3 [5.289]	2.609(.406) 4 [6.419]

TABLE 4.1 (Continued) Louisiana—Group I

Estimated Parameter	1880	1890	1900	1910
C_1	1.988(.865) 3 [2.297]	2.602(.681) 2 [3.819]	2.901(.632) 4 [4.590]	2.890(.671) 6 [4.307]
C_2	2.126(.900) 2 [2.361]	2.780(.708) 1 [3.925]	3.014(.646) 2 [4.666]	3.080(.714) 3 [4.312]
C_3	2.142(.892) 1 [2.401]	2.571(.690) 5 [3.727]	3.341(.623) 1 [5.363]	3.225(.692) 1 [4.660]
C_4	1.760(.890) 6 [1.979]	2.586(.704) 4 [3.672]	2.766(.664) 6 [4.166]	2.592(.708) 7 [3.661]
C_5	1.628(.944) 7 [1.725]	2.449(.743) 7 [3.297]	2.945(.696) 3 [4.230]	3.158(.760) 2 [4.157]
C_6	1.849(.847) 4 [2.182]	2.599(.671) 3 [3.873]	2.772(.626) 5 [4.432]	3.041(.680) 4 [4.472]
C_7	1.828(.900) 5 [2.031]	2.492(.712) 6 [3.501]	2.672(.676) 7 [3.953]	2.993(.713) 5 [4.200]

TABLE 4.1 (Continued) Texas—Group I

Estimated Parameter	1880	1910
C_1	−.160(.830) 5 [−.193]	.404(.628) 6 [.643]
C_2	.249(.846) 2 [.295]	1.245(.658) 1 [1.893]
C_3	−.143(.924) 4 [−.155]	.571(.686) 3 [.833]
C_4	−.268(.826) 8 [−.325]	.239(.630) 7 [.380]
C_5	−.293(.836) 10 [−.350]	.180(.641) 9 [.281]
C_6	−.195(.754) 6 [−.259]	.182(.632) 8 [.288]
C_7	−.0355(1.003) 3 [−.0354]	.488(.719) 4 [.679]
C_8	−.227(1.166) 7 [−.195]	.444(.786) 5 [.565]
C_9	−.427(1.102) 11 [−.388]	.789(.769) 2 [1.026]
C_{10}	.467(.571) 1 [.817]	.126(.592) 10 [.212]
C_{11}	−.268(.240) 9 [−1.116]	.125(.579) 11 [.216]

Interpretation of the Results of the Group I Regressions

1. *Fit and a priori reasonableness*. These estimates of the production function coefficients show generally an excellent fit and estimated coefficients significantly different from zero in most cases. There are only five instances of estimated input elasticities outside the zero-to-one range and two of these are in the same state and year. Altogether 114 input elasticities were estimated, so these a priori unreasonable estimates could easily be due to chance alone. The t-statistics associated with the estimated input elasticities are less than 2 in only 21 of the 114 possible cases. The calculated R^2 values are greater than .9 in every one of the Group I regressions. On grounds of fit and conformity to a priori expectations, the production model is very successful.

2. *Exploitation of labor*. Appendix B reports the results of a sampling of the reported values of the output shares received by the factors of production in Southern agriculture after the Civil War. Every example of the shares of output received by the factors which was found during the course of the research was recorded. This sample includes the systematic report of factor shares contained in the 1880 Census *Survey of Cotton Production*. The figures are not strictly comparable with each other, of course, since uniform definitions of the services rendered by each factor were not used and the carefulness of the observers varied greatly. In this sample, out of 56 observations corresponding roughly to the share of output received for labor services alone, only one lies outside the range from 1/4 to 1/2. The unweighted average of all these observations is .415. The relative uniformity of these observations, given the wide variation in their location, point in time, factor definitions, and reliability, constitutes very strong evidence that the share received by agricultural laborers was somewhere between 1/4 and 1/2. One-half would seem to be the upper limit of the share of output paid for labor alone.

The estimated labor input elasticities in the Group I regressions show substantial variation both across states and over time. Even if each state's production function were unchanged over the forty-year period covered by the four censuses, some variation in the estimates would be expected, because of the fact that four different samples were drawn for each state. Therefore, some care is required in determining whether the results support the competition hypothesis or the exploitation hypothesis. It may be observed initially that of the 38 estimated labor elasticities, 18 lie within the [1/4,1/2] range, 17 lie below this range, while only 3 lie above it. This simple frequency breakdown by itself means very little, however, since it includes no information concerning the confidence that can be attached to any of the estimates.

If a 95 percent confidence interval is constructed around each estimated labor elasticity, only four intervals out of 38 fail to include some portion of the range [1/4,1/2]. Since a 95 percent confidence interval around an estimate contains those hypothetical values of the parameter which the estimated value would not cause to be rejected at the 5 percent significance level, this means that only in 4 cases out of 38 can the hypothesis that the true value of α belongs to the [1/4,1/2] range be rejected at the 5 percent level. At the 10 percent significance level (which involves a narrower confidence interval around each estimated value $\hat{\alpha}$), only 5 estimates fail to pass the null hypothesis that $1/4 \leq \alpha \leq 1/2$. Five rejections out of 38 is 13 percent, slightly greater than the frequency that a valid null hypothesis would be rejected at the 10 percent significance level by chance alone. At the 5 percent level, there are about twice as many instances of rejection as would be expected on chance grounds alone, even though the number of cases of rejection is small. However, *every case* of rejection of the [1/4,1/2] range at the 5 percent level involves a production function estimate in which one of the estimated input elasticities is negative. These estimates are implausible on a priori grounds, since input elasticities of well-behaved production functions are invariably positive.

Without undertaking the additional computations required formally to combine the four-census cross-section samples,[5] it is possible to construct a set of descriptive statistics which eliminate the intercensus variation in the parameter estimates. Those statistics are simply the averages of the four estimates of each input elasticity for each state. If the covariance between the estimated elasticity of an input in one year and the estimated elasticity of the same input in any other year is zero, then it is also possible to compute approximate standard errors of these four-census averages.[6] Since this procedure bypasses most of the theoretical

5. For a discussion of the combining of cross-sectional data from different points in time, see Arnold Zellner, "An Efficient Method of Estimating Seemingly Unrelated Regressions and Tests for Aggregation Bias," *Journal of the American Statistical Association* 57, no. 298 (June 1962): 348–368; Marc Nerlove, *Estimation and Identification of Cobb-Douglas Production Functions*, pp. 157–190.

6. If $X_1, X_2, \ldots, X_n$ are n random variables, with $E(X_i) = \mu_i$, Var $(X_i) = \sigma_i^2$, and Cov $(X_i, X_j) = 0$ when $i \neq j$, then for any n constants a_i,

$$E(\sum_i a_i X_i) = \sum_i a_i E(X_i) \qquad \text{and}$$

$$\text{Var}(\sum_i a_i X_i) = \sum_i a_i^2 \text{ Var } (X_i)$$

TABLE 4.2 Group I Intercensus Averages, Variant I

State	α	β	γ
North Carolina	.345(.0390)	.440(.0424)	.225(.0454)
South Carolina	.158(.0774)	.494(.0728)	.307(.0642)
Georgia	.412(.0303)	.398(.0292)	.242(.0277)
Florida	.194(.0859)	.168(.0693)	.641(.0650)
Tennessee	.215(.0391)	.438(.0449)	.333(.0372)
Alabama	.468(.0475)	.514(.0366)	.128(.0373)
Mississippi	.229(.0416)	.424(.0406)	.336(.0417)
Arkansas	.307(.0514)	.302(.0485)	.376(.0389)
Louisiana	.290(.0622)	.340(.0543)	.354(.0368)
Texas	.210(.0592)	.508(.0517)	.427(.0706)
Overall unweighted average	.283	.403	.337

issues involved in combining the information contained in the different samples, it should be firmly kept in mind that statistical tests based on the intercensus averages are only provisional. These statistics do, however, present a condensed picture of the information contained in the individual regressions, and as such may serve to clarify the general direction of the individual regression results. The four-census averages and associated approximate standard errors are presented in table 4.2. These averages are denoted the "Group I Intercensus Averages, Variant I."

Thus, the standard deviation of $\dfrac{1}{n} \sum_i X_i$ is

$$\sigma = \frac{1}{n}\left[\sum_i \sigma_i^2\right]^{1/2}$$

If the exact standard deviations of the input elasticity estimates were known, this expression would give the standard deviation of their four-census average exactly. Since the standard deviations are not known, the standard error of the average is approximated by

$$s = \frac{1}{n}\left[\sum_i s_i^2\right]^{1/2}$$

If it is assumed that each census cross section is a sample drawn from the same population, with α the common value of the labor elasticity, then the statistic

$$m = \frac{\frac{1}{4}(\hat{\alpha}_1 + \hat{\alpha}_2 + \hat{\alpha}_3 + \hat{\alpha}_4) - \alpha}{s}$$

will be distributed approximately normally with mean zero and variance equal to one. The significance tests reported in the text are based on approximating the distribution of m by a normal distribution, and in view of this approximation and of the assumptions made to combine the individual parameter estimates in the first place, it should be emphasized that the significance tests are intended to be only provisional and suggestive.

It is immediately apparent from table 4.2 that the Variant I average labor elasticities are uniformly less than 1/2. More important, none of them are so far outside the [1/4,1/2] range to lead, at either the 5 percent or 10 percent significance levels, to rejection of the hypothesis that the true α values for each state belonged to this range. Thus, for no state is it possible to reject the hypothesis that the estimated labor input elasticity was in the same range as that of sharecrop shares obtained from the direct sample. Since the share of output received by labor equals the labor input elasticity if the wage equals the marginal product of labor, the estimates of α are consistent with existence of a perfectly competitive labor market in every state.

It has already been observed that negative input elasticities are intrinsically implausible. If all four production function estimates containing a negative input elasticity are eliminated from the four-census averages, these conclusions are reinforced even more strongly. Table 4.3 contains the averages of the input elasticities of each state and their associated approximate standard errors, excluding from the averages all elasticities from any production function possessing a negative estimated input elasticity. These averages are denoted the "Group I Intercensus Averages, Variant II." Again, for no state can the hypothesis that the true α was contained in the [1/4,1/2] interval be rejected at either the 5 percent or 10 percent level of significance. For the Variant II averages, the overall unweighted mean of the labor elasticities is .309; while for land and capital the mean elasticities are .396 and .321, respectively.

It bears repeating that all of these results only confirm a *necessary*

TABLE 4.3   Group I Intercensus Averages, Variant II

State	α	β	γ
North Carolina	.345(.0390)	.440(.0424)	.225(.0454)
South Carolina	.273(.0926)	.444(.0901)	.261(.0801)
Georgia	.412(.0303)	.398(.0292)	.242(.0277)
Florida	.371(.0851)	.171(.0784)	.477(.0670)
Tennessee	.297(.0475)	.364(.0532)	.331(.0445)
Alabama	.355(.0474)	.572(.0348)	.177(.0415)
Mississippi	.229(.0416)	.424(.0406)	.336(.0417)
Arkansas	.307(.0514)	.302(.0485)	.376(.0389)
Louisiana	.290(.0622)	.340(.0543)	.354(.0368)
Texas	.210(.0592)	.508(.0517)	.427(.0706)
Overall unweighted average	.309	.396	.321

use

condition for competition in the labor market. Competition had to be assumed in order to disregard any allocational or distributional impact of sharecropping per se and to form the aggregate production functions. Given that the actual share of output received by Southern agricultural workers was in the [1/4,1/2] range, estimated labor elasticities significantly outside that range would imply a failure of the competitive assumptions. When the full amount of information for each state is taken into account (by means of the intercensus averages), no state fails to pass the test of this important necessary condition for the competition hypothesis. At the level of the individual production function estimates, the number of failures of the same test is small compared with the number of functions estimated, and at the 5 percent level of significance every failure involves an estimated production function with at least one negative input elasticity, estimates which are highly suspect on a priori grounds.

Of course, it is possible that an adventitious combination of market imperfections and structural rigidities might have resulted in production function estimates with the labor elasticity within the [1/4,1/2] range. No statistical test can ever establish its null hypothesis; it can only lead to rejection of the hypothesis. This general limitation is shared by the tests performed here. However, if the production function parameter estimates are robust in the face of market imperfections, that is, if the estimates correspond to the true parameters of the production functions despite imperfections in the factor and output markets, interpretation of the results can proceed even farther. In this case the hypothesis of the exploitation of labor can definitely be ruled out. Almost all deviations of the estimated labor input elasticities from the [1/4,1/2] interval occur at the lower end of the range. No state's Variant I or Variant II average production function exhibits a labor elasticity greater than 1/2. The overall average of these elasticities is actually lower than the average share paid to labor computed from the sample of direct observations, although that finding may not mean very much because of the lack of uniformity in the sample of sharecrop contracts as compiled. Stiglitz[7] has shown that in a competitive sharecropping economy with uncertainty, deviations from ordinary marginal product factor pricing can be attributed to different risk preferences on the part of landlords and tenants; so it is possible that workers received a risk premium sufficient to increase their wages above the average marginal productivity level.

7. Joseph E. Stiglitz, "Incentives and Risk-Sharing in Sharecropping," mimeographed.

no exploitation

Even if the discrepancy between the estimated labor input elasticity and the actual share of output received by labor was due to other causes, the fact that the competitive labor share was *less* than the actual share (in the absence of uncertainty) only *strengthens* the case for rejection of the exploitation hypothesis, provided the parameter estimates are robust.

These conclusions regarding the absence of exploitation apply only to the labor market. They imply nothing about possible exploitation of the agricultural workers by monopolistic furnishing merchants, or about the equity of the distribution of ownership of the nonhuman factors of production among the various groups in the population. Also, while marginal product factor pricing is suggestive of at least some degree of competition (since competition is a simple mechanism leading to equalization of the marginal productivities and the factor prices), it is not sufficient to guarantee full competitive equilibrium. The marginal product of labor may vary with soil quality, population density, and other local conditions, and there may have been insufficient factor mobility to equalize the differences. In this case, marginal productivity wage levels would partially reflect favorable or unfavorable location, and the wage rate would not be the same everywhere. Alternatively, it is possible for the wage/employment combination to lie on the demand curve for labor (so that the wage equals the marginal product of labor) yet still lie off the supply curve of labor. Such a marginal productivity wage level could correspond to a situation of "forced labor" if the wage level were below the competitive equilibrium wage. Enforcement of such a labor market "equilibrium" could very easily necessitate repressive laws and institutions.

These qualifications emphasize the need for caution in drawing conclusions from these tests of a necessary condition for labor market competition, no matter how important the necessary condition may be or how unambiguous are the results of the tests. Nevertheless, it is clear that the results support the hypothesis of competition in the labor market. They certainly provide no grounds for believing that Southern agricultural workers were exploited. The competition hypothesis passes the test that the estimated production function parameters must be consistent with the sharecrop payments actually made. The data on inputs and outputs contained in the agricultural censuses over the forty-year period are consistent with marginal productivity wage levels. On the basis of these results, it would seem at the very least that the burden of proof has been shifted to advocates of the contrary view that Southern agricultural laborers were exploited by their employers in the postbellum period, and that this exploitation formed the basis of the Southern legal and social climate.

3. *Returns to scale.* These results can also be used to test the hypothesis of constant returns to scale. The sum of the estimated values of the coefficients, minus the expected value of the sum, divided by the sample standard error of the sum will be distributed as t with the same degrees of freedom as the t-statistics for the individual coefficients.[8] The Group I tables show these test statistics for the null hypothesis that $\nu = 1$ for each production function.

It should be recalled that the estimation process did not constrain the returns to scale at all—ordinary least squares was simply applied to the input and output data. Nevertheless, 18 out of 34 calculated values of ν were greater than one, while 16 were less than one. (The returns to scale parameter ν was not calculated if any of the input elasticities lay outside the zero-to-one range.) The test statistic for the null hypothesis that $\nu = 1$ is greater than 2 in absolute value in only 6 out of the 34 cases, and is greater than one in absolute value in only 12 of 34 cases. Instances of $\hat{\nu}$ significantly different from one were concentrated in Alabama and Texas, and even in these states the largest deviation of $\hat{\nu}$ from one was only .151. In general, the estimates indicate no strong departure from constant returns to scale in agriculture.

While it is true that constant returns is required for meaningful aggregation, and therefore also for estimation of the production functions from the county data, the finding that the unconstrained estimates show constant returns is not vacuous. As with the labor input elasticity, if the estimated returns to scale had been substantially different from one, it would show that some sort of discordance existed between the data and the assumptions required for aggregation and estimation. The constant returns of the estimated functions cannot prove the assumption of constant returns required to derive them, but finding constant returns in the unconstrained estimates does in a sense vindicate the assumption. The data are not inconsistent with the assumption of constant returns.

4. *Soil fertility parameters.* The results can be used to determine whether the Hilgard soil-type classifications represented by the S_i dummy variables do in fact correspond to soils of different intrinsic fertilities. Two questions need to be answered: (a) Does inclusion of the dummy variables significantly decrease the unexplained variance in each regression compared to regressions including only a single constant? (b) Do the coefficients of the S_i maintain a stable relationship to one another in

8.   J. Johnston, *Econometric Methods,* pp. 131–135.

successive census years? In other words, does their overall significance (if such is found) follow from *fertility* differences, or is it due to some transitory county differences not connected at all to the composition of the soil?

The first of these two questions can be answered by performing a series of Chow-type F-tests on the overall significance of the coefficients of the dummy variables, as compared with a single constant.[9] In a general model where the S_i's are the soil-type dummy variables and X represents the vector of all the other independent variables, with the relation between the variables given (except for the disturbance) by

$$Y = X\beta_1 + S_1\beta_{21} + S_2\beta_{22} + S_3\beta_{23} + \ldots + S_N\beta_{2N}, \qquad (4.25)$$

recall that, by definition

$$S_N = 1 - \sum_{i=1}^{N-1} S_i \qquad (4.26)$$

Then

$$Y = X\beta_1 + S_1\beta_{21} + S_2\beta_{22} + \ldots + (1 - \sum_{i=1}^{N-1} S_i)\beta_{2N}$$

$$= X\beta_1 + \beta_{2N} + S_1(\beta_{21} - \beta_{2N}) + S_2(\beta_{22} - \beta_{2N}) + \ldots \qquad (4.27)$$

$$+ S_{N-1}(\beta_{2,N-1} - \beta_{2N})$$

So let $\beta_{2N} = C$. To test the hypothesis that the remaining $N - 1$ coefficients of $S_1, S_2, \ldots, S_{N-1}$ are different from zero, compute

$$F(m, n) = \frac{(u'u - u^{*\prime}u^*)/(N - 1)}{u^{*\prime}u^*/[Z - (k + N - 1)]} \qquad (4.28)$$

where $k =$ the number of variables in X plus one, $N =$ number of soil types, $Z =$ number of observations, $m = N - 1, n = Z - (k + N - 1)$, $u'u$ is the sum of squares of the residuals from a regression in which the coefficients of $S_1, \ldots, S_{N-1}$ are restricted to be zero, and $u^{*\prime}u^*$ is the sum of squares of residuals from the regression in which these coefficients are not all restricted to zero. These F values are given in table 4.4.

In most cases, the test statistic is significant at the 5 percent level, but even more pertinent is the significance of the four F values for each state taken together. The cumulative area under any continuous probability

9. Franklin M. Fisher, "Tests of Equality Between Sets of Coefficients in Two Linear Regressions: An Expository Note," *Econometrica* 38, no. 2 (March 1970) contains a particularly useful method for carrying out the Chow test. Fisher's development is followed here.

TABLE 4.4 F-test on Overall Significance of Coefficients of S_i as Compared to a Single Constant—Group I Regressions

State	1880	1890	1900	1910
North Carolina	1.735(3,84)	1.398(3,86)	5.053(3,86)	4.716(3,82)
max. P-value	.25	.50	.005	.01
South Carolina	2.103(4,22)	3.636(4,24)	10.662(4,28)	24.725(4,29)
	.25	.025	.001	.001
Georgia	3.807(7,121)	1.932(7,119)	4.563(7,118)	19.467(7,128)
	.001	.10	.001	.001
Florida	4.529(3,29)	1.897(3,35)	3.663(3,32)	2.865(3,34)
	.025	.25	.025	.10
Tennessee	6.185(11,75)	6.219(11,75)	3.395(11,75)	9.773(11,74)
	.001	.001	.005	.001
Alabama	2.203(8,51)	11.857(8,49)	2.315(8,49)	5.002(8,49)
	.05	.001	.05	.001
Mississippi	.540(8,60)	6.406(8,61)	6.065(8,61)	10.729(8,63)
	.90	.001	.001	.001
Arkansas	2.510(5,62)	1.686(5,63)	1.654(5,63)	6.887(5,61)
	.05	.25	.25	.001
Louisiana	1.475(6,45)	1.567(6,46)	3.925(6,46)	2.297(6,45)
	.25	.25	.005	.10
Texas	1.060(10,206)			1.582(10,218)
	.50			.25

The number listed below each F value in the table is a P-value which is at least as large as the area under the appropriate F distribution to the right of the tabled F value. The exact P-values were not given because the F tables used gave only the "critical" F values for P-values equal to .75, .50, .25, .10, .05, .025, .01, .005, and .001. F. James Rohlf and Robert R. Sokal, *Statistical Tables*, Table S: "Critical values of the F-distribution," pp. 168–197.

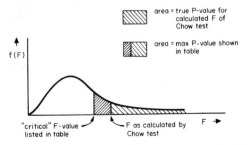

If the proper degrees of freedom were not listed in the table, the max P-value was again chosen to be at least as large as the true P-value.

density function is uniformly distributed over the interval 0 to 1.[10] For each of the F-statistics, the cumulative distribution function equals $1 -$ P-value. It can be shown (see appendix D) that if $\xi =$ the sum of the P-values for the four test statistics of each state, the probability that $\xi < 1$ will be less than .05. In the table, $\xi < 1$ for all nine states that have four test statistics. Hence, the results of the Chow tests show that over the entire period, the soil-type dummy variables were more significant as a group than a single constant for every state but Texas.

However, examination of the coefficients of the S_i in successive census years reveals a certain amount of fluctuation in the relative rankings of those coefficients. In order to determine the degree of stability in the relative rankings, a Friedman two-way analysis of variance by ranks[11] was performed. This test determines the probability that the ranks of the C_i (for a given state) were drawn from the same population over the four census years. The null hypothesis is that there was no stable ranking of coefficients, so that in each census year, the likelihood that a given C_i would have a high rank was the same as the probability that it would have a low rank. Hence, the mean rank of each C_i over the four censuses should be the same under the null hypothesis.

The test statistic is

$$\chi_r^2 = \frac{12}{Nk(k + 1)} \sum_{j=1}^{k} (R_j)^2 - 3N(k + 1) \qquad (4.29)$$

where

$k =$ the number of soil types

$N = 4$, the number of census years—1880, 1890, 1900, and 1910

$R_j =$ sum of ranks for soil-type j coefficient over the four census years.

The statistic χ_r^2 is distributed approximately as chi-square with $k - 1$ degrees of freedom. The values of χ_r^2 with appropriate degrees of freedom, and their associated P-values, are listed below in table 4.5. These low P-values are sufficient to reject the null hypothesis of no rank-stability at the .05 level in eight of the ten states, and certainly do not support the null hypothesis in the other two cases. Furthermore, the largest P-value is for Texas, which provided only a pair of coefficient rankings to base the test upon, rather than the four sets of rankings in the other states. All in all, the situation here is similar to that in the case of the F-tests on the overall significance of the coefficients; the evidence is sufficient to reject the null hypothesis in most cases, and is certainly

10.   Robert V. Hogg and Allen T. Craig, *Introduction to Mathematical Statistics*, p. 178.
11.   Sidney Siegel, *Nonparametric Statistics for the Behavioral Sciences*, pp. 166–172.

TABLE 4.5   Test Statistics for Friedman Two-Way Analysis of Variance by Ranks, Group I Regressions

State	χ_r^2(d.f.)	P-value
North Carolina	χ^2 (3) = 3.90	between 0.1 and 0.5, .34 by interpolation
South Carolina	χ^2 (4) = 12.60	< .025
Georgia	χ^2 (7) = 22.17	< .005
Florida	χ^2 (3) = 9.30	< .05
Tennessee	χ^2(11) = 39.92	< .005
Alabama	χ^2 (8) = 16.07	< .05
Mississippi	χ^2 (8) = 17.07	< .05
Arkansas	χ^2 (5) = 11.43	< .05
Louisiana	χ^2 (6) = 12.64	< .05
Texas	χ^2(10) = 11.82	between 0.5 and 0.1, .35 by interpolation

The P-value is defined as the area under the appropriate χ^2 distribution to the right of the observed value of the test statistic χ_r^2:

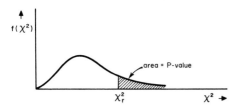

not favorable to the null hypothesis in the remainder. This preponderance of evidence suggests that indeed the soil-type categories corresponded to soils of different net fertilities, and that these differences persisted in a stable pattern over the forty-year period.

The S_i coefficients measure the "net fertility" or "net residual fertility" of the Hilgard soil types because the specification of the production function including race- and crop-associated differences may result in some differences in soil quality being measured by the coefficients of the variables B/R and H/T, not by the coefficients of the S_i. Conversely, the coefficients of B/R and H/T may be thought to measure race- and crop-associated differences *within* each of the chemically and physically distinct soil categories. Because neither the S_i variables nor the race and crop variables are likely to correspond perfectly to the soil heterogeneities, a problem arises in attempting to ascertain the relative fertilities of the different soils. Since some soil differences may be captured by the coefficients of the race and crop variables, ranking of the coefficients of the S_i will not necessarily correspond to the ranking of fertilities of the different soil types. Nevertheless, the S_i coefficients can only correspond to intrinsic fertility differences, and these coefficients are significantly different from each other and from a constant. It is therefore possible that the coefficients of B/R and H/T measure race- and crop-associated differences that exist only *within* counties (each county belonging to a different soil type). This identification problem persists throughout the subsequent discussion. Fortunately it makes little difference in what follows whether a race- or crop-associated difference represents a "global" difference or only one prevailing within counties of similar soil composition. The results simply do not allow a full resolution of the soil quality differences.

5. *Crop-associated productivity differences.* The estimated coefficient of H/T, the proportion of improved acres devoted to cotton, provides information on the relative output of cotton land compared to other improved land, ceteris paribus. Referring back to the development of (4.20), we see that the coefficient of H/T is $\frac{\beta}{c_0}(c-d)$. Since there is no way to know a priori the value of c_0, the starting point for the Taylor series expansion, there is no meaningful way to compare the magnitudes of these coefficients either across states or over time. The parameters c and d include an unknown amount of "scaling," and there is no constraint forcing the scale to be the same across states or over different census years. Hence the maximum amount of information that can be recovered from the coefficient is the sign of the difference $c-d$, and whether or not this difference is significantly different from zero. Even with these limitations, the results of the Group I regressions are unambiguous. All 38 estimated coefficients of H/T are positive. The t-statistics of these estimates are greater than 2 in 28 out of 38 cases. Clearly there was a productivity advantage associated with cotton growing.

These results are contrary to the hypothesis that overproduction of cotton was a source of poverty and agricultural distress in the South. Given the pattern of production as it actually was, cotton culture was responsible for relatively greater value of output than the alternative crops or livestock products, factor inputs being equal. To sustain the "overproduction" hypothesis, it would be required for the cotton farmers to have been able to produce *even more* output had they switched to other crops. Suppose the cotton productivity advantage were due entirely to the fact that cotton was produced on the better lands. It might have been the case that the farmers on those lands could have produced a greater value of output had they diversified. More likely, however, is the notion that land was good land partly because it was *cotton* land, that is, because it could be planted in the valuable staple.

It is not possible to test directly the association of cotton with soil fertility because the difference between parameters c and d may partly reflect a fertility difference and the coefficients of the soil-type variables S_i measure only net fertility. However, if diversification would have produced even more value of output than cotton culture, a positive association between cotton concentration and net residual fertility would be expected. If cotton were concentrated in fertile counties, and if farmers had been able to realize more output from cultivation of the alternative crops and livestock in these counties, then cotton should appear to have been concentrated in the counties of greatest net residual fertility. Cultivators of the alternative crops in the cotton counties should have been generally more productive than cultivators of the alternative crops in counties where cotton was not grown.

Instead, there appears to be no association between cotton concentration and net residual fertility. The difference between the average proportion of acres planted to cotton in the counties with greatest net residual fertility, and the average proportion of acres planted to cotton in the counties with lowest net residual fertility, is positive in 19 out of 38 possible cases, and negative in 19 out of 38 cases. (See appendix C for the details of these calculations.) That is, cotton acres were not concentrated in the counties of greatest net residual fertility as measured by the S_i coefficients. In addition, this difference in mean proportion of cotton acres between the residually "best" and "rest" of the counties as measured by the C_i is not statistically significant in any states but North Carolina, Tennessee, and Florida, none of which was an important cotton-producing state. The overproduction hypothesis would seem to require an involved and intricate justification in order to be brought into accord with the results.

A preferable explanation of the observed productivity advantage is simply that cotton was well suited for Southern conditions. The agricultural population may have accumulated special skills in cotton production over the years. Even more likely, certain Southern soils and the climate may have been ideal for cultivation of a crop in great demand. The positive values of the parameter difference $c - d$ are, in this view, nothing but a reflection of these advantages of cotton reflected in the amount of dollar output from the agricultural sector.

Clearly such an explanation implies that rational farmers would have been motivated to concentrate even more heavily in cotton production, if there were no scarcities, bottlenecks, or other limitations preventing them from doing so. There is some evidence that such a trend actually was underway, but it was weak and not universal. For example, table 4.6 shows that over the entire South the proportion of improved acres planted to cotton increased with each census from 1880 to 1910. Texas was being opened to settlement during this period, and grew tremendously in improved acres, but even more in cotton acres. When Texas is excluded the share of improved acres in cotton increased from 1880 to 1910, but fell in 1900 from its 1890 high. Disaggregating, North Caro-

TABLE 4.6   Statewide Values of H/T

State	1880	1890	1900	1910	4-Census Averages	Sign of Trend in Cotton Supply Function
North Carolina	.138	.147	.121	.145	.138	+
	9	9	9	8	9	
South Carolina	.330	.378	.359	.419	.372	+
	3	2	3	1	2	
Georgia	.319	.349	.331	.397	.349	+
	4	4	5	2	4	
Florida	.259	.198	.147	.146	.188	−
	7	7	8	9	8	
Tennessee	.085	.080	.061	.072	.075	+
	10	10	10	10	10	
Alabama	.365	.359	.370	.385	.370	+
	2	3	2	3	3	
Mississippi	.404	.421	.382	.377	.396	−
	1	1	1	4	1	
Arkansas	.290	.311	.236	.267	.276	+
	6	6	7	6	6	
Louisiana	.316	.336	.295	.181	.282	−
	5	5	6	7	5	
Texas	.172	.190	.356	.363	.270	+
	8	8	4	5	7	
Total	.244	.257	.280	.301		
Total without Texas	.264	.282	.257	.278		

The number below each state value of H/T is that state's rank in cotton concentration for the indicated census year.

lina, South Carolina, Georgia, Alabama, and Texas displayed an overall increase in proportion of improved acres in cotton, while Florida, Tennessee, Mississippi, Arkansas, and Louisiana showed a decrease. Out of 30 possible increases or decreases in this proportion from one census year to the next, it increased in 16 instances. Finally, in a subsequent chapter cotton supply functions are estimated in which the share of acres in cotton compared to total acres in all crops is the dependent variable. The supply functions cover the period 1883–1914, and include a pure trend term. The coefficient of this trend is positive in seven of the ten states. All in all, the evidence for increasing specialization in cotton is inconclusive. There was surely no overwhelming shift out of other crops into cotton.

The South's failure to specialize completely is evidence that the cotton productivity advantage was due to the location in the South of some factor which could not be increased easily. If the productivity advantage was due to the existence of good cotton-growing land in the South, then over time there would be a tendency to increase the proportion of acres devoted to cotton, in order to capture the greater returns available in cotton compared to other crops. Counteracting this tendency would be the fact that the best cotton lands would have been settled *first,* given the long-standing brisk demand for cotton and consequent profitability of the staple back even to the prewar years. Hence, as the expansion of improved acres went on, a relatively lower proportion of those lands would be suitable for cotton culture than of the lands already improved by 1880. The outcome of these two conflicting tendencies is impossible to predict, and probably accounts for the mixed behavior of the overall proportion of cotton acres over time and within each state.

It should be noted that Texas was really the only "frontier" state of the ten, and Texas shows the strongest increase in proportion of improved acres planted in cotton. It might be hypothesized that the reason for this is that Texas still contained virgin lands in 1880, and that the best cotton country had not all been settled. As Texas land was improved toward the end of the nineteenth century, the farmers responded to the strong world demand for cotton by increasing their cotton acres faster than they increased their improved acreage for other uses. This is only a conjecture, however.

To summarize, cotton displayed a sustained and unmistakable productivity advantage in the South over the period 1880–1910. The most plausible explanation of this is that cotton culture enjoyed a comparative advantage over the alternative agricultural activities during this period. Specialization in cotton was not complete, because some factors required for it (good cotton land most probably) could not be expanded easily. Cotton was King because it was profitable to the agricultural sector as a whole. The local furnishing merchants may have preferred cotton to the alternatives, but only because there was more money in it than in producing anything else. In all likelihood, independent farmers would have also favored concentration in cotton, provided they had access to land suitable for its cultivation. Again, these results say nothing about the distribution of the profits from cotton culture among the various individuals in the agricultural sector. The crop choice decision as an issue in the exercise of monopoly power by merchants will be taken up in chapter 7.

6. *Race-associated productivity differences.* In contrast to the coefficient of H/T, the coefficient of B/R displays no immediate pattern. In some cases it is positive, in others negative; sometimes the estimated difference $b - a$ is significant, sometimes not. For reasons analogous to those given regarding the $c - d$ difference, only the sign and significance of the difference $b - a$ can be determined in this model, not the absolute magnitudes of the parameters b and a. The following frequencies summarize the estimates:

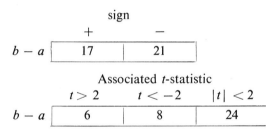

No clear productivity advantage is associated with either race over the

TABLE 4.7   Simple Correlation Coefficient between B/R and H/T

State	1880	1890	1900	1910
North Carolina	.683	.624	.562	.597
South Carolina	.049	−.0097	.0039	.107
Georgia	.633	.551	.548	.548
Florida	.665	.481	.393	.107
Tennessee	.704	.679	.684	.665
Alabama	.836	.762	.794	.818
Mississippi	.720	.762	.709	.684
Arkansas	.862	.870	.897	.797
Louisiana	.380	.415	.511	.371
Texas	.651			.274

entire South. Nevertheless, it does appear that blacks were concentrated in the most fertile counties. First of all, the proportion of blacks in the total population is positively correlated with the proportion of improved acres devoted to cotton in every state and every census year except for South Carolina in 1890. Second, the average proportion of blacks tended to be larger in the counties of greatest residual fertility (those counties having soil types with the largest C_i coefficients). The table in appendix C showing the difference in means between $\overline{B/R}$ in the "best" counties $(=\mu_B)$ and $\overline{B/R}$ in the "rest" of the counties $(=\mu_R)$ reveals the following sign frequencies (the indicated t ranges in the second table are for the t statistics associated with $\mu_B - \mu_R$):

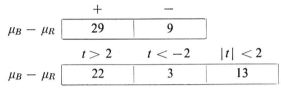

	$+$	$-$
$\mu_B - \mu_R$	29	9

	$t > 2$	$t < -2$	$\|t\| < 2$
$\mu_B - \mu_R$	22	3	13

These frequencies indicate that blacks were concentrated in the counties of greatest residual fertility.

In addition to the pattern of blacks being located in the cotton counties and in the counties of greatest residual fertility, there is an intraregional pattern in the signs of the $b - a$ coefficients. Blacks tended to be less productive than whites in the cotton belt, and more productive than whites in the border or peripheral states. This can be seen after first constructing an index of a state's concentration in cotton. The states fall into three rough groups. Mississippi, South Carolina, Ala-

TABLE 4.8 Four-Census Average Proportion of Improved Acres in Cotton, by Rank

State	Proportion of Cotton Acres
Mississippi	.396
South Carolina	.372
Alabama	.370
Georgia	.349
Louisiana	.282
Arkansas	.276
Texas	.270
Florida	.188
North Carolina	.138
Tennessee	.075

bama, and Georgia, all east of the Mississippi River, clearly showed concentration in cotton; Florida, North Carolina, and Tennessee were "peripheral" both in location and in cotton production. It is not clear whether Louisiana, Arkansas, and Texas belong to one group or the other, and these are grouped as "intermediate" states. The frequencies of the signs of $b - a$ for each of these groups of states are as follows:

East of Mississippi River Cotton States	+	−	
	3	13	Pr = .0106

Intermediate States	+	−	
	6	4	Pr = .3770

Eastern Periphery	+	−	
	8	4	Pr = .1938

Under the null hypothesis that the sign of $b - a$ is a random variable with equal probability of being positive or negative, and independent within states and over time, the one-tailed probabilities of the observed sign frequencies or ones more unbalanced are given by the cumulative binomial distribution. These probabilities are listed to the right of each frequency table. The low probabilities under the null hypothesis for the East of the Mississippi Cotton States and Periphery, combined with the different balance of signs between those two regions, are suggestive of a systematic variation in the sign of $b - a$ according to region.

A stronger test can be performed if the number of intraregional groups is decreased. On purely geographical grounds, Texas is more a peripheral state than a cotton belt state, and in addition, its average proportion of improved acres in cotton was the lowest of the intermediate states. On casual grounds a priori, it seems reasonable to group Louisiana and Arkansas with the rest of the cotton belt states. If these assignments are made, the sign pattern in a 2 × 2 contingency table is even more striking:

Region	Sign of $b - a$	
	+	−
Cotton Belt (South Carolina, Georgia, Alabama, Mississippi, Arkansas, Louisiana)	7	17
Periphery (North Carolina, Florida, Tennessee, Texas)	10	4

A Fisher Exact Probability Test can be used to test the null hypothesis that there is no systematic association between region and the sign of $b - a$.[12] The probability of observing a particular set of frequencies in a 2 × 2 table, when the marginal totals are regarded as fixed, is given by the hypergeometric distribution. The Fisher test consists of calculating the probabilities of the observed frequency distribution or one more extreme, keeping the marginal totals fixed, that is, of

7	17		6	18		5	19		4	20		3	21
10	4	or	11	3	or	12	2	or	13	1	or	14	0

This probability is

$$P = \frac{24!\ 14!\ 17!\ 21!}{38!\ \ 7!\ 17!\ 10!\ 4!} + \frac{24!\ 14!\ 17!\ 21!}{38!\ \ 6!\ 18!\ 11!\ 3!} + \frac{24!\ 14!\ 17!\ 21!}{38!\ \ 5!\ 19!\ 12!\ 2!}$$

$$+ \frac{24!\ 14!\ 17!\ 21!}{38!\ \ 4!\ 20!\ 13!\ 1!} + \frac{24!\ 14!\ 17!\ 21!}{38!\ \ 3!\ 21!\ 14!\ 0!}$$

$$= .0120 + .0017 + .0001 + .0000 + .0000, \text{ to four places}$$

$$= .0138$$

This probability value is extremely low and justifies rejection of the null hypothesis of no association between the sign of $b - a$ and region, with as low as 2 percent probability of a Type I error.

The same test performed for only those values of $b - a$ which have associated t-statistics greater than 2 yields the same result.

Region

	$t > 2$	$t < -2$	$|t| < 2$
Cotton Belt	3	8	13
Periphery	4	0	10

The probability of the significant portion of this table under the null hypothesis of no association between the sign of $b - a$ and region is given by

$$P = \frac{11!\ 4!\ 7!\ 8!}{15!\ 3!\ 8!\ 4!\ 0!} = .0256$$

which again is very low.

12. Ibid., pp. 96–104.

Individually the states conform reasonably well to this pattern. The estimate of $b - a$ is positive in a majority of the four census years in North Carolina, Tennessee, Louisiana, and Texas; it is negative in a majority of the years in South Carolina, Georgia, Florida, Alabama, Mississippi, and Arkansas. Florida is an exception to the regional pattern, but Florida was not an important cotton state. The other exception, Louisiana, belonged to the "intermediate" group of states with proportion of improved acres in cotton in the middle of the range for the ten states.

The conclusion seems inescapable. Whites appear to have been more productive overall than blacks in the cotton belt, but less productive overall than blacks in the peripheral states.

This pattern, combined with the previous results, would seem to suggest a paradox. Consider the following findings:

a. Cotton was more productive in value terms than the alternative agricultural outputs.

b. Blacks were concentrated on the cotton lands, as well as on the lands of greatest residual fertility.

c. Nevertheless, blacks appear less productive than whites in the *cotton belt,* but more productive than whites in the peripheral states.

How can these findings be reconciled? If blacks were concentrated on cotton lands, and if cotton lands tended to be more fertile than the lands devoted to other crops, why does the coefficient $b - a$ not reflect some of this locational advantage? It must be kept in mind that the parameters a and b reflect race-associated productivity differences. If blacks were concentrated on more fertile lands than whites, this advantage could just as easily appear as a positive $b - a$ value as could a black productivity advantage based on a difference in skill. The identification problem cannot be escaped; the parameters a, b, c, and d measure only productivity differences, not the *source* of the productivity differences.

Similarly, if the black/white differences were due to the "legacy of slavery" manifested in lower productivity of black workers because of deprivation in education, entrepreneurship, or initiative, why should there be a *regional* pattern to the black/white productivity difference? Did the "legacy of slavery" weigh heavier on the freedmen in the deep South than in the border states?

The results are too strong to be ignored, yet these are real problems of interpretation. In particular, the identification problem cannot be surmounted with the given specification of the production function. In order to confront this identification problem explicitly, it is possible to modify the production function to recognize the systematic association of race and crop.

5
A Modification of the Production Function

The natural generalization of the production function of the previous chapter is to allow productivity differences between members of the same race, depending on which crop is grown, as well as fertility differences for the lands devoted to each crop, depending on the race of the farmers working them. Such a production function, still of the generalized Cobb-Douglas type, is

$$\log Q = (\sum_{i=1}^{N} A_i S_i) + \alpha \log (a_1 W_1 + a_2 W_2 + b_1 B_1 + b_2 B_2)$$

$$+ \beta \log (c_1 H_1 + c_2 H_2 + d_1 J_1 + d_2 J_2) + \gamma \log K + u_o \quad (5.1)$$

where

$W_1 =$ white labor devoted to growing cotton
$W_2 =$ white labor devoted to growing alternative crops
$B_1 =$ black labor devoted to growing cotton
$B_2 =$ black labor devoted to growing alternative crops
$H_1 =$ cotton acres farmed by whites
$H_2 =$ cotton acres farmed by blacks
$J_1 =$ other improved acres farmed by whites
$J_2 =$ other improved acres farmed by blacks
$Q =$ value of output not fed to livestock
$S_i =$ the soil-type dummy variables
$K =$ agricultural capital input and
$u_o =$ a random disturbance with the same properties as the disturbance in chapter 4.

(To simplify the notation somewhat, u_o will not be carried through the subsequent derivations. This omission should not be a source of confusion.)

Next, write $W_1 + W_2 = W$; $B_1 + B_2 = B$; $H_1 + H_2 = H$; $J_1 + J_2$

$= J;$ $W + B = R$ and $H + J = T$. W, B, H, and J are all observable, that is, are reported for each county in the census.

Unfortunately, W_1, W_2, B_1, B_2, H_1, H_2, J_1, and J_2 are not observed. It probably would not be too far wrong to assume that

$$W_1 \cong (H/T)W \tag{5.2}$$

that is, the number of whites growing cotton was roughly the total number of whites times the proportion of total land in cotton, with a similar relationship holding true for the other unobservable variables. To preserve generality, however, introduce a new set of "predilection" parameters k_i, l_i, m_i, and n_i such that

$$W_1 = k_1 \frac{H}{T} W; \quad W_2 = k_2 \frac{J}{T} W; \quad B_1 = l_1 \frac{H}{T} B; \quad B_2 = l_2 \frac{J}{T} B \tag{5.3}$$

$$H_1 = m_1 \frac{W}{R} H; \quad H_2 = m_2 \frac{B}{R} H; \quad J_1 = n_1 \frac{W}{R} J; \quad J_2 = n_2 \frac{B}{R} J \tag{5.4}$$

These parameters express the "predilection" of whites to grow cotton, whites to grow alternative crops, blacks to grow cotton, etc. The predilection parameters are not intended to represent some sort of alleged psychological preference of a group for one type of farming or another. Even if such preferences did exist, it is likely that they were based on experience or specialized knowledge of the techniques of growing the different crops. The "predilections" of the different groups could also have involved locational factors leading to differential specialization. Throughout the subsequent discussion, "predilection" should be interpreted to mean nothing more nor less than the deviation of the proportion of farmers of one race who grew cotton (or the alternatives) from the proportion of total improved acres devoted to cotton (or the alternatives).

Not all the new parameters are independent. Since

$$k_1 \frac{H}{T} W + k_2 \frac{J}{T} W + l_1 \frac{H}{T} B + l_2 \frac{J}{T} B = R \tag{5.5}$$

and

$$m_1 \frac{W}{R} H + m_2 \frac{B}{R} H + n_1 \frac{W}{R} J + n_2 \frac{B}{R} J = T \tag{5.6}$$

it follows that

$$k_1 \frac{HW}{RT} + k_2 \frac{JW}{RT} + l_1 \frac{HB}{RT} + l_2 \frac{JB}{RT}$$

$$= m_1 \frac{WH}{RT} + m_2 \frac{BH}{RT} + n_1 \frac{WJ}{RT} + n_2 \frac{BJ}{RT} \tag{5.7}$$

or

$$\frac{WH}{RT}(k_1 - m_1) + \frac{WJ}{RT}(k_2 - n_1) + \frac{BH}{RT}(l_1 - m_2)$$

$$+ \frac{BJ}{RT}(l_2 - n_2) = 0 \tag{5.8}$$

The only way this expression can be equal to zero whatever the values of R, T, B, and H (remembering that these four values will determine W and J as well) is if $k_1 = m_1$, $k_2 = n_1$, $l_1 = m_2$, and $l_2 = n_2$. The production function can now be written

$$\log Q = \left(\sum_{i=1}^{N} A_i S_i \right) + \alpha \log \left(a_1 k_1 \frac{H}{T} W + a_2 k_2 \frac{J}{T} W \right.$$

$$\left. + b_1 l_1 \frac{H}{T} B + b_2 l_2 \frac{J}{T} B \right) + \beta \log \left(c_1 m_1 \frac{W}{R} H + c_2 m_2 \frac{B}{R} H \right.$$

$$\left. + d_1 n_1 \frac{W}{R} J + d_2 n_2 \frac{B}{R} J \right) + \gamma \log K \tag{5.9}$$

Obviously a_1 and k_1, a_2 and k_2—in fact all of the efficiency and predilection or fertility and predilection parameter pairs—are not separately distinguishable in this form. It remains useful to write both of them for convenience in the discussion.

Linearizing this production function in Taylor series around $a_0 k_0 = a_{10} k_{10} = a_{20} k_{20} = b_{10} l_{10} = b_{20} l_{20}$ for the labor term and $c_0 m_0 = c_{10} m_{10} = c_{20} m_{20} = d_{10} n_{10} = d_{20} n_{20}$ for the land term yields

$$\log Q = \sum_{i=1}^{N} B_i S_i + \alpha \log R + \beta \log T + \gamma \log K$$

$$+ \frac{\alpha a_1 k_1}{a_0 k_0} \frac{H}{T} \frac{W}{R} + \frac{\alpha a_2 k_2}{a_0 k_0} \frac{J}{T} \frac{W}{R} + \frac{\alpha b_1 l_1}{a_0 k_0} \frac{H}{T} \frac{B}{R} + \frac{\alpha b_2 l_2}{a_0 k_0} \frac{J}{T} \frac{B}{R}$$

$$+ \frac{\beta c_1 m_1}{c_0 m_0} \frac{W}{R} \frac{H}{T} + \frac{\beta c_2 m_2}{c_0 m_0} \frac{B}{R} \frac{H}{T} + \frac{\beta d_1 n_1}{c_0 m_0} \frac{W}{R} \frac{J}{T}$$

$$+ \frac{\beta d_2 n_2}{c_0 m_0} \frac{B}{R} \frac{J}{T} \tag{5.10}$$

Consider only the last three lines of this expression. If dependencies are eliminated, the last three lines become

$$\frac{\alpha a_1 k_1}{a_0 k_0} \frac{H}{T} \frac{(R - B)}{R} + \frac{\alpha a_2 k_2}{a_0 k_0} \frac{(T - H)}{T} \frac{(R - B)}{R} + \frac{\alpha b_1 l_1}{a_0 k_0} \frac{H}{T} \frac{B}{R}$$

$$+ \frac{\alpha b_2 l_2}{a_0 k_0} \frac{(T - H)}{T} \frac{B}{R} + \frac{\beta c_1 m_1}{c_0 m_0} \frac{(R - B)}{R} \frac{H}{T} + \frac{\beta c_2 m_2}{c_0 m_0} \frac{B}{R} \frac{H}{T}$$

$$+ \frac{\beta d_1 n_1}{c_0 m_0} \frac{(R - B)}{R} \frac{(T - H)}{T} + \frac{\beta d_2 n_2}{c_0 m_0} \frac{B}{R} \frac{(T - H)}{T}$$

$$= \left[\frac{\alpha a_2 k_2}{a_0 k_0} + \frac{\beta d_1 n_1}{c_0 m_0} \right] + \left[-\frac{\alpha a_2 k_2}{a_0 k_0} + \frac{\alpha b_2 l_2}{a_0 k_0} - \frac{\beta d_1 n_1}{c_0 m_0} + \frac{\beta d_2 n_2}{c_0 m_0} \right] \frac{B}{R}$$

$$+ \left[\frac{\alpha a_1 k_1}{a_0 k_0} - \frac{\alpha a_2 k_2}{a_0 k_0} + \frac{\beta c_1 m_1}{c_0 m_0} - \frac{\beta d_1 n_1}{c_0 m_0} \right] \frac{H}{T}$$

$$+ \left[-\frac{\alpha a_1 k_1}{a_0 k_0} + \frac{\alpha a_2 k_2}{a_0 k_0} + \frac{\alpha b_1 l_1}{a_0 k_0} - \frac{\alpha b_2 l_2}{a_0 k_0} - \frac{\beta c_1 m_1}{c_0 m_0} + \frac{\beta c_2 m_2}{c_0 m_0} \right.$$

$$+ \left. \frac{\beta d_1 n_1}{c_0 m_0} - \frac{\beta d_2 n_2}{c_0 m_0} \right] \frac{B}{R} \frac{H}{T} \tag{5.11}$$

Collecting terms and recalling that $k_1 = m_1$, $k_2 = n_1$, $l_1 = m_2$, and $l_2 = n_2$ yields the final form of the equation to be estimated:

$$\log Q = \sum_{i=1}^{N} C_i S_i + \alpha \log R + \beta \log T + \gamma \log K + \eta \frac{B}{R} + \theta \frac{H}{T}$$

$$+ \phi \frac{B}{R} \cdot \frac{H}{T} \tag{5.12}$$

with

$$\eta = \frac{\alpha}{a_0 k_0} (b_2 l_2 - a_2 k_2) + \frac{\beta}{c_0 m_0} (d_2 l_2 - d_1 k_2) \tag{5.13}$$

$$\theta = \frac{\alpha}{a_0 k_0} (a_1 k_1 - a_2 k_2) + \frac{\beta}{c_0 m_0} (c_1 k_1 - d_1 k_2) \tag{5.14}$$

$$\phi = \frac{\alpha}{a_0 k_0} (a_2 k_2 - a_1 k_1 + b_1 l_1 - b_2 l_2) \tag{5.15}$$

$$+ \frac{\beta}{c_0 m_0} (c_2 l_1 - c_1 k_1 + d_1 k_2 - d_2 l_2)$$

The estimates of the parameters of (5.12) will be referred to as the Group II results.

The first thing to observe about these results is that the conclusions based on the Group I results regarding fit and reasonableness, exploitation of labor, returns to scale, and the overall significance of the soil-type coefficients are substantially unchanged. There are only three estimated land, labor, and capital elasticities outside the zero-to-one range, and these occur in the same states and years as in the Group I regressions. Both the individual production function estimates and the Variant I and Variant II intercensus averages are favorable to the competition hypothesis as opposed to the exploitation hypothesis. At the

TABLE 5.1   The Group II Regressions

All definitions of the tabled entries are the same as for the Group I results, except for the coefficients of B/R, H/T and $(B/R)(H/T)$, which are different because of the change in specification.

The four tables following the main regression results are analogous to the corresponding tables of the previous chapter. The Variant I and Variant II intercensus averages and their associated approximate standard errors were computed on the same assumptions as the Group I averages, omitting from the Variant II averages all estimated elasticities arising in a state and year with an estimated input elasticity outside the zero-to-one range. The max P-values just below the F statistics in the test of overall significance of the C_i compared to a single constant are maximum values for the area under the appropriate F distribution to the right of the calculated F value. The approximate P-values of the χ^2 test statistics for the Friedman Two-Way Analysis of Variance by Ranks were calculated by linear interpolation.

TABLE 5.1   (Continued) North Carolina

Estimated Parameter	1880	1890	1900	1910
α	.281(.0781)	.480(.0922)	.324(.0643)	.347(.0688)
	[3.601]	[5.209]	[5.038]	[5.037]
β	.413(.0641)	.335(.111)	.504(.0780)	.515(.0730)
	[6.439]	[3.010]	[6.467]	[7.053]
γ	.291(.0657)	.243(.114)	.155(.0882)	.144(.0843)
	[4.427]	[2.132]	[1.759]	[1.706]
η	1.109(.212)	.779(.253)	.361(.179)	.531(.190)
	[5.227]	[3.084]	[2.019]	[2.791]
θ	2.758(.533)	1.733(.605)	.264(.459)	1.550(.418)
	[5.173]	[2.864]	[.576]	[3.705]
ϕ	−3.434(1.089)	−3.280(1.390)	.591(1.106)	−.633(.969)
	[−3.155]	[−2.360]	[.535]	[−.653]
ν	.985(.0444)	1.058(.0581)	.983(.0378)	1.006(.0409)
	[−.338]	[.998]	[−.450]	[.147]
R^2	.965	.924	.958	.966
$F(m, n)$	252.3(9,83)	115.2(9,85)	215.1(9,85)	254.7(9,81)
obs	93	95	95	91
$u^{*\prime}u^*$	2.12914	3.51969	1.68395	1.85582
$u'u$	2.37030	3.82705	1.94015	2.15589

TABLE 5.1 (Continued) South Carolina—Group II

Estimated Parameter	1880	1890	1900	1910
α	.224(.153) [1.465]	.416(.196) [2.116]	.203(.139) [1.466]	-.187(.140) [-1.336]
β	.267(.131) [2.031]	.517(.192) [2.694]	.533(.146) [3.660]	.645(.111) [5.819]
γ	.359(.101) [3.546]	.148(.163) [.909]	.230(.153) [1.502]	.448(.0932) [4.804]
η	1.061(.542) [1.956]	-.227(.845) [-.269]	-.507(.379) [-1.336]	-.491(.440) [-1.116]
θ	2.415(.950) [2.541]	.905(1.400) [.647]	1.140(.714) [1.598]	1.746(.665) [2.623]
ϕ	-2.475(1.588) [-1.559]	.0458(2.423) [.0189]	.211(1.121) [.188]	.0984(1.131) [.0870]
ν	.850(.0801) [-1.873]	1.081(.114) [.711]	.966(.0566) [-.601]	—
R^2	.971	.936	.965	.978
$F(m, n)$	69.02(10,21)	33.71(10,23)	74.94(10,27)	124.6(10,28)
obs	32	34	38	39
$u^{*\prime}u^{*}$	.256867	.592387	.239759	.186573
$u'u$	.347336	.923953	.597322	.783471

TABLE 5.1   (Continued) Georgia—Group II

Estimated Parameter	1880	1890	1900	1910
α	.546(.0600)	.440(.0591)	.433(.0694)	.168(.0467)
	[9.093]	[7.443]	[6.245]	[3.604]
β	.351(.0584)	.407(.0590)	.402(.0715)	.504(.0405)
	[6.016]	[6.897]	[5.626]	[12.463]
γ	.201(.0481)	.171(.0496)	.211(.0721)	.351(.0454)
	[4.172]	[3.452]	[2.921]	[7.725]
η	.818(.183)	.390(.202)	−.0969(.165)	−.235(.142)
	[4.472]	[1.933]	[−.587]	[−1.654]
θ	2.670(.323)	1.771(.326)	1.133(.275)	1.081(.200)
	[8.257]	[5.434]	[4.123]	[5.398]
ϕ	−3.424(.588)	−.535(.584)	−.532(.491)	.483(.357)
	[−5.820]	[−.917]	[−1.085]	[1.353]
ν	1.098(.0326)	1.018(.0319)	1.046(.0283)	1.023(.0209)
	[3.006]	[.564]	[1.625]	[1.100]
R^2	.969	.970	.969	.986
$F(m, n)$	289.7(13,120)	292.4(13,118)	278.7(13,117)	705.6(13,127)
obs	134	132	131	141
$u^{*\prime}u^*$	2.40091	2.25981	1.65847	1.16542
$u'u$	2.72415	2.42691	1.96734	2.34433

TABLE 5.1 (Continued) Florida—Group II

Estimated Parameter	1880	1890	1900	1910
α	.376(.127) [2.949]	.521(.160) [3.253]	.165(.162) [1.016]	−.346(.231) [−1.500]
β	.335(.117) [2.870]	.111(.184) [.604]	.0551(.102) [.541]	.178(.149) [1.200]
γ	.203(.0787) [2.572]	.488(.144) [3.395]	.755(.119) [6.368]	1.138(.165) [6.877]
η	−.691(.508) [−1.359]	−.00444(.640) [−.00694]	−.898(.439) [−2.048]	.561(.701) [.800]
θ	1.473(1.030) [1.430]	.731(1.302) [.561]	.809(1.461) [.554]	2.709(1.930) [1.403]
ϕ	1.865(2.261) [.825]	−.913(3.316) [−.275]	3.896(2.974) [1.310]	−3.900(4.288) [−.910]
ν	.914(.0941) [−.914]	1.120(.0966) [1.242]	.975(.0920) [−.272]	—
R^2	.956	.919	.939	.917
$F(m, n)$	67.95(9,28)	42.71(9,34)	52.62(9,31)	40.64(9,33)
obs	38	44	41	43
$u^{*\prime}u^*$	1.58713	4.36052	1.73744	3.74942
$u'u$	2.27680	4.90785	2.18361	4.80509

TABLE 5.1   (Continued) Tennessee—Group II

Estimated Parameter	1880	1890	1900	1910
α	.398(.113) [3.515]	−.0324(.0646) [−.502]	.247(.0631) [3.917]	.238(.0618) [3.856]
β	.154(.125) [1.228]	.661(.0860) [7.694]	.511(.0727) [7.030]	.471(.0819) [5.745]
γ	.406(.0954) [4.261]	.337(.0702) [4.801]	.226(.0704) [3.216]	.312(.0754) [4.138]
η	.341(.260) [1.310]	.284(.205) [1.390]	−.0695(.212) [−.329]	.298(.253) [1.181]
θ	1.549(.529) [2.928]	.520(.356) [1.460]	.691(.453) [1.525]	.565(.453) [1.249]
ϕ	−.469(1.076) [−.436]	−.0869(.790) [−.110]	−.567(.919) [−.617]	−1.077(.977) [−1.102]
ν	.958(.0361) [−1.163]	—	.984(.0283) [−.565]	1.021(.0305) [.689]
R^2	.978	.984	.980	.980
$F(m, n)$	196.7(17,74)	264.8(17,74)	208.8(17,74)	210.1(17,73)
obs	92	92	92	91
$u^{*\prime}u^*$	1.34395	.792645	.834327	1.02892
$u'u$	2.32767	1.44126	1.19037	2.35344

TABLE 5.1   (Continued) Alabama—Group II

Estimated Parameter	1880	1890	1900	1910
α	.765(.123) [6.199]	.431(.101) [4.272]	.443(.0829) [5.339]	.197(.0627) [3.142]
β	.306(.101) [3.048]	.537(.0652) [8.244]	.540(.0592) [9.121]	.623(.0615) [10.124]
γ	.0282(.0825) [.342]	.161(.0713) [2.258]	.109(.0839) [1.295]	.263(.0612) [4.295]
η	.597(.401) [1.488]	-.0229(.309) [-.0741]	-.302(.209) [-1.443]	-.352(.192) [-1.830]
θ	2.447(.509) [4.807]	1.176(.393) [2.993]	1.007(.295) [3.412]	1.284(.340) [3.778]
ϕ	-2.314(1.049) [-2.206]	-.264(.830) [-.318]	.0511(.542) [.0943]	-.296(.513) [-.577]
ν	1.099(.0663) [1.493]	1.129(.0619) [2.084]	1.092(.0434) [2.120]	1.083(.0407) [2.039]
R^2	.976	.982	.984	.979
$F(m, n)$	144.7(14,50)	182.6(14,48)	210.8(14,48)	157.2(14,48)
obs	65	63	63	63
$u^{*\prime}u^*$	.928375	.522949	.250216	.208466
$u'u$	1.06562	1.47770	.324767	.309178

TABLE 5.1 (Continued) Mississippi—Group II

Estimated Parameter	1880	1890	1900	1910
α	.223(.105) [2.115]	.112(.110) [1.020]	.356(.0529) [6.738]	.230(.0600) [3.834]
β	.286(.0998) [2.862]	.679(.117) [5.824]	.338(.0475) [7.106]	.414(.0605) [6.840]
γ	.530(.0819) [6.480]	.148(.107) [1.384]	.301(.0666) [4.528]	.350(.0773) [4.532]
η	.103(.533) [.193]	.531(.380) [1.399]	−.156(.195) [−.798]	−.491(.248) [−1.979]
θ	2.219(.836) [2.654]	.750(.623) [1.204]	.917(.332) [2.759]	1.220(.370) [3.299]
ϕ	−.898(1.233) [−.729]	.147(.865) [.170]	.0975(.506) [.193]	.503(.638) [.788]
ν	1.039(.0713) [.547]	.939(.0651) [−.937]	.995(.0288) [−.174]	.994(.0338) [−.178]
R^2	.959	.960	.989	.990
$F(m, n)$	98.78(14,59)	102.4(14,60)	368.6(14,60)	422.0(14,62)
obs	74	75	75	77
$u^{*\prime}u^*$	2.87837	2.07385	.355703	.486083
$u'u$	3.10534	3.81516	.616220	1.05682

TABLE 5.1   (Continued) Arkansas—Group II

Estimated Parameter	1880	1890	1900	1910
α	.455(.0882) [5.157]	.307(.106) [2.908]	.273(.104) [2.628]	.239(.103) [2.319]
β	.286(.0864) [3.310]	.312(.0917) [3.401]	.131(.113) [1.162]	.377(.0891) [4.237]
γ	.290(.0642) [4.526]	.309(.0665) [4.649]	.644(.104) [6.176]	.366(.0756) [4.835]
η	.572(.243) [2.355]	.281(.203) [1.385]	-.0161(.249) [-.0648]	-.454(.246) [-1.847]
θ	2.620(.200) [13.102]	1.410(.175) [8.040]	1.264(.198) [6.385]	2.000(.189) [10.585]
ϕ	-2.261(.492) [-4.593]	-.233(.344) [-.678]	-.157(.524) [-.299]	-.168(.506) [-.332]
ν	1.031(.0324) [.957]	.928(.0335) [-2.149]	1.048(.0363) [1.322]	.982(.0468) [-.385]
R^2	.968	.970	.964	.968
$F(m, n)$	169.2(11,61)	184.6(11,62)	152.0(11,62)	164.3(11,60)
obs	73	74	74	72
$u^{*\prime}u^*$	.624040	.591193	.569125	.627102
$u'u$	.953464	.672615	.627412	.926825

TABLE 5.1   (Continued) Louisiana—Group II

Estimated Parameter	1880	1890	1900	1910
α	.300(.160) [1.873]	.394(.113) [3.489]	.314(.110) [2.855]	.210(.109) [1.933]
β	.342(.139) [2.456]	.228(.0829) [2.744]	.446(.107) [4.155]	.273(.0928) [2.945]
γ	.403(.0923) [4.370]	.375(.0623) [6.014]	.185(.0543) [3.413]	.448(.0834) [5.372]
η	1.477(.522) [2.828]	.752(.384) [1.957]	−.260(.344) [−.755]	−.323(.424) [−.762]
θ	2.069(.830) [2.493]	.744(.542) [1.372]	−.406(.548) [−.740]	.523(.819) [.638]
ϕ	−2.352(1.096) [−2.146]	−.249(.826) [−.301]	1.796(.896) [2.003]	1.388(1.607) [.864]
ν	1.045(.0935) [.481]	.997(.0751) [−.0399]	.945(.0650) [−.846]	.931(.0727) [−.949]
R^2	.924	.927	.930	.925
$F(m, n)$	44.65(12,44)	47.85(12,45)	50.03(12,45)	45.34(12,44)
obs	57	58	58	57
$u^{*\prime}u^*$	3.46765	2.16334	1.60968	1.74941
$u'u$	4.31804	2.59331	2:28250	2.29340

TABLE 5.1   (Continued) Texas—Group II

Estimated Parameter	1880	1910
α	.154(.0764) [2.012]	.236(.0917) [2.575]
β	.315(.0685) [4.593]	.686(.0782) [8.777]
γ	.676(.0949) [7.118]	.200(.106) [1.881]
η	.979(1.224) [.800]	1.859(.929) [2.001]
θ	3.133(1.913) [1.637]	2.442(.410) [5.956]
ϕ	−2.302(4.384) [−.525]	−3.579(2.121) [−1.687]
ν	1.145(.0831) [1.745]	1.122(.0605) [2.017]
R^2	.954	.912
$F(m, n)$	267.6(16,205)	140.6(16,217)
obs	222	234
$u^{*\prime}u^*$	274.829	71.6597
$u'u$	288.995	75.6390

TABLE 5.1   (Continued) North Carolina—Group II

Estimated Parameter	1880	1890	1900	1910
C_1	1.945(.389)	1.532(.523)	2.654(.352)	2.767(.383)
	4 [4.997]	4 [2.931]	4 [7.538]	2 [7.225]
C_2	2.083(.418)	1.622(.565)	2.841(.380)	2.876(.412)
	3 [4.987]	3 [2.871]	1 [7.485]	1 [6.981]
C_3	2.141(.425)	1.721(.567)	2.718(.380)	2.697(.408)
	2 [5.034]	2 [3.036]	3 [7.150]	3 [6.605]
C_4	2.182(.409)	1.823(.547)	2.750(.366)	2.581(.388)
	1 [5.337]	1 [3.334]	2 [7.505]	4 [6.659]

TABLE 5.1   (Continued) South Carolina—Group II

Estimated Parameter	1880	1890	1900	1910
C_1	3.455(.742)	1.730(1.066)	3.020(.555)	3.308(.533)
	5 [4.655]	4 [1.623]	3 [5.438]	2 [6.211]
C_2	3.508(.731)	2.210(.983)	3.286(.562)	3.474(.563)
	3 [4.799]	1 [2.248]	1 [5.848]	1 [6.173]
C_3	3.649(.786)	1.935(1.125)	3.109(.572)	3.267(.530)
	1 [4.640]	2 [1.720]	2 [5.431]	3 [6.168]
C_4	3.465(.751)	1.684(1.080)	2.870(.561)	3.147(.528)
	4 [4.612]	5 [1.560]	4 [5.113]	4 [5.959]
C_5	3.582(.783)	1.741(1.132)	2.778(.563)	2.917(.529)
	2 [4.572]	3 [1.538]	5 [4.932]	5 [5.518]

TABLE 5.1   (Continued) Georgia—Group II

Estimated Parameter	1880	1890	1900	1910
C_1	1.411(.314)	2.101(.316)	2.1242(.289)	2.162(.225)
	4 [4.487]	6 [6.657]	7 [7.344]	7 [9.620]
C_2	1.446(.298)	2.041(.304)	2.1239(.278)	2.153(.212)
	2 [4.858]	8 [6.714]	8 [7.646]	8 [10.162]
C_3	1.385(.313)	2.132(.318)	2.130(.288)	2.273(.222)
	6 [4.424]	4 [6.696]	6 [7.404]	6 [10.241]
C_4	1.406(.311)	2.119(.315)	2.241(.296)	2.375(.226)
	5 [4.527]	5 [6.726]	3 [7.571]	5 [10.505]
C_5	1.074(.329)	2.147(.335)	2.173(.316)	2.379(.241)
	8 [3.260]	3 [6.411]	5 [6.877]	4 [9.877]
C_6	1.374(.304)	2.100(.312)	2.212(.296)	2.439(.227)
	7 [4.513]	7 [6.734]	4 [7.480]	2 [10.751]
C_7	1.450(.290)	2.242(.300)	2.281(.284)	2.521(.221)
	1 [5.000]	1 [7.470]	2 [8.040]	1 [11.402]
C_8	1.427(.280)	2.149(.289)	2.296(.265)	2.402(.211)
	3 [5.088]	2 [7.426]	1 [8.675]	3 [11.362]

TABLE 5.1   (Continued) Florida—Group II

Estimated Parameter	1880	1890	1900	1910
C_1	3.166(.843)	1.742(.951)	2.501(.852)	1.378(1.267)
	4 [3.757]	2 [1.831]	4 [2.936]	4 [1.088]
C_2	3.185(.767)	1.502(.860)	2.737(.823)	1.727(1.212)
	3 [4.151]	4 [1.746]	3 [3.324]	2 [1.425]
C_3	3.431(.810)	1.714(.902)	2.815(.823)	1.483(1.183)
	2 [4.236]	3 [1.899]	2 [3.422]	3 [1.253]
C_4	3.707(.712)	2.030(.761)	3.129(.743)	2.115(1.111)
	1 [5.210]	1 [2.668]	1 [4.213]	1 [1.904]

TABLE 5.1   (Continued) Tennessee—Group II

Estimated Parameter	1880	1890	1900	1910
C_1	3.573(.389)	2.332(.287)	3.002(.335)	3.170(.373)
	1 [9.173]	1 [8.140]	1 [8.952]	1 [8.500]
C_2	3.084(.382)	2.152(.280)	2.856(.329)	2.700(.343)
	2 [8.074]	3 [7.682]	2 [8.669]	2 [7.870]
C_3	3.028(.392)	2.024(.280)	2.766(.324)	2.439(.336)
	4 [7.727]	5 [7.219]	3 [8.541]	4 [7.255]
C_4	2.957(.395)	2.070(.275)	2.651(.314)	2.362(.325)
	5 [7.491]	4 [7.522]	6 [8.447]	6 [7.258]
C_5	3.063(.360)	2.164(.259)	2.739(.292)	2.449(.307)
	3 [8.499]	2 [8.344]	4 [9.381]	3 [7.982]
C_6	2.957(.366)	2.022(.259)	2.642(.295)	2.372(.308)
	6 [8.079]	6 [7.807]	7 [8.967]	5 [7.690]
C_7	2.753(.381)	1.878(.269)	2.616(.302)	2.298(.318)
	9 [7.235]	11 [6.986]	8 [8.650]	8 [7.238]
C_8	2.918(.387)	1.888(.274)	2.709(.305)	2.301(.317)
	7 [7.542]	10 [6.902]	5 [8.890]	7 [7.251]
C_9	2.662(.345)	1.893(.246)	2.546(.278)	2.234(.291)
	12 [7.708]	9 [7.706]	10 [9.172]	9 [7.672]
C_{10}	2.760(.368)	1.947(.258)	2.542(.289)	2.125(.306)
	8 [7.502]	8 [7.538]	11 [8.794]	11 [6.947]
C_{11}	2.744(.383)	1.819(.268)	2.536(.300)	2.050(.315)
	10 [7.172]	12 [6.788]	12 [8.442]	12 [6.508]
C_{12}	2.719(.377)	1.949(.266)	2.548(.301)	2.152(.318)
	11 [7.216]	7 [7.316]	9 [8.471]	10 [6.773]

TABLE 5.1   (Continued) Alabama—Group II

Estimated Parameter	1880	1890	1900	1910
C_1	1.665(.630)	1.139(.571)	1.734(.428)	1.664(.425)
	2 [2.641]	5 [1.994]	3 [4.054]	4 [3.917]
C_2	1.638(.631)	1.073(.586)	1.652(.439)	1.583(.429)
	4 [2.594]	6 [1.832]	6 [3.765]	7 [3.688]
C_3	1.533(.617)	.949(.568)	1.621(.432)	1.562(.433)
	9 [2.483]	8 [1.672]	9 [3.754]	9 [3.611]
C_4	1.641(.637)	.779(.573)	1.632(.436)	1.610(.434)
	3 [2.578]	9 [1.360]	8 [3.744]	6 [3.705]
C_5	1.721(.617)	1.062(.558)	1.737(.422)	1.574(.418)
	1 [2.790]	7 [1.902]	1 [4.119]	8 [3.762]
C_6	1.540(.604)	1.171(.562)	1.693(.429)	1.668(.421)
	8 [2.549]	3 [2.084]	5 [3.950]	3 [3.960]
C_7	1.585(.612)	1.269(.567)	1.718(.431)	1.709(.424)
	7 [2.589]	2 [2.236]	4 [3.989]	2 [4.031]
C_8	1.608(.632)	1.144(.575)	1.644(.427)	1.630(.424)
	5 [2.545]	4 [1.991]	7 [3.849]	5 [3.844]
C_9	1.601(.545)	1.361(.534)	1.735(.414)	1.733(.415)
	6 [2.937]	1 [2.547]	2 [4.188]	1 [4.176]

TABLE 5.1   (Continued) Mississippi—Group II

Estimated Parameter	1880	1890	1900	1910
C_1	1.626(.729)	2.266(.620)	2.678(.277)	2.555(.339)
	8 [2.231]	9 [3.653]	9 [9.677]	8 [7.542]
C_2	1.632(.742)	2.336(.630)	2.7380(.281)	2.627(.340)
	7 [2.200]	8 [3.707]	5 [9.744]	6 [7.722]
C_3	1.764(.730)	2.389(.622)	2.7382(.275)	2.769(.333)
	2 [2.415]	7 [3.842]	4 [9.964]	2 [8.323]
C_4	1.701(.715)	2.650(.616)	2.720(.274)	2.602(.336)
	5 [2.380]	4 [4.306]	7 [9.920]	7 [7.754]
C_5	1.590(.698)	2.641(.598)	2.789(.272)	2.418(.328)
	9 [2.276]	5 [4.415]	2 [10.269]	9 [7.371]
C_6	1.723(.674)	2.800(.579)	2.972(.271)	2.934(.342)
	4 [2.557]	2 [4.836]	1 [10.964]	1 [8.577]
C_7	1.733(.716)	2.531(.618)	2.707(.274)	2.726(.333)
	3 [2.421]	6 [4.095]	8 [9.894]	5 [8.177]
C_8	1.696(.711)	2.753(.617)	2.747(.276)	2.739(.338)
	6 [2.385]	3 [4.459]	3 [9.957]	4 [8.113]
C_9	1.857(.611)	2.936(.573)	2.730(.268)	2.769(.323)
	1 [3.038]	1 [5.128]	6 [10.198]	3 [8.585]

TABLE 5.1   (Continued) Arkansas—Group II

Estimated Parameter	1880	1890	1900	1910
C_1	2.224(.312)	3.174(.292)	1.858(.344)	2.849(.436)
	1 [7.129]	1 [10.869]	1 [5.404]	1 [6.537]
C_2	2.178(.313)	3.044(.297)	1.767(.348)	2.735(.430)
	2 [6.968]	4 [10.252]	2 [5.071]	2 [6.356]
C_3	1.961(.334)	3.078(.316)	1.691(.368)	2.457(.443)
	6 [5.878]	2 [9.734]	6 [4.592]	6 [5.551]
C_4	1.981(.320)	2.998(.303)	1.703(.351)	2.601(.427)
	5 [6.186]	6 [9.911]	4 [4.854]	3 [6.096]
C_5	2.034(.324)	3.049(.306)	1.702(.355)	2.533(.428)
	4 [6.269]	3 [9.948]	5 [4.799]	5 [5.922]
C_6	2.125(.314)	3.038(.300)	1.744(.347)	2.591(.413)
	3 [6.771]	5 [10.132]	3 [5.030]	4 [6.278]

TABLE 5.1   (Continued) Louisiana—Group II

Estimated Parameter	1880	1890	1900	1910
C_1	1.434(.872)	2.500(.765)	3.430(.667)	3.068(.704)
	3 [1.644]	2 [3.267]	4 [5.144]	6 [4.359]
C_2	1.551(.907)	2.670(.803)	3.605(.692)	3.296(.759)
	2 [1.711]	1 [3.327]	2 [5.211]	3 [4.344]
C_3	1.682(.885)	2.475(.765)	3.859(.657)	3.399(.722)
	1 [1.902]	5 [3.235]	1 [5.877]	1 [4.704]
C_4	1.176(.898)	2.478(.797)	3.302(.697)	2.799(.749)
	6 [1.310]	4 [3.110]	6 [4.740]	7 [3.735]
C_5	1.118(.939)	2.345(.826)	3.499(.729)	3.354(.795)
	7 [1.191]	7 [2.838]	3 [4.799]	2 [4.219]
C_6	1.263(.860)	2.495(.761)	3.319(.665)	3.245(.722)
	4 [1.469]	3 [3.279]	5 [4.994]	4 [4.496]
C_7	1.230(.909)	2.379(.812)	3.283(.722)	3.210(.757)
	5 [1.353]	6 [2.931]	7 [4.545]	5 [4.238]

TABLE 5.1   (Continued) Texas—Group II

Estimated Parameter	1880	1910
C_1	−.196(.834) 6 [−.235]	.370(.626) 4 [.591]
C_2	.198(.853) 2 [.232]	1.019(.669) 1 [1.524]
C_3	−.184(.929) 5 [−.199]	.348(.695) 5 [.501]
C_4	−.314(.832) 8 [−.378]	.154(.629) 8 [.245]
C_5	−.336(.841) 9 [−.399]	.150(.638) 9 [.234]
C_6	−.184(.756) 4 [−.243]	.129(.631) 10 [.205]
C_7	−.0882(1.010) 3 [−.0874]	.448(.716) 3 [.625]
C_8	−.339(1.187) 10 [−.285]	.160(.800) 7 [.200]
C_9	−.373(1.109) 11 [−.336]	.849(.767) 2 [1.107]
C_{10}	.497(.575) 1 [.865]	.128(.590) 11 [.216]
C_{11}	−.272(.241) 7 [−1.127]	.165(.577) 6 [.286]

5 percent level of significance, only four of the individual estimates of the labor elasticity would justify rejection of the hypothesis that the true elasticity was in the [1/4,1/2] range, and three of these four cases involve an estimated input elasticity less than zero. No state produced more than one such extreme estimated value of α. As with the Group I estimates, the intercensus averages are all less than 1/2. Again, if the production function estimates are robust, the exploitation hypothesis may be rejected on the basis of either the individual single-census results or the intercensus averages. For the entire South, the overall Variant II average labor elasticity is .319, compared with .309 for the Group I average, and the average estimates of β and γ are not very different, either.

TABLE 5.2 Group II Intercensus Averages, Variant I

State	α	β	γ
North Carolina	.358(.0383)	.442(.0417)	.208(.0449)
South Carolina	.164(.0794)	.491(.0740)	.296(.0656)
Georgia	.397(.0297)	.416(.0292)	.234(.0274)
Florida	.179(.0871)	.170(.0708)	.646(.0653)
Tennessee	.213(.0393)	.449(.0468)	.320(.0393)
Alabama	.459(.0475)	.501(.0368)	.140(.0377)
Mississippi	.230(.0430)	.429(.0430)	.332(.0423)
Arkansas	.319(.0503)	.277(.0478)	.402(.0396)
Louisiana	.305(.0624)	.322(.0538)	.353(.0373)
Texas	.195(.0596)	.500(.0520)	.438(.0712)
Overall unweighted average	.282	.400	.337

TABLE 5.3 Group II Intercensus Averages, Variant II

State	α	β	γ
North Carolina	.358(.0383)	.442(.0417)	.208(.0449)
South Carolina	.281(.0949)	.439(.0915)	.246(.0818)
Georgia	.397(.0297)	.416(.0292)	.234(.0274)
Florida	.354(.0869)	.167(.0802)	.482(.0676)
Tennessee	.294(.0478)	.379(.0554)	.315(.0468)
Alabama	.459(.0475)	.501(.0368)	.140(.0377)
Mississippi	.230(.0430)	.429(.0430)	.332(.0423)
Arkansas	.319(.0503)	.277(.0478)	.402(.0396)
Louisiana	.305(.0624)	.322(.0538)	.353(.0373)
Texas	.195(.0596)	.500(.0520)	.438(.0712)
Overall unweighted average	.319	.387	.315

If the three production function estimates containing a negative input elasticity are omitted, the results are consistent with constant returns to scale. Nineteen of 35 estimated returns to scale parameters are greater than one; 16 are less than one. The t-statistic for testing the hypothesis that $\nu = 1$ is larger than 2 in absolute value in only 6 cases. Again, the coefficients of the soil-type dummy variables are usually significant as a group compared to a single constant term, and the four F values taken together are significant at the 5 percent level for every state but Texas. The values of the test statistic for the Friedman Two-Way Analysis of Variance by Ranks also show that the Hilgard categories still represent stable levels of residual fertility in this specification.

TABLE 5.4 F-test on Overall Significance of Coeffiicents of S_i as Compared to a Single Constant—Group II Regressions

State	1880	1890	1900	1910
North Carolina	3.134(3,83)	2.474(3,85)	4.311(3,85)	4.366(3,81)
max. P-value	.05	.10	.01	.01
South Carolina	1.849(4,21)	3.218(4,23)	10.067(4,27)	22.395(4,28)
	.25	.05	.001	.001
Georgia	2.308(7,120)	1.246(7,118)	3.113(7,117)	18.353(7,127)
	.05	.50	.01	.001
Florida	4.056(3,28)	1.423(3,34)	2.654(3,31)	3.097(3,33)
	.025	.50	.10	.05
Tennessee	4.924(11,74)	5.505(11,74)	2.871(11,74)	8.543(11,73)
	.001	.001	.005	.001
Alabama	.924(8,50)	10.954(8,48)	1.788(8,48)	2.899(8,48)
	.51*	.001	.25	.025
Mississippi	.582(8,59)	6.297(8,60)	5.493(8,60)	9.100(8,62)
	.90	.001	.001	.001
Arkansas	6.440(5,61)	1.708(5,62)	1.270(5,62)	5.735(5,60)
	.001	.25	.50	.001
Louisiana	1.798(6,44)	1.491(6,45)	3.135(6,45)	2.280(6,44)
	.25	.25	.025	.10
Texas	1.057(10,205)			1.205(10,217)
	.50			.50

*By interpolation

TABLE 5.5 Test Statistics for Friedman Two-Way Analysis of Variance by Ranks, Group II Regressions

State	χ_r^2(d.f.)	Approximate P-value (by interpolation)
North Carolina	$\chi^2(3) = 3.60$	.32
South Carolina	$\chi_2(4) = 9.00$	.06
Georgia	$\chi^2(7) = 15.58$	.03
Florida	$\chi^2(3) = 8.40$	.04
Tennessee	$\chi^2(11) = 39.77$	< .01
Alabama	$\chi^2(8) = 14.73$	.07
Mississippi	$\chi^2(8) = 17.87$	.02
Arkansas	$\chi^2(5) = 12.71$	.03
Louisiana	$\chi^2(6) = 12.64$	.05
Texas	$\chi^2(10) = 9.45$	.49

It is interesting to note that the max P-values for the F-test on the overall significance of the S_i coefficients are generally larger in the Group II regressions than in the Group I regressions. This is a reflection of the fact that the "interaction" term $(B/R) \cdot (H/T)$ in (5.12) joins the B/R and H/T terms in measuring some elements of soil fertility, leaving fewer intrinsic soil quality differences to be expressed by the C_i coefficients than in the Group I specification. As before, the Hilgard variables seem to have little meaning in the case of Texas.

At first glance, the inclusion of the interaction term $(B/R) \cdot (H/T)$ does not seem to accomplish very much. Only two of the t-statistics associated with its coefficient are greater than two in absolute value after 1880, and the pattern in the sign of its coefficient is not obviously or immediately apparent. But compared to equation (4.20) of chapter 4, inclusion of the more detailed labor and land variables of (5.1) and their associated productivity and predilection parameters changes the meaning of the coefficients of B/R and H/T in equation (5.12) in a subtle way. As a result of the Taylor series linearization of the production function, the coefficients of B/R, H/T and $(B/R) \cdot (H/T)$ are given by the expressions (5.13)–(5.15). Examination of these expressions shows that the simple interpretation, for example, of the coefficient of B/R as indicating the relative productivities of blacks and whites, is no longer possible. A certain amount of further analysis is required to untangle the meaning of estimates of η, θ, and ϕ, but it will be shown that these three coefficients contain a significantly greater amount of information than the coefficients of B/R and H/T in the specification of chapter 4. Even though the individual estimates of ϕ are not particularly significant, taken as a group and in conjunction with the estimates of the other two coefficients η and θ, they permit recovery of information on the relative productivities of white cotton farmers, black cotton farmers, black farmers of other crops and white farmers of other crops. The new specification (5.12) resolves the productivities of the various groups in post-bellum Southern agriculture in greater detail than was possible with the specification of chapter 4. This additional information justifies the additional effort that must be undertaken to interpret the estimates properly.

Consider the expressions

$$\eta = \frac{\alpha}{a_0 k_0} (b_2 l_2 - a_2 k_2) + \frac{\beta}{c_0 m_0} (d_2 l_2 - d_1 k_2) \tag{5.16}$$

$$\theta = \frac{\alpha}{a_0 k_0} (a_1 k_1 - a_2 k_2) + \frac{\beta}{c_0 m_0} (c_1 k_1 - d_1 k_2) \tag{5.17}$$

$$\eta + \phi = \frac{\alpha}{a_0 k_0} (b_1 l_1 - a_1 k_1) + \frac{\beta}{c_0 m_0} (c_2 l_1 - c_1 k_1) \tag{5.18}$$

$$\theta + \phi = \frac{\alpha}{a_0 k_0} (b_1 l_1 - b_2 l_2) + \frac{\beta}{c_0 m_0} (c_2 l_1 - d_2 l_2) \tag{5.19}$$

As with the Group I results, the unknown Taylor series expansion point prevents recovery of any information from estimates of these expressions except for their signs and statistical significance as compared to zero. Nevertheless, even this minimal amount of information is important.

It is possible for η to be greater than zero if $b_2 > a_2$, $d_2 > d_1$, $l_2 > k_2$ or some combination of these inequalities. In other words, $\eta > 0$ if black noncotton growers were more productive than white noncotton growers, if the noncotton lands farmed by blacks were more productive than the noncotton lands farmed by whites, or if blacks had a greater predilection for noncotton farming than whites. It should be noted that even the more detailed specification of (5.12) does not avoid the fundamental identification problem: there is no way to distinguish between the efficiency of farmers and the fertility of the land they worked, from knowledge of total productivity alone.

However, there are strong grounds a priori for believing that blacks had a predilection for cotton farming and not for the alternative types of farming. According to the definitions of the parameters,

$$l_2/k_2 = [(B_2/B) \cdot (T/J)]/[(W_2/W) \cdot (T/J)]$$
$$= (B_2/B)/(W_2/W) = (B_2/W_2)/(B/W) \tag{5.20}$$

That is, $l_2 > k_2$ if the proportion of blacks who farmed crops other than cotton was greater than the proportion of whites who farmed crops other than cotton, or alternatively if the ratio of black noncotton farmers to white noncotton farmers was greater than the ratio of blacks to whites in the population as a whole. Strictly speaking, these farmers may have grown both cotton and alternative crops, in which case the interpretation of $l_2 > k_2$ would be that the proportion of black labor time devoted to crops other than cotton was greater than the corresponding proportion of white labor time. However, all indications point to *blacks* being more heavily committed to cotton culture. The positive correlation between the proportion of blacks in the rural population and the proportion of improved acres planted to cotton was pointed out in the previous chapter. Also, many contemporary observers commented on the close and pervasive association of blacks with cotton culture.[1] Of course, in light of the findings of chapter 2, such testimony is at best only suggestive. Nevertheless, it does confirm the expectation a priori, supported by the concentration of blacks in the cotton counties, of a black predilection for cotton.

This will prove to be important in interpreting the results. The predilection of blacks for cotton ($k_2 > l_2$) tends to make $\eta < 0$, working against the potential rankings of efficiency and fertility ($b_2 > a_2$ and $d_2 > d_1$) tending to make $\eta > 0$. If the preponderance of the estimates indicate $\eta > 0$, the conclusion that black noncotton farmers were in general more productive than white noncotton farmers would be strengthened by the supposition a priori that $k_2 > l_2$.

Similarly, $\theta > 0$ if $a_1 > a_2$, $c_1 > d_1$, $k_1 > k_2$, or some combination of these inequalities. If the definition of the predilection parameters is recalled, it is clear that

$$k_1/k_2 = [(W_1/W) \cdot (T/H)]/[(W_2/W) \cdot (T/J)]$$
$$= (W_1/W_2) \cdot (H/J) \tag{5.21}$$

1. U. S. Industrial Commission, *Reports of the Industrial Commission*, vol. 15: *Reports of the Industrial Commission on Immigration and on Education*, p. 553. See also chapter 2, third section, *passim*, particularly the testimony before the Industrial Commission (note 192), "A Georgia Plantation" (note 201), and *Southern Cultivator* (note 209).

Hence $k_1 > k_2$ if the ratio of white labor time devoted to cotton over white labor time devoted to alternative crops was greater than the ratio of cotton land to noncotton land overall. Thus, $\theta > 0$ if white cotton farmers were more efficient than white noncotton farmers, if the cotton lands farmed by whites were more fertile than the noncotton lands farmed by whites, or if whites had a predilection for *cotton*.

In the same way, $\eta + \phi < 0$ if $a_1 > b_1$, $c_1 > c_2$, $k_1 > l_1$ or some combination of the inequalities. In words, $\eta + \phi < 0$ if white cotton farmers were more skillful than black cotton farmers, if the cotton lands farmed by whites were more fertile than the cotton lands farmed by blacks, or if whites had a predilection for cotton as compared to blacks.

Finally, $\theta + \phi > 0$ if $b_1 > b_2$, $c_2 > d_2$, $l_1 > l_2$, or some combination of the inequalities. That is, $\theta + \phi > 0$ if blacks were more productive in cotton than in alternative crops and livestock, if cotton land worked by blacks was more fertile than other land worked by blacks, or if blacks had a predilection for cotton. It will be seen momentarily that only in this case does blacks' predilection for cotton incline the sign of the coefficient or coefficient combination in the direction actually observed.

Table 5.6 presents the signs of expressions (5.16)–(5.19) based on the estimated values of the coefficients η, θ, and ϕ. It is possible also to compute the probability that the observed sign frequency or a more unbalanced frequency would occur given the null hypothesis that the distribution of the signs is random, with plus and minus equally likely.[2] The observed frequencies and associated probabilities are as follows:

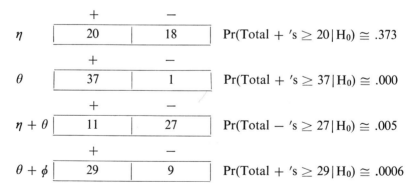

	+	−	
η	20	18	$\Pr(\text{Total} + \text{'s} \geq 20\,|\,H_0) \cong .373$
θ	37	1	$\Pr(\text{Total} + \text{'s} \geq 37\,|\,H_0) \cong .000$
$\eta + \theta$	11	27	$\Pr(\text{Total} - \text{'s} \geq 27\,|\,H_0) \cong .005$
$\theta + \phi$	29	9	$\Pr(\text{Total} + \text{'s} \geq 29\,|\,H_0) \cong .0006$

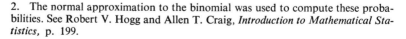

2. The normal approximation to the binomial was used to compute these probabilities. See Robert V. Hogg and Allen T. Craig, *Introduction to Mathematical Statistics*, p. 199.

TABLE 5.6 Estimated Coefficient Sign Pattern—Group II Regressions

State			1880	1890	1900	1910
North Carolina	η	θ	+ +	+ +	+ +	+ +
	$\eta+\phi$		−	−	+	−
	$\theta+\phi$		−	−	+	+
South Carolina			+ +	− +	− +	− +
			−	−	−	−
			−	+	+	+
Georgia			+ +	+ +	− +	− +
			−	−	−	+
			−	+	+	+
Florida			− +	− +	− +	+ +
			+	−	+	−
			+	−	+	−
Tennessee			+ +	+ +	− +	+ +
			−	·+	−	−
			+	+	+	−
Alabama			+ +	− +	− +	− +
			−	−	−	−
			+	+	+	+
Mississippi			+ +	+ +	− +	− +
			−	+	−	+
			+	+	+	+
Arkansas			+ +	+ +	− +	− +
			−	+	−	−
			+	+	+	+
Louisiana			+ +	+ +	− −	− +
			−	+	+	+
			−	+	+	+
Texas			+ +			+ +
			−			−
			+			−

Clearly, the null hypothesis can be rejected in the last three cases and cannot be rejected in the first case, regardless of whether a one-tailed test or a two-tailed test is performed. (The two-tailed P-values of the observed sign frequencies or ones more extreme would simply be double the one-tailed P-values.) Write WC for white cotton farming, BC for black cotton farming, WN for white noncotton farming, and BN for black noncotton farming. Let the relation $>$ stand for "is more productive than," $\approx$ for "is roughly as productive as," and $\geq$ for "is at least as productive as." Then for the South as a whole over the entire period, these sign frequencies lead to the conclusion that

$$WC > BC > BN \approx WN \qquad\qquad (5.22)$$

Also, the predilection of blacks for cotton reinforces the strength of this relation in every case but that of $BC > BN$. Nevertheless, the preponderance of positive values of $\theta + \phi$ strongly suggests the indicated direction of the relation. It might be safest to say that $BC \geq BN$, however. It should be noted that in all cases of comparisons across race, the blacks' predilection for cotton would tend to incline the productivity relation in the direction opposite from that indicated by the actual sign frequencies, strengthening the conclusions regarding productivity comparisons across race.

Expression (5.22) is a striking relationship, with white farmers occupying both the top and the bottom of the agricultural productivity ladder. But before discussing it in more detail, it should be observed that basically the *same* relation between the productivities of the different groups of farmers holds when the subregions of the South are considered separately:

South Carolina + Georgia + Alabama + Mississippi + Arkansas + Louisiana ("Cotton Belt")

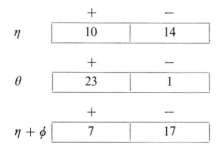

	+	−
$\theta + \phi$	21	3

North Carolina + Florida + Tennessee + Texas (Periphery + Texas)

	+	−
η	10	4

	+	−
θ	14	0

	+	−
$\eta + \phi$	4	10

	+	−
$\theta + \phi$	8	6

The η coefficient displays a majority of positive signs in one case and a majority of negative signs in the other. The other three expressions show the same sign majorities as for the South as a whole, even though the majority of positive signs of $\theta + \phi$ is slim for the peripheral states. The probabilities of these sign frequencies or frequencies more extreme are not as small as for the South as a whole, which is to be expected for the smaller samples. Of greater importance than the exact binomial probabilities are the similarities of the implied productivity rankings of the different groups of farmers within the subregions to the ranking over the entire South:

$$\text{WC} > \text{BC} > \text{BN} \approx \text{WN} \quad \text{for the South as a whole, 1880–1910} \quad (5.23)$$

$$\text{WC} > \text{BC} > \text{BN} \approx \text{WN} \quad \text{for the cotton belt} \quad (5.24)$$

$$\text{WC} > \text{BC} \approx \text{BN} > \text{WN} \quad \text{for the periphery} \quad (5.25)$$

It should be kept in mind that relations (5.24) and (5.25) are not as firmly established as (5.23) because they are based on smaller samples of coefficients. It is also interesting that the same pattern of sign majorities holds in the case of $\theta, \eta + \phi$ and $\theta + \phi$ for the three subregions consisting of South Carolina + Georgia + Alabama + Mississippi, Arkansas + Louisiana + Texas, and North Carolina + Florida + Tennessee. For η one group has a majority of positive signs, one group a majority of negative signs, and one group only the slightest majority of positive signs. Again, the small sample sizes make exact probability calculations less valuable than for the South overall:

South Carolina + Georgia + Alabama + Mississippi (cotton states east of the Mississippi River)

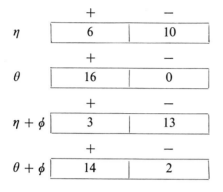

	+	−
η	6	10

	+	−
θ	16	0

	+	−
$\eta + \phi$	3	13

	+	−
$\theta + \phi$	14	2

Arkansas + Louisiana + Texas (the "intermediate" states)

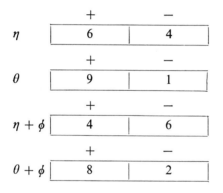

	+	−
η	6	4

	+	−
θ	9	1

	+	−
$\eta + \phi$	4	6

	+	−
$\theta + \phi$	8	2

North Carolina + Florida + Tennessee (the eastern "periphery")

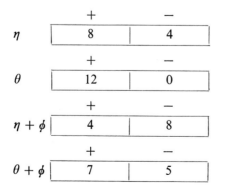

	+	−
η	8	4

	+	−
θ	12	0

	+	−
$\eta + \phi$	4	8

	+	−
$\theta + \phi$	7	5

Another interesting way of looking at these results is to examine the sign frequncey pattern over time. If the period is divided into two sub-periods, 1880–1890 and 1900–1910, the sign frequency patterns are:

1880–1890   1900–1910

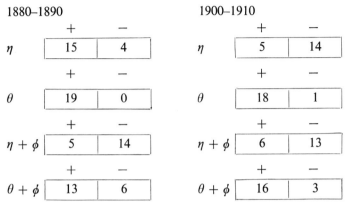

These frequencies seem to indicate that the relative positions of white and black noncotton farmers reversed themselves over the period—while all the other relationships remained the same, and were the same as for the South as a whole. The relations could be written:

$$WC > BC > BN \approx WN \qquad 1880\text{–}1910, \text{ the entire period} \qquad (5.26)$$

$$WC > BC > BN > WN \qquad 1880\text{–}1890 \qquad (5.27)$$

$$WC > BC > BN < WN \qquad \text{and } WC > WN \quad 1900\text{–}1910 \qquad (5.28)$$

The white noncotton farmers' position improved in the latter subperiod. White cotton growers remained more productive than white noncotton growers ($\theta > 0$) in both subperiods, and therefore there is no way of assessing the relative productivities of white noncotton and black cotton farmers in the 1900–1910 subperiod. Again, because of the small size of the samples for the subperiods, the productivity rankings (5.27) and (5.28) cannot be considered as firmly established as the overall aggregate productivity rankings for the South as a whole.

Since the Group II regressions include a set of soil-type dummy variables for each state, the productivity rankings discussed up to this point may apply only within counties of similar soil composition. This is all that is necessary to sustain the interpretations that will be proposed in the next chapter, but to test the sensitivity of the rankings to the soil quality "control" represented by the dummy variables, the sign frequencies of η, θ, $\eta + \phi$, and $\theta + \phi$ were computed for a set of regressions identical to (5.12) except that a single constant was substituted for the S_i:

All Southern states, 1880–1910

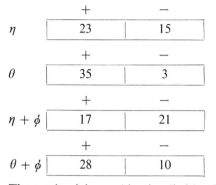

η	+	−
	23	15

θ	+	−
	35	3

$\eta + \phi$	+	−
	17	21

$\theta + \phi$	+	−
	28	10

The productivity ranking implied by these frequencies is

$$\text{WC} \approx \text{BC} > \text{BN} > \text{WN} \qquad (5.29)$$

which is identical to the ranking when the soil types are included, except that the relative position of the whites compared to the blacks is weakened. Given the concentration of blacks in counties of high residual fertility, this is precisely what should be expected. When the soil-type dummy variables are omitted, some of the association across soil types between blacks and land quality is captured by the race variables. The overall ranking of the different groups is unchanged, however, with cotton superior to alternative crops and whites occupying the extreme ends of the productivity scale. This indicates that the productivity ranking is generally valid both within the different soil-type categories and across those categories as well. Within groups of counties belonging to the same Hilgard soil classifications the advantage of white cotton growers compared to their black counterparts is strong while the advantage of black noncotton farmers compared to white noncotton farmers largely disappears.

It should be emphasized that the rather involved discussion of the meaning of the coefficients η, θ, and ϕ is necessary for a proper interpretation of the Group II estimates. Suppose that equation (5.12) had been proposed without deriving it as an approximation to the basic specification (5.1), and that its coefficients were estimated and interpreted without benefit of the preceding analysis of the meaning of the coefficients. The economic significance of the coefficient ϕ of the interaction term would be difficult enough to determine, since a variable such as $(B/R) \cdot (H/T)$ has no immediately obvious economic interpretation in the logarithmic transformation of a Cobb-Douglas production function. But even the coefficients of B/R and H/T could not be interpreted as simply indicating the relative productivities of blacks and whites or cotton land and other improved land in production, *because of the presence of the interaction term* $(B/R) \cdot (H/T)$ *in the regressions.* These difficulties would render any "naive" interpretation of the estimated coefficients of the three ratio terms highly suspect.

On the other hand, the procedure followed in the text is logical and unambiguous. The initial specification of the production function (5.1) is intuitively plausible and in the spirit of the requirements for Southern agricultural production functions set forth at the outset of chapter 4. Equation (5.12) was derived mathematically, by Taylor series approximation, from (5.1) after the introduction of predilection parameters to eliminate the unobservable input variables. Because of this, the economic meaning of the estimated coefficients of the ratio terms is determined by the meaning of the productivity and predilection parameters in the original specification. No ad hoc theorizing is required to interpret the results, because the estimates contain information on the relative magnitudes of the well-defined productivity parameters of (5.1). As has been pointed out earlier, the gain in resolution of the relative productivities of the different groups of farmers is well worth the extra care that must be taken to interpret the Group II results properly. The technique employed in this chapter may be applicable in other situations where the relative productivities of different groups or activities are being determined, and such future applications should provide additional examples of its usefulness.

This concludes the presentation of the main empirical findings of the production function estimations. However, in order to place these results in the context of the hypotheses under investigation, it is necessary first to suggest a plausible sequence of actual historical events which accounts for the observed productivity differences. This will be the task of the next chapter.

6
Interpretation of the Results: The Land Occupancy and Ownership Hypothesis

The results of the Group II estimates suggest a hypothesis which is consistent with all the statistical evidence presented so far, and which resolves the apparent paradoxes of the Group I results as well. This explanation rests on the following three conjectures:

1. *Before the Civil War, the large plantations occupied most of the best cotton land.* The big slaveholders were able to capture this land because their ownership of slaves conferred on them a profit advantage derived from the exploitation of their slave labor. Some small white yeoman farmers and a certain number of whites with a few slaves also owned fertile cotton lands, however. The worst lands were occupied almost entirely by whites who did not own slaves or whites who owned only a relatively small number of slaves.

2. *After the war and emancipation, the different population groups remained largely where they had lived before the war.* There may have been mobility of individual blacks from plantation to plantation, but the blacks as a whole continued to work for former slaveholders as sharecroppers or tenants. Similarly, the prewar "poor whites" continued to occupy the least fertile lands of each state.

3. *When cotton plantations were divided into smaller operating units after the war, whites tended to be located on the best of these lands.* For example, if a plantation owner was forced himself to undertake farming in the period of postwar destitution, he would pick for his own use the best acres of the plantation. Similarly, noninheriting sons, relatives, former overseers, or other whites would have the choice of rental plots over freedmen. If plantations were driven onto the distressed sales market, whites would have a better opportunity to buy the best sections of the plantation, since the blacks emerged from slavery with no capital and no credit. The same division of cotton lands would be expected of small ex-slaveholders.

A man who had owned one slave might hire the former slave as a tenant, but he would himself work the best acres of his small farm. In short, there was a general tendency for whites to gain control of the better cotton lands as the unsettled agricultural situation returned to equilibrium after the war.

These three propositions imply a pattern of land occupancy that explains all the results of the Group II regressions. White cotton farmers were the most productive group because they occupied the best land. Blacks followed in productivity, since they had initially been located on the best lands, and as a group remained concentrated in the fertile cotton belt. The poor whites, whose land could not support cotton culture, had the lowest overall productivity because of the poor quality of the land they occupied. The main determinant of any group's overall productivity was the fertility of the land its members worked.

In addition to being consistent with the Group II results, this land occupancy and ownership hypothesis (hereafter referred to as the LOOH) accounts for the Group I findings and apparent paradoxes. Concentration of the blacks on the old plantation lands accounts for the uniform correlation of the percentage of blacks in the total rural population and proportion of improved acres in cotton, as well as the location of the blacks on lands of greatest residual fertility, without requiring that the blacks occupied the very best of the available lands within counties of a given soil type. Similarly, the LOOH explains why whites would appear to be more productive than blacks in the cotton belt, and less productive than blacks on the periphery. There were relatively few cotton-farming whites in the peripheral states, compared to large numbers of whites growing other agricultural products, simply because of the scarcity of cotton land in those states. On the other hand, the blacks in those states were concentrated in the cotton counties, even if they did not occupy the prime cotton lands after the war. The relatively large number of low-productivity whites growing other crops would tend to lower the overall white productivity level in the border states as compared with the overall black productivity level, leading to the apparent finding that blacks were more productive than whites in those states. Conversely, in the cotton belt, more land was available for cotton, so that a relatively larger proportion of the white population was engaged in high-productivity cotton culture. Blacks in some instances were relegated to the second-best cotton lands, possibly even to plantation lands not suited for cotton. Thus, in the cotton belt, overall white productivity appears greater than overall black productivity in the Group I regressions.

The fact that the intraregional difference in overall productivities disappears in the Group II specification is strong evidence for the correctness of that specification. The Group II model captures all the race- and crop-associated productivity differences found by the Group I model, while eliminating the paradoxes which seem to be generated by the Group I model. The LOOH is consistent with *both* sets of results.

The Group II regressions maintain the previous finding that a productivity advantage was associated with cotton. The LOOH would indicate that the source of this advantage was in the peculiar suitability of certain Southern lands for cotton culture, but does not require this. In any case, the overproduction hypothesis fares as badly under the specification of the Group II model as under the specification of the Group I model.

In addition, these results create insurmountable problems for any simple legacy of slavery hypothesis. If differences in "human capital" were the source of productivity differentials, and if the blacks as a group emerged to freedom deficient in education, entrepreneurship, and farming trade skills, how can the position of white farmers not growing cotton on the *bottom* of the productivity ladder be explained? The estimates show that white cotton farmers were most productive, white grain farmers least productive; and they show substantial productivity differences between *black* cotton farmers and black grain farmers as well. Blacks as a group were simply not less productive than whites as a group.

Similarly, how could the "legacy of slavery" explain the Group I regional differences? One possible indicator of human capital differences might be different literacy levels among blacks and whites, but examination of the census reports on literacy is sufficient to indicate that these differences had no pronounced regional component, though literacy levels did vary with race and over time. Except for 1880, the whites as well as the blacks were, if anything, more literate in the periphery, though the statistical significance of the difference in regional literacy levels is impossible to ascertain.[1] In any case, if literacy was any measure of productivity-raising human capital, whites should have been more productive than blacks *everywhere,* not only in the cotton belt.

An argument could be made that the freedmen had actually learned

---

1. These census reports are summarized for the ten Southern states in table 6.1. The percentages were computed from United States Census Office, *Twelfth Census, 1900,* vol. 2: *Population,* part 2, pp. ciii–cv; and United States Bureau of the Census, *Thirteenth Census, 1910,* vol. 1: *Population,* pp. 1204–1205, 1230. The category of "Blacks" in table 6.1 includes Indians, Chinese, and Japanese, who were a negligible part of the "colored" population of the Southern states in these years.

TABLE 6.1 Percentage of Population Ten Years of Age and Over Recorded as Illiterate

States	1880	1890	1900	1910
Blacks				
South Carolina, Georgia, Alabama, Mississippi, Arkansas, Louisiana	78.8	65.4	53.2	38.1
North Carolina, Florida, Tennessee, Texas	74.7	55.3	42.1	27.6
Native Whites				
South Carolina, Georgia, Alabama, Mississippi, Arkansas, Louisiana	22.5	17.0	12.8	8.8
North Carolina, Florida, Tennessee, Texas	24.1	15.4	11.8	7.6

more about farming during their servitude than was known by the poor whites of the backwoods. The high productivity of the white cotton farmers would be attributed, in this view, to the knowledgeability of this group, drawn as it was from former planters, overseers, yeoman cotton farmers, and small slaveholders. Because of the now-familiar identification problem, there is no way to reject this possibility on the basis of the productivity evidence. However, such localization of productivity differences would be so different from the simple "legacy of slavery" idea that it would require a totally different description and rationale.

Another advantage of the LOOH is that it corresponds to the competitive model of income distribution based on factor ownership. The absence of exploitation in the factor markets, combined with the estimates of the input elasticities of the agricultural production functions (with the competitive output shares they imply) makes it clear that the degree of capital and land ownership was a crucial determinant of a farmer's income. The actual or imputed wage rate, which depended on the marginal product of labor, was important in determining the farmer's income; but farm ownership was equally important, since the competitive land share was comparable to the competitive labor share of output. Thus a white corn farmer might be less productive than a black cotton farmer because he worked poorer land, yet still receive a higher income due to his ownership of that poor land. Even relatively infertile land was a valuable asset.

Wages may have been equalized between the different counties of each state, but this is not required for the LOOH or for any of the results established so far. (Production function aggregation requires that the wages, rents, and capital costs be the same from farm to farm *within* counties—see chapter 3—but not that these factor prices be the same across counties.) The results indicate that the factors were paid according to the value of their marginal products, but this does not imply equalization of factor prices everywhere. It only means that the extent of the area over which competition equalized factor prices was at least as large as the county. If total productivity differences were due to soil fertility differences, as is the case under the LOOH, these differences would be reflected as differential rents accruing to the landowners, or possibly as higher wages earned by the fortunate residents of the more fertile cotton-growing counties, if there was not enough trade or factor mobility to equalize wage rates between counties. Indeed, incomplete equalization of factor prices across counties may have been a source of variation in the factor ratios, thus contributing to the feasibility of estimating the production functions by ordinary least squares. Determination of the extent of the areas over which competition equalized factor prices is an interesting problem for future research, but it will not be pursued here.

Since the blacks were emancipated without capital or land, even poor whites who owned their own land after the war probably had better opportunity to obtain good land as time went on than did landless blacks. This would help account for the ultimate location of the whites on the better lands (as postulated by the LOOH). Furthermore, natural abilities being distributed equally in the white and black populations, the "head start" enjoyed by the whites in factor ownership could account for the reversal in the productivities of black and white noncotton farmers between the beginning and the end of the period. Since the whites started the postbellum period with more resources, they could have begun to displace blacks on the better lands over the years. This is only conjecture, however. If black-white productivity differences were due to the legacy of slavery, it seems that these differences would have been greater the nearer in time to emancipation, so that if any productivity reversal were to take place, the blacks would be in their worst position *soon* after the Civil War. An explanation of the productivity reversal based on human capital could be constructed, but it would have to be far more complicated than any simple slavery-induced disability.

A further advantage of the LOOH is that it is possible to find support for it in the historical literature and in the narrative evidence from the period. As should be amply clear from chapter 2, such evidence is neither necessary nor sufficient for the LOOH or any other hypothesis. Nevertheless, it is encouraging to find scattered examples of exactly the kind of land occupancy and ownership patterns required for the LOOH.

To begin with, there appears to be a consensus among both historians and contemporary observers that the slave plantations were located on the best lands prior to the Civil War. Roger Shugg, who collected information on the fertility of Louisiana lands in documenting the history of economic conflicts in Louisiana, found that

in few parts of the world has there been deposited so much alluvial soil as in Louisiana. . . . The black and brown clay is so prodigally fertile that it yields more cotton and sugar than other Southern soil. . . . *
Such rich land could be profitably exploited only by rich planters. It early brought prices beyond the reach of newcomers without plenty of capital. Indeed, none but the wealthy could afford to cultivate, much less to buy, these river bottoms.**[2]

Shugg also saw the link between the advantages of slaveholding and control of these premium lands.

Nonslaveholders were depressed and excluded from the plantation system not only because they failed to secure good land, but also because they gradually lost the ability to buy Negroes . . . .
. . . Since nonslaveholding farmers were unable to operate on a large scale and with cheap labor, they could not specialize in profitable staples such as cotton and sugar, nor cultivate land especially valuable for their production.
A host of farmers were therefore expelled from fertile regions by the expanding plantation system.* The best soil was needed for commercial agriculture, and planters were able to command it at a premium because of the profit derived from slavery.** Yeomen and nonslaveholders had no choice but to move westward or retreat to sandy patches in the woods and narrow margins along the swamps and bayous.***[3]

2.   Roger W. Shugg, *Origins of Class Struggle in Louisiana: A Social History of White Farmers and Laborers During Slavery and After, 1840–1875*, pp. 4–5. Shugg's footnotes in this passage are:
* *U.S. Census, 1860, Preliminary Report*, 200–1. Shugg asserts in the footnote that "After 1870 the black, waxy prairie of Texas rivaled Mississippi alluvium; since 1900 the boll weevil has hurt both regions."
** U. B. Phillips, "Plantations with Slave Labor and Free," *A.H.R.*, XXX (July 1925), 746.
3.   Shugg, *Origins of Class Struggle*, pp. 86, 94–95. Shugg's sources for the latter passage are:
* F. L. Olmsted, *A Journey in the Back Country* (London: 1860), 306–7.
** L. C. Gray, "Economic Efficiency and Competitive Advantages of Slavery under the Plantation System," *Agricultural History*, IV (April 1930), 41.

Nevertheless, Shugg reports that even in the leading cotton and sugar parishes before the war, 1/3 to 1/2 of the farmers owned fewer than six slaves, indicating that relatively small farms existed alongside the large plantations before the war.[4] Shugg's findings are corroborated by another historian of Louisiana:

> The great bulk of Louisiana's poor, white, rural population lived outside of the wealth-laden valleys. The small farmers' land was usually in sections of the state where the soil was thin and sandy or where it was difficult to use the steamboats which carried agricultural produce to New Orleans and returned with imported supplies. It is true that there were some small farms in the alluvial valleys, but their aggregate value and production was negligible when compared with that of the neighboring plantations.[5]

There is no reason to believe that Louisiana was atypical in this regard.

Enoch Banks, the economist, found roughly the same situation in Georgia prior to the war.

> The region in which farms worked by their proprietors tended to prevail more than elsewhere was outside the region characterized by large possessions of lands and slaves. Moreover, such farms prevailed in the rugged region of the north and the pine flats of the south, each of which was relatively uninviting from the economic point of view. . . . It was, therefore, in the cotton and rice sections that the slavery plantation system predominated. Even here, however, it must be remembered, the small farm existed side by side with the large plantation.[6]

Banks also stated that some of the less aggressive whites who were reluctant to become pioneers became "in a few cases, tenants on the poorer parts of the large plantations."[7] This assessment of the prewar patterns of landownership was shared by so unlikely a source as the *Presbyterian Banner* of Pittsburgh, which saw in the gradual takeover of the best Southern lands by slaveholders the origin of the late nineteenth-century poverty and ignorance of the Southern mountain whites:

*** Olmsted, *A Journey in the Back Country,* 310; *The Cotton Kingdom,* II (New York: 1861), 44; F. Lieber, *Slavery, Plantations and the Yeomanry* (New York: 1863), 5.

4. Shugg, *Origins of Class Struggle,* p. 26. His calculation is based on *U.S. Census, 1860, Agriculture,* p. 230.

5. William E. Highsmith, "Louisiana Landholding During War and Reconstruction," *The Louisiana Historical Quarterly* 38, no. 1 (January 1955): 39.

6. Enoch M. Banks, *The Economics of Land Tenure in Georgia,* Studies in History, Economics and Public Law, vol. 23, no. 1, p. 24.

7. Ibid., p. 82.

In 1792 Whitney invented the cotton gin. Cotton lands became more valuable; slaves did the work. The non-slaveholders could not find employment, either as artisans or as field hands. Those that were embarrassed and trying to hold their lands had to sell out; and thus an increased number had to betake themselves to the mountains. . . .There were no schools in the mountains. There were few church privileges. . . . Each succeeding generation was more illiterate than the preceding one. Idleness, hunting and poor soil, with their isolation, absence of schools, and churches without an educated ministry, have produced that condition of thriftlessness and poverty in which they are now found. . . .

. . ."The present condition of these people is directly traceable to slavery; for, in making the slave the planter's blacksmith, carpenter, wheelwright, and man-of-all-work, slavery shut every avenue of honest employment against the working white man and drove him to the mountains or the barren sandhills."[8]

It should be noted that this passage contains a mixture of "human capital" and "land occupancy" explanations of the low productivity of the mountain whites.

Ulrich Phillips observed that as late as the 1920s,

everywhere east of Texas the best cotton districts are peopled by a majority of Negroes today, because within the space of threescore years and seven from the invention of the gin, planters had carried slaves in predominant numbers to all these districts and had maintained market inducements causing slave traders to supplement the effects of their own migration. In the same period they placed the American cotton belt in an unchallenged primacy in the world's production of the staple.[9]

In the same article, Phillips remarked:

Now no one who could pay any price for farm land would dally with the pine barrens [poor soil] before the introduction of commercial fertilizers. Certainly the planters avoided them with one accord. At the other extreme, the alluvial tracts were occupied by planters from the beginning, with little participation by farmers—partly because the problem of flood control put a premium upon large-scale undertakings.[10]

Modern economic historians have also concluded that the most fertile

8. A Scotch-Irishman [pseud.], *The Mountain Whites of the South* (Pittsburgh, Pa.: James McMillan, printer, 1893), pp. 14–15. The quoted passage is attributed to J. R. Gilmore (n.p., n.d.). *The Mountain Whites of the South* is a collection of articles reprinted from the *Presbyterian Banner* of Pittsburgh, Pa., with a letter from Rev. John Hall of New York, to the *Banner*.
9. Ulrich B. Phillips, "Plantations with Slave Labor and Free," *Agricultural History* 12, no. 1 (January 1938): 85.
10. Ibid., p.86.

lands were in the hands of the large planters before the war. According to William Parker,

> not superior physical efficiency, but the power of a larger capital, expanding in fixed channels and exploiting labor at a lower level of existence, permitted the plantation to take the best land and most of the cotton market from the family-sized farm.[11]

Gavin Wright, in his exhaustive empirical study of the concentration of wealth and landholding in the antebellum South, reports among other conclusions "that farm value was significantly more concentrated than improved acreage in the cotton South, suggesting that the planters not only held more land, but also more valuable land than their small-farm neighbors."[12]

More pertinent to the LOOH are accounts of what happened to the pattern of land occupancy and ownership after the Civil War. The evidence for the LOOH is of three types:

1. Evidence that after the war many "poor whites" remained on lands relatively inferior to the old plantation cotton lands.
2. Evidence that blacks as a group remained largely where they had been located before the war, on the lands of the old plantations.
3. Evidence that some plantation lands, particularly the better lands, came under the control of whites.

Both direct and indirect evidence for all three of these propositions can be found.

A. B. Hart portrayed the condition of the various groups after the war in exactly the same terms as could have been applied prior to 1860. In fact, Hart implicitly subscribed to the theory that whites who did not own slaves suffered a competitive disadvantage against slaveholders, and thus were driven to the hills in the prewar years. That is where they stayed, so after the war the "mountaineers" of the South occupied "the most sterile of 'upright' and stony farms, farms the very sight of which would make an Indiana farmer sick with nervous prostration."[13] Hart went on to say:

> The Mountain Whites ought not to be confused with the Poor Whites of the lowlands. Although there are many similarities of origin and life,

11. William N. Parker, "The Slave Plantation in American Agriculture," in *Essays in American Economic History,* ed. A. W. Coats and Ross M. Robertson, p. 134.
12. Gavin Wright, " 'Economic Democracy' and the Concentration of Agricultural Wealth in the Cotton South, 1850–1860," in *The Structure of the Cotton Economy of the Antebellum South,* ed. William Parker, p. 84.
13. Albert Bushnell Hart, *The Southern South,* p. 35.

the main difference is that the mountaineers have almost no Negroes among them and are therefore nearly free from the difficulties of the race problem. In the lowlands as in the mountains, men whose fathers had settled on rich lands, as the country developed were unable to compete with their more alert and successful neighbors, who were always ready to outbid them for land or slaves; therefore they sold out and moved back into the poor lands in the lowlands, or into the belt of thin soil lying between the Piedmont and the low country. Hence the contemptuous names applied to them by the planting class—"Tar Heels" in North Carolina; "Sand Hillers" in South Carolina; "Crackers" in Georgia; "Clay Eaters" in Alabama; "Red Necks" in Arkansas; "Hill Billies" in Mississippi; and "Mean Whites," "White Trash," and "No 'Count" everywhere.[14]

Hart also pointed out that many of the postwar plantations employed "managers," whose role was analogous to the prewar overseer, and that some of these managers had "some opportunity to plant on their own account."[15]

A similar view of the Southern poor whites was expressed, without as much sympathy, by Timothy T. Fortune, the black radical journalist:

As the poor whites of the South were fifty years ago, so they are to-day— a careless, ignorant, lazy, but withal, arrogant set, who add nothing to the productive wealth of the community because they are too lazy to work, and who take nothing from that wealth because they are too poor to purchase. They have graded human wants to a point below which man could not go without starving. They live upon the poorest land in the South, the "piney woods," and raise a few potatoes and corn, and a few pigs, which never grow to be hogs, so sterile is the land upon which they are turned to "root, or die." These characteristic pigs are derisively called "shotes" by those who have seen their lean, lank and hungry development. They are awful counterparts of their pauper owners. It may be taken as an index of the quality of the soil and the condition of the people, to observe the condition of their live stock. Strange as it may appear, the faithful dog is the only animal which appears to thrive on "piney woods" land.[16]

These assessments are typical of the widely held view that the poor whites of the Southern backlands continued to occupy the relatively infertile lands after the war, just as they had before the war.[17]

14. Ibid., p. 38.
15. Ibid., p. 263.
16. Timothy Thomas Fortune, *Black and White: Land, Labor and Politics in the South*, p. 199.
17. See also Walter Fleming, *Documentary History of Reconstruction: Political, Military, Social, Religious, Educational and Industrial, 1865 to the Present Time*, vol. 2: 273 and 320, reprinting segments of Nordhoff, *Cotton States*, pp. 10, 21, 55, 76, 96, 107, and 111.

Many writers commented on the ultimate return of the blacks to the plantations after they had "tested their freedom" upon emancipation. In some cases the blacks returned to the very plantations where they had worked as slaves; in other cases they seem to have changed places with other blacks.

Carl Schurz noted in his *Report* that despite the widespread black migrations and congregations of freedmen at the Union army camps, "still others, and their number was by no means inconsiderable, remained with their former masters and continued their work on the field, but under new and as yet unsettled conditions, and under the agitating influence of a feeling of restlessness."[18] Fleming's *Documentary History of Reconstruction* contains several examples of this same phenomenon. Mrs. Frances Butler Leigh, who managed a plantation on the Georgia coast for several years after the war, wrote: "The negroes seem perfectly happy at getting back to the old place and having us there, and I have been deeply touched by many instances of devotion on their part."[19] The same story was told by Mrs. V. V. Clayton, in another plantation reminiscence.[20] A Northern missionary to the South also found that after the war "the one-time masters undertook to run the plantations by hiring the former slaves."[21]

In *The Plantation Negro as Freeman*, Philip Bruce argued that even in the face of the massive black migrations following emancipation, freedmen soon were again providing labor on the plantations.

Many of the largest plantations were almost depopulated of their former laborers, the places they vacated being filled by those who had immigrated from other sections or had come in from the same countryside.[22]

The perceptive English traveler Robert Somers disagreed as to the freedmen's preferences in employers, but concurred in the belief that they remained on the plantations:

The old proprietors have an advantage in this respect [securing their labor supply] over new planters. The negroes seem to prefer their employ-

18. Carl Schurz, *Report on the Condition of the South*, p. 15.
19. Fleming, *Documentary History*, p. 301, citing Leigh, *Ten Years on a Georgia Plantation* (1866).
20. Fleming, *Documentary History*, p. 309, citing Mrs. V. V. Clayton, *White and Black under the Old Regime*, (1899).
21. Fleming, *Documentary History*, p. 439, citing C. G. Smith, *Colonization of Negroes in Central Alabama* (pamphlet from about 1900).
22. Philip A. Bruce, *The Plantation Negro as Freeman*, p. 177. This passage is embedded in a longer quote given in full in chapter 2.

ment, and, after various changes, come back and settle down to work in their old places.[23]

At least one modern historian saw in the desire of the freedmen to remain in the "sections with which they were familiar," an impetus toward establishment of the sharecropping system.[24]

Testimony before the government committees confirmed both the ownership of the best lands by planters and the continued location of blacks on those lands. In Mississippi,

the owners of the large plantations do not wish to cut up their plantations at all, and all the good land in Mississippi is generally owned by the large planters. The small planters generally have poor land, hilly land, while the large plantations are generally bottom lands. In other words, there is in the central portion of the State considerable rich land called "hummock lands," which is generally held in large plantations. The valley of the Tombigbee contains a very large negro population, and the planters have always hoped to work their plantations with the negroes since the surrender. . . . I myself told the negroes at the time of the surrender that it would be much better for them to go back on the plantations to work, and that they would be secured under their contracts as long as I was there and the troops were there; and a large portion of the negroes did so. This was some time before the Freedmen's Bureau took charge of them.[25]

A witness before the Industrial Commission indicated both that when blacks moved they went from one plantation to another, and that many did not even go that far:

In a general way our labor throughout that section of Georgia is very content and permanent in its home life. They move about from plantation to plantation every 2 or 3 years—some of them; but to-day I have men on my place who were slaves on the place, living there during the reconstruction troubles, who were very much alarmed because a stranger came in and bought a farm. They thought they would have to move off, and they could not keep their old ways. . . . They have always lived there and will probably die there, right on the plantation where they were born.[26]

23. Robert Somers, *Southern States Since the War, 1870–71*, p. 146.
24. Marjorie S. Mendenhall, "The Rise of Southern Tenancy," *Yale Review* 27, no. 1 (Autumn 1937): 125.
25. U.S. Congress, Joint Committee on Reconstruction, *Report of the Joint Committee on Reconstruction*, 39th Cong., 1st sess., part 3, p. 6. Testimony of Brevet Major General Edward Hatch. This report will hereafter be referred to as the *RJCR*.
26. U.S. Industrial Commission, *Reports of the Industrial Commission*, vol. 10: *Report of the Industrial Commission on Agriculture and Agricultural Labor*, p. 379. Testimony of J. H. Hale, farmer, of Fort Valley, Georgia, and South Glastonbury, Connecticut. This volume of the Industrial Commission's *Reports* will hereafter be referred to as *ROIC*, 10.

Again, the point that blacks remained on lands which had formerly been plantations is hardly to be denied. Emancipated without resources, the blacks had to survive. The only sources of subsistence were working for a planter, rations issued by the Freedmen's Bureau, or employment outside the agricultural sector. Under these circumstances it could only be expected that after the Freedmen's Bureau had been disbanded, most blacks who remained in agriculture would find employment on the productive lands of the old plantations.

Perhaps the most questionable of the assumptions of the LOOH is the assumption that cotton-growing whites had access to some of the most fertile available lands. Nevertheless, there are indications scattered through the narrative accounts suggesting that just such a pattern of land occupancy emerged after the Civil War.

The discussion in the 1880 census of the reliability of its statistics on cotton production included an offhand reference to the cultivation of the best plantation lands by the landowners themselves:

Cotton, more over, is now very largely raised "on shares," or by special arrangements of a great variety of forms, which tend to endanger the accuracy of a popular enumeration. Thus, to take a comparatively simple case, a large planter not infrequently cultivates a part of his estate under his own management, while letting other, perhaps the more distant or less valuable, parts to be cultivated on shares by others.[27]

More explicit support for the LOOH would be difficult to imagine. Other observers attested to similar division of the former plantation lands between the different groups of farmers. For example, Robert Somers identified several new sources of white labor on the old plantation lands after the war—white "croppers," sons of the planters themselves, and ambitious poor whites of the hill districts who came down from the mountains to buy or rent lands of the ravaged plantations.

I have seen more than one great plantation absolutely deserted, and as void of fence or labour as it was at the end of the war. [Somers is writing in 1870–1871.] This state of affairs has given rise to assiduous efforts to rent out land to cultivators; and a class of people called "croppers," mostly whites, enter into annual tenancies of land.[28]

Somers believed that this type of labor was not generally successful, unlike operation of some plantations by the sons of planters:

27. U.S. Census Office, *Report on the Productions of Agriculture as Returned at the Tenth Census* (June 1, 1880), vol. 3 of 1880 Census, p. xviii.
28. Somers, *Southern States,* p. 116.

Yet behind all this difficulty there is an undergrowth of wholesome influences at work that promise ultimately a great revival and deliverance. The sceptre falling from the hands of fathers is being grasped by vigorous and stalwart sons, who are rallying labour round them, and, while plodding in the cotton field, are also riding and hunting, courting and marrying, and casting all the past behind them with hopeful outlook to the future.[29]

Finally, the distress of the planters provided a source of hope and an incentive to the poor whites of the hills. After a successful year due to high cotton prices,

these small hill farmers come down occasionally into the plain, looking for land to rent or buy; and it is not improbable that many of the better and more industrious class of families in "the mountains," as the gently swelling uplands are called, will eventually come down altogether, and help to renovate the waste places, and build up the agricultural prosperity of the Valley.[30]

Somers also attributed the increase in the cotton crop in the years following the Civil War to the rise of white cotton farmers. These whites were small farmers who had not grown cotton before the war, white laborers who availed themselves of the opportunity to rent and sharecrop, white villagers who joined in the cotton harvest or grew small garden plots of the staple, and

the cloud of white planters and their families, reduced to poverty, who have been the foremost to go down into the Western bottoms, and there and elsewhere have bent with noble fortitude and ardour to labour in the fields.[31]

Other commentators saw the same trends. Henry W. Grady made the point that many whites and even some blacks were able to buy former plantation lands at distressed postwar prices:

Led into the market by the low prices to which the best lands had fallen, came a host of small buyers, to accommodate whom the plantations were subdivided, and offered in lots to suit purchasers. Never perhaps was there a rural movement, accomplished without revolution or exodus,

29. Ibid.
30. Ibid., p. 117. In these three passages, Somers was speaking specifically of conditions he found in Tennessee, though there is no reason why his comments cannot be taken as applying more generally.
31. Ibid., pp. 272–273.

that equalled in extent and swiftness the partition of the plantations of the ex-slave-holders into small farms. As remarkable as was the eagerness of the negroes . . . the earth-hunger of the poorer class of the whites, who had been unable under the slave-holding oligarchy to own land, was even more striking.[32]

Another writer found former overseers following the same route to landownership.[33] Matthew Brown Hammond told the same story:

The purchasers of these [distressed] lands came in part from the North, being chiefly men whom political or military affairs had brought to the South and who were induced by the high prices of cotton and the low prices of the land to attempt the cultivation of this staple. In the main, however, the purchasers were found within the South itself. The poor whites whose inability to own slaves had kept them largely out of cotton growing before the war, were now eager to undertake the cultivation of this staple on the better lands offered for sale on such favorable terms. A great increase in the number of small farms took place during the years following the war.[34]

The twentieth-century historian of Populism, John D. Hicks, also asserted that the former overseers and small farmers who had owned land adjacent to the plantations before the war acquired plantation lands at the depressed postwar land prices.[35]

Vernon Wharton found in Mississippi a movement of both white tenants and buyers onto vacant plantations. In some instances, these whites located on lands deserted by migrating Negroes.[36] Shugg found manuscript records referring to rich bottom lands that allegedly could be occupied without paying a cent and without risking anything but a lawsuit, but he said that many piney-woods natives shunned the diseases,

32. Henry W. Grady, "Cotton and Its Kindgom," *Harper's New Monthly Magazine* 63 (October 1881): 721–722.
33. Ernest Hamlin Abbott, "The South and the Negro," *Outlook* 77 (1904): 228.
34. Matthew Brown Hammond, "Cotton Production in the South," *The South in the Building of the Nation,* vol. 6, prepared by The Southern Historical Publication Society (Richmond: 1909), 89. This volume will hereafter be referred to as *SBN,* 6.
35. John D. Hicks, *The Populist Revolt,* pp. 37–38. Hicks, in addition to citing Grady's *Harper's* article (note 32) dealing with the acquisition of plantation lands by freedmen and whites, refers also to Francis B. Simkins, *The Tillman Movement in South Carolina* (Durham, North Carolina: 1926), pp. 8–9; and Robert P. Brooks, *The Agrarian Revolution in Georgia, 1865–1912* (Madison, Wisconsin: 1914), ch. 3.
36. Vernon Wharton, *The Negro in Mississippi, 1865–1890,* vol. 28 of The James Sprunt Studies in History and Political Science, p. 104. Wharton's references are to the Hinds County *Gazette,* February 17, 24, March 17, December 15, 29, 1875; February 6, 1878; and it is interesting to note that another one of Wharton's sources is Somers, *Southern States,* pp. 142–143.

different methods of cultivation, and Negroes of the lowlands.[37] Such fastidiousness is not entirely plausible.

Shugg also alludes to a reversion to actual farming by some of the planters ruined by the war:

[Some of the planters] regained a fair measure of comfort by the proverbial sweat of their brows.* With "their sons and grandsons following the plow and wielding the hoe," it soon came to be noticed that "in many of the descendants of the old planters a yeomanry is springing up as honorable as our planting aristocracy of yore."**[38]

One such planter adopted owner-operation of his farm for reasons other than wartime devastation, and wrote to the Southern Cultivator:

The war left me an old but valuable plantation, a large stock of horses, mules, mares and colts; also cattle, sheep and hogs, and about forty freed negroes—fat, sleek and well cared for, but who unfortunately took it into their woolly pates that I had committed an unpardonable sin in ever having held them in slavery, and consequently considered it their religious duty to take everything they could lay their hands on from me, as properly belonging to them. By stealing, slander, &c., I was reduced in five years to running a two-horse farm, with very limited means to do it with. During all these years, I had tried hiring in all the usual ways, of wages and part of the crop. . . . So at the commencement of last year, I saw that, unless a change took place, I would be a ruined man. I determined, therefore, to hire no hands that year, but to do the best I could by my own labor and that of my son, a youth 19 years of age.[39]

This planter found himself "too little accustomed to manual labor" and settled on hiring black workers by the day, but there were undoubtedly others who tried the same thing. The Cultivator later reprinted an article by J. C. DeLavigne from DeBow's Review, which claimed that there were enough abandoned plantation lands waiting for labor to be applied to make everyone "independent, happy and rich."[40]

In testimony before the Industrial Commission during the 1890s, the Georgia State Commissioner of Agriculture remarked that "the most of the landowners down there live on the farms themselves and cultivate

37.   Shugg, Origins of Class Struggle, p. 255, citing Samuel H. Lockett, Louisiana As It Is (unpublished book, 1873), pp. 215–217.
38.   Ibid., pp. 276–277. The references are:
* [New Orleans] Picayune (September 3, 1867).
** Ibid. (September 5, 1873).
39.   An Old Beginner [pseud.], "Labor, Mode of Managing, &c.," Southern Cultivator 30 (April 1872): 127–128.
40.   "The Labor Question," ibid. 32 (October 1874): 390. The article originally appeared in DeBow's Review (February 1870).

what they can, then they turn out or rent out the balance of the land under these systems."[41] Under normal circumstances, it might be expected that these landlord/cultivators would locate themselves on the choicest plots in their holdings.

Even the Hampton Institute's *Southern Workman* provides support for the LOOH. Orra Langhorne wrote a series of background articles on various aspects of Southern life for the *Workman*. One of these articles, "A Poor White Man's Experience Since the War," consisted of a short biography of one James Johnson, a former overseer. Johnson lived in Virginia, and had bought a few slaves and some poor land before the war broke out. He lost the slaves and was drafted into the Confederate army, but deserted before Lee's surrender. Returning home, he and his wife survived by planting a garden, some corn, and tobacco. Johnson was not absolutely penniless—he was able to trade some old harnesses and a saddle for a plow without a point; then he bought a plow point with what money he had.

Two or three years after the close of the war, Johnson found himself going back to his old dreams of owning land, and it was not long before he purchased an excellent creek bottom farm, to which he has from time to time made additions, until he now owns seven hundred acres of land.[42]

James Johnson's progress from overseer and owner of poor land to prosperous white farmer owning rich land must have been repeated throughout the South.

All the historical references in support of the LOOH to this point have dealt with the pattern of land *occupancy* by the various groups. It is also clear that many diverse individuals were conscious of the importance of land *ownership* in the determination of farmers' incomes. The best examples of this consciousness came out during the debate over land reform that followed the collapse of the Confederate armies. Proposals for confiscation and redistribution of the lands of the defeated rebels were made by Thaddeus Stevens and others at the close of the war. These proponents of confiscation anticipated the LOOH, at least insofar as its emphasis on factor ownership in income distribution is concerned.

While the supporters of land reform in the South were able to generate little support in the North, articulate Radical Republicans were not the only advocates of confiscation and redistribution of rebels' lands. Large numbers of freedmen themselves ardently hoped for "forty acres and a

41. *ROIC*, 10: 909, testimony of the Honorable O. B. Stevens.
42. Orra Langhorne, "A Poor White Man's Experience Since the War," *Southern Workman* 10 (April 1881): 38.

mule" to accompany their emancipation.[43] Frederick Douglass perhaps expressed best the feelings of frustration and bitterness which must have overtaken the blacks as the realization dawned on them that their dreams of land and capital ownership were to be denied:

History does not furnish an example of emancipation under conditions less friendly to the emancipated class than this American example. Liberty came to the freedmen of the United States not in mercy, but in wrath—not by moral choice but by military necessity—not by the generous action of the people among whom they were to live, and whose good will was essential to the success of the measure, but by strangers, foreigners, invaders, trespassers, aliens, and enemies. The very manner of their emancipation invited to the heads of the freedmen the bitterest hostility of race and class. They were hated because they had been slaves, hated because they were now free, and hated because of those who had freed them. Nothing was to have been expected other than what has happened, and he is a poor student of the human heart who does not see that the old master class would naturally employ every power and means in their reach to make the great measure of emancipation unsuccessful and utterly odious. It was born in the tempest and whirlwind of war, and has lived in a storm of violence and blood. When the Hebrews were emancipated, they were told to take spoil from the Egyptians. When the serfs of Russia were emancipated, they were given three acres of ground upon which they could live and make a living. But not so when our slaves were emancipated. They were sent away empty-handed, without money, without friends, and without a foot of land upon which to stand. Old and young, sick and well, were turned loose to the open sky, naked to their enemies. The old slave quarter that had before sheltered them and the fields that had yielded them corn were now denied them. The old master class, in its wrath, said, "Clear out! The Yankees have freed you, now let them feed and shelter you!"[44]

The advocates of the land reform proposals often made the connection between political democracy and landownership in classical Jeffersonian terms. Implicit in their arguments is the idea that in a competitive market economy, ownership of the land is a crucial determinant of income and economic independence. An ex-Confederate army officer would seem to be an unlikely proponent of confiscation. Nevertheless, Sidney Andrews, correspondent to the *Boston Advertiser* and the *Chicago Tribune,* reported

43. C. W. Tebeau, "Some Aspects of Planter-Freedman Relations, 1865–1880," *Journal of Negro History* 21, no. 2 (April 1936): 131; Oscar Zeichner, "The Transition from Slave to Free Agricultural Labor in the Southern States," *Agricultural History* 13 (January 1939): 22–32. Zeichner gives several references for this sentiment among the freedmen.
44. Frederick Douglass, *Life and Times of Frederick Douglass,* pp. 503–504. The passage was taken from a speech delivered by Douglass at Elmira, New York, August 1, 1880, to a meeting of blacks celebrating West Indian emancipation.

to the Joint Committee on Reconstruction a conversation he held during a railroad journey with an ex-rebel army captain, a man who had been a lawyer before the war. Andrews did not reveal the identity of his train companion. He did record the conversation immediately after it had been concluded, however, and this is what the anonymous Confederate officer had to say:

"No, I have not much faith in the idea that capital and labor will reconcile themselves. Things are exceptional here. Our capital is all in the hands of a few, and invested in great plantations. Our labor is all in the hands of a race supremely ignorant, and against whom we all have a strong prejudice. In my opinion, you can't reconcile these two interests unless you put the labor in subjection to the capital—that is, unless you give the white man control of the negro. Of course that can't again be allowed, and therefore there's an almost impassable gulf between the negro and freedom unless the government aids him.

"I'll tell you what I think you [the victorious North] should have done. The policy of confiscation should be rigidly carried out at once. Mercy to the individual is death to the State; and in pardoning all the leading men, the President is *killing the free State he might have built here.* The landed aristocracy have always been the curse of the State. I say that as a man born and reared in Georgia and bound to her by every possible tie. Till that is broken down there can be no real freedom here for either the negro or the poor white. The result of the war gave you a chance you never will get again to overthrow that monopoly. The negroes and the poor whites are bitter enemies in many respects, but they agree in wanting land. You should have carried out your confiscation policy—divided up the great plantations into fifty-acre lots, and sold them to the highest. . . bidders. That would have thrown some of the land into other large plantations, but it would have been fair, and would have given the poor whites and the negroes a chance. Give a man a piece of land, let him have a cabin of his own upon his own lot, and then you make him free. Civil rights are good for nothing, the ballot is good for nothing, till you make some men of every class landholders. You must give the negroes and the poor whites a chance to live—that's the first thing you should do. The negro has a great notion to get a piece of land, and you should help him along by that notion."[45]

The former rebel told Andrews, "I should be shot before to-morrow morning if I were to publicly say what I've said to you";[46] so there is little wonder that Andrews would not reveal the identity of his source.

The most eloquent advocate of confiscation was Thaddeus Stevens. He argued forcefully that such an opportunity to build a more egalitarian society in the conquered South would never come again:

45. *RJCR,* part 3, pp. 174–175.
46. Ibid., p. 175.

But, it is said, by those who have more sympathy with rebel wives and children than for the widows and orphans of loyal men, that this stripping the rebels of their estates and driving them to exile or to honest labor would be harsh and severe upon innocent women and children. It may be so; but that is the result of the necessary laws of war. But it is revolutionary, say they. This plan would, no doubt, work a radical reorganization in southern institutions, habits and manners. It is intended to revolutionize their principles and feelings. This may startle feeble minds and shake weak nerves. So do all great improvements in the political and moral world. It requires a heavy impetus to drive forward a sluggish people. When it was first proposed to free the slaves, and arm the blacks, did not half the nation tremble? The prim conservatives, the snobs, and the male waiting-maids in Congress, were in hysterics.

The whole fabric of southern society *must* be changed, and never can it be done if this opportunity is lost. Without this, this Government can never be, as it never has been, a true republic. Heretofore, it had more the features of aristocracy than of democracy.—The Southern States have been despotisms, not governments of the people. It is impossible that any practical equality of rights can exist where a few thousand men monopolize the whole landed property. The larger the number of small proprietors the more safe and stable the government. As the landed interest must govern, the more it is subdivided and held by independent owners, the better. . . . How can republican institutions, free schools, free churches, free social intercourse exist in a mingled community of nabobs and serfs; of the owners of twenty thousand acre manors with lordly palaces, and the occupants of narrow huts inhabited by "low white trash?"—If the south is ever to be made a safe republic let her lands be cultivated by the toil of the owners or the free labor of intelligent citizens. This must be done even though it drive her nobility into exile. If they go, all the better.[47]

To summarize, then, the land occupancy and ownership hypothesis is consistent with the econometric findings of the previous chapter, and has a basis in the narrative accounts of contemporary observers and careful historians as well. Because of an identification problem, it is fundamentally impossible to attribute productivity differences *solely* to differences in land quality or to differences in skill levels of the different groups of agricultural workers. Nevertheless, the results conclusively eliminate the naive "legacy of slavery" notion that blacks as a whole were less productive than whites as a whole because they were deprived of human capital. The observed differences in productivity (with white cotton farmers most productive, followed by black cotton farmers, black noncotton farmers, and white noncotton farmers at the bottom of the scale either less or no more productive than the black noncotton farmers) may, of

47. Thaddeus Stevens, "Reconstruction." This speech was originally delivered in Lancaster, Pennsylvania, on September 7, 1865.

course, have been due to some *combination* of locational fertility factors and human capital disparities, but again, there can be no simple categorization of blacks as less productive than whites as a result of the "legacy of slavery."

Similarly, whichever specification is used, a strong productivity advantage is associated with cotton. The strength and uniformity of this advantage are sufficient grounds to reject the hypothesis that cotton was a relatively unprofitable staple. Rather, it would appear that cotton enjoyed such a comparative advantage that anyone who had land suitable for cotton culture could have generated more output in value terms by concentrating on cotton than in alternative lines of agricultural production. Nevertheless, there must have been marginal lands, which were about equally able to sustain cotton or the alternative crops. Crop rotation alternating cotton and corn was surely practiced, and the two crops were even occasionally grown side by side on the same piece of land.[48]

The LOOH is consistent with all these findings, as well as with the major result of marginal product factor pricing in contradiction of the exploitation hypothesis. In fact, one of the greatest attractions of the LOOH is that it requires no market imperfections, no institutional peculiarities, no deviations from an ordinary competitive private enterprise economy to explain all the econometric results. The very simplicity and naturalness of the LOOH, flowing as it does out of normal competitive behavior given the factor endowments of the various segments of the population at the close of the war, recommend it as the null hypothesis for future investigations of Southern agricultural productivity and income distribution.

48. For an example of rotation, see J.A.H., "Cotton and Corn—Rotation Of," *Southern Cultivator* 32 (June 1874): 212; for an example of side-by-side cultivation, see Thomas E. Gregg, "Tobacco—Sweet Potatoes—Cotton and Corn Together," *Southern Cultivator* 36 (June 1878): 212. These are typical examples, and other farmers wrote to the *Cultivator* reporting the same practices. And all the propaganda in favor of agricultural diversification would have been pointless if there had not been some flexibility in the crop choice. At least some cotton land must have been suitable for growing other crops.

7
Cotton Supply Functions, 1882–1914

The Model

The conclusions of the previous chapters were based on production functions estimated from cross-sectional data. As such, these results reveal nothing about the price-responsiveness of Southern farmers in making their crop-choice decisions *over time*. It has been shown in chapters 4 and 5 that there was an overall productivity advantage in value terms associated with cotton culture from at least 1880 onward. Given that the general level of cotton production was not too high, however, the South may still have suffered from "overproduction" of cotton if farmers were slow or inflexible in responding to changes in the relative prices of cotton and the alternative crops.

Even if it were advantageous for some farmers to concentrate on cotton regardless of its price (because of their possession of premier cotton lands such as in the Mississippi delta), other farmers' optimum crop mix must have depended on the relative prices of the alternative outputs. The advantage enjoyed by producers on the ideal cotton lands could result in the statistical estimation of an aggregate cotton-associated productivity advantage over the South as a whole from the cross-sectional data, even though farmers who should have been shifting between cotton and other crops *over time* (as relative output prices changed) were unwilling or unable to do so. This type of overproduction may have been due to farmers' irrationality and traditionalism or to merchants' insistence on cotton, but if it did take place to any significant extent it would have been manifested in an unresponsiveness of cotton supply to changes in the relative crop prices. In this situation, farmers might be said to have been "locked in" to cotton culture. Estimates of cotton supply functions for each state based on time series data should provide enough information for a judgment about price-responsiveness and therefore should contribute materially to the (somewhat belated) settlement of the over-production debate.

The proposed model of suppliers' reactions to changing relative prices belongs to the class of widely and successfully applied dynamic adjustment models introduced first by Nerlove.[1] In this model, either acreage in cotton or the share of tilled acres in cotton is the dependent variable, serving as a measure of cotton supply. The model includes both a mechanism for formation of price expectations and one for the adjustment of planted acreage to desired acreage with lags. The final equation which is estimated can be derived from several different "underlying" behavioral models, but it is useful to examine one such model in detail in order to determine just what the estimates can and cannot reveal about the decision-making process. In what follows, the random disturbance term will not be included until later, because there is no reason for believing a priori that a statistical disturbance with desirable properties should appear at any one stage of the derivation as contrasted with any other.

The behavioral equations of the model are

$$X_t^* = \alpha + \beta P_t^e + \delta t \tag{7.1}$$
$$X_t = X_{t-1} + \gamma(X_t^* - X_{t-1}) \tag{7.2}$$
$$P_t^e = P_{t-1}^e + \lambda(P_{t-1} - P_{t-1}^e) \tag{7.3}$$

where

X_t^* = the cotton acreage level desired by the agriculturalists in year t. There are two forms of the model: one in which $X_t^* = S_t^*$ = the desired proportion of total acres in cotton, the other in which $X_t^* = A_t^*$ = desired total acres in cotton.

P_t^e = expected cotton price relative to an index of the prices of the major alternative crops in year t, and

X_t and P_t are the actual or realized values of these quantities in the year t. The data used to compute these variables are described and discussed in appendix A.

The variables can be measured either in their natural units or in loga-

1. See, for example, Marc Nerlove, *The Dynamics of Supply: Estimation of Farmers' Response to Price;* Vahid Nowshirvani, *Agricultural Supply in India: Some Theoretical and Empirical Studies;* and Jere Richard Behrman, *Supply Response in Underdeveloped Agriculture: A Case Study of Four Major Annual Crops in Thailand, 1937–1963.* Chapter 1 of Behrman includes a bibliography of other supply studies, particularly in underdeveloped agriculture. The model has been employed in historical situations, particularly in Franklin M. Fisher and Peter Temin, "Regional Specialization and the Supply of Wheat in the United States, 1867–1914," *Review of Economics and Statistics* 52, no. 2 (May 1970). The work in the present chapter follows Fisher and Temin closely, both in theoretical approach and in statistical technique.

rithms. In this chapter, they are all measured in logarithms except for t, so that the parameters can be interpreted directly as elasticities. For example, the parameter β is the elasticity of the desired cotton acreage or proportion of acreage with respect to expected relative price.

Equations (7.2) and (7.3) show the response of actual acreage to desired acreage with speed of adjustment γ, and the revision of price expectations based on past experience with speed of adjustment λ. Equation (7.1) shows the desired cotton acreage variable (either share of cotton acres or total cotton acres) to be a function of both the expected relative price of cotton and a trend. It is easy to see why producers would base their decisions on expected relative prices, but inclusion of the trend term requires more explanation. At a general level, the trend can be thought of as representing changes in the underlying conditions of supply which are not captured by the expected price variable. More specifically, the specification of the supply function could be deficient either because of the presence of structural change over the period or because other variables besides expected relative price affected the determination of supply. In the latter case, the use of time as a proxy for such omitted variables as the relative rates of technical progress in growing the different crops or the exhaustion of new land suitable for cotton reduces the specification error that would be committed by leaving them out altogether. It will also be seen subsequently that it is advantageous to include the trend for purposes of comparison of the results with other supply studies; so the trend in (7.1) is required on both theoretical and practical grounds.

The variables X_t^* and P_t^e are unobservable and must be eliminated before the model's parameters can be estimated. Easy algebraic manipulation shows that from (7.2)

$$X_t^* = \frac{1}{\gamma}(X_t - X_{t-1}) + X_{t-1} \tag{7.4}$$

If both sides of (7.3) are multiplied by β and rearranged,

$$\beta P_t^e = (1 - \lambda)\beta P_{t-1}^e + \lambda\beta P_{t-1}$$

From (7.1), (7.1) lagged, and (7.5)   (7.5)

$$X_t^* - \alpha - \delta t = (1 - \lambda)[X_{t-1}^* - \alpha - \delta(t - 1)] + \lambda\beta P_{t-1} \tag{7.6}$$

From (7.4), (7.4) lagged, and (7.6)

$$\frac{1}{\gamma}(X_t - X_{t-1}) + X_{t-1} - \alpha - \delta t$$

$$= (1 - \lambda)\left[\frac{1}{\gamma}(X_{t-1} - X_{t-2}) + X_{t-2} - \alpha - \delta(t - 1)\right] + \lambda\beta P_{t-1} \tag{7.7}$$

If both sides are multiplied by γ and the terms in (7.7) are rearranged,

$$X_t = (\alpha\gamma\lambda + \gamma\delta - \gamma\delta\lambda) + \beta\gamma\lambda P_{t-1} + [(1 - \gamma) + (1 - \lambda)] X_{t-1}$$
$$- [(1 - \gamma)(1 - \lambda)] X_{t-2} + \delta\gamma\lambda t \tag{7.8}$$

Now since γ and λ enter equation (7.8) symmetrically, models in which either γ or $\lambda = 1$ will be observationally indistinguishable. Furthermore, suppose the estimated coefficient of X_{t-1} is a and the estimated coefficient of X_{t-2} is b. Then

$$[(1 - \gamma) + (1 - \lambda)] = a \tag{7.9}$$

$$-(1 - \gamma)(1 - \lambda) = b \tag{7.10}$$

So

$$-(1 - \gamma)[a - (1 - \gamma)] = b \tag{7.11}$$

$$\gamma^2 + (a - 2)\gamma + (1 - a - b) = 0 \tag{7.12}$$

$$\gamma = \frac{(2 - a) \pm (a^2 + 4b)^{1/2}}{2} \tag{7.13}$$

Similarly,

$$\lambda = \frac{(2 - a) \mp (a^2 + 4b)^{1/2}}{2} \tag{7.14}$$

In principle, therefore, estimates of (7.8) could be used to calculate γ and λ, but there would be no way of determining which was which. In fact the data suggest that either γ or λ is one. Estimates of (7.8) give coefficients of X_{t-1} and X_{t-2} which together imply values of γ and λ which in every case but one are imaginary or outside the range from 0 to 1. In addition the estimated coefficients of X_{t-2} are generally small relative to their standard errors,[2] so that $(1 - \gamma)(1 - \lambda)$ is not significantly different from zero. These two facts indicate that either γ or λ is equal to one, though it is impossible to determine which.[3]

Thus (7.8) reduces to

$$X_t = \alpha\mu + \beta\mu P_{t-1} + \delta\mu t + (1 - \mu) X_{t-1} \tag{7.15}$$

where all variables and parameters are as previously defined, except for μ and α. Since it is impossible to determine which of the two speeds of adjustment is unity and which is not, μ will denote the speed of adjustment which is less than one, and will subsequently be referred to simply

2. It will be explained subsequently that the estimated standard errors are biased downward. (See note 5 following.) This fact only strengthens the conclusion that the estimated coefficient of X_{t-2} is not significantly different from zero, however.
3. Fisher and Temin reached the same conclusion in their study of the supply of wheat in the United States over roughly the same period. Fisher and Temin, "Regional Specialization and the Supply of Wheat," p. 138.

TABLE 7.1   Simultaneous Estimation of γ and λ [S_t form], 1884–1914

| $S_t = c_1 + c_2 P_{t-1} + c_3 t + a S_{t-1} + b S_{t-2} + u_t; \quad u_t = \rho u_{t-1} + v_t$ | | | | |
State	a	b	$a^2 + 4b$	γ, λ
North Carolina [quasi-t]	.651	−.255 [−1.922]	−.596	γ, λ not real
South Carolina	.767	−.342 [−2.621]	−.780	//
Georgia	.920	−.386 [−2.388]	−.698	//
Florida	.577	−.138 [−.856]	−.219	//
Tennessee	.953	−.303 [−1.603]	−.304	//
Alabama	.656	−.311 [−2.174]	−.814	//
Mississippi	.518	.0958 [.594]	.652	$\gamma, \lambda = 1.145, .338$
Arkansas	.613	−.0527 [−.296]	.165	$\gamma, \lambda = .897, .491$
Louisiana	.881	−.236 [−1.362]	−.168	γ, λ not real
Texas	.453	−.151 [−.944]	−.399	//

S_t = *proportion* of total acres planted to cotton; S_t and P_t in logs. The numbers in square brackets below the b estimates are the ratios of the estimates of b to their estimated standard errors, u_t is a first-order autocorrelated disturbance, and the v_t are uncorrelated. (See the subsequent discussion of the disturbance in the text.)

as "the" speed of adjustment. For purposes of testing the price-responsiveness of the agricultural system, it really makes little difference whether acreage allotments or price expectations are adjusted. Merchants insisting on cotton culture can be thought of as being decision-makers who prevented farmers from shifting crops to the desired alternatives to cotton, or as decision-makers who maintained optimistic expectations of the relative cotton price, thus insisting on continuation of its culture. In other words, the identification of which speed of adjustment is equal to one and which is not is really not important for the problem at hand—the determination of whether or not the supply of cotton responded to price changes or was restrained from responding because farmers were

TABLE 7.2   Simultaneous Estimation of γ and λ [A_t form], 1884–1914

$A_t = c_1 + c_2 P_{t-1} + c_3 t + a A_{t-1} + b A_{t-2} + u_t; \quad u_t = \rho u_{t-1} + v_t$

State	a	b	$a^2 + 4b$	γ, λ
North Carolina [quasi-t]	.645	−.302 [−2.281]	−.792	γ, λ not real
South Carolina	.492	−.235 [−1.684]	−.698	//
Georgia	.705	−.193 [−1.113]	−.275	//
Florida	.631	−.252 [−1.371]	−.610	//
Tennessee	.751	−.211 [−1.212]	−.280	//
Alabama	.747	−.283 [−1.865]	−.574	//
Mississippi	.0901	−.0293 [−.177]	−.109	//
Arkansas	.390	−.106 [−.636]	−.272	//
Louisiana	.630	.0245 [.144]	.495	$\gamma, \lambda = 1.037, .333$
Texas	.659	.145 [.763]	1.014	$\gamma, \lambda = 1.174, .167$

A_t = total acres planted to cotton. Other comments are the same as in the previous table.

locked in to cotton. The new value of α is defined so as to make the constant term in (7.8) equal a multiple of μ when the unit speed of adjustment is substituted into (7.8).

It was mentioned previously that there is no a priori reason for introducing a statistical disturbance term at any particular stage of the derivation of (7.8). If a disturbance which is not autocorrelated is introduced in the underlying model (for example, in (7.1)), then the disturbance which will be present in (7.8) or (7.15) will be autocorrelated. This can be seen by carrying the disturbance through the derivation of (7.8). Alternatively, if the disturbance term is first introduced in (7.15), there is no a priori reason why it should not be autocorrelated. Therefore, it will be assumed that the disturbance is linearly autocorrelated, so that the structure to be estimated is

$$X_t = \alpha\mu + \beta\mu P_{t-1} + \delta\mu t + (1 - \mu) X_{t-1} + u_t \tag{7.16}$$

$$u_t = \rho u_{t-1} + v_t \tag{7.17}$$

with the v_t uncorrelated and normally distributed in the usual way.

The parameters of (7.16) and (7.17) were estimated by choosing the value of ρ to minimize the sum of squares of the v_t over all but the first observation. This procedure differs from maximum likelihood in its treatment of the first observation, but is at least asymptotically equivalent to maximum likelihood.[4] However, the standard errors were calculated as if the serial correlation coefficient were known, rather than being estimated along with the other parameters. Cooper has shown that in the presence of a lagged dependent variable the standard errors of the regression coefficients will be biased downward even asymptotically when this assumption is made.[5] The asymptotic correction derived by Cooper for this situation could not be applied because the asymptotic properties of the correction formulas failed to hold for the small samples (32 observations per state) used in the estimates. Thus the reported standard errors are biased downward and the ratios of the estimated coefficients to their standard errors ("t-statistics") are biased upward.[6] The coefficient estimates themselves are not biased, however, and no

---

4. The estimation procedure follows Fisher and Temin. Their description of it can hardly be improved upon, and with notation and equation numbering changed to conform to the notation used here, they say:

"[G]iven ρ, [(7.16) was lagged and multiplied by ρ, the product was subtracted from the original equation, and ordinary least squares was applied], choosing that value of ρ which gave the smallest resulting error sum of squares. This procedure uses the first observation only as a subtraction from the second. If one believes that the process generating the disturbances. . . was going on for a long time when the observation period started, then our procedure differs from maximum likelihood (assuming the v_t normally distributed in the usual way) in its treatment of the first observation, but is asymptotically equivalent to maximum likelihood. If, on the other hand, one believes that disturbances in the recent past before the first observation were differently generated, then our procedure yields the maximum likelihood estimator even in small samples."
Fisher and Temin, "Regional Specialization," pp. 140–141.
5. J.P. Cooper, "Asymptotic Covariance Matrix of Procedures for Linear Regression in the Presence of First Order Serially Correlated Disturbances," *Econometrica* 40, no. 2 (March 1972): 305–310.
6. It should be noted that the "quasi-t-statistics" reported in Fisher and Temin were calculated after the Cooper correction had been applied to the estimated standard errors. The sample sizes for the wheat supply functions (47 observations in most cases) were sufficiently large for the asymptotic properties of the Cooper correction formulas to apply. The difference is not important for the subsequent comparisons between the estimates of the wheat supply functions and cotton supply functions which will be undertaken below, since the (unbiased) estimated coefficients themselves will be compared, not their standard errors.

great weight will be placed on the size of the "t-statistics" in the subsequent discussion.

Up to this point it has been assumed that (7.16) and (7.17) were derived from an underlying behavioral model embodied by equations (7.1)–(7.3) combined with the least restrictive assumptions about the disturbance (except for confining it to no higher than first-order autocorrelation). In this case, estimation of (7.8) shows that adjustment either of price expectations or of the difference between desired and actual planted acreages was very rapid. However, it is also possible that (7.16) itself is the appropriate behavioral equation—that the current level or percentage of cotton acreage was determined by the previous period's relative price and the previous year's level of the dependent variable. If so, the model includes only one speed of adjustment: μ. In both cases the coefficient of P_{t-1} is the short-run elasticity of X_t with respect to price.

The long-run elasticity with respect to price can also be determined. In a model such as this one, which includes a trend term, the condition for long-run equilibrium is that X_t be growing smoothly according to trend; that is,

$$X_t - X_{t-1} = \delta \tag{7.18}$$

The logarithmic difference $X_t - X_{t-1}$ is the proportional rate of growth in period terms, and the rate of growth of the desired level X_t^* in the underlying model is δ. Because the model is one of adaptive expectations, it is not possible to achieve $X_t = X_t^*$ in long-run equilibrium. If $\gamma \neq 1$, $X_t = X_t^*$ would require $X_t = X_{t-1}$ from (7.2). But in long-run equilibrium, X_t continues to grow because of the trend factor. There actually is no paradox here. In the "steady state" long-run equilibrium, the desired level X_t^* grows with trend, and X_t can never quite "catch up" to it because X_t adjusts only with a lag. Equilibrium is reached, however, when X_t is growing at the steady trend rate δ. Thus, for any given price level $\bar{P}$, substitution of (7.18) into (7.16) gives for long-run equilibrium $\bar{X}_t$,

$$\bar{X}_t = \left[\alpha - \frac{(1-\mu)\delta}{\mu}\right] + \beta\bar{P} + \delta t \tag{7.19}$$

Thus β is the long-run elasticity of $\bar{X}_t$ with respect to price. Note that $\bar{X}_t$ is slightly smaller than X_t^*, reflecting that X_t can never quite "catch up" to its desired level, even in long-run equilibrium. If $\gamma = 1$, then X_t always equals X_t^* and (7.19) is replaced by

$$\bar{X}_t = \alpha + \beta\bar{P} + \delta t \tag{7.20}$$

Again, β is the long-run elasticity of $\bar{X}_t$ with respect to $\bar{P}$.[7]

The Results

Parameter estimates corresponding to both forms of (7.16) are given in tables 7.3 and 7.4. In these tables, S_t = the share of total acres in cotton, and A_t = total cotton acreage in year t, with both variables (and all other variables except the trend) in logs. The span of time covered by the estimates is 1883–1914. The initial year is 1883 because the state-wide cotton price series of the United States Department of Agricul-

TABLE 7.3   Cotton Supply Functions, 1883–1914 [S_t form]

$S_t = \alpha\mu + \beta\mu\, P_{t-1} + \delta\mu t + (1 - \mu)S_{t-1} + ut$;
$u_t = \rho u_{t-1} + v_t$; all variables in logs except t.

The numbers in ordinary parentheses to the right of each parameter estimate are the (biased downward) standard errors; the numbers in brackets below the standard errors are the associated (and biased upward) "t-statistics."

Estimated Parameter	North Carolina	South Carolina	Georgia	Florida
$\alpha\mu$	−9.186(3.983) [−2.306]	−2.763(1.364) [−2.025]	−4.176(2.117) [−1.972]	9.664(3.076) [3.142]
$\beta\mu$	.318(.0598) [5.323]	.126(.0265) [4.745]	.134(.0385) [3.473]	.149(.0376) [3.975]
$\delta\mu$	.00419(.00205) [2.046]	.00117(.000692) [1.695]	.00191(.00108) [1.758]	−.00562(.00170) [−3.298]
$1 - \mu$	.591(.139) [4.247]	.576(.131) [4.386]	.589(.147) [4.015]	.464(.121) [3.823]
ρ	.383	.0390	.108	−.343
β	.778	.297	.326	.278
δ	.0102	.00276	.00465	−.0105
μ	.409	.424	.411	.536
R^2	.827	.713	.734	.695
$F(3,27)$	42.921	22.333	24.775	20.477

7. In subsequent discussion of the results, ratios of estimated coefficients of (7.16) will be computed to form estimates of parameters such as $\beta = \beta\mu/\mu$. The mean of such a ratio (under the usual assumptions about the disturbance) is approximately equal to the ratio of the means of the two coefficients, and approximate methods are known for calculating the standard error of the ratio of two regression coefficients. (H. Gregg Lewis, "On the Distribution of the Partial Elasticity Coefficient," *Journal of the American Statistical Association* 36, no. 215 (September 1941): 413–416.)However, because the standard errors of the β estimates are not really necessary for the subsequent argument, and because the estimated standard errors of the estimates of $\beta\mu$ and μ are themselves biased, the standard errors of the β ratios were not computed.

TABLE 7.3 (Continued) Cotton Supply Functions, 1883–1914 [S_t form]

Estimated Parameter	Tennessee	Alabama	Mississippi
$\alpha\mu$	–3.974(3.380) [–1.176]	–2.738(1.407) [–1.946]	4.736(2.855) [1.659]
$\beta\mu$	.321(.0767) [4.191]	.114(.0266)] [4.288]	.116(.0298) [3.894]
$\delta\mu$	.00147(.00179) [.817]	.00116(.000704) [1.652]	–.00277(.00151) [–1.834]
$1-\mu$	.747(.130) [5.728]	.539(.169) [3.181]	.453(.166) [2.735]
ρ	.220	–.0829	.550
β	1.269	.247	.212
δ	.00581	.00252	–.00506
μ	.253	.461	.547
R^2	.711	.683	.709
$F(3,27)$	22.119	19.403	21.912

TABLE 7.3 (Continued) Cotton Supply Functions, 1883-1914 [S_t form]

Estimated Parameter	Arkansas	Louisiana	Texas
$\alpha\mu$	–2.801(2.672) [–1.048]	11.198(7.431) [1.507]	–12.170(4.734) [–2.571]
$\beta\mu$	.160(.0476) [3.371]	.133(.0468) [2.851]	.0995(.0317) [3.137]
$\delta\mu$	.00110(.00139) [.795]	–.00615(.00394) [–1.562]	.00614(.00245) [2.505]
$1-\mu$	.560(.157) [3.553]	.679(.159) [4.267]	.457(.174) [2.618]
ρ	.147	.590	.0842
β	.364	.414	.183
δ	.00250	–.0192	.0113
μ	.440	.321	.543
R^2	.544	.886	.910
$F(3,27)$	10.748	69.761	90.955

TABLE 7.4   Cotton Supply Functions, 1883–1914 [A_t form]

$A_t = \alpha\mu + \beta\mu P_{t-1} + \delta\mu t + (1 - \mu)A_{t-1} + u_t$;
$u_t = \rho u_{t-1} + v_t$; all variables in logs except t.

The numbers in ordinary parentheses to the right of each parameter estimate are the (biased downward) standard errors; the numbers in brackets below the standard errors are the associated (and biased upward) "t-statistics."

Estimated Parameter	North Carolina	South Carolina	Georgia	Florida
$\alpha\mu$	−6.509(3.504)	−8.477(2.546)	−11.255(3.892)	.0644(3.211)
	[−1.857]	[−3.329]	[−2.892]	[.0201]
$\beta\mu$	.327(.0637)	.156(.0384)	.179(.0526)	.147(.0511)
	[5.140]	[4.054]	[3.407]	[2.878]
$\delta\mu$	.00491(.00215)	.00661(.00188)	.00765(.00264)	.00148(.00178)
	[2.281]	[3.525]	[2.900]	[.832]
$1 - \mu$	.512(.144)	.429(.144)	.560(.146)	.419(.146)
	[3.542]	[2.973]	[3.830]	[2.876]
ρ	.338	−.0925	−.0789	−.184
β	.670	.273	.407	.253
δ	.0101	.0116	.0174	.00255
μ	.488	.571	.440	.581
R^2	.818	.910	.926	.484
$F(3,27)$	40.447	91.387	112.538	8.429

TABLE 7.4   (Continued) Cotton Supply Functions, 1883–1914 [A_t form]

Estimated Parameter	Tennessee	Alabama	Mississippi
$\alpha\mu$	−.248(3.758) [−.0660]	−5.345(2.251) [−2.374]	5.509(8.449) [.652]
$\beta\mu$	.330(.0729) [4.525]	.166(.0416) [3.988]	.152(.0434) [3.512]
$\delta\mu$	.00110(.00188) [.585]	.00453(.00177) [2.564]	.000645(.00453) [.142]
$1 - \mu$	.618(.144) [4.305]	.558(.151) [3.686]	.126(.175) [.720]
ρ	.295	−.208	.766
β	.864	.376	.174
δ	.00288	.0102	.000738
μ	.382	.442	.874
R^2	.662	.876	.809
$F(3,27)$	17.596	63.635	38.175

TABLE 7.4   (Continued) Cotton Supply Functions, 1883–1914 [A_t form]

Estimated Parameter	Arkansas	Louisiana	Texas
$\alpha\mu$	−12.198(4.360) [−2.798]	4.421(8.363) [.529]	−9.746(9.082) [−1.073]
$\beta\mu$	.143(.0560) [2.557]	.192(.0665) [2.885]	.0812(.0434) [1.870]
$\delta\mu$	.00885(.00285) [3.102]	−.00129(.00439) [−.294]	.00578(.00528) [1.096]
$1 - \mu$	.348(.164) [2.123]	.674(.158) [4.261]	.848(.107) [7.953]
ρ	.0591	.574	−.377
β	.219	.589	.534
δ	.0136	−.00396	.0380
μ	.652	.326	.152
R^2	.834	.802	.984
$F(3,27)$	45.345	36.363	558.040

ture do not begin until 1882; and the final year was chosen to avoid possible structural changes accompanying World War I. Also, the period 1882–1914 includes those years (except for 1880) covered by the production function estimates.

Examination of these results shows that the parameter estimates for both forms of the supply functions are reasonable in sign and magnitude. The coefficients of the relative price and the lagged acreage variable are positive in every state. The coefficients of P_{t-1} are large compared to their (biased) standard errors in most cases. The estimated speeds of adjustment μ lie between zero and one. The values of the test statistic F are significantly different from zero at the .01 level for every state's supply function. The model works well in explaining either S_t or A_t, and Southern agricultural producers appear to have been flexible and sensitive in responding to changes in the relative price of cotton.

The general plausibility of the estimated parameters does not settle the cotton overproduction dispute, however. Further analysis of the results is necessary. The coefficient of the trend is positive in seven out of ten states for the S_t functions and for nine out of ten states for the A_t functions, although in most cases the associated "t-statistic" is not very large. These positive coefficients indicate that there was a general increase in total acreage devoted to cotton, and that a majority of states gave over an increasing share of their acreage to the cultivation of cotton. The trend of increasing cotton acreage in the A_t functions is hardly surprising, since 1882–1914 was a period of general agricultural expansion throughout the South. For this reason, the extension of the area devoted to cotton has little bearing on the overproduction question.

The apparent tendency for the share of acreage in cotton to increase in most states is also inconclusive, because it is consistent with either the overproduction hypothesis or with farmers' responding normally to changes in the underlying conditions of supply. If merchants insisted that any farmer who fell into the toils of debt had to grow cotton, the ordinary variance in farmers' fortunes would result in a few more of them each year becoming caught in the cotton trap. On the other hand, if technical progress were more rapid in cotton culture than in the alternative crops, and if world demand for cotton grew more rapidly than the demand for the South's alternative agricultural outputs, then it would be possible *both* for Southern farmers to concentrate more on cotton *and* for the relative price of cotton and the alternatives to be unchanged. This situation would be reflected in a positive coefficient of the trend term in the S_t regressions. Since the relative rates of growth of technical progress and world demand for cotton and the Southern alternatives are not known, the sign of the trend term alone is insufficient basis for accepting or rejecting the overproduction hypothesis. Furthermore, if the trend term merely reflects a specification error of some unknown type, then its sign has no bearing at all on the overproduction issue.

Nevertheless, the estimates of the other parameters do bear on the question of overproduction. From the estimates of the supply functions it is possible to calculate the amount of time that would have been required for farmers to adjust to a given once-and-for-all change in the relative cotton price. A lengthy period of adjustment to such a price change would constitute evidence of some sort of institutional or structural rigidity that could have resulted in cotton overproduction. Assume that at $t = \tau$, the suppliers were in long-run equilibrium at relative price level P. Then assume a once-and-for-all shift in the price level to P'. Define $k(n)$ as the proportion of the adjustment completed after n years. To compute $k(n)$ it is necessary to compare $X_{\tau+n}$ to what X would have been if the price had remained at P, as well as to the level X would have reached if it had achieved its long-run equilibrium value. In the notation of figure 7.1,

$$k(n) = \frac{X_{\tau+n} - V_{\tau+n}}{W_{\tau+n} - V_{\tau+n}} \tag{7.21}$$

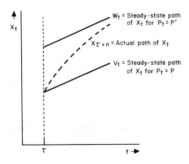

Figure   7.1

If the disturbance is ignored for purposes of calculating values of $k(n)$,

$$X_{\tau+n} = \alpha\mu + \beta\mu P' + \delta\mu(\tau + n) + (1 - \mu) X_{\tau+n-1}$$
$$= \alpha\mu + \beta\mu P' + \delta\mu(\tau + n) + (1 - \mu)[\alpha\mu + \beta\mu P' + \delta\mu(\tau + n - 1)$$
$$+ (1 - \mu) X_{\tau+n-2}]$$
$$\vdots$$

$$= [\alpha\mu + \beta\mu P' + \delta\mu\tau] \sum_{j=0}^{n-1} (1 - \mu)^j + \delta\mu \sum_{j=0}^{n-1} (n - j)(1 - \mu)^j$$
$$+ (1 - \mu)^n X_\tau$$

$$= [\alpha + \beta P' + \delta\tau]\mu \sum_{j=0}^{n-1} (1 - \mu)^j + \delta\mu \sum_{j=0}^{n-1} (n - j)(1 - \mu)^j$$
$$+ (1 - \mu)^n[c + \beta P + \delta\tau]. \tag{7.22}$$

where $c = \alpha - \dfrac{(1 - \mu)\delta}{\mu}$ or $c = \alpha$, depending on whether $\gamma \neq 1$ or $\gamma = 1$.

Then from the definition of $k(n)$

$$k(n) = \{(\alpha + \beta P' + \delta\tau)\,\mu \sum_{j=0}^{n-1} (1 - \mu)^j + \delta\mu \sum_{j=0}^{n-1} (n - j)(1 - \mu)^j$$
$$+ (1 - \mu)^n[c + \beta P + \delta\tau] - [c + \beta P + \delta(\tau + n)]\} /$$
$$\{[c + \beta P' + \delta(\tau + n)] - [c + \beta P + \delta(\tau + n)]\} \tag{7.23}$$

Since

$$\sum_{j=0}^{n-1} (1 - \mu)^j = \frac{1 - (1 - \mu)^n}{\mu} \tag{7.24}$$

(7.23) reduces to

$$k(n) = \{[\alpha + \beta P' + \delta\tau][1 - (1 - \mu)^n] + \delta\mu \sum_{j=0}^{n-1} (n - j)(1 - \mu)^j$$
$$+ (1 - \mu)^n(c + \beta P + \delta\tau) - [c + \beta P + \delta(\tau + n)]\} / \beta(P' - P) \tag{7.25}$$

$$k(n) = \{(\alpha - c) + \beta(P' - P) - (1 - \mu)^n[(\alpha - c) + \beta(P' - P)]$$
$$- \delta n + \delta\mu \sum_{j=0}^{n-1} (n - j)(1 - \mu)^j\} / \beta(P' - P) \tag{7.26}$$

Observe that if $\delta = 0$, $k(n)$ reduces to

$$k(n) = 1 - (1 - \mu)^n \tag{7.27}$$

Also, if δ is small and n is not too large (so that $\alpha \approx c$ and the last two terms in the numerator of (7.26) are small relative to the middle terms) then (7.27) will hold approximately. It should be noted that in this case $k(n)$ does not depend on the magnitude of the price change. This is a reflection of the assumptions of constant elasticity of supply and proportional adjustment in the model. It can be seen from the estimates in tables 7.3 and 7.4 that δ is indeed small, exceeding .02 in only one case. For these reasons the convenient approximation (7.27) will be used to calculate $k(n)$, rather than the exact expression (7.26). These approximate values of $k(n)$ for n from one through five years are given in tables 7.5 and 7.6.

The table of $k(n)$ for the S_t form of the supply function shows that every state but Tennessee and Louisiana would have completed over 90 percent of its final adjustment after only five years. After three years, all the states except these two would have completed over three-fourths of the final adjustment to a once-and-for-all price change. When the unweighted average of the $k(n)$ values is calculated for all states, it can be seen that the South as a whole would have completed two-thirds of its final adjustment to a relative price change after only two years, and over 80 percent of the final adjustment after three years. Essentially similar conclusions can be drawn from the $k(n)$ values in the A_t model. These values of $k(n)$ indicate that even though the cotton suppliers adjusted to price changes with a lag, there is no reason to believe that a state of chronic overproduction could have persisted over any lengthy period after a price decline.

Of course, farmers may have been distressed by not being able to achieve their desired planting mix immediately. Similarly, anything short of instantaneous adjustment of price expectations may have led to overoptimistic plans and frustrated hopes. On the other hand, completely rational behavior can allow for adjustment with lags. To get any perspective on the behavior of late nineteenth-century Southern farmers, it is necessary to find a standard to judge them against. Specifically, it would be useful to know how their short- and long-run price elasticities and their speeds of adjustment compared to the same parameters for

TABLE 7.5 Approximate $k(n)$ for $n = 1$ through 5, Cotton Supply Functions in S_t Form

State	1	2	3	4	5
North Carolina	.409	.651	.794	.878	.928
South Carolina	.424	.668	.809	.890	.937
Georgia	.411	.653	.796	.880	.929
Florida	.536	.785	.900	.954	.978
Tennessee	.253	.442	.583	.689	.767
Alabama	.461	.709	.843	.916	.955
Mississippi	.547	.795	.907	.958	.981
Arkansas	.440	.686	.824	.902	.945
Louisiana	.321	.539	.687	.787	.856
Texas	.543	.791	.905	.956	.980
Overall average	.429	.667	.801	.879	.924

TABLE 7.6   Approximate $k(n)$ for $n = 1$ through 5, Cotton Supply Functions in A_t Form

State	1	2	3	4	5
North Carolina	.488	.738	.866	.931	.965
South Carolina	.571	.816	.921	.966	.985
Georgia	.440	.686	.824	.902	.945
Florida	.581	.824	.926	.969	.987
Tennessee	.382	.618	.764	.854	.910
Alabama	.442	.689	.826	.903	.946
Mississippi	.874	.984	.998	1.000	1.000
Arkansas	.652	.879	.958	.985	.995
Louisiana	.326	.546	.694	.794	.861
Texas	.152	.281	.390	.483	.561
Overall average	.491	.706	.817	.879	.916

other United States farmers during roughly the same period.

Fortunately the material for such a comparison is at hand. Fisher and Temin estimated a model of the behavior of wheat suppliers in the United States over the period 1866–1914 which is identical to the S_t form of the cotton supply functions in specification.[8] The dependent variable in the Fisher and Temin study is the log of the proportion of acres in major crops devoted to wheat, their relative price is the wheat price paid to farmers divided by an index of the prices of the major alternatives (to wheat), and they also included a trend as an independent variable. The parameter estimates of the wheat supply functions are plausible and significant, but differ in certain respects from the cotton estimates.

In wheat supply functions of seventeen states, Fisher and Temin found the trend coefficient to be negative in thirteen. This contrasts with seven of ten trend terms positive for the cotton supply functions. The Northern and Western wheat-producing states were not increasingly specializing in wheat the way the Southern states may have been specializing in cotton. Thus it can hardly be argued that wheat farmers were "locked in" to the production of their leading cash crop; so differences between the other parameters of the cotton and wheat supply functions might be expected.

Before actually comparing the estimates, consider what the alternative

8. Fisher and Temin, "Regional Specialization," pp. 142–143. Fisher and Temin actually reported estimates of two models, one of which included the log of lagged relative yield as an independent variable. Only the estimates from their specification identical in form to (7.16) of the text are used in the subsequent comparisons, however.

hypotheses would predict. If cotton overproduction prevailed, farmers presumably were prevented from growing alternative crops by their own ignorance or by merchants who controlled short-term credit lines and who insisted on cotton. In this case, therefore, the short-run response of cotton farmers to price changes should have been weaker than the response of Western and Northern farmers. In the long run, the price elasticity of the cotton farmers may have also been lower than the price elasticity of wheat farmers, but it would not necessarily be so. Even monopolistic merchants would eventually respond to changes in price conditions; so no firm prediction can be made about the long-run price elasticity under the overproduction hypothesis. The important prediction is that if farmers were locked into cotton, they must have been locked in over the short run, because credit was extended on a yearly basis and because planting decisions had to be made every year.

On the other hand, if Southern farmers were as flexible and responsive as their Western and Northern counterparts, there should have been little difference in the short-run price elasticities between regions. Even if certain Southern lands had an enormous comparative advantage in cotton culture, the lands which would be shifted between alternative crops would have been those which were not so cotton-specific.

Similarly, the overproduction hypothesis would predict a lower speed of adjustment for Southern farmers than for farmers in the rest of the country, under the supposition that institutional and/or attitudinal rigidities prevented them from rapidly adjusting their actual plantings or price expectations in response to market conditions. Conversely, unrestricted farmers should have been able to adjust with roughly equal rapidity in either region.

The short-run price elasticity, the speed of adjustment, and the long-run price elasticity are not all independent, since any two are sufficient to calculate the third. Even given the expectations a priori concerning the relative magnitudes of the short-run price elasticities and speeds of adjustment outlined above, the relative magnitudes of the long-run price elasticities are not determined, since $\beta = \beta\mu/\mu$. The smaller the long-run elasticity, the smaller the ultimate producers' response to a price change; so the long-run price elasticity may be thought of as an inverse measure of the relative comparative advantage of a region in the production of its major crop. Thus, a relatively small long-run price elasticity for cotton compared with wheat would indicate that the South's comparative advantage in cotton was stronger than the West's comparative advantage in wheat. This would be the case if Southern lands were so ideally suited to cotton that a relatively small proportion of those lands would be switched to alternative crops even in the face of a permanent cotton price decline, compared with the shift of wheat lands in response to a comparable wheat price decline. But the relative magnitudes of these long-run price elasticities would not resolve the overproduction issue. Once the values of $k(n)$ show that permanent adjustment would be completed in a reasonable length of time, it is comparison of the short-run price elasticities and the speeds of adjustment between wheat and cotton that is relevant to the overproduction question.

Comparison of these parameters estimated in supply functions of the S_t form fails to support the predictions of the overproduction hypothesis. Table 7.7 shows that the short-run price elasticities for the cotton-producing states all lie above the median short-run wheat price elasticity. Similarly, Table 7.8 shows that the speeds of adjustment for the Southern states all lie in the upper range of speeds of adjustments for the wheat states.

The long-run price elasticities implied by the estimated values of $\beta\mu$ and μ also reveal an interesting pattern. Except for the border states of Tennessee and North Carolina, the long-run cotton price elasticities are all in the *lower* range of long-run wheat price elasticities. It would appear that the deep South's comparative advantage in cotton was stronger

TABLE 7.7   Comparison of Short-Run Price Elasticities

Cotton				Wheat
State	$\beta\mu =$ short-run price elasticity $= \beta\mu$			State
Tennessee	.321		.284	Wisconsin
North Carolina	.318		.277	Michigan
Arkansas	.160		.249	Kansas
Florida	.149		.191	Ohio
Georgia	.134	All-South	.162	Iowa
Louisiana	.133	Range	.144	North Dakota
South Carolina	.126		.136	Minnesota
Mississippi	.116		.121	New York
Alabama	.114		.0891	California
Texas	.0995		.0852	Nebraska
			.0804	South Dakota
			.0712	Virginia
			.0704	Maryland
			.0488	Illinois
			.0453	Pennsylvania
			.0278	Missouri
			.0229	Indiana

TABLE 7.8 Comparison of Speeds of Adjustment

Cotton				Wheat
State	$\mu =$ speed of adjustment $= \mu$			State
Mississippi	.547		.932	Indiana
Texas	.543		.410	Missouri
Florida	.536		.350	North Dakota
Alabama	.461		.280	Illinois
Arkansas	.440	All-South	.272	Wisconsin
South Carolina	.424	Range	.254	Kansas
Georgia	.411		.245	Michigan
North Carolina	.409		.235	Minnesota
Louisiana	.321		.216	Virginia
Tennessee	.253		.212	Ohio
			.185	Maryland
			.153	New York
			.152	Iowa
			.120	South Dakota
			.0909	Pennsylvania
			.0711	Nebraska
			.0667	California

TABLE 7.9 Comparison of Long-Run Price Elasticities

Cotton				Wheat
State	$\beta =$ long-run price elasticity $= \beta$			State
Tennessee	1.269		1.336	California
North Carolina	.778		1.198	Nebraska
Louisiana	.414		1.132	Michigan
Arkansas	.364		1.067	Iowa
Georgia	.326		1.043	Wisconsin
South Carolina	.297	Deep South	.982	Kansas
Florida	.278	Range	.902	Ohio
Alabama	.247		.792	New York
Mississippi	.212		.669	South Dakota
Texas	.183		.579	Minnesota
			.498	Pennsylvania
			.412	North Dakota
			.380	Maryland
			.329	Virginia
			.174	Illinois
			.0678	Missouri
			.0246	Indiana

than the comparative advantage of the rest of the agricultural states in wheat. This is certainly not incompatible with casual contemporary impressions of the dominance of cotton culture in nineteenth-century Southern agriculture, nor with the widespread productivity advantage associated with cotton culture throughout the period 1880–1910, demonstrated in chapters 4 and 5. Also, the largest long-run cotton price elasticities are displayed by the border states of North Carolina and Tennessee, and this too is consistent with a comparative advantage explanation of the long-run price elasticity.

The results strongly suggest that Southern cotton farmers were as flexible and as price-responsive as wheat farmers in the rest of the United States during the late nineteenth and early twentieth centuries. The supply functions whose parameters were compared were identical in specification, including the error structure. They were estimated by identical statistical techniques, even using the same program for the computations. The cotton supply functions and wheat supply functions were similar except for the trend differences and parameter patterns discussed above. Both sets of supply functions fit the data well, with coefficient signs and values which are plausible a priori. Nothing in the results contradicts the flexible specialization hypothesis; yet to find support for the overproduction hypothesis in the South requires construction of a tortuous explanation of the "paradoxical" results.[9] While comparison of these particular supply functions does not exhaust all possibilities for finding evidence of the overproduction hypothesis in the behavior of Southern agricultural producers,[10] the pattern that does seem to emerge is that the concentration in cotton by Southern farmers derived from regional advantages of geography and climate. Rural furnishing merchants may or may not have exercised a credit monopoly in local markets, but apparently they did not force overproduction of cotton in the face of given price levels or changes in the relative prices of the alternative crops. The supply function comparisons, combined with the unequivocal productivity advantage associated with cotton described in chapters 4 and 5, suggest that by rejecting the panacea of diversification, Southern farmers implicitly displayed a solid grasp of the realities of their regional economy.

9. See appendix E, section (5).
10. Ibid.

Appendix A
The Data

The Data for the Production Function Estimates

The county cross sections of values of each of the variables were taken from the published censuses of 1880, 1890, 1900, and 1910.[1] The census definitions of each of these variables, their units of measurement, and the census sources of the cross sections are listed in the following table. The volume numbers of the sources for each variable in each year refer to volumes of the census for that year.

Great problems are attendant on any use of census data, even though

1. The Census volumes which formed the basic data source for the production function estimates were the following:

U.S. Census Office, *Tenth Census, 1880,* vol. 1: *Statistics of the Population of the United States;* vol. 3: *Report on the Production of Agriculture;* vols. 5–6: *Report on Cotton Production in the United States, also Embracing Agricultural and Physicogeographical Descriptions of the Several Cotton States and of California,* ed. by Eugene W. Hilgard.

U.S. Census Office, *Eleventh Census, 1890,* vol. 1: *Report on Population of the United States;* vol. 5: *Reports on the Statistics of Agriculture in the United States, Agriculture by Irrigation in the Western Part of the United States, and Statistics of Fisheries in the United States; Compendium of the Eleventh Census: 1890,* 3 parts.

U.S. Census Office, *Twelfth Census, 1900,* vols. 1–2: *Population;* vols. 5–6: *Agriculture.*

U.S. Bureau of the Census, *Thirteenth Census of the United States: 1910,* vol. 2: *Population, 1910. Reports by States, with Statistics for Counties, Cities and Other Civil Divisions—Alabama-Montana;* vol. 3: *Population, 1910. Reports by States, with Statistics for Counties, Cities and Other Civil Divisions—Nebraska-Wyoming, Alaska, Hawaii, and Porto Rico* [sic]; vol. 5: *Agriculture, 1909 and 1910. General Report and Analysis;* vol. 6: *Agriculture, 1909 and 1910. Reports by States, with Statistics for Counties—Alabama-Montana;* vol. 7: *Agriculture, 1909 and 1910. Reports by States, with Statistics for Counties—Nebraska-Wyoming, Alaska, Hawaii, and Porto Rico* [sic].

In subsequent references to the Census, only the number and year of the Census, and a shortened title of the volume of the Census (for example, *Agriculture, Population,* etc.) along with the appropriate page or table reference will be given.

TABLE A.1   Census Definition, Units, and Source—1880

Variable

Q "Estimated value of all farm productions (sold, consumed, or on hand), 1879," in dollars, vol. 3: *Agriculture*. . . , Table VII.

W Total white rural population = Total white population − white population of cities and towns of 4,000 inhabitants and upward.

Total white population, in number of people, vol. 1: *Population*. . . , Table V.

White population of cities and towns of 4,000 inhabitants and upward, in number of people, vol. 1: *Population*. . . , Table VI.

B Total black rural population = Total black population − black population of cities and towns of 4,000 inhabitants and upward. The sources of these variables are the same as for the variables used in computing W.

R $R = W + B$

H Acres in Cotton, 1879, vol. 3: *Agriculture*. . . , Table XIII.

T "Total improved land in farms," in acres, vol. 3, *Agriculture*. . . , Table VII.

J $J = T - H$

K "Value of farming implements and machinery," in dollars, vol. 3: *Agriculture*. . . , Table VII.

S_i Soil-type dummy variables, vols. 5–6: *Report on Cotton Production*. . . , Table I (for each state's report).

TABLE A.1   (Continued) Census Definition, Units, and Source—1890

Variable

Q "Estimated value of farm products, 1889," in dollars, vol. 5: *Agriculture*. . . , Table 6.

W Total white rural population = total white population − white population of places of 2,500 inhabitants or more.

Total white population, in number of people, vol. 1: *Population*. . . , Table 15.

White population of places of 2,500 inhabitants or more, number of people, *Compendium*. . . , part 1, Table 17.

B Same as for W, with blacks instead of whites.

R $R = W + B$

H Cotton acres, 1889, vol. 5: *Agriculture*. . . , Table 16.

T "Improved acres in farms," vol. 5: *Agriculture*. . . , Table 6.

J $J = T - H$

K "Valuation: Implements and Machinery," in dollars, vol. 5: *Agriculture*. . . , Table 6.

S_i Soil-type dummy variables, same as 1880.

TABLE A.1 (Continued) Census Definition, Units, and Source—1900

Variable	

Q "Value of products not fed to livestock, [1899]," in dollars, vol. 5: *Agriculture*. . . , Table 19.

W Total white rural population = total white population − white population of places of 2,500 inhabitants or more.

   Total white population, in number of people, vol. 1: *Population*. . . , Table 19.

   White population of places having 2,500 inhabitants or more, in number of people, vol. 1: *Population*. . . , Table 23.

B Same as for W, with blacks instead of whites.

R $R = W + B$

H Cotton acres, 1899, and sea island cotton acres, 1899, both from vol. 6: *Agriculture*. . . , Table 10.

T "Improved acres in farms," vol. 5: *Agriculture*. . . , Table 19.

J $J = T - H$

K "Value of farm property: Implements and Machinery," in dollars, vol. 5: *Agriculture*. . . , Table 19.

S_i Soil-type dummy variables, same as 1880.

TABLE A.1 (Continued) Census Definition, Units, and Source—1910

Variable	

Q "Total value of all crops, 1909," in dollars, vols. 6–7: *Agriculture*. . . , Table 4 (for each state).

W Total white population, in number of people, vols. 2–3: *Population*. . . , Table I (for each state).

B Same as for W, with blacks instead of whites.

R Rural population = Total county population − population of places of 2,500 or more, vols. 2–3: *Population*. . . , Table 1 (for each state).

   Note that the proportion of blacks in this census year is computed as $B/(W + B)$, not as B/R as in the previous years.

H Cotton acres, 1909, vols. 6–7: *Agriculture*. . . , Table 4 (for each state).

T "Improved land in farms," in acres, vols. 6–7: *Agriculture*. . . , Table 1 (for each state).

J $J = T - H$

K Value of implements and machinery, in dollars, vols. 6–7: *Agriculture*. . . , Table 1 (for each state).

S_i Soil-type dummy variables, same as 1880.

such data are the best and most extensive quantitative record of agriculture for the period. The first difficulty with the census cross sections is that not all variables are measured at the same point in time. For example, the output variable Q is an estimated value of output in the year prior to the enumeration. Since the actual enumeration was scheduled before all the census year's crops had been harvested, estimated output of the previous year was the best measure of production which could be obtained. Similarly, the acreages planted to cotton and to all the other crops separately tabled, as well as value of fertilizers applied, are all estimated values for the year prior to the census year. On the other hand the input variables of population, total improved acres, and capital stock were all measured directly by the census-takers in the years of the censuses. Thus an error is introduced by the timing discrepancy. There is no way around this difficulty. Even so, the various input and output variables probably did not change too drastically from one year to the next, so that the error in measurement incurred by using the XXX9 value of output or cotton acreage as a proxy for the (unobserved) XXX0 census year values will not be too great.

A second difficulty with the output variable is that it is not identically defined in the four census years, particularly with regard to its treatment of the value of animal products produced on the farm. In commenting on the inadequacies of this recorded output to measure real farm income accurately, the superintendent of the 1880 census observed that the returns from both 1870 and 1880 were likely to be on the conservative side because (1) the products were valued at the farm, not in the market; (2) double counting was avoided by excluding the value of products fed to livestock [actually this is a virtue rather than a drawback of the data]; (3) the farmers were indisposed to report the value of the products they consumed on the farm; and (4) farmers tended to underestimate the value of their output out of fear of taxation.[2] The 1890 census used the same form of inquiry relating to the value of farm products as the tenth census. These values were also undoubtedly underestimated, since for the U.S. as a whole the reported values of the "six cereals, with hay and cotton, had a farm value in excess of that total [of all farm products] and . . . it, therefore, was deficient to an amount in excess of the value of all animals sold, and animals slaughtered on farms, and of all miscellaneous products of the farm."[3] Of course, this does not mean that the six cereals and hay and cotton were meticulously reported and

2. *Tenth Census, 1880,* vol. 3: *Agriculture,* p. xxv, cited in *Twelfth Census, 1900,* vol. 5: *Agriculture,* p. cxx.
3. *Twelfth Census, 1900,* vol. 5: *Agriculture,* p. cxxi.

the value of animal products systematically omitted, although for the reasons given, the degree of underreporting of livestock products was probably greater than for the major crops.

Recognizing these difficulties, the compilers of the twelfth census (1900) "made an effort to obtain, if possible, a more complete statement of the value of farm products. To secure such a statement, the farmers and enumerators were requested to state the value of all the important staple crops raised on farms, that of all animals sold, and animals slaughtered on farms, that of the poultry raised, and that of the various products not otherwise reported." While "the values of the great staple crops, as cereals, cotton, and hay, were obtained with a comparatively narrow margin of error," the compilers of this census still felt that miscellaneous products and livestock sales and slaughters were underestimated. Nevertheless: "The aggregate of such omissions is believed to be not less than 5 nor more than 10 percent of the total reported value of farm products."[4] In the 1910 census, the aggregate value of all farm products was not collected. The 1910 census supervisors apparently despaired of being able to measure livestock output accurately:

It is impossible to give a total representing the value of the annual production of all live stock products, for the reason that the total value of products of the business of raising domestic animals can not be calculated from the census returns. Even if a total representing the value of the annual production of live stock products could be obtained and were added to the value of all crops, the sum would not accurately represent the total value of farm products for the year, because much duplication would result from the fact that part of the crops are fed to the live stock.[5]

In using the total value of all crops as the output variable in this year, the double counting of adding the value of crops fed to livestock to the value of livestock sold, consumed, or added to is again avoided, but at the cost of underestimating the contribution of the livestock to total production.

To summarize: for each census the output variable tends to underestimate total agricultural output. The most persistent systematic underestimation is probably of the contribution of livestock to output, due to exclusion of "betterments and additions to stock" for 1880–1900 and to using the value of crops fed to livestock in 1910 to approximate the total value of livestock products.

4. Ibid., pp. cxxi–cxxii.
5. *Thirteenth Census, 1910*, vol. 5: *Agriculture, General Report*, p. 473.

The labor inputs consist of total black and white rural populations. The difficulty here is in distinguishing the agricultural labor force from the rural population. First of all, counties containing a city in which either the black or white population of the city exceeded 10,000 were excluded from the sample altogether. This was done to avoid contamination of the sample of rural counties by inclusion of the counties containing cities such as Atlanta and New Orleans. In addition, in 1880 the inhabitants of all cities with populations greater than 4,000 were deducted from the county populations to arrive at the rural population figure; in 1890 and 1900 the inhabitants of all cities with a total population greater than 2,500 were deducted; in 1910 the rural population was reported directly. The 1910 rural population is directly comparable with the 1890 and 1900 definitions, since the census definition of rural population excludes inhabitants of places of 2,500 or more people.[6] Of course, this procedure is open to two sources of error. First, by deducting the town dwellers from the total rural population, agricultural workers who lived in the towns but worked regularly in the surrounding fields were omitted, as well as some seasonal agricultural workers who lived in the towns and who performed agricultural labor only at peak periods. Counteracting this undercounting of agricultural laborers, the procedure employed includes in the agricultural labor force the inhabitants of the smaller towns and villages who were employed full time in activities other than agriculture.

As well as not attempting to assess the relative participation of town and city dwellers in agriculture, no adjustment was made for the difference between total population and working population. In other words, the same participation rate was assumed for the white and black populations, and no correction was made for age-structure differences. It was simply assumed that total rural population was a proxy measure for the total agricultural labor force of each race. (See appendix E, section 2, for further discussion of the labor force measurements.)

The acreage variables are the reported acres in cotton, and total improved acres in farms. The census definition of "improved acres" corresponds most closely of any of the census land variables to the land input to total agricultural production:

Improved Land includes all land regularly tilled or mowed, land in pasture which has been cleared or tilled, land lying fallow, land in gardens,

6. *Thirteenth Census, 1910,* vols. 2–3: *Population,* table 2 contains for each state a list of the county locations of incorporated places, which proved invaluable in locating the towns of 2,500 inhabitants or more (4,000 or more in 1880) in their respective counties.

orchards, vineyards, and nurseries, and land occupied by farm build-ings. . . . Substantially the same classification of farm land has been employed at the different censuses beginning with 1880, except that in 1890 and 1900 no distinction was made between woodland and other unimproved land.[7]

Using total land in farms as the agricultural land input would include some lands that made little, if any, contribution to output (that is, it would include lands which were claimed, but not worked at all), while any land input more restricted than total improved acres might exclude some pasturage or other land which did contribute to total output. The inclusion of land lying fallow in the improved-acres category probably introduces some error into this variable as a measure of land input to production, however.

When acres devoted to sea island cotton and uplands cotton were re-ported separately, the total cotton acreage figure was obtained by simply adding the two cotton acreages. This ignores any difference between the quality or land requirements of the two types of cotton.

The agricultural capital variable used in all four census years was the "value of implements and machinery" total reported for each county. Obviously, implements and machinery were not the only component of agricultural capital. Farm animals were a vital part of the total capital stock, and fertilizers were also used. Nevertheless, the value of imple-ments and machinery was chosen as the single measure of farm capital. Land, labor, and the possible capital measures were highly correlated with each other. In test regressions this collinearity was manifested in er-ratic behavior of the coefficient of total number of draft animals when that variable was included in regressions containing the other inputs. The coefficient of the draft animals (horses and mules) variable was often negative, and seldom was it large compared to its standard error. Similarly, no substantial improvement in fit was obtained when both the value of fertilizers and the value of implements and machinery were in-cluded in the regressions. No clear superiority in performance between value of fertilizers and value of implements and machinery emerged. In addition, many counties utilized no fertilizer at all, and the form of the production function is such that output is zero if the capital input is zero. Hence, either the production function would have to be respecified or the counties not using fertilizer would have to be omitted from the sam-ple, if fertilizer were used to measure capital or entered the production function as another input.

7. U.S. Bureau of the Census, *Fourteenth Census of the United States Taken in the Year 1920,* vol. 5: *Agriculture: General Report and Analytical Tables,* p. 17.

For these reasons it was decided to use the value of implements and machinery as the sole measure of agricultural capital input. Given the high degree of collinearity between the potential candidates for measuring this variable, as well as the difficulty of many counties' not using any fertilizer, this choice of a capital measure is probably no great source of error in the estimates.

Finally, the soil types are those of the 1880 *Survey of Cotton Production,* edited by Eugene W. Hilgard. This 1880 survey classified each county of the South as belonging to one of twenty-eight soil categories.[8] Each state contained from four to twelve of these different types of soil. Since the sample for each estimate of the production function consisted of a particular state in a particular census year, dummy variables for each state were defined on the basis only of the soil types in each state. The definitions of the soil types corresponding to the dummy variables for each state are as follows:[9]

Alabama:
S1 — Metamorphic Region
S2 — Coosa Valley Region
S3 — Coal-Measures Region
S4 — Tennessee Valley Region
S5 — Oak and Hickory Uplands, with Shortleaf Pine
S6 — Gravelly Hills, with Longleaf Pine
S7 — Oak and Hickory Uplands, with Longleaf Pine
S8 — Central Prairie Region
S9 — Longleaf Pine Region

Arkansas:
S1 — Alluvial Region, Mississippi Bottomlands
S2 — Alluvial Region, Crowley's Ridge
S3 — Gray Silt Prairie Region
S4 — Yellow-Loam Region
S5 — Red-Loam Region
S6 — Northern Barrens and Hills

8. Richard C. Sutch and Roger L. Ransom, "Economic Regions of the South in 1880," Working Paper no. 3 of Southern Economic History Project Working Paper Series, p. 12.
9. *Tenth Census, 1880,* vols. 5–6: *Report on Cotton Production,* ed. Eugene W. Hilgard, table 1 (for each state). The *smallest* soil type divisions reported in these state tables are assigned dummy variables, even when these subdivisions are part of a more inclusive soil type (for example, S1 and S2 in Arkansas, etc.)

Florida:
S1 — Oak, Hickory, and Pine Upland Region
S2 — Longleaf Pine Region, Short Staple Cotton
S3 — Longleaf Pine Region, Sea-Island Cotton
S4 — Pitch Pine, Treeless, and Alluvial Region, Sea-Island Cotton

Georgia:
S1 — Northwest Georgia
S2 — Metamorphic Region, Blue Ridge Counties
S3 — Metamorphic Region, Middle Georgia Counties
S4 — Central Cotton Belt
S5 — Southern Oak, Hickory, and Pine Uplands
S6 — Longleaf Pine and Wire-Grass Region, Limesink Division
S7 — Longleaf Pine and Wire-Grass Region, Pine Barrens Division
S8 — Pine Flats and Coast Counties

Louisiana:
S1 — Alluvial Region, North of Red River
S2 — Alluvial Region, South of Red River
S3 — Tidewater Parishes
S4 — Bluff Region
S5 — Attakapas Region
S6 — Longleaf Pine Region
S7 — Oak Uplands

Mississippi:
S1 — Northeastern Prairie Region, Prairie Belt
S2 — Northeastern Prairie Region, Pontotoc Ridge
S3 — Yellow-Loam Region, Brown-Loam Tablelands
S4 — Yellow-Loam Region, Shortleaf Pine, and Oak, Upland Region
S5 — Cane Hills
S6 — Mississippi Alluvial Region
S7 — Central Prairie Region
S8 — Longleaf Pine and Coast Region, Longleaf Pine, Oak, and Hickory
     Uplands
S9 — Longleaf Pine and Coast Region, Longleaf Pine Hills and Flats

North Carolina:
S1 — Seaboard Region
S2 — Longleaf Pine Region
S3 — Oak Uplands Region
S4 — Transmontane Region

South Carolina: [See note below]
S1 — Longleaf Pine Flats and Savannahs
S2 — Marshes, Swamps, and Live-Oak Lands
S3 — Oak, Hickory and Longleaf Pine Hills
S4 — Sand Hills Belt
S5 — Granite and Metamorphic Gray and Red Lands of the Piedmont

Tennessee:
S1 — Alluvial Plain of the Mississippi River
S2 — Alluvial Plain of the Mississippi River and Plateau Slope of West
       Tennessee, Alluvial Plain and Bluff
S3 — Alluvial Plain of the Mississippi River and Plateau Slope of
       West Tennessee, Brown-Loam Tablelands, Midland Counties
S4 — Alluvial Plain of the Mississippi River and Plateau Slope of
       West Tennessee, Summit Region of Watershed
S5 — Western Valley of Tennessee River
S6 — The Highlands, or Highland Rim of Middle Tennessee, West-
       ern Subdivision
S7 — The Highlands, or Highland Rim of Middle Tennessee, Eastern
       Subdivision
S8 — Central Basin
S9 — Cumberland Tableland
S10 — Cumberland Tableland, Valley of East Tennessee, and Unaka
       Mountain Region, Tableland and Valley
S11 — Cumberland Tableland, Valley of East Tennessee, and Unaka
       Mountain Region, Valley
S12 — Cumberland Tableland, Valley of East Tennessee, and Unaka
       Mountain Region, Valley and Unaka

Texas:
S1 — Oak, Hickory, and Pine Uplands
S2 — Longleaf Pine Region
S3 — Southern and Coast Prairie Region, Region East of the Brazos
       River
S4 — Southern and Coast Prairie Region, Region West of the Brazos
       River
S5 — Central Black Prairie Region
S6 — Northwestern Red-Loam Prairie Region
S7 — Red River Alluvial Counties
S8 — Brazos Alluvial or "Sugar Bowl" Region
S9 — Rio Grande Valley
S10 — Noncotton-Producing Counties [not a physical soil type]
S11 — Unorganized Counties [not a soil type]

The counties belonging in each classification were taken directly from state tables in the 1880 *Survey,* with the exception of South Carolina. For some reason no soil categorization table appeared for South Carolina in the copy of the census used, so the South Carolina soil types and county groupings were taken from the reproduction of the Hilgard classifications in Sutch and Ransom's "Economic Regions of the South."[10]

It would have been preferable to assign counties to more than one soil-type category in accordance with the proportions of their farm areas belonging to the different soil classifications. This was not done because it would have required geometric measurements from the soil-type maps of each state to determine the relative proportions, and even this would not guarantee that the *farmlands* were divided in proportions equal to the division of total land area. Some lands were economically useless swamps, mountains, or forested areas.

No comparable survey of soil types exists for the subsequent three censuses. For these years it was assumed that a county's soil type was the same as it had been in 1880. Since the soil-type classifications were based on chemical and geographical analyses, it is unlikely that these characteristics changed much over the forty-year period. Counties created after 1880 present a different problem. The 1910 census includes a list of all county boundary changes which took place after 1880.[11] Using this list it is possible to determine the counties from which new counties were created. Suppose that the new county was created out of pieces of n old counties. If a plurality of these old counties was of a particular soil type, the new county was classified as belonging to that soil-type category. If there was no such plurality the new county was arbitrarily assigned to one of the soil-type categories which the old counties belonged to. There were very few such cases. It would have been better to assign the newly created counties according to the preponderance of area of each type of soil, but this would have required use of detailed boundary-change maps, and it was felt not to be worth the data-collecting effort that would have been involved to obtain such maps. As can be seen from the results, these simplifications of the soil-type classifications do not vitiate the usefulness of the Hilgard categories.

Data for the Supply Function Estimates

In order to estimate cotton supply functions for each Southern state of the type proposed in chapter 7, two basic sets of data are required. The

10. Sutch and Ransom. "Economic Regions of the South," table 2, pp. 13–14; table B-1, pp. 64–68; table B-2, p. 94.
11. *Thirteenth Census,* 1910, vols. 2–3: *Population,* table 5 (for each state).

first is a yearly time series of measurements of the acreages in the various crops. The second is a comparable time series of prices paid to producers for their crops. The time span 1882–1914 chosen for the sample was based on the availability of the data and to correspond as closely as possible to the years covered by the production function estimates.

The period 1882–1914 is of sufficient length to permit statistically meaningful estimation of the supply function. The year 1914 was taken as the end point to eliminate disturbances in price and/or structure induced by World War I. The war may have disrupted Southern agriculture in many ways, such as draining agricultural labor away from the farms into the army or marking the beginning of the migration of blacks to the Northern cities.[12] The sample could not begin earlier than 1882 because no state-by-state series of consecutive yearly cotton prices could be found prior to that year. (See below for source and definition of the price variables.)

The data on crop acreages harvested are the revised statistics of the United States Department of Agriculture.[13] When the dependent vari-

12.   Paul S. Taylor, "Slave to Freedman," Working Paper no. 7 of the Southern Economic History Working Paper Series.

13.   The sources for both acreage and yield data are as follows:

Cotton: U.S. Department of Agriculture, Agricultural Marketing Service, *Cotton and Cottonseed: Acreage, Yield, Production, Disposition, Price, Value, by States, 1866–1952*, Statistical Bulletin no. 164.

Wheat: U.S. Department of Agriculture, Agricultural Marketing Service, *Wheat: Acreage, Yield, Production, by States, 1866–1943*, Statistical Bulletin no. 158.

Potatoes: U.S. Department of Agriculture, Bureau of Agricultural Economics, *Potatoes: Acreage, Production, Value, Farm Disposition, Jan. 1 Stocks, 1866–1950*, Statistical Bulletin no. 122.

Acreage and yield data for the other crops were not found in any of the regular Department of Agriculture series such as the Statistical Bulletins or the Miscellaneous Bulletins. These acreages were instead found in mimeographed circulars, printed by the U.S. Department of Agriculture, Bureau of Agricultural Economics, titled and dated as follows:

Revised Estimates of Barley Acreage, Yield and Production, 1866–1929 (February 1935).

Revised Estimates of Corn Acreage, Yield and Production, 1866–1929 (May 1934).

Revised Estimates of Oats Acreage, Yield and Production, 1866–1929 (July 1934).

Revised Estimates of Tobacco Acreage, Yield and Production, 1866–1929 (August 1935).

Revised Estimates of Buckwheat Acreage, Yield and Production, 1866–1929 (August 1936).

Revised Estimates of Tame Hay Acreage, Yield and Production, 1866–1929 (December 1936).

Revised Estimates of Rye Acreage, Yield and Production, 1866–1929 (October 1935).

Revised Estimates of Sweet Potatoes Acreage, Yield and Production, 1866–1929 (February 1937).

These bulletins will subsequently be referred to as *USDA Revised Estimates*.

able was the share of cotton acreage in total acreage of all crops, total acreage was computed as the sum of all crop acreages available in the Department of Agriculture series, which consisted of cotton, corn, wheat, oats, tame hay, barley, rye, sweet potatoes, potatoes, tobacco, and buckwheat. The total crop acreages calculated in this way include most of the improved acres reported in the census, as can be seen from comparing the two totals at the four census years.[14] The low figures for Louisiana may reflect the exclusion of sugar from the sum of harvested acres; the low percentages for Texas in the earlier years are probably due to the inclusion of cleared grazing lands in the census definition of improved acres.[15]

The failure to include sugar in the Louisiana totals is probably the most serious weakness in the acreage data, since sugar was an important cash crop. A sugar acreage series comparable to those for the other crops was not found. No attempt was made to consider cattle or other livestock as a possible alternative to cotton in the model, and this may lead to some distortions of the results. However, since corn was the main food for livestock this is probably not a serious omission except in Texas, where many cattle grazed on open range land.

The United States Department of Agriculture series are of acreage harvested in each crop, while the supply function specification would indicate acres *planted* as the appropriate variable in farmers' decision-mak-

TABLE A.2   Sum of Acres Harvested in Eleven Major Crops as Percent of Total Improved Land in Farms, 1880–1910

	1880	1890	1900	1910
North Carolina	73	67	64	60
South Carolina	79	75	74	76
Georgia	78	73	75	72
Florida	71	69	58	57
Tennessee	66	65	62	57
Alabama	78	76	73	70
Mississippi	78	73	71	67
Arkansas	80	73	70	61
Louisiana	63	58	62	54
Texas	46	40	75	63

14.   The various state totals of improved acres were taken from U.S. Census Bureau, *Abstract of the Fourteenth Census of the United States, 1920*, pp. 595–597.
15.   See note 7 above.

ing. However, the difference between acres planted and acres harvested (abandonment) is in part a function of the same factors that influence supply (mainly the relevant price). The remainder of the abandonment error may be subsumed in the disturbance term, since it is a function of weather, pests, and other unpredictable events. Some trial regressions were run using yield as a proxy for the weather factors leading to abandonment,[16] but the yield coefficient was rarely significant, and did not display any intraregional pattern. Hence, yield was not included in the final specification, and the measurement error involved in using acres harvested rather than acres planted was treated as part of the disturbance.

The price data are crop prices paid to producers on December 1.[17] They are not strictly prices at the farm gate:

The prices reported to the Department of Agriculture are the prices at which the products first changed hands when sold by the producer, usually the price the farmer receives in his local market. For most farm products there is no price "at the farm"; the prices called such include the variable item of cost to the farmer of transporting the product to the place where it changes hands.[18]

Thus, with elastic demand for agricultural products in the local markets, the net prices received by the farmers themselves diverged from the reported prices by the amount of the local transportation costs. But since the determinants of unit transportation costs for the various crops were largely identical and were also stable in the short run, the *ratios* of net prices received by farmers for different crops must have been nearly the same as the ratios of those prices in the local market.

The relative price appearing in the models is the price of cotton divided by an index of the prices of the major alternative crops. This index was constructed as a value-weighted index with 1899 as the base year. If Y_t is defined as the index of the prices of the alternative crops,

$$Y_t = \sum_i \frac{P_t^i}{P^i_{1899}} w^i$$

where $i =$ corn, wheat, oats, and tame hay; and $w^i =$ the proportion of value from all four of the major alternative crops due to the ith crop

16. Following Geoffrey Moore's suggestion to Fisher and Temin, "Regional Specialization and the Supply of Wheat. . . ," p. 138.
17. The source for all the price series was U.S. Department of Agriculture, *Prices of Farm Products Received by Producers, 3. South Atlantic and South Central States,* Statistical Bulletin no. 16.
18. Ibid., p. 2.

TABLE A.3   Percent of Value of Cotton, Corn, Wheat, Oats, and Tame Hay in Total Value of All Eleven Crops in the USDA Acreage Series, 1899

State	%	
North Carolina	77	(tobacco = 17 percent)
South Carolina	91	
Georgia	95	
Florida	77	(sweet potatoes = 14 percent)
Tennessee	87	
Alabama	96	
Mississippi	97	
Arkansas	96	
Louisiana	96	(but sugar not included in the "total")
Texas	98	

TABLE A.4   Correlation Matrix of Relative Price Variable between States, 1882–1914

	NC	SC	GA	FL	TE	AL	MI	AR	LA	TX
North Carolina	1.0	.96	.92	.48	.92	.94	.89	.88	.84	.82
South Carolina			.95	.58	.94	.97	.94	.90	.90	.89
Georgia				.64	.92	.93	.91	.89	.92	.87
Florida					.56	.59	.61	.55	.61	.56
Tennessee						.94	.92	.94	.88	.88
Alabama							.97	.94	.93	.93
Mississippi								.93	.95	.89
Arkansas									.91	.93
Louisiana										.88
Texas										1.0

in 1899. The procedure omits the crops other than cotton and the four in Y_t, but those five crops comprised the major part of the output of the eleven crops in the acreage series, as shown in table A. 3.

The relative price variable used in the estimations was $P_t = P_t^{cotton}/Y_t$. While this variable is correlated between states, there is some degree of independent variation between states, as the correlation matrix in table A. 4 shows.

Finally the proper *dating* of the observations must be followed. The acreage figures are given for the crop year. A crop year includes a full growing season; so, for example, crop year 1882 begins in 1882. Since the prices are December 1 prices, the P_{t-1} appearing with X_t in (7.16) is the price given for the year prior to the year of X_t. Farmers making decisions about acreage allotments in 1883 based their decisions on the last available observed prices, those of December 1882. Alternatively, the cotton planting for 1883 would be based on the expected price of cotton at the time of the harvest, which would be roughly the same as the December 1883 price.

Appendix B
A Sample of Direct Observations on the Division of Shares between the Factors of Production

For each observation the source, terms of contract (when known) and share of output received by the sharecropper are given. The sample includes all instances of observations on the division of the crop in sharecropping arrangements that were found in the course of the research. It is extensive, but not exhaustive by any means.

TABLE B.1 A Sample of Sharecrop Contracts, Showing Division of Output among the Factors

Source	Terms of Contract	Share to Laborer
1.		
John Caldwell Calhoun, testimony, in Timothy Thomas Fortune, *Black and White: Land, Labor and Politics in the South* (New York: Fords, Howard & Hulbert, 1884; reprinted by Arno Press, New York, 1960), p. 246.	"The proprietor furnishes the land and houses, including dwelling, stables, and outhouses, pays the taxes, makes all necessary improvements, keeps up repairs and insurance, gives free of cost a garden spot, fuel, pasturage for the stock owned by the laborers, and allows the use of his teams for hauling fuel and family supplies, provides mules or horses, wagons, gears, implements, feed for teams, the necessary machinery for ginning, or, in short, every expense of making the crop and preparing it for market. . . ."	1/2

TABLE B.1   (Continued)

Source	Terms of Contract	Share to Laborer
2.		
Ibid., p. 247.	"[Under renting] where the laborer owns his own teams, gears, and implements necessary for making a crop. . . . "	2/3 or 3/4, depending on the fertility of the land.
3.		
Robert Somers, *Southern States Since the War, 1870–71* (London and New York: Macmillan Co., 1871), p. 146.	Not specified.	1/2
4.		
A. R. Lightfoot, "Condition and Wants of the Cotton Raising States," *DeBow's Review* (Feb. 1869), p. 153.	Not specified. The given share value is the last value given by Lightfoot, and pertains to 1867.	1/4
5.		
Frances Butler Leigh, *Ten Years on a Georgia Plantation* [1866], cited in Walter Fleming, *Documentary History of Reconstruction,* vol. 2 (Cleveland: Arthur H. Clark Company, 1907), p. 300.	Not specified.	1/2
6.		
Enoch Banks, *The Economics of Land Tenure in Georgia,* Studies in History, Economics and Public Law, vol. 23, no. 1 (New York: Columbia University Press, 1905), p. 79	The landlord furnishes land, house, livestock, farming implements and seed. [sometimes 1/2 the seed]	1/2
7.		
Ibid., p. 80	The landlord supplies only land and house; the tenant furnishes all other forms of capital as well as the labor required in the production of the crop.	2/3 of grain, 3/4 of cotton.

TABLE B.1 (Continued)

Source	Terms of Contract	Share to Laborer
8.		
Vernon Wharton, *The Negro in Mississippi, 1865–1890,* vol. 28 of The James Sprunt Studies in History and Political Science (Chapel Hill: University of North Carolina Press, 1947), pp. 69–70. Wharton's sources are: U.S. Commissioner of Agriculture, *Report, 1867,* p. 417; and "Report of the Planters of Washington County," *Appleton's Cyclopedia,* 1879, p. 634.	a. Landlord supplies rations [plus everything else?]	a. 1/4
	b. Landlord does not supply rations.	b. 1/3
	c. Tenant also supplies half the feed for stock [plus rations]. a, b, and c apply to Greenville and Yazoo sections.	c. 1/2
	d. Laborer supplies only labor (neighborhood of Louisville).	d. 3/10
	e. Laborer supplies labor, rations and feed (Tippah County).	e. 1/2
9.		
James B. Runnion, "The Negro Exodus," *Atlantic Monthly* 44 (Aug. 1879), p. 224.	Landlord supplies only "the use of the land, without stock, tools, or assistance of any kind."	1/2 to 3/4, perhaps averaging 2/3
10.		
U.S. Industrial Commission, *Reports of the Industrial Commission,* vol. 11: *Report of the Industrial Commission on Agriculture and on Taxation in the Various States* (Washington: Government Printing Office, 1901), p. 135.	a. Varies, depending on laborer's "ability to furnish more than his muscle" [North Carolina].	a. 1/4 to 1/2
	b. Alabama: Laborer provides labor alone.	b. 1/3 of cotton, 1/4 of corn
	c. Alabama: Laborer feeds himself and pays for half the fertilizer if any is used.	c. 1/2
	d. Tennessee: On [fertile] bottom lands, new or highly improved grounds, landlord furnishing nothing but soil.	d. 1/2
	e. Tennessee: Lands of average productivity and condition, landlord furnishing stock and seed.	e. 1/2

TABLE B.1   (Continued)

Source	Terms of Contract	Share to Laborer
	f. Mississippi, Arkansas, and Louisiana: Landlord furnishing team, laborer feeding himself and team.	f. 1/2
11. U.S. Industrial Commission, *Reports of the Industrial Commission,* vol. 10: *Report of the Industrial Commission on Agriculture and Agricultural Labor* (Washington: Government Printing Office, 1901), p. 918 Testimony of Hon. Robert Ransom Poole, Commissioner of Agriculture of the State of Alabama.	a. "The owner of the land furnishes the land and the tenant house and all the teams and implements necessary to make a crop. The tenant furnishes the labor."	a. 1/2 of cotton, 1/3 of corn and other crops.
	b. "Landowner or landlord furnishes everything, and furnishes the tenant so many provisions, say provisions for 6 months. . . "	b. 1/3
12. Benjamin Hibbard, "Tenancy in the Southern States," *Quarterly Journal of Economics* 27, no. 3 (May 1913): 485–486.	a. Tenants who furnished little or nothing in the way of equipment.	a. 1/2
	b. Tenants who furnish a considerable part of the equipment, usually including one or two mules.	b. 2/3 or 3/4
13. Theodore Saloutos, "Southern Agriculture and the Problems of Readjustment: 1865–1877," *Agricultural History* 30, no. 2 (April 1956): 71. Saloutos refers to D. Wyatt Aiken, "Agriculture in Mississippi," *The Rural Carolinian* 1 (May 1870): 476; Robert P. Brooks, *The Agrarian Revolution in Georgia, 1865–1912* (Madison, 1914), pp. 47–54; and source 15 below.	a. "The 'cropper' working on 'halves,' normally did all the work himself and generally furnished his own provisions. The owner, as his part of the bargain, furnished the land, a house, seed, plows, hoes, teams, wagons, ginned the cotton, and paid half the fertilizer bill. . . . "	a. 1/2
	b. Landlord furnished everything but labor.	b. 1/4
	c. Landlord furnished everything except labor and provisions.	c. 1/3
14. Marjorie S. Mendenhall, "The Rise of Southern Tenancy,"		

TABLE B.1   (Continued)

Source	Terms of Contract	Share to Laborer
Yale Review 27, no. 1 (Autumn, 1937): 125–126, citing:		
a. "Report made upon the condition of the South to General Grant by Theodore C. Peters, the former President of the New York State Agricultural Society, includ[ing] a letter from a planter who was head of an agricultural club in South Carolina" (1867).	a. Tenants fed themselves, and paid for one-third of the commercial manures. "Apparently the landlord commonly furnished mules, forage, utensils, housing, and fuel, together with six or eight acres gratis, to be cultivated by the tenant's wife and children."	a. 1/2 of the bread-stuffs and 1/3 of the cotton lint
b. Report of federal Commissioner of Agriculture, based on information received from correspondents throughout the South (1867).	b. South Carolina, with labor furnishing its own rations.	b. 1/3
c. Harry Hammond (1866)	c. Landlord furnishing food and shelter.	c. 1/4
d. Harry Hammond (1869)	d. Not specified.	d. 1/2
e. Harry Hammond (later than 1869, but date not specified)	e. Not specified.	e. 3/4
15.		
Rosser H. Taylor, "Post-Bellum Southern Rental Contracts," *Agricultural History* 17, no. 2 (April 1943): 121.	Not specified.	1/3

The following observations on the division of shares are all taken from U.S. Census Office, *Tenth Census, 1880,* vols. 5–6: *Report on Cotton Production in the United States: Also Embracing Agricultural and Physico-geographical Descriptions of the Several Cotton States and of California,* edited by Eugene W. Hilgard (Washington: Government Printing Office, 1884). For each state's survey, the information below is taken from the "Cultural and Economic Survey," subsection titled "Labor and System of Farming." Each state survey is separately paginated, and these are the page numbers indicated in parentheses just following the state names. The groups of names beneath the state name are the counties for which the particular description of contracts and shares applies.

16.

| Alabama (p. 155) | a. Landlord furnishes everything but the laborers' board. | a. 1/2 |

TABLE B.1 (Continued)

Source	Terms of Contract	Share to Laborer
	b. Landlord furnishes only land.	b. 3/4 of cotton, 2/3 of corn
17. Arkansas (p. 105)		
a. Arkansas Craighead Cross Crittenden Desha Garland Pulaski Lee Mississippi Union Miller	a. Owner furnishes supplies and working implements (including one horse or mule for every 15–20 acres).	a. 1/2
b. Sevier Pope Columbia	b. Owner furnishes working implements and horse or mule; laborer furnishes supplies.	b. 1/2
c. Saint Francis Clark Conway Franklin	c. The tenant boards himself and provides the gin and press; the owner furnishes all other implements.	c. 1/2
d. Dallas White Woodruff	d. Owner supplies everything.	d. 1/2
e. same counties as in d.	e. Tenant provides all supplies and implements.	e. 3/4
f. Chicot Scott	f. Owner supplies everything but provisions.	f. 1/2
g. Grant Marion Faulkner Howard Crawford	g. Owner provides only land.	g. 2/3 or 3/4
h. Same counties as in g.	h. Owner furnishes everything except gin and press.	h. 1/2
i. Sebastian Boone Fulton Baxter	i. Owner provides land and gin only.	i. 2/3

TABLE B.1   (Continued)

Source	Terms of Contract	Share to Laborer
j. Jefferson	j. "Owner furnishes everything but board. . . gardens are given to the negroes rent free."	j. 1/2
k. Hot Spring Prairie	k. Same as d, e, and f [note the discrepancy—the terms in d, e, and f are dissimilar].	k. Same as d, e, and f, except 1/3 of corn is included in rent
18. Florida (p. 70)	a. Landowner furnishes teams and implements.	a. 1/2
	b. Landowner furnishes teams, implements, and all supplies.	b. 1/4 to 1/3
19. Georgia (p. 172)	a. Landlord provides land alone.	a. 3/4 of cotton and 2/3 of corn
	b. Landlord provides land, implements and teams; laborer boards himself.	b. 1/2
	c. Landlord provides land, implements, teams, and board.	c. 1/3
d. Appling County	d. [See last column.]	d. Labor alone = 1/3 of crop. Land = 1/3 of crop. Stock, feed, and implements = 1/3.
20. Louisiana (p. 83)	a. Owner furnishes land, teams, and implements.	a. 1/2
	b. Owner furnishes land alone.	b. 3/4
	c. Owner furnishes land, implements, and board.	c. 1/3
21. Mississippi (p. 154)	a. Landowner furnishes land, implements, and teams.	a. 1/2

TABLE B.1   (Continued)

Source	Terms of Contract	Share to Laborer
	b. Landowner furnishes only land.	b. 2/3 to 3/4 of cotton, 2/3 of corn
	c. Landowner furnishes board and everything else.	c. 1/4
22. North Carolina (p. 77)	a. Landowner furnishes all necessary supplies except food for the laborer, and one-half of any fertilizers that may be used.	a. 1/2
	b. Landowner furnishes land alone, without supplies.	b. 2/3 corn 3/4 cotton
23. South Carolina (pp. 60–66) a. Coast Region	a. Landowner provides house, fuel, and 6 acres of arable land.	a. 2/3 of labor *time* (4 days/week for 10 months)
b. Lower Pine Belt	b. Landholder furnishes all supplies.	b. 2/3 cotton, 1/2 provision crop
c. Williamsburgh County (in b)	c. Landlord provides land alone.	c. 2/3 to 3/4
d. Clarendon County (in b)	d. Landlord "advances" all supplies [Note: Unclear what " 'net' of the crop" means.]	d. 2/3 "net" of crop
e. Upper Pine Belt, Silverton Township	e. Landowner provides house, rations, and three acres of land.	e. Slightly more than 1/4
f. Barnwell Hampton Darlington Marlborough (Counties)	f. Employer furnishes land, teams, and implements.	f. 1/3 to 1/2
g. Aiken County (of e)	g. Landlord provides everything but food.	g. 1/3
h. Same as g.	h. Landlord provides everying including food.	h. 1/4

TABLE B.1   (Continued)

Source	Terms of Contract	Share to Laborer
i. Metamorphic Region: Laurens Chester Abbeville York portions of Fairfield & Spartanburgh	i. Landlord furnishes tools, stock, and stock-feed.	i. 1/2
j. Metamorphic Region: Greenville portions of Fairfield & Spartanburgh	j. Same as i.	j. 1/3
k. Greenville	k. Landlord furnishes only land.	k. 2/3
l. Metamorphic Region	l. Landlord furnishes land alone.	l. 2/3 to 3/4
24. Tennessee (p. 104)	a. Owner furnishes land only.	a. 2/3 of crop, or 3/4 cotton & 2/3 corn
	b. Owner furnishes also supplies, such as teams, implements, seed, etc.	b. 1/2
25. Texas (p. 161)	a. Owner furnishes implements, teams, and feed; buildings and improvements are *generally* included in Texas farms.	a. 1/2
	b. Renter furnishes own supplies.	b. 3/4 cotton, 2/3 grain and other products
	c. Owner provides board in addition to farm and implements.	c. 1/3

From this compilation it is clear that the share of output received in payment for labor services alone fluctuated between 1/4 and 1/2 of the crop. In order to condense the mass of references to a few figures, it is useful to calculate the unweighted average of all labor share values under roughly comparable conditions as to the factors supplied by the landlords. The observations listed under Category I below are those of the share of output received for labor alone, as nearly as can be determined from the often skimpy information provided on the terms of contract. In cases where the shares of the different crops where different, both numbers were included in the unweighted average. Similarly, Category II observations correspond as closely as possible to the shares received by the tenant when the landlord supplied only land. Again, when several shares are given for the same observation, all are included in the unweighted average. Given these average labor and land shares, and assuming constant returns and exhaustion of the product, the average capital share can be calculated as well. (It simply equals one minus the sum of the land and labor shares.)

TABLE B.2 Category I Labor Shares—Laborer provides labor alone, with or without provisions, including or not some portion of cost of fertilizer, feed, seed, part or all of ginning

Observation Number	Labor Share	Observation Number	Labor Share	Observation Number	Labor Share
1	1/2	14c	1/4	23e	1/4
6	1/2	16a	1/2	23f	1/3, 1/2
8a	1/4	17a	1/2	23g	1/3
8b	1/3	17b	1/2	23h	1/4
8c	1/2	17c	1/2	23i	1/2
8d	3/10	17d	1/2	23j	1/3
8e	1/2	17f	1/2	24b	1/2
10a	1/4, 1/2	17h	1/2	25a	1/2
10b	1/3, 1/4	17j	1/2	25c	1/3
10c	1/2	18a	1/2		
10e	1/2	18b	1/4, 1/3		
10f	1/2	19b	1/2		
11a	1/2, 1/3	19c	1/3		
11b	1/3	19d	1/3		
12a	1/2	20a	1/2		
13a	1/2	20c	1/3		
13b	1/4	21a	1/2		
13c	1/3	21c	1/4		
14a	1/2, 1/3	22a	1/2		
14b	1/3	23b	2/3, 1/2		
Unweighted average = .415					

TABLE B.3   Category II Tenant Shares—Landlord provides land alone

Observation Number	Tenant Share
7	2/3, 3/4
9	1/2, 3/4, 2/3
10d	1/2
12b	2/3, 3/4
16b	3/4, 2/3
17g	2/3, 3/4
17i	2/3
19a	3/4, 2/3
19d	2/3
20b	3/4
21b	2/3, 3/4, 2/3
22b	2/3, 3/4
23a	2/3
23c	2/3, 3/4
23k	2/3
23l	2/3, 3/4
24a	2/3, 3/4, 2/3
25b	3/4, 2/3

Unweighted average = .689

Average land share, assuming constant returns and exhaustion of the product = .311

The factor shares found from these direct observations, and the overall average competitive factor shares computed from the production function estimates, correspond rather closely:

Factor shares:	labor	land	capital
Direct Observation of Share Payments	.415	.311	.274
Group I Production Functions, Variant II Averages	.309	.396	.321
Group II Production Functions, Variant II Averages	.319	.387	.315

(See chapters 4 and 5 for full discussion of these results.)

Appendix C
The Difference in Means of H/T and B/R in Counties Ranked by Overall S_i Coefficients, with Test of Significance

To begin with, the soil types were divided into the "best" and "rest" soils according to the overall rank of the coefficients of the S_i. The ranks of each soil type were averaged over the four census years, with half of the soil types with the lowest overall rank (hence highest net residual fertility) grouped together as the "best" soils and the other half grouped as the "rest" of the soils in each state. Since the soil-type categories do not all contain the same number of counties, there are usually different numbers of counties in the "best" and "rest" categories.

The results of this division are given in the following tables. The "best" soil categories are ranked according to their coefficients from the Group I regressions in the left-hand column. The right-hand column of figures gives the corresponding ranking of each tabled soil type for the Group II regression coefficients (introduced in chapter 5 of the text). It should be noted that even though some soil quality differences might have been measured by the coefficients of the race and crop variables, the Mississippi River alluvial counties possess the soils of greatest net fertility in the four states where those soils are present (Tennessee, Arkansas, Mississippi, and Louisiana).

Define a new variable BEST $= \sum S_i$ where the index i runs over those soil types whose coefficients rank in the top half of the magnitude-ranking of the coefficients. The variable BEST is 1 for a county whose soil belongs to the most fertile half of the soil types. Define REST $= \sum S_i$ for the remainder of the soil-type categories. [Note: In cases where there was an odd number $(2N + 1)$ of soil types, the BEST category was taken to be N soil types with the largest estimated coefficients—2 out of 5 S_i classifications, 3 in the case of 7 S_i, etc.]

It is well known that (omitting county observation subscripts) an equation $y = \beta_1 \text{BEST} + \beta_2 \text{REST} + u$, when estimated by least squares, yields $\hat{\beta}_1 = \bar{y}$ for the counties belonging to the BEST soil-type classifi-

TABLE C.1   Listing of the "Best" Soils by State, Four-Census Averages, in Order of Net Residual Fertility

State	Group I	Group II
North Carolina	S2 – Longleaf pine region	(1)–(2) [tie]
	S3 – Oak uplands region	
	S4 – Transmontane region	(1)–(2)
South Carolina	S2 – Marshes, swamps and live-oak lands of the coast	(1)
	S3 – Oak, hickory, and longleaf pine hills in the Central Belt	(2)
Georgia	S7 – Longleaf pine and wire-grass region, pine barrens division	(1)
	S8 – Pine flats and coast counties	(2)
	S6 – Longleaf pine and wire-grass region, limesink division	(4)
	S4 – Central cotton belt	(3)
Florida	S4 – Pitch-pine, treeless, and alluvial region, sea island cotton	(1)
	S3 – Longleaf pine region, sea island cotton	(2)
Tennessee	S1 – Alluvial plain of the Mississippi River	(1)
	S2 – Alluvial plain of the Mississippi River and plateau slope of West Tennessee, alluvial plain, and bluff	(2)
	S5 – Western valley of the Tennessee River	(3)
	S3 – Alluvial plain of the Mississippi River and plateau slope of West Tennessee, brown-loam tablelands, midland counties	(4)
	S4 – Alluvial plain of the Mississippi River and plateau slope of West Tennessee, summit region of watershed	(6)
	S6 – The Highlands, or highland rim of middle Tennessee, western subdivision	(5)
Alabama	S9 – Longleaf pine region	(1)
	S7 – Oak and hickory uplands, with longleaf pine	(3)
	S1 – Metamorphic region	(2)
	S5 – Oak and hickory uplands, with shortleaf pine	(4)
Mississippi	S6 – Mississippi alluvial region	(1)
	S9 – Longleaf pine and coast region,	

TABLE C.1   (Continued)

State	Group I	Group II
	longleaf pine hills and flats	(2)
	S8 – Longleaf pine and coast region, longleaf pine, oak, and hickory uplands	(4)
	S3 – Yellow-loam region, brown-loam tablelands	(3)
Arkansas	S1 – Alluvial region, Mississippi bottomlands	(1)
	S2 – Alluvial region, Crowley's Ridge	(2)
	S6 – Northern barrens and hills	(3)
Louisiana	S2 – Alluvial region, south of Red River [= S3]	(1)–(2)
	S3 – Tidewater parishes	(1)–(2)
	S1 – Alluvial region, north of Red River	(3)
Texas	S2 – Longleaf pine region	(1)
	S3 – Southern and coast prairie region, region east of the Brazos River [= S7]	(3)–(4)
	S7 – Red River alluvial counties	(2)
	S1 – Oak, hickory, and pine uplands [= S10]	(3)–(4)
	S10 – Non-cotton-producing counties	(5)

TABLE C.2   Listing of the "Rest" Soils by State, Four-Census Averages, in Order of Net Residual Fertility

State	Group I	Group II
North Carolina	S4 – Transmontane region	
		S3 – Oak uplands region (3)
	S1 – Seaboard region	(4)
South Carolina	S1 – Longleaf pine flats and savannahs	(3)
	S5 – Granite and metamorphic gray and red lands of the Piedmont	(4)
	S4 – Sand hills belt	(5)
Georgia	S5 – Southern oak, hickory, and pine uplands	(5)
	S3 – Metamorphic region, middle Georgia counties	(6)
	S1 – Northwest Georgia	(7)
	S2 – Metamorphic region, Blue Ridge counties	(8)

TABLE C.2 (Continued)

State	Group I	Group II
Florida	S2 – Longleaf pine region, short staple cotton	(3)
	S1 – Oak, hickory, and pine upland region	(4)
Tennessee	S8 – Central basin	(7)
	S7 – The Highlands, or highland rim of middle Tennessee, eastern subdivision	(8)
	S12 – Cumberland tableland, valley of East Tennessee, and Unaka Mountain region, valley and Unaka	(9)
	S10 – Cumberland tableland, valley of East Tennessee, and Unaka Mountain region, tableland and valley	(10)
	S9 – Cumberland tableland	(11)
	S11 – Cumberland tableland, valley of East Tennessee, and Unaka Mountain region, valley	(12)
Alabama	S6 – Gravelly hills, with longleaf pine region	(5)
	S2 – Coosa valley region	(7)
	S8 – Central prairie region	(6)
	S4 – Tennessee valley region	(8)
	S3 – Coal-measures region	(9)
Mississippi	S7 – Central prairie region	(5)
	S4 – Yellow-loam region, shortleaf pine and oak upland region	(6)
	S5 – Cane hills	(7)
	S2 – Northeastern prairie region, Pontotoc ridge	(8)
	S1 – Northeastern prairie region, prairie belt	(9)
Arkansas	S3 – Gray silt prairie region	(6)
	S5 – Red-loam region	(4)
	S4 – Yellow-loam region	(5)
Louisiana	S6 – Longleaf pine region	(4)
	S5 – Attakapas region	(5)
	S4 – Bluff region [= S7]	(6)–(7)
	S7 – Oak uplands	(6)–(7)
Texas	S8 – Brazos alluvial or "Sugar Bowl" region	(10)
	S9 – Rio Grande valley	(6)–(7)
	S6 – Western red-loam prairie region	(8)

TABLE C.2   (Continued)

State	Group I	Group II
	S4 – Southern and coast prairie region, region west of the Brazos River	(9)
	S5 – Central black-prairie region	(11)
	S11 – Unorganized counties	(6)–(7)

cation, while $\hat{\beta}_2 = \bar{y}$ over the rest of the counties. This is easily seen by calculating the least squares estimates. With i denoting the county,

$$\hat{y}_i = \hat{\beta}_1(\text{BEST})_i + \hat{\beta}_2(\text{REST})_i$$

Define $X_i = (\text{BEST})_i$; $Z_i = (\text{REST})_i$ for convenience of notation.

$$e_i^2 = (y_i - \hat{y}_i)^2 = (y_i - \hat{\beta}_1 X_i - \hat{\beta}_2 Z_i)^2$$

$$E = \sum e_i^2$$

First-order conditions for a minimum sum of squares are

$$\frac{\partial E}{\partial \hat{\beta}_1} = \sum_i 2(y_i - \hat{\beta}_1 X_i - \hat{\beta}_2 Z_i) \cdot X_i = 0$$

$$\frac{\partial E}{\partial \hat{\beta}_2} = \sum_i 2(y_i - \hat{\beta}_1 X_i - \hat{\beta}_2 Z_i) \cdot Z_i = 0$$

From the first of these conditions,

$$\sum_i (y_i X_i - \hat{\beta}_1 X_i^2) = 0 \qquad \text{since } X_i Z_i = 0 \text{ for all } i$$

But $X_i^2 = 1$ when $X_i = 1$ and $X_i^2 = 0$ when $X_i = 0$. So if $n_1 =$ the number of counties whose soils are in the "best category:

$$\sum_{i \varepsilon BEST} y_i - n_1 \hat{\beta}_1 = 0$$

$$\hat{\beta}_1 = \frac{1}{n_1} \sum_{i \varepsilon BEST} y_i$$

Similarly,

$$\hat{\beta}_2 = \frac{1}{n_2} \sum_{i \varepsilon REST} y_i$$

Hence $\hat{\beta}_1$ and $\hat{\beta}_2$ are the "group means" of the variable y_i for its values when considering the counties with the "best" soils and with the "rest" of the soils, respectively.

One further transformation will simplify the subsequent tests. BEST + REST = 1 for each county, or REST = 1 − BEST. So

$$y = \beta_1 (\text{BEST}) + \beta_2 (\text{REST}) + u$$

$$= \beta_1 (\text{BEST}) + \beta_2 (1 - \text{BEST}) + u$$
$$= \beta_2 + (\beta_1 - \beta_2)(\text{BEST}) + u$$

Therefore, ordinary least squares estimates of

$$y = \psi_0 + \psi_1(\text{BEST}) + u$$

will give as ψ_1 the difference in means of the variable y between the two groups of counties. The t-statistic associated with the estimate of ψ_1 will test the significance of this difference of means.

Obviously, exactly the same transformations could be performed to test the significance of the difference of means for any other variable between any other mutually exclusive and exhaustive classification of the counties into two groups.

Tables C.3 and C.4 show the differences in means and associated t-statistics both for the proportion of acres planted in cotton and for the proportion of blacks in the total population. It should be noted again that the overall "best" and "rest" soil-type categories are the same for every state in the Group I and Group II regressions except North Carolina, for which the different results are both reported.

TABLE C.3   Group I and Group II Regressions, Overall Best Soils, $(\overline{H/T})_{\text{BEST}} - (\overline{H/T})_{\text{REST}}$

State	1880	1890	1900	1910
North Carolina				
Group I:	.0804	.0825	.0826	.0922
[t]	[3.318]	[3.332]	[4.165]	[3.650]
Group II:	.0311	.0288	.0175	.0298
	[1.246]	[1.129]	[.837]	[1.138]
South Carolina	.000994	.00420	−.0368	.0372
	[.0233]	[.0927]	[−.830]	[1.027]
Georgia	−.0186	.00837	−.0413	−.0147
	[−.745]	[.353]	[−1.643]	[−.563]
Florida	−.0861	−.0863	−.0561	−.116
	[−2.208]	[−2.292]	[−1.765]	[−4.010]
Tennessee	.138	.131	.113	.131
	[7.222]	[6.815]	[6.312]	[6.319]
Alabama	−.00427	−.00678	−.0383	−.0541
	[−.141]	[−.274]	[−1.371]	[−.830]

TABLE C.3 (Continued)

State	1880	1890	1900	1910
Mississippi	.0157	.0261	.0158	.0526
	[.458]	[.733]	[.483]	[1.729]
Arkansas	−.0156	.00395	−.0111	.0342
	[−.469]	[.100]	[−.316]	[.946]
Louisiana	−.0746	−.107	−.0665	−.0782
	[−1.283]	[−1.970]	[−1.407]	[−2.548]
Texas	.100			−.0309
	[5.824]			[−1.224]

TABLE C.4   Group I and Group II Regressions, Overall Best Soils
$(\overline{B/R})_{\text{BEST}} - (\overline{B/R})_{\text{REST}}$

State	1880	1890	1900	1910
North Carolina				
Group I:	.122	.110	.115	.101
[t]	[3.116]	[2.846]	[3.016]	[2.534]
Group II:	−.0258	−.0336	−.0183	−.00280
	[−.643]	[−.853]	[−.471]	[−.0693]
South Carolina	.152	.146	.150	.119
	[2.508]	[2.247]	[2.529]	[2.288]
Georgia	.0939	.142	.164	.152
	[2.460]	[3.727]	[4.260]	[4.222]
Florida	−.151	−.177	−.129	−.0706
	[−2.014]	[−2.702]	[−2.022]	[−1.313]
Tennessee	.123	.131	.137	.130
	[4.210]	[4.628]	[4.766]	[4.585]
Alabama	−.0973	−.0764	−.0674	−.0541
	[−1.532]	[−1.169]	[−1.008]	[−.830]
Mississippi	.0564	.0687	.0821	.0907
	[1.101]	[1.262]	[1.503]	[1.739]
Arkansas	−.0196	.00714	.0130	.0233
	[−.339]	[.115]	[.204]	[.379]
Louisiana	.151	.165	.143	.107
	[3.033]	[3.098]	[2.610]	[2.071]
Texas	.132			.109
	[5.368]			[5.395]

Appendix D
A Test of Significance of the Sum of Values of Cumulative Distribution Functions

The derivation of this test is elementary, but it still seems to be useful in situations such as the one in the text, when a group of test statistics taken together proves to be significant even when some of them taken individually are not, and the number of test statistics involved is too small to allow straightforward application of the Central Limit Theorem.

In the derivations that follow, the X_i are independent random variables distributed uniformly over the interval 0 to 1. These X_i can be interpreted as values of the cumulative distribution function of any continuous random variable.[1] In the examples of chapters 4 and 5, the X_i represent areas under the appropriate F density functions to the left of the calculated F-values for each state in each census year. In the notation of those chapters $X_i = 1 -$ P-value for each test.

Consider first the case of two such variables. Let

$$Y_1 = X_1$$

$$Y_2 = X_1 + X_2$$

The probability density function of Y_2 is to be found. The change-of-variable technique[2] will be employed:

$$X_1 = Y_1$$

and

$$X_2 = Y_2 - Y_1$$

The appropriate Jacobian for the change of variables equals 1, and if f and g are the joint density functions of X_1 and X_2 and of Y_1 and Y_2 respectively, then $g(y_1, y_2) = 1 \cdot f(x_1, x_2)$ over the appropriate region. X_1

1. Robert V. Hogg and Allen T. Craig, *Introduction to Mathematical Statistics*, p. 178.
2. Ibid., pp. 115–125.

and X_2 are independently distributed uniform random variables over $[0,1]$; hence $f(x_1, x_2) = 1$ over the unit square in the x_1, x_2 plane. This region corresponds in the y_1, y_2 plane (see figure D.1) to

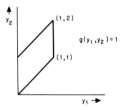

Figure D.1

$$0 \le y_2 \le 1; 0 \le y_1 \le y_2$$

and

$$1 < y_2 \le 2; y_2 - 1 \le y_1 \le 1$$

Thus, the marginal density function h of y_2 alone is given by

$$h(y_2) = \int_0^{y_2} 1 \cdot dy_1 \qquad\qquad 0 \le y_2 \le 1$$

$$h(y_2) = \int_{y_2-1}^1 1 \cdot dy_1 \qquad\qquad 1 < y_2 \le 2$$

So that (see figure D.2):

$$h(y_2) = y_2 \qquad\qquad 0 \le y_2 \le 1$$

$$\qquad\quad = 2 - y_2 \qquad\qquad 1 < y_2 \le 2$$

Figure D.2

The same approach can be applied to larger numbers of variables. Consider three uniformly distributed variables X_1, X_2 and X_3. Let

$$Y_1 = X_1 \qquad\qquad\qquad X_1 = Y_1$$
$$Y_2 = X_1 + X_2 \qquad\qquad X_2 = Y_2 - Y_1$$
$$Y_3 = X_1 + X_2 + X_3 \qquad X_3 = Y_3 - (Y_2 - Y_1) - Y_1$$
$$\qquad\qquad\qquad\qquad\qquad = Y_3 - Y_2$$

The Jacobian for the change of variables is again equal to one. To simplify notation, let g indicate the joint or marginal density functions of the argument variables.

So $g(y_1, y_2, y_3) = 1$ over the appropriate region in y_1, y_2, y_3 space. To find $g(y_3)$ it is first necessary to find $g(y_2, y_3)$:

$$g(y_2, y_3) = \int_0^{y_2} g(y_1, y_2, y_3) dy_1 \quad \text{when} \quad 0 \le y_2 \le 1$$

$$= \int_{y_2-1}^1 g(y_1, y_2, y_3) dy_1 \quad \text{when} \quad 1 < y_2 \le 2$$

By reasoning analogous to that preceding, the range of y_1 and y_2 must be the same as in the 2-variable case. Therefore,

$$g(y_2, y_3) = y_2 \qquad 0 \le y_2 \le 1$$
$$= 2 - y_2 \qquad 1 < y_2 \le 2$$

All that remains is to describe the range of y_2 and y_3. (See figure D.3) This is easy to do:

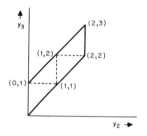

Figure D.3

If $0 \le y_3 \le 1$, $0 \le y_2 \le y_3$

If $1 < y_3 \le 2$, $y_3 - 1 \le y_2 \le y_3$

If $2 < y_3 \le 3$, $y_3 - 1 \le y_2 \le 2$

Therefore,

$$g(y_3) = \int_0^{y_3} y_2 \, dy_2 = \frac{y_3^2}{2} \qquad\qquad \text{when} \qquad 0 \le y_3 \le 1$$

$$g(y_3) = \int_{y_3-1}^1 y_2 \, dy_2 + \int_1^{y_3} (2 - y_2) dy_2 \quad \text{when} \qquad 1 < y_3 \le 2$$

$$= \frac{y_2^2}{2}\Big|_{y_3-1}^1 + \left(2y_2 - \frac{y_2^2}{2}\right)\Big|_1^{y_3}$$

$$= \frac{1}{2} - \frac{(y_3-1)^2}{2} + 2y_3 - \frac{y_3^2}{2} - 2 + \frac{1}{2}$$

$$= -\frac{1}{2}(2y_3^2 - 6y_3 + 3) \qquad \text{when} \qquad 1 < y_3 \le 2$$

and

$$g(y_3) = \int_{y_3-1}^{2} (2 - y_2)dy_2 \qquad \text{when} \qquad 2 < y_3 \le 3$$

$$= \frac{1}{2}(y_3 - 3)^2$$

So the probability density function of y_3 is given by figure D.4.

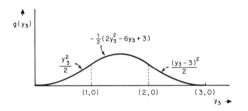

Figure D.4

    The derivation can be checked by calculating the total area under the curve (which equals one) and the maximum value of the middle section (which occurs at $1\frac{1}{2}$). Also, the segments of the function actually meet at $y_3 = 1$ and $y_3 = 2$.

    Finally, consider the case of four variables. The procedure is by now familiar, so the steps will be abbreviated:

$Y_1 = X_1$	$X_1 = Y_1$
$Y_2 = X_1 + X_2$	$X_2 = Y_2 - Y_1$
$Y_3 = X_1 + X_2 + X_3$	$X_3 = Y_3 - Y_2$
$Y_4 = X_1 + X_2 + X_3 + X_4$	$X_4 = Y_4 - Y_3$

Jacobian $= 1$

$$g(y_2, y_3, y_4) = y_2 \qquad\qquad 0 \le y_2 \le 1$$

$$= 2 - y_2 \qquad\qquad 1 < y_2 \le 2$$

$$g(y_3, y_4) = \frac{y_3^2}{2} \qquad\qquad 0 \le y_3 \le 1$$

$$= -\frac{1}{2}(2y_3^2 - 6y_3 + 3) \qquad 1 < y_3 \le 2$$

$$= \frac{(y_3 - 3)^2}{2} \qquad\qquad 2 < y_3 \le 3$$

The relevant region in y_3, y_4 space is shown in figure D.5:

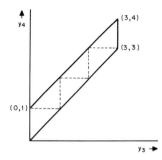

Figure D.5

$$g(y_4) = \int_0^{y_4} \frac{y_3^2}{2}\, dy_3 = \frac{y_4^3}{6} \qquad\qquad \text{when} \qquad 0 \le y_4 \le 1$$

$$g(y_4) = \int_{y_4-1}^{1} \frac{y_3^2}{2}\, dy_3 + \int_1^{y_4} -\frac{1}{2}(2y_3^2 - 6y_3 + 3)dy_3$$

$$= \frac{1}{6}(-3y_4^3 + 12y_4^2 - 12y_4 + 4) \qquad \text{when} \qquad 1 < y_4 \le 2$$

Rather than continue the somewhat laborious computation, it is sufficient to observe that the probability density function is symmetric around $y_4 = 2$. (See figure D.6)

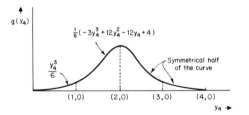

Figure D.6

Calculation of any area under the density function is merely a matter of integration, but the area of concern here is the area from $y_4 = 3$ to $y_4 = 4$. This area equals the probability that the sum of 4 P-values will be less than or equal to one. By symmetry, the area is

$$A = \int_0^1 \frac{y_4^3}{6}\, dy_4 = \frac{y_4^4}{24}\Big|_0^1 = \frac{1}{24} = .042 < .05$$

This is the result used in the text.

Appendix E
Some Criticisms and Reservations

There are several issues that need to be raised in order to achieve a completely balanced assessment of the methodology and results of this study. These qualifications do not by any means invalidate the conclusions drawn in the main body of the text, but they do reinforce the commonplace that the results of any empirical investigation are only as good as the data and the assumptions upon which they are based. Naturally the author of any work is not necessarily his own best critic; so the list of objections that will be raised here should not be thought of as the only criticisms that can be made, or the most telling ones. Even so, by illustrating the nature of some of the biases which may have infected the estimates, it should be possible to form a better judgment regarding their validity and their usefulness in interpreting Southern economic history.

1. Arbitrary Sample Delimitation

The choice of single states and single census years as the samples of counties from which the production functions were estimated was partly arbitrary and partly dictated by the nature of the data. Since the definitions of the variables were prone to change from census to census, any pooling of data over time would have been subject to severe errors of measurement. On the other hand, there is no intrinsic reason why larger sample regions than the individual states could not have been chosen. Chow-type F-tests could have been employed to determine whether several state cross sections could have been pooled, but these tests were not done. The state sample regions were used primarily because of the ease of describing the results in terms of the "natural" political units.

In conjunction with this decision, many statistical tests were performed on the signs or values of parameters from the sample of *regressions,* in order to discern overall trends and regionwide tendencies. The tests on the sample of coefficients require the *independence* of the coefficient estimates from year to year and state to state under null hypotheses typically tested—that no significant pattern was present in the coefficients or their signs. Given the arbitrary choice of single states in single census years as the data sets for each regression, the assumption of independence may not be plausible. Rejection of the null hypotheses of no pattern in the coefficients led to acceptance of the simplest alternative: that the preponderance of signs indicated the true direction of a systematic pattern. This was not the only possible alternative hypothesis, however. In particular, more complicated alternative hypotheses involving the failure of the independence assumption could have been accepted on the basis of the findings.

The basic point here is that, given the mass of data contained in the census cross sections, there are several methods available for processing it and casting it into tractable groupings. The method chosen in the text is only one such method, and was somewhat arbitrary at that.

2. Errors of Measurement in the Labor Force Variables

In order to interpret the difference $b - a$ as a race-associated productivity difference, it is necessary that the variables W and B actually measure the labor inputs attributable to the two groups of agricultural workers, whites and blacks. There are two reasons why this might not be the case: (i) There might have been a systematic difference in the participation rates of the two races. For example, if blacks were discriminated against and paid lower wages than whites, the black participation rate might have been higher than the corresponding white rate, in order for the black families living at the edge of subsistence to be able to survive. Thus a given number of rural black inhabitants would be providing a larger amount of labor than the same number of white rural inhabitants. In this case a positive value of $b - a$ might not indicate any productivity difference: only a difference in the participation rates, with blacks having the higher rate. (ii) If there was a systematic difference in the quality or intensity of labor provided by workers under various tenure arrangements, and if these tenure arrangements were systematically associated with racial differences (as, for example, a positive correlation between the incidence of tenant farming and of black agricultural workers), then a significant $b - a$ might reflect only this labor intensity difference.

Similar objections could be raised regarding the labor input measurements in the Group II model. This measurement error associated with the use of total rural population as a measure of labor input might explain a pattern to the sign of $b - a$, but it is hard to see how it could account for the systematic regional differences which were found. As in the case of the simple "legacy of slavery" idea, it is diffcult to see how a participation-rate explanation of the sign of $b - a$ could account for $b - a$ positive in the periphery, negative in the cotton belt; or how participation rates alone could explain the overall productivity ranking based on the Group II results, showing whites occupying the top and bottom of the productivity scale.

3. Possible Bias in the Relative Crop Productivity Estimates

It might be argued that the strength of the cotton-associated productivity advantage was overestimated because not all improved acres were farmed with equal intensity. The difference in intensity could be due to greater labor requirements per acre for cotton culture than for other crops. Also, the census definition of improved acres included lands lying fallow and used for grazing, lands which may not have been worked as intensively as cotton acres. (See appendix A.)

The labor intensity argument is probably not too serious, since the labor input is explicitly included in the production function. Even if cotton required more labor per acre, it is hardly likely that a cotton farmer worked harder than a grain farmer. Any extra labor requirements should be reflected in a greater population in cotton counties.

The possible error in using improved acres as the land input is potentially more serious. To meet the objections, both the Group I and Group II production functions were reestimated, replacing $T =$ improved acres by $T =$ total acres planted in corn, wheat, oats, and cotton. The results of these estimations were designated Group I-PA and Group II-PA, respectively (PA designating "planted acres" rather than improved acres). In the Group I-PA regressions, the coefficient of H/T would tend to *underestimate* any potential cotton productivity advantage, because in addition to the output of the four crops, the total agricultural output of each county included the output of other crops and the excess of the value of animal products over the value of the corn and oats consumed by the livestock. Animals increased in value owing to their consumption of other grains, their grazing on improved acres not counted in this definition of T, and their natural biological increase of growth and reproduction. The total acreage planted to the four major crops underestimates the input of noncotton land; hence the coefficient d will tend to be *overestimated* in the regressions because of the measurement error in the noncotton land input.

The results of the Group I-PA and Group II-PA regressions are not

TABLE E.1   Group I-PA Intercensus Averages, Variant II

State	α	β	γ
North Carolina	.405	.290	.326
South Carolina	.303	.335	.309
Georgia	.460	.315	.276
Florida	.322	.141	.479
Tennessee	.241	.402	.347
Alabama	.462	.473	.166
Mississippi	.310	.279	.395
Arkansas	.254	.361	.377
Louisiana	.356	.214	.355
Texas	.121	.490	.495
Overall	.323	.330	.353

TABLE E.2   Group II-PA Intercensus Averages, Variant II

State	α	β	γ
North Carolina	.417	.292	.309
South Carolina	.316	.338	.289
Georgia	.413	.398	.256
Florida	.290	.126	.479
Tennessee	.242	.401	.345
Alabama	.445	.474	.175
Mississippi	.312	.282	.394
Arkansas	.249	.366	.383
Louisiana	.337	.212	.360
Texas	.118	.490	.499
Overall	.314	.338	.349

TABLE E.3   Coefficients of H/T with Associated t-Statistics, Group I-PA
Regressions

State	1880	1890	1900	1910
North Carolina	.610	−.133	.168	.297
[t]	[3.289]	[−.629]	[1.018]	[1.784]
South Carolina	.162	−.253	.768	1.438
	[.326]	[−.471]	[2.035]	[5.525]
Georgia	.546	1.065	.360	.390
	[2.082]	[5.028]	[1.770]	[2.635]
Florida	1.385	1.339	1.464	1.416
	[2.098]	[3.014]	[3.785]	[3.204]

TABLE E.3   (Continued)

State	1880	1890	1900	1910
Tennessee	.785	−.0509	−.148	−.218
	[2.908]	[−.262]	[−.604]	[−.998]
Alabama	2.431	.284	.394	.335
	[7.182]	[1.133]	[1.732]	[1.481]
Mississippi	1.375	.211	.854	.782
	[2.426]	[.467]	[4.172]	[2.586]
Arkansas	1.914	.967	.845	.778
	[10.928]	[7.276]	[4.766]	[5.910]
Louisiana	−.236	−.262	−.237	.654
	[−.592]	[−.957]	[−.547]	[1.992]
Texas	−.695			−.000288
	[−.645]			[−.00216]

TABLE E.4   Coefficients of B/R with Associated t-Statistics, Group I-PA Regressions

State	1880	1890	1900	1910
North Carolina	.764	.554	.661	.774
[t]	[4.320]	[3.024]	[4.715]	[4.624]
South Carolina	.597	.308	−.306	−.514
	[1.995]	[.933]	[−1.910]	[−3.391]
Georgia	.0184	.303	−.119	.111
	[.144]	[3.071]	[−1.506]	[1.704]
Florida	−.440	−.437	−.499	−.133
	[−1.124]	[−1.109]	[−1.597]	[−.254]
Tennessee	.313	.463	.114	.231
	[1.646]	[2.816]	[.623]	[1.215]
Alabama	−.718	.108	−.132	−.305
	[−3.679]	[.778]	[−1.209]	[−3.095]
Mississippi	−.213	.734	−.131	−.222
	[−.628]	[2.872]	[−1.407]	[−1.921]
Arkansas	−.539	.218	−.0533	−.290
	[−3.768]	[1.953]	[−.416]	[−2.982]
Louisiana	1.133	.971	.399	.0550
	[2.697]	[4.071]	[1.642]	[.227]
Texas	.709			.706
	[.859]			[2.005]

TABLE E.5 Estimated Sign Patterns for Group II-PA Regressions

State			1880	1890	1900	1910
North Carolina	η	θ	+ +	+ +	+ −	+ +
	$\eta + \phi$		−	−	+	+
	$\theta + \phi$		−	−	+	−
South Carolina			+ +	+ +	− +	− +
			−	−	−	−
			−	−	+	+
Georgia			+ +	+ +	+ +	− +
			−	−	−	+
			−	+	−	+
Florida			− −	− +	− +	+ +
			+	+	+	−
			+	+	+	+
Tennessee			+ +	+ − ·	+ −	+ −
			+	+	+	−
			+	+	−	−
Alabama			− +	+ +	− +	− +
			−	−	+	−
			+	−	+	+
Mississippi			+ +	+ +	− +	− +
			−	+	+	−
			+	+	+	+
Arkansas			+ +	− +	− +	− +
			−	+	+	−
			+	+	+	+
Louisiana			+ +	+ −	− −	− −
			+	+	+	+
			−	+	+	+
Texas			+ −			+ +
			+			+
			−			−

very different from the Group I and Group II results. The average input elasticities are hardly changed; so the conclusions regarding exploitation and returns to scale need not be touched. As expected, the cotton productivity advantage is not as pronounced. It is still unmistakable, however. Out of 38 estimated coefficients of H/T in the Group I-PA equations, 28 are positive. If the sign of this coefficient were a random variable with equal probability of being positive or being negative, the probability of 28 or more positive signs would be approximately:

$$\Pr\left[Z \geq \frac{28 - 19}{\sqrt{38 \cdot \frac{1}{2} \cdot \frac{1}{2}}}\right] = \Pr(Z \geq 2.92) \cong .002$$

where Z is the standard normal variable, using the normal approximation to the binomial. Such a sign distribution is highly unlikely, even considering that the test employed was a one-tailed test. In this specification, the t-statistic of the coefficient of H/T was greater than 2 in 19 of 38 cases, and greater than 1 in 26 of 38 cases. In *none* of the cases in which the coefficient was negative was the absolute value of the t-statistic greater than 1. Thus, even measuring the cotton and noncotton land inputs in such a way as to bias the results strongly *against* indicating a cotton productivity advantage, the advantage was still apparent.

Similarly, the advantage in productivity of white cotton farmers over black cotton farmers is weakened by the redefinition of "total" acres in the Group II-PA results, although every other pattern found in the Group II tables was essentially unchanged, as the following sign frequencies and associated productivity relations show:

1880–1910, All South

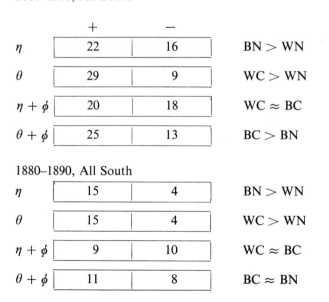

	+	−	
η	22	16	BN > WN
θ	29	9	WC > WN
$\eta + \phi$	20	18	WC ≈ BC
$\theta + \phi$	25	13	BC > BN

1880–1890, All South

η	15	4	BN > WN
θ	15	4	WC > WN
$\eta + \phi$	9	10	WC ≈ BC
$\theta + \phi$	11	8	BC ≈ BN

1900–1910, All South

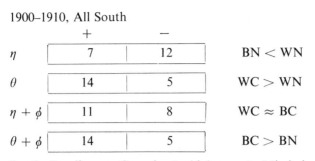

	+	−	
η	7	12	BN < WN
θ	14	5	WC > WN
$\eta + \phi$	11	8	WC ≈ BC
$\theta + \phi$	14	5	BC > BN

South Carolina + Georgia + Alabama + Mississippi + Arkansas + Louisiana, 1880–1910

	+	−	
η	11	13	BN ≈ WN
θ	21	3	WC > WN
$\eta + \phi$	10	14	WC ≧ BC
$\theta + \phi$	18	6	BC > BN

North Carolina + Tennessee + Texas + Florida, 1880–1910

	+	−	
η	11	3	BN > WN
θ	8	6	WC ≈ WN
$\eta + \phi$	10	4	BC > WC
$\theta + \phi$	7	7	BC ≈ BN

This last case of the results for the periphery is the only one of the subregional and subperiod breakdowns in which the actual ranking of the productivities is different from that of the Group II results. It can be seen that in all the Group II-PA results white cotton farmers appear to have "lost" in productivity, but that the overall ranking of the productivities of the different groups of farmers is essentially unchanged. White cotton farmers are still generally among the most productive farmers, other white farmers among the least productive; with blacks in between and with black cotton farmers generally more productive than black farmers of other crops.

The insensitivity of the main conclusions to such a major change in the variable definitions is important. The acreage planted to corn, wheat, and oats greatly underestimated the land input to agricultural products other than cotton. Nevertheless, the cotton productivity advantage continued to show through clearly, despite the fact that the estimate of $c - d$ was biased downward by the measurement error. Similarly, with some weakening of the productivity advantage to white cotton farmers, the basic productivity rankings of the Group II model were again found in most cases. The most important conclusions of all, those regarding exploitation and the marginal product of labor, were unchanged. For these reasons the results reported in the text on crop-associated productivity cannot be too far wrong at worst. Total improved acreage is a priori a better measure of the land area input than the acreage planted to the four crops, and even the severest sort of bias deliberately introduced fails to eradicate the comparative advantage of cotton in the South.

4. The Taylor Series Approximation

Only the linear approximations of the production functions were estimated. It was shown earlier (see chapter 4) that these linear approximations were better approximations, the smaller the productivity differences between the different types of land and labor employed. It would have been ideal to perform nonlinear estimations of the production functions, or alternatively to include more terms of the Taylor series expansions in the equations finally fitted. The fact that the linear approximations fitted well and revealed significant patterns in the coefficient signs is really the only justification for not attempting the nonlinear estimations. Of course, given the massive amount of data involved, the computational problems involved in nonlinear estimation would have been severe.

5. Alternative Parameterizations of the Overproduction Hypothesis in the Cotton Supply Functions

It is usually the case in parameterizing a somewhat vague collection of ideas such as the overproduction hypothesis that more than one model may be taken as a fair representation of the hypothesis. For example, in using the farmers' speed of adjustment and price-responsiveness to distinguish between the lock-in and flexible specialization possibilities, it was assumed in the text that farmers' responses were symmetrical with respect to either rising or falling prices. The magnitudes of the respective speeds of adjustment and price elasticities were then taken as indicative of the flexibility of the farmers in making crop selection decisions. This is not the only possible specification, however. A plausible version of the lock-in hypothesis might be that farmers were able to shift rapidly into cotton culture when the (expected) relative cotton price was *rising,* but that they were not so able to shift out of it when the (expected) price was *falling.* If such a specification were closer to the truth than the symmetrical adjustment of the model actually used, relatively high speeds of adjustment might be merely a reflection of a greater number of years of increasing cotton prices than of decreasing cotton prices.

It does not seem possible to maintain the autocorrelated error structure while dividing the sample into one part consisting of those years in which the relative cotton price was increasing and another of those years with decreasing cotton price, because successive observations in these partitioned samples will not correspond to successive crop years in many cases. A specification employing dummy variables to distinguish between years with increasing and decreasing relative cotton price might be tried, however. More generally, the parameters of the model may be undergoing changes over time. If this is the case, the trend variable should measure (albeit imperfectly) some of this parameter variation. The estimated elasticities and speeds of adjustment will represent only averages over the entire period, and as such may fail to reveal important changes taking place in the underlying structure.[1]

This is not the only possible variant in parameterizing the overproduction hypothesis. The trend variable in the cotton supply function may actually be a proxy for some other variable. For example, in an earlier version of the supply model[2] the trend was replaced by a "tenancy-trend" variable constructed by linear interpolation between the census years of the percent of farms operated by tenants of all kinds. Because of the strong trend component in this variable, the estimated supply functions including it were very similar to those with a pure trend. In particular, the ranges of long- and short-run price elasticities and speeds of adjustment were roughly the same. This earlier version of the model was employed at the outset of the research, when this investigator was convinced of the validity of the overproduction hypothesis a priori. Tenancy was included as a proxy for merchants' control of the planting decisions. The argument presented in that earlier paper was that the tenancy-trend proxy picked up all lock-in effects, so that the estimated elasticities and speeds

1. Thomas F. Cooley and Edward C. Prescott, "Varying Parameter Regression: A Theory and Some Applications," *Annals of Economic and Social Measurement* 2, no. 4 (October 1973): 463–473 contains a general discussion of this possibility and develops estimation methods for dealing with it.
2. Stephen DeCanio, "Tenancy and the Supply of Cotton in the South: 1882–1914," unpublished paper presented at the Cliometrics Conference in Madison, Wisconsin, April 1971.

of adjustment should not have been radically different from similar values for Western wheat farmers. The tenancy-trend coefficient was positive for every state in the A_t (total cotton acreage) model, and was positive in seven of ten states in the S_t (share of total acreage in cotton) model. These results were interpreted as indicating merchants' pressure for cotton cultivation. However, it was pointed out at the 1971 Cliometrics Conference in Madison, Wisconsin, that the link between the tenancy-trend variable and any meaningful measure of merchants' control was problematical at best. The theoretical results referred to in chapter 3 undermined every link between tenure and other variables, and the production function estimates further reduced expectations presumptive of a lock-in effect. The interpretation of the supply function estimates proposed in the text is both simpler and more consistent with the other strong results than any complicated interpretation based on tenancy.

This list of objections is not complete by any means. All things considered, it would seem that the objections do not seriously call into question any of the important conclusions in the body of the text. At least, the burden of proof now rests with adherents to the hypotheses rejected as a result of analysis of the estimates.

Bibliography

Abbott, Ernest Hamlin. "The South and the Negro." *The Outlook* 77 (1904).

Alexander's Magazine. Boston: Charles Alexander, editor and publisher.

Banks, Enoch M. *The Economics of Land Tenure in Georgia*. Studies in History, Economics and Public Law, vol. 23, no. 1. New York: Columbia University Press, 1905.

Bardhan, P. K., and Srinivasan, T. N. "Cropsharing Tenancy in Agriculture: A Theoretical and Empirical Analysis." *The American Economic Review* 61, no. 1 (March 1971): 48–64.

Behrman, Jere Richard. *Supply Response in Underdeveloped Agriculture: A Case Study of Four Major Annual Crops in Thailand, 1937–1963*. Amsterdam: North Holland Publishing Company, 1968.

Berthoff, R. T. "Southern Attitudes Toward Immigration." *Journal of Southern History* 17 (1951): 328–360.

Brandfon, Robert L. *Cotton Kingdom of the New South*. Cambridge, Massachusetts: Harvard University Press, 1967.

Bressler, Raymond G., Jr., and Hopkins, John A. *Trends in Size and Production of the Aggregate Farm Enterprise, 1909–36*. Works Projects Administration, National Research Project, Report no. A-6. Philadelphia: July 1938.

Bruce, Philip A. *The Plantation Negro as Freeman*. New York and London: G.P. Putnam's Sons, The Knickerbocker Press. 1889.

Buck, Paul H. *The Road to Reunion, 1865–1900*. Boston: Little, Brown, 1937.

Buck, Solon J. *The Agrarian Crusade*. New Haven: Yale University Press, 1920.

Burkett, Charles William, and Poe, Clarence Hamilton. *Cotton: Its Cultivation, Marketing, Manufacture, and the Problems of the Cotton World*. New York: Doubleday Page & Company, 1906.

Carstensen, Vernon, ed. *The Public Lands: Studies in the History of the Public Domain*. Madison: University of Wisconsin Press, 1963.

Cash, Wilbur Joseph. *The Mind of the South*. New York: A.A. Knopf, 1941.

Cheung, Steven N. S. *The Theory of Share Tenancy*. Chicago: University of Chicago Press, 1969.

Clark, Thomas Dionysius. *Pills, Petticoats, and Plows: The Southern Country Store*. Indianapolis and New York: Bobbs-Merrill Company, 1944.

———. "The Furnishing and Supply System in Southern Agriculture since 1865." *The Journal of Southern History* 12 (1946): 22–44.

Cooley, Thomas F., and Prescott, Edward C. "Varying Parameter Regression: A Theory and Some Applications." *Annals of Economic and Social Measurement* 2, no. 4 (October 1973): 463–473.

Cooper, J. P. "Asymptotic Covariance Matrix of Procedures for Linear Regression in the Presence of First Order Serially Correlated Disturbances." *Econometrica* 40, no. 2 (March 1972): 305–310.

Cox, LaWanda Fenalson. "Tenancy in the United States, 1865–1900." *Agricultural History* 18, no. 3 (July, 1944): 97–104.

———. "The American Agricultural Wage Earner, 1865–1900." *Agricultural History* 22, no. 2 (April 1948): 95–113.

Crisis: A Record of the Darker Race. [Magazine of the National Association for the Advancement of Colored People] New York City.

Danhof, Clarence. "Farm-Making Costs and the 'Safety-Valve': 1855–1860." Reprinted with permission from the *Journal of Political Economy*, vol. 49 (1941): 317–359, in *The Public Lands: Studies in the History of the Public Domain*. Edited by Vernon Carstensen. Madison: University of Wisconsin Press, 1963.

DeBow's Review. New Orleans: After-the-war series.

DeCanio, Stephen. "Tenancy and the Supply of Cotton in the South: 1882–1914." Unpublished paper presented at the Cliometrics Conference in Madison, Wisconsin, April 30, 1971.

Domar, Evsey. "The Causes of Slavery or Serfdom: A Hypothesis." *Journal of Economic History* 30, no. 1 (March 1970): 18–32.

Douglass, Frederick. *Life and Times of Frederick Douglass*. New York: Bonanza Books, reprinted from the revised edition of 1892.

Dubester, Henry J. *Catalog of United States Census Publications: 1790–1945*. Washington: Government Printing Office, 1950.

DuBois, W.E.B. *Black Reconstruction in America*. New York: Atheneum, [1935], 1969.

Econometric Software Package: User's Manual. Cambridge, Mass.: M.I.T. Information Processing Center, April 1971 (mimeographed).

Englesman, John Cornelius. "The Freedmen's Bureau of Louisiana." *The Louisiana Historical Quarterly* 32, no. 1 (January 1949): 145–224.

Extracts from Letters of Teachers and Superintendents of the New England Educational Commission for Freedmen. Vol. 39 of *Pamphlets on Slavery,* Harvard Widener Library. Boston: David Clapp, printer, 1864.

Fisher, Franklin M. "The Existence of Aggregate Production Functions." *Econometrica* 37, no. 4 (October 1969): 553–577.

———. "Tests of Equality Between Sets of Coefficients in Two Linear Regressions: An Expository Note." *Econometrica* 38, no. 2 (March 1970): 361–366.

———, and Temin, Peter. "Regional Specialization and the Supply of Wheat in the United States, 1867–1914." *Review of Economics and Statistics* 52, no. 2 (May 1970): 134–149.

Fleming, Walter L. "Immigration to the Southern States." *Political Science Quarterly* 20, no. 2 (June 1905): 276–297.

———. *Documentary History of Reconstruction: Political, Military, Social, Religious, Educational and Industrial. 1865 to the Present Time.* 2 vols. Cleveland: Arthur H. Clark Company, 1907.

Fogel, Robert W., and Engerman, Stanley L., eds. *The Reinterpretation of American Economic History.* New York: Harper and Row, 1971.

———. *Time on the Cross: The Economics of American Negro Slavery.* Boston: Little, Brown and Company, 1974.

———. *Time on the Cross: Evidence and Methods—A Supplement.* Boston: Little, Brown and Company, 1974.

Fortune, Timothy Thomas. *Black and White: Land, Labor and Politics in the South.* New York: Fords, Howard, & Hulbert, 1884. Reprinted by Arno Press, 1968.

Franklin, John Hope. *From Slavery to Freedom.* Second edition, revised and enlarged. New York: Alfred A. Knopf, 1956.

Galambos, Louis. "The Agrarian Image of the Large Corporation, 1879–1920: A Study in Social Accommodation." *Journal of Economic History* 28 (September 1968): 341–362.

"A Georgia Plantation." *Scribner's Monthly* 21, no. 6 (April 1881).

Grady, Henry. "Cotton and Its Kingdom." *Harper's New Monthly Magazine* 63 (1881). New York: Harper & Brothers.

Greene, Lorenzo J., and Woodson, Carter G. *The Negro Wage Earner.* Washington, D.C.: The Association for the Study of Negro Life and History, 1930.

Griliches, Zvi. "Distributed Lags: A Survey." *Econometrica* 35, no. 1 (January 1967): 16–49.

Hall, Robert E. "The Specification of Technology with Several Kinds of Output." *Journal of Political Economy* 81, no. 4 (July/August 1973): 878–892.

Hammond, Matthew B. *The Cotton Industry: An Essay in American Economic History.* New York: Macmillan Co. 1897. Reprinted by Johnson Reprint Corporation.

Handlin, Oscar; Schlesinger, Arthur Meier; Morison, Samuel Eliot; Merk, Frederick; Schlesinger, Arthur Meier Jr.; and Buck, Paul Herman. *Harvard Guide to American History.* New York: Atheneum, 1967.

Hart, Albert Bushnell. *The Southern South.* New York and London: D. Appleton and Company, 1910.

Hesseltine, William B. "Economic Factors in Abandonment of Reconstruction." *Mississippi Valley Historical Review* 22 (1935): 191–210.

Hibbard, Benjamin. "Tenancy in the Southern States." *Quarterly Journal of Economics* 27 (1913): 482–496.

Hicks, John D. *The Populist Revolt.* University of Nebraska Press, 1961; originally published by University of Minnesota Press, 1931.

Higgs, Robert. "Race, Tenure, and Resource Allocation in Southern Agriculture, 1910." *Journal of Economic History* 33, no. 1 (March 1973): 149–169.

Highsmith, William E. "Louisiana Landholding During War and Reconstruction." *The Louisiana Historical Quarterly* 38, no. 1 (January 1955): 39–54.

Hofstadter, Richard, and Lipset, Seymour Martin, eds. *Turner and the Sociology of the Frontier.* New York: Basic Books, 1968.

Hogg, Robert V., and Craig, Allen T. *Introduction to Mathematical Statistics.* Second Edition. New York: Macmillan Co., 1965.

Holley, William C., and Arnold, Lloyd E. *Changes in Technology and Labor Requirements in Crop Production: Cotton.* Works Projects Administration, National Research Project, Report no. A–7. Philadelphia: September 1938.

James, Glenn, and James, Robert C., eds. *Mathematics Dictionary.* Princeton, N.J.: D. Van Nostrand Company, 1949, 1959.

Johnston, J. *Econometric Methods.* New York: McGraw-Hill Book Company, 1963.

Kelsey, Carl. *The Negro Farmer.* Chicago: Jennings & Pye, 1903.

Kirwan, Albert D. *Revolt of the Rednecks: Mississippi Politics, 1876–1925.* New York: Harper Torchbooks, 1965; first published by University of Kentucky Press, 1951.

Kmenta, J. "On Estimation of the CES Production Function." *International Economic Review* 8, no. 2 (June 1967): 180–189.

————. "The Approximation of CES Type Functions: A Reply." *International Economic Review* 8, no. 2 (June 1967): 193.

Laird, William E., and Rinehart, James R. "Deflation, Agriculture, and Southern Development." *Agricultural History* 42, no. 2 (April 1968): 115–124.

Lancaster, Kelvin. *Mathematical Economics.* London: Macmillan Company, Collier-Macmillan Limited, 1968.

Leowenberg, Bert J. "Efforts of the South to Encourage Immigration, 1865–1900." *South Atlantic Quarterly* 33 (October 1934): 363–385.

Lewis, Edward E. *The Mobility of the Negro*. New York: Columbia University Press, 1931.

Lewis, H. Gregg. "On the Distribution of the Partial Elasticity Coefficient." *Journal of the American Statistical Association* 36, no. 215 (September 1941), 413–416.

McCarthy, Michael D. "Approximation of the CES Production Function: A Comment." *International Economic Review* 8, no. 2 (June 1967): 190–192.

McKitrick, Eric L. *Andrew Johnson and Reconstruction*. Chicago: University of Chicago Press, 1960.

McPherson, Edward. *The Political History of the United States of America During the Period of Reconstruction, from April 15, 1865 to July 15, 1870*. Washington, D.C.: Philp & Solomons, 1871.

Mangum, Charles S., Jr. *The Legal Status of the Negro*. Chapel Hill: University of North Carolina Press, 1940.

Mendenhall, Marjorie S. "The Rise of Southern Tenancy." *Yale Review* 27, no. 1 (Autumn 1937): 110–129.

Mundlak, Yair. "Specification and Estimation of Multiproduct Production Functions." *Journal of Farm Economics* 45, no. 2 (May 1963): 433–443.

————, and Hoch, Irving. "Consequences of Alternative Specifications in Estimation of Cobb-Douglas Production Functions." *Econometrica* 33, no. 4 (October 1965).

Nerlove, Marc. *The Dynamics of Supply: Estimation of Farmers' Response to Price*. Baltimore: Johns Hopkins Press, 1958.

————. *Estimation and Identification of Cobb-Douglas Production Functions*. Chicago: Rand McNally & Company; Amsterdam: North Holland Publishing Company, 1965.

"Nicholas Worth" [pseudonym]. "The Autobiography of a Southerner Since the Civil War." *Atlantic Monthly* 98 (1906).

North, Douglass C. *Growth & Welfare in the American Past*. Second Edition. Englewood Cliffs, N.J.: Prentice-Hall, 1974.

Nowshirvani, Vahid. *Agricultural Supply in India: Some Theoretical and Empirical Studies*. Ph.D. dissertation, Massachusetts Institute of Technology, February 1968.

Owen, W. F. "The Development Squeeze on Agriculture." *American Economic Review* 56, no. 1 (March 1966): 43–70.

Parker, William N. "The Slave Plantation in American Agriculture." A. W. Coats and Ross M. Robertson, eds. *Essays in American Economic History*. New York: Barnes & Noble, 1969.

Passell, Peter. "The Impact of Cotton Land Distribution on the Antebellum Economy." *Journal of Economic History* 31, no. 4 (December 1971): 917–937.

Phillips, Ulrich B. "Plantations with Slave Labor and Free." *Agricultural History* 12, no. 1 (January 1938): 77–95.

Pollack, Norman. *The Populist Response to Industrial America: Midwestern Populist Thought.* Cambridge, Mass.: Harvard University Press, 1962.

Raper, Arthur F. *Preface to Peasantry.* Chapel Hill: The University of North Carolina Press, 1936.

Ransom, Roger L., and Sutch, Richard. "Debt Peonage in the Cotton South After the Civil War." *Journal of Economic History* 32, no. 3 (September 1972): 641–669.

————. "The Ex-Slave in the Post-Bellum South: A Study of the Economic Impact of Racism in a Market Environment." *Journal of Economic History* 33, no. 1 (March 1973): 131–148.

Reid, Joseph D., Jr. "Sharecropping As An Understandable Market Response: The Post-Bellum South." *Journal of Economic History* 33, no. 1 (March 1973): 106–130.

————. "Sharecropping and Agricultural Uncertainty." Department of Economics Discussion Paper no. 257. Philadelphia: University of Pennsylvania, April 1973.

Rohlf, James F., and Sokal, Robert R. *Statistical Tables.* San Francisco: W.H. Freeman and Company, 1969.

Runnion, James B. "The Negro Exodus." *Atlantic Monthly,* August 1879.

Saloutos, Theodore. "Southern Agriculture and the Problems of Readjustment: 1865–1877." *Agricultural History* 30, no. 2 (April 1956): 58–76.

Schurz, Carl. *Report on the Condition of the South.* New York: Arno Press reprint, 1969. The original version of the *Report* was submitted December 19, 1865 as 39th Congress, 1st Session, Senate, Ex. Doc. no. 2.

"A Scotch-Irishman." *The Mountain Whites of the South.* Pittsburgh: James McMillan, printer, 1893.

Shannon, Fred A. "The Homestead Act and the Labor Surplus." *The Public Lands: Studies in the History of the Public Domain.* Edited by Vernon Carstensen. Madison: University of Wisconsin Press, 1963.

Shaw, Eldon E., and Hopkins, John A. *Trends in Employment in Agriculture, 1909–36.* Works Projects Administration, National Research Project, Report no. A–8. Philadelphia: November 1938.

Shugg, Roger W. "Survival of the Plantation System in Louisiana." *Journal of Southern History* 3 (1937): 311–325.

————. *Origins of Class Struggle in Louisiana: A Social History of White Farmers and Laborers During Slavery and After, 1840–1875.* Baton Rouge: Louisiana State University Press, 1939 and 1968.

Siegel, Sidney. *Nonparametric Statistics for the Behavioral Sciences.* New York, Toronto, & London: McGraw-Hill Book Company, 1956.

Sinclair, William A. *The Aftermath of Slavery.* Boston: Small, Maynard & Company, 1905.

Solow, Robert M. "Capital, Labor, and Income in Manufacturing." *The Behavior of Income Shares,* National Bureau of Economic Research Conference on Research in Income and Wealth, Studies in Income and Wealth, 27. Princeton: Princeton University Press, 1964.

Somers, Robert. *Southern States Since the War, 1870–71.* London and New York: Macmillan Co., 1871.

Southern Cultivator 7 (1849). Augusta, Georgia; 27 (1869); 30 (1872); 32 (1874); 36 (1878). Athens, Georgia; *Southern Cultivator and Dixie Farmer* 47 (1889). Atlanta, Georgia.

Southern Historical Publication Society. *The South in the Building of the Nation,* vol. 6. [13 volumes] Richmond, Virginia: 1909.

Southern Workman, vols. 1–19 (1872–1890). Hampton, Virginia.

"Southerner" [pseudonym]. "Agricultural Labor at the South." *The Galaxy* 12, no. 3 (September 1871). New York: Sheldon & Company.

Stampp, Kenneth M. *The Peculiar Institution: Slavery in the Ante-Bellum South.* New York: Vintage Books, 1956.

———. *The Era of Reconstruction: 1865–1877.* New York: Vintage Books, 1967.

Stephenson, Gilbert Thomas. *Race Distinctions in American Law.* New York: AMS Press, 1969. Reprinted with permission of Appleton-Century-Crofts, New York, 1910.

Stevens, Thaddeus. "Reconstruction." Speech by the Hon. Thaddeus Stevens, delivered in the city of Lancaster, September 7, 1865. Lancaster, Pa.: Examiner & Herald Printers, 1865.

———. "Reconstruction." Speech delivered in the House of Representatives of the United States, December 18, 1865. Washington: H.P. Polkinhorn & Son, Printers.

Stiglitz, Joseph E. "Incentives and Risk-Sharing in Sharecropping." Mimeographed. New Haven: Yale University, 1972.

Sutch, Richard C., and Ransom, Roger L. "Economic Regions of the South in 1880." Working Paper no. 3 of Southern Economic History Project Working Paper Series. Mimeographed. Berkeley: Institute of Business and Economic Research, 1971.

———. "Debt Peonage as a Cause of Economic Stagnation in the Deep South Following the Civil War." Working Paper no. 9 of Southern Economic History Project Working Paper Series. Mimeographed. Berkeley: Institute of Business and Economic Research, September 1970.

Taylor, Paul S. "Slave to Freedman." Working Paper no. 7 of Southern Economic History Project Working Paper Series. Mimeographed. Berkeley: Institute of Business and Economic Research, 1970.

Taylor, Rosser H. "Post-Bellum Rental Contracts." *Agricultural History* 17, no. 2 (April 1943): 121–128.

Tebeau, C. W. "Some Aspects of Planter-Freedman Relations, 1865–1880." *Journal of Negro History* 21, no. 2 (April 1936): 130–150.

Temin, Peter. "The Causes of Cotton-Price Fluctuations in the 1830's." *Review of Economics and Statistics* 49, no. 4 (November 1967): 463–470.

Thomas, George B. *Calculus and Analytic Geometry.* Second edition. Reading, Mass.: Addison-Wesley Publishing Company, 1951, 1953.

Turner, H. A. "A Graphic Summary of Farm Tenure." United States Department of Agriculture *Miscellaneous Publications,* no. 261. Washington: 1936.

United States Census Office. *Tenth Census, 1880.* Vol. 1: *Statistics of the Population of the United States.* Washington: Government Printing Office, 1883.
Vol. 3: *Report on the Production of Agriculture.* Washington: Government Printing Office, 1883.
Vols. 5–6: *Report on Cotton Production in the United States; also Embracing Agricultural and Physico-geographical Descriptions of the Several Cotton States and of California.* Edited by Eugene W. Hilgard. Washington: Government Printing Office, 1884.

———. *Eleventh Census, 1890.* Vol. 1: *Report on Population of the United States.* Washington: Government Printing Office, 1895–1897.
Vol. 5: *Reports on the Statistics of Agriculture in the United States, Agriculture by Irrigation in the Western Part of the United States, and Statistics of Fisheries in the United States.* Washington: Government Printing Office, 1895.
Compendium of the Eleventh Census: 1890 [3 Pts.]. Washington: Government Printing Office, 1892–1897.

———. *Twelfth Census, 1900.* Vols. 1–2: *Population.* Washington: Government Printing Office, 1901–1902.
Vols. 5–6: *Agriculture.* Washington: Government Printing Office, 1902.

United States Bureau of the Census. *Thirteenth Census of the United States: 1910.*
Vol. 2: *Population, 1910. Reports by States, with Statistics for Counties, Cities and Other Civil Divisions—Alabama-Montana.* Washington: Government Printing Office, 1913.
Vol. 3: *Population, 1910. Reports by States, with Statistics for Counties, Cities and Other Civil Divisions—Nebraska-Wyoming, Alaska, Hawaii, and Porto Rico* [sic]. Washington: Government Printing Office, 1913.
Vol. 5: *Agriculture, 1909 and 1910. General Report and Analysis.* Washington: Government Printing Office, 1913.
Vol. 6: *Agriculture, 1909 and 1910. Reports by States with Statistics for Counties—Alabama-Montana.* Washington: Government Printing Office, 1913.
Vol. 7: *Agriculture, 1909 and 1910. Reports by States with Statistics for Counties—Nebraska-Wyoming, Alaska, Hawaii, and Porto Rico* [sic]. Washington: Government Printing Office, 1913.

———. *Fourteenth Census of the United States Taken in the Year 1920.*
Vol. 5: *Agriculture: General Report and Analytical Tables.* Washington: Govern-

ment Printing Office, 1922. *Abstract of the Fourteenth Census of the United States, 1920.* Washington: Government Printing Office, 1923.

United States Congress, Joint Committee on Reconstruction. *Report of the Joint Committee on Reconstruction.* 39th Congress, 1st Session. Washington: Government Printing Office, 1866.

United States Congress, Senate. *Report of the Committee on Agriculture and Forestry on Condition of Cotton Growers in the United States, the Present Prices of Cotton, and the Remedy; and on Cotton Consumption and Production.* 53d Congress, 3d Session, Report 986. 2 vols. Washington: Government Printing Office, 1895.

United States Congress, Senate. *Report of the Joint Select Committee to Inquire Into the Condition of Affairs in the Late Insurrectionary States.* 42d Congress, 2d Session, Report No. 41, Pt. 1. Attached to the *Report* is the *Testimony Taken by the Joint Committee to Inquire Into the Condition of Affairs in the Late Insurrectionary States.* The entire *Report* is in 13 vols., the last 12 being the *Testimony.* Washington: Government Printing Office, 1872.

United States Department of Agriculture. *Prices of Farm Products Received by Producers, 3. South Atlantic and South Central States.* Statistical Bulletin no. 16. Washington: Government Printing Office, 1927.

United States Department of Agriculture, Agricultural Marketing Service. *Wheat: Acreage, Yield, Production, by States, 1866–1943.* Statistical Bulletin no. 158. Washington: Government Printing Office, 1955.

————. *Cotton and Cottonseed: Acreage, Yield, Production, Disposition, Price, Value, by States, 1866–1952.* Statistical Bulletin no. 164. Washington: Government Printing Office, 1955.

United States Department of Agriculture, Bureau of Agricultural Economics. *Potatoes: Acreage, Production, Value, Farm Disposition, January 1 Stocks, 1866–1950.* Statistical Bulletin no. 122. Washington: Government Printing Office, 1953.

United States Department of Agriculture, Bureau of Agricultural Economics. [Each following publications is mimeographed, and dated as indicated.]
Revised Estimates of Barley Acreage, Yield and Production, 1866–1929 (February 1935).
Revised Estimates of Buckwheat Acreage, Yield and Production, 1866–1929 (August 1936).
Revised Estimates of Corn Acreage, Yield and Production, 1866–1929 (May 1934).
Revised Estimates of Oats Acreage, Yield and Production, 1866–1929 (July 1934).
Revised Estimates of Rye Acreage, Yield and Production, 1866–1929 (October 1935).
Revised Estimates of Sweet Potatoes Acreage, Yield and Production, 1866–1929 (February 1937).
Revised Estimates of Tame Hay Acreage, Yield and Production, 1866–1929 (December 1936).
Revised Estimates of Tobacco Acreage, Yield and Production, 1866–1929 (August 1936).

United States Department of Agriculture, Division of Statistics. *Wages of Farm Labor In the United States.* Miscellaneous Series, Report no. 4. Washington: Government Printing Office, 1892.

United States Industrial Commission. *Reports of the Industrial Commission.*
Vol. 5: *Report of the Industrial Commission on Labor Legislation.* Washington:
Government Printing Office, 1900.
Vol. 7: *Report of the Industrial Commission on the Relations and Conditions of Capital
and Labor Employed in Manufactures and General Business.* Washington: Government Printing Office, 1901.
Vol. 10: *Report of the Industrial Commission on Agriculture and Agricultural Labor.*
Washington: Government Printing Office, 1901.
Vol. 11: *Report of the Industrial Commission on Agriculture and on Taxation in the
Various States.* Washington: Government Printing Office, 1901.
Vol. 15: *Reports of the Industrial Commission on Immigration and on Education.* Washington: Government Printing Office, 1901.

Wharton, Vernon Lane. *The Negro in Mississippi, 1865–1890,* Vol. 28 of the James
Sprunt Studies in History and Political Science. Chapel Hill: University of North
Carolina Press, 1947.

Wiley, B. I. "Salient Changes in Southern Agriculture Since the Civil War," *Agricultural History* 13 (1939): 65–76.

Willcox, Walter F. *Negro Criminality.* Boston: Geo. H. Ellis, printer, 1899.

Woodman, Harold D. *King Cotton and His Retainers.* Lexington: University of Kentucky Press, 1968.

———, ed. *Slavery and the Southern Economy: Sources and Readings.* New York:
Harcourt, Brace & World, 1966.

Woodward, C. Vann. *Tom Watson, Agrarian Rebel.* New York: Oxford University
Press, 1963. First published by Macmillan Co., 1938.

———. *Origins of the New South, 1877–1913,* vol. 9 of *A History of the South.* Edited
by Wendell Holmes Stephenson and E. Merton Coulter. [Baton Rouge]: Louisiana
State University Press, 1951. First paperback edition, 1966.

———. *The Strange Career of Jim Crow.* New York: Oxford University Press, 1955.

Woolfolk, George Ruble. *The Cotton Regency: The Northern Merchants and Reconstruction, 1865–1880.* New York: Bookman Associates, 1958.

The World's Work, June, 1907. New York and Chicago: Doubleday, Page & Company.

Wright, Gavin. " 'Economic Democracy' and the Concentration of Agricultural
Wealth in the Cotton South, 1850–1860." In *The Structure of the Cotton Economy
of the Antebellum South.* Edited by William N. Parker. Washington: The Agricultural History Society, 1970.

Zeichner, Oscar. "The Transition from Slave to Free Agricultural Labor in the
Southern States." *Agricultural History* 13 (1939): 22–32.

———. "The Legal Status of the Agricultural Laborer in the South." *Political Science Quarterly* 55, no. 3 (September 1940): 412–428.

Zellner, A.; Kmenta, J.; and Drèze, J. "Specification and Estimation of Cobb-Douglas Production Function Models." *Econometrica* 34, no. 4 (October 1966): 784–795.

Zellner, Arnold. "An Efficient Method of Estimating Seemingly Unrelated Regressions and Tests for Aggregation Bias." *Journal of the American Statistical Association* 57, no. 298 (June 1962): 348–368.

Index

Elasticities
  in production functions, 165–170,
    189, 207
  in supply functions, 243, 248, 255–
    261, 310
  See also specific types of elasticities
Emancipation, 6, 14, 72–73
Employers, 22, 30. *See also* Planters
Employment opportunities, outside
    agriculture, 51, 69
Endowments, of nonhuman factors of
    production, 14, 240
Enserfment, 3
Entrepreneurship, 7, 118, 184
Equal treatment of blacks and whites
    under Black Codes, 21
  as laborers, 92–93
  as tenants, 93
Equilibrium
  conditions of, 123–130
  long-run, 248–254
Error structure, 121, 261, 310. *See
    also* Disturbance
Errors of measurement
  of production function variables,
    265–269
  of supply function variables, 274–
    275
Estimation techniques
  factor shares method, 132
  ordinary least squares, 131–132, 141,
    171, 224, 289, 293–294
  other than ordinary least squares,
    132, 309
  unconstrained, 141, 146–147, 171
Exhaustion of the product, 287
"Exodus" movements, 37, 72, 75
Exploitation, 2, 6, 10, 13, 16, 26, 170
  in the aggregate, 12, 50, 76, 118
  blacks' concern over, 49
  cause of Exodus movement, 75
  consciousness of, 17, 42
  of convict labor, 41
  in the credit market, 94–95
  denunciation of, 46
  elimination of, after Civil War, 14
  of farmers by merchants, 8–9, 11,
    13, 111, 170
  laws and violence as instruments of,
    13
  "Marxian" definition of, 4
  not the same as risk premium, 130
  not the source of poverty of blacks,
    68
  profits to be made by, 116

"Robinsonian" definition of, 4
  of slave labor, 14
  source of political and social ten-
    sions, 118
  use of term, 5
  of whites, 8
Exploitation hypothesis, 24, 28, 37–
    39, 44, 50, 76, 120, 165
  necessary condition for, 122
  statement of, 10, 27, 45
  test of, 120, 165–171, 189, 207, 309

Factor prices
  equalization of, 224
  See also Share of output; Wages
Factor shares. *See* Share of output
Factors of production, 2. *See also*
    Capital; Endowments; Labor;
    Land
"False pretenses" laws, 32–33, 36
Farm animals, 268. *See also*
    Livestock
Farmers
  acquisition of lands by, 234
  adaptability of, 109–110
  of cotton and wheat compared, 257–
    261
  flexibility of, 10–11, 14, 258, 261,
    309. *See also* Supply functions
  ignorance of, 94, 108–109, 258
  irrationality of, 9, 94, 96, 100, 241
  price-responsiveness of, 13–14, 94–
    95, 108, 110–111, 114, 121, 241,
    245, 253, 261, 309–310
  rationality of, 11, 177–178
  traditionalism of, 11, 118–119
  See also Blacks; Whites
Farmers' Alliances, 64–65
Farming, objective of, 101
Federal military governors, 21
Federal occupation armies, 30
Fertility
  of land
    farmed by various groups, 186,
      210–219
    as main determinant of produc-
      tivity, 221
  locational factors in, 240
  measurement of, 143
  of Mississippi River alluvial
    counties, 289
  of soils, 82, 121, 139
  See also Productivity; Soils
Fertilizers, 265, 268–269